Praise for

Eric Lax's

Woody Allen

"A fascinating look into both the making of movies and the mind of a very gifted artist." —*Dallas Morning News*

"[A] thoughtful, fascinating, well-informed, wildly entertaining chronicle of Woody's life and times. Here is almost everything you ever wanted to know about Woody but were afraid to ask."
—*St. Petersburg Times*

"The behind-the-scenes insights . . . and extensive knowledge Lax displays of the entire Allen cinematic canon . . . make this biography an indispensable source. . . . It is also a feast for Allen fans."
—*Cleveland Plain Dealer*

"*Woody Allen* is a wonderfully thorough piece of work."
—*Boston Globe*

"Well worth reading." —*Economist*

"Exhaustive . . . a work of intelligence and diligence."
—*Houston Post*

"A laugh on every page? In Eric Lax's biography of filmmaker Woody Allen, it's more like a piece of wisdom on every page."
—*Orlando Sentinel*

"*Woody Allen* digs much further than anyone ever has to explain the genius behind the genius. The book is a splendidly written view of Allen's life and career." —*Indianapolis Star*

Eric Lax

Woody Allen

Eric Lax was born in British Columbia in 1944 and grew up near San Diego. After graduating from Hobart College, he spent five years as a Peace Corps volunteer and staff member. He is the author of *On Being Funny: Woody Allen and Comedy* and *Life and Death on 10 West*, as well as *Bogart* (with A. M. Sperber). His articles have appeared in *The Atlantic, The New York Times Magazine, The Washington Monthly, Life* and *Esquire*, where he was a contributing editor. He lives in Beverly Hills with his wife, Karen Sulzberger, and their two sons.

Woody
Allen

Woody Allen

a biography

Eric Lax

DA CAPO PRESS

Grateful acknowledgment is made to the following for permission to use
excerpts from copyrighted work: Carson Productions, for material from
The Tonight Show; Allen Funt Productions, Inc., for segments from *Candid
Camera*; and NBC, for sketches from *The Chevy Show* and *Saturday Night
Revue*.

A CIP record for this book is available from the Library of Congress.

First Da Capo Press Edition 2000
ISBN 0-306-80985-0

Published by Da Capo Press
A Member of the Perseus Books Group
http://www.dacapopress.com

1 2 3 4 5 6 7 8 9 10——04 03 02 01 00

To
Karen Sulzberger

Contents

Illustrations follow pages 148 and 276.

Preface to
the Second Edition

This book was first published in 1991 and covered Woody Allen's life and career through 1990. Da Capo Press has kindly plucked it from the books-out-of-print cemetery and asked if I would perform a death-defying act by making it a bit more current. Part Six was written in early 2000. It is an encapsulation of the past ten years and is not intended to be as thorough as the body of the book. Obviously much happened to Woody Allen personally: the disintegration of his relationship with Mia Farrow, their very public child-custody battle in court, his marriage to Soon-Yi Previn and their becoming parents of two baby girls—as well as professionally: the end of his long-term film financing and distribution partnership with Orion, a short stint with TriStar, and the production financing deal with Sweetland Films, his friend Jean Doumanian's company, which began in 1993 and ended in early 2000, when he moved to DreamWorks SKG. An in-depth treatment of all these events, plus his own ten films and the several other projects he was involved with in this period, is not possible here and rather is something for another time.

Over the decade, Woody and I continued to talk about his work, as we have for thirty years now. This is a particularly apt moment to take stock of him, for he seems to have come to the end of a time of personal upheaval and change and settled into a new and calmer period. But this new edition is also just an update to a life that continues to unfold, and therefore it lacks the perspective of time and the context of whatever events follow. What is most interesting to me at this point, and I would think most useful to anyone interested in a continually evolving artistic career, is what Woody has to say about his films, his writing, and his life. So along with some added commentary from me, that is what you'll find here.

Eric Lax
July 2000

Woody
Allen

Introduction:
The Digger Ant's Vacation

Woody Allen lay on a double bed in the Grand Hotel in Stockholm, writing a film script in longhand. This was not unique. He composes many of his films while spread out on the big brass bed in a guest room of his duplex penthouse on Fifth Avenue in New York City. But now he was on vacation—this *was* unique—and instead of the yellow legal pad he normally writes on, his face was nearly as close as his pen to a piece of the hotel stationery. While he scribbled intently, alone in the room, Mia Farrow and the seven children who had come with them on this trip in the summer of 1988 were out enjoying the morning.

He had not planned to do any scriptwriting while away; he had left a clean copy of the first thirty pages of this screenplay next to the portable manual typewriter in his workroom overlooking Central Park. And also, the day before leaving New York, an idea for another, possibly more appealing movie came to him and he wanted to examine it. He spent his next-to-last morning before departure pacing about his apartment, considering the new story's possibilities. Then, after looking at several different proposed coming-attraction trailers for *Another Woman* and editing part of the *Oedipus Wrecks* segment of *New York Stories*, his two pieces of work scheduled to open within the next few months, he spent some of the afternoon with an acquaintance, walking the streets (always the shady side to avoid the dreaded sun) in the East

Sixties and Seventies and thinking aloud about the new idea. By the end of the day he had uncovered its potential flaws but he still liked it. Unsure of which story to film, he decided that rather than continue with either, he would let them sort themselves out in his mind while he traveled. But as for him a vacation without work is a vacation without pleasure, he intended to write along the way an essay he had promised *The New York Times Book Review* on Ingmar Bergman's autobiography, *The Magic Lantern*.

The tourists flew from New York to Norway. In Bergen they boated through fjords and visited Edvard Grieg's birthplace. Then they drove to a countryside inn, taking, because of Woody's claustrophobia, two extra hours to go around the coastal mountains rather than drive the several-mile-long tunnel through them. In Helsinki they spent hours in the park so the children, ages eight months to fifteen years, could play. Finland was their entryway to the Soviet Union, a destination they eagerly anticipated; they even had a bagful of such desirables as cigarettes and baseball cards from the picture *Bull Durham* to pass out as tips during their planned several days' stay.

But once in Russia, anticipation quickly gave way to disappointment and disappointment rapidly turned into desire for flight. Although Woody found Leningrad as beautiful a city as any in the world, he liked nothing about the Hotel Pribaltiskaya: the accommodations; the service; the standing on line to get a cafeteria-style breakfast; even the lobby, which reminded him of an old, cavernous airport. The confines of the hotel aside, there was the confining nature of Soviet society to overcome.

"I've got to get my passport back," he heard another guest say to a hotel functionary.

"We don't open the safe until two o'clock," the clerk answered.

"But my bus is leaving. I've *got* to get it," the man pleaded.

For someone not inclined to vacations under the best of circumstances, the specters this raised caused sheer anxiety. Only hours after checking in, Woody and Jane Martin, his assistant, were at the services counter in the hotel to inquire about all the flights that left town the next day, regardless of destination; with so many people to board he wasn't particularly choosy. He wished they could go to Paris, but they had not gotten the then required visas in advance. There was, however, a flight to Stockholm that looked open, and although it was not a scheduled stop on their trip, it is a favorite city. For bureaucratic reasons the concierge could not confirm reservations for them, so at 2 a.m.

Leningrad time, Jane was on the phone to their travel agent at his summer house on Long Island, urging him in the strongest language to get them out of Russia immediately—which might explain why her call was disconnected in mid-expletive and why all attempts to reestablish contact through the hotel switchboard were futile.

At 6 a.m. Woody was at Jane's door, frantic to leave for the airport, where they learned of their travel agent's success from a surly Aeroflot agent who was angry at having to rewrite ten tickets by hand. She seemed unimpressed with the notion that by taking an hour and a quarter to do the job the plane might leave before she finished, thus causing her to rewrite the tickets yet again, but in the end they made the flight with a few minutes to spare. Twenty-three hours after entering the Soviet Union, they were on their way out.

In Stockholm they checked into the eponymous Grand Hotel and ate a pleasant and relaxed lunch in what Woody always finds a lovely city full of nice people. He is generally comfortable in Scandinavia: The quality of life, the terrain, and the sensibilities of the people all appeal to him. A bonus on the stop was the opportunity for a visit with the cinematographer Sven Nykvist, who had shot the last two Woody Allen pictures and would do the next.

Woody assumed before he left New York that he'd be too distracted by the travel and the new places to give much thought to his two script ideas, but that wasn't the case. He couldn't get the one with the thirty completed pages off his mind and it became clear that it was the story to proceed on. His surroundings surely added an extra push. The disparate issues of religious faith, the measurement of success, and moral responsibility in the face of an absent or silent God that his film idea raised, occur again and again in the works of those Scandinavian artists he likes—Bergman, Ibsen, and Strindberg. (He is also fond of the music of Sibelius.) Being in the midst of their culture could in turn only force those issues to the front of his mind.

Not having the already completed pages with him was no problem; they were fresh in his memory. So most mornings, after the room service breakfast carts were rolled out, he told everyone he'd catch up with them in a couple of hours. Then he set to work on the bed, his normally generous and rounded handwriting reduced by concentration to a tiny, crabbed but neat script on whatever paper was handy. When he finished, he folded the various-sized pages into quarters, put them in his coat breast pocket, and went out to meet the others.

The cities changed but the pattern didn't. Snapshots prove Woody's participation in familial touring, but whereas whoever else being photographed is invariably smiling, he never is. Instead his gaze is suspicious, his lips pursed. (The exception is a group photo in Leningrad in which *everyone* is scowling in the rain.) But he swears he enjoyed himself despite the contrary appearances. "God, I look like such a pill," he said after his return, laughing as he pointed to a photo of himself in a striped tie, jacket, and frown beside a radiant Mia Farrow in a Venetian gondola. A busload of tourists on a nearby bridge had just spotted the two and were angling for pictures, but Woody's disgruntled look was more from being in a boat than from being ogled, which happens constantly, especially in Europe. A friend who has traveled with him there says he's like the Statue of Liberty walking down the street.

As the trip progressed, the scratch-pad-sized paper of the Grand Hotel became folded together with the long, rectangular sheets of the Villa d'Este on Lake Como; the wide, pure-white, gold-embossed stationery from the Gritti Palace in Venice; the smaller, barely engraved paper of the Hotel Hassler in Rome; various telex forms; and several sheets of lined paper ripped from a school notebook bought on the street in Copenhagen. By the time they reached London his pocket bulged as though he had a loaf of bread in it. Finally Jane Martin convinced him to stash the work in the hotel safe rather than continue to cart it around, if only to avoid spilling soup on it in a restaurant, so each day pieces of the small, elegant, blue Claridge's stationery were folded in half, piled on the heap, and locked away before he went out to wander the streets or play with the children in one of the parks.

When the ten checked out to return to New York, the Bergman essay remained unwritten but he had completed the first draft of *Crimes and Misdemeanors*, a dramatic and comic novel-like, densely textured script about, among other things, intellectually, morally, and insofar as not being suspected, personally getting away with murder. While he made many refinements over the following months, it was a blueprint for the nineteenth film in twenty years written and directed by Woody Allen. Its themes, and the determined, focused way Woody wrote it, are also keys for understanding much of his personal and artistic complexity.

Part
One

Snared in the Web of Escape

Forgive me if I romanticize. My old neighborhood wasn't always
this stormy and rainswept, but that's the way I remember it.

— RADIO DAYS

Woody Allen was born in Brooklyn, New York, in the spring of 1952, when Allan Stewart Konigsberg, who was born in the Bronx on December 1, 1935, settled on the name as a suitable cover. Allan, who was raised in Brooklyn, decided that spring to become a comedy writer and he sent jokes and one-liners to several of the gossip columnists at the New York newspapers whose items were a daily staple for millions of readers. But being shy, he didn't want his classmates to pick up the papers and see his name. Besides, he thought, everyone in show business changes his name; it's part of the myth, part of the glamour. And Allan Konigsberg is not the light name of a funny person. So he tried to formulate one that was.

He liked Allan and thought the more commonly spelled Allen made a good last name. But what for a first one? He thought of Max, after the writer Max Shulman, one of his idols. He thought of Mel, but Mel Allen was the broadcaster for the New York Yankees. Eventually he thought of Woody and settled on it because it had, he says, "a slightly comic appropriateness and is not completely off the tracks." Contrary to the popular belief that his choice was an *hommage* to one musician or another, it was, he insists, purely arbitrary and wholly unrelated to Woody Herman, Woody Guthrie, Woody Woodpecker, or even Woodrow Wilson.

Arbitrary as the choice was, it began a process of self-invention common in the theatrical world, where names traditionally are changed either to erase telltale signs of immigration or simply for euphony. The notion that an audience might be more kindly disposed to someone named Woody Allen than they would to Allan Konigsberg (or, for that matter, to Cary Grant rather than Archie Leach) is common among performers and producers, who think audiences are more likely to accept someone with a "normal" name. (Then again, Cary Grant *does* seem more appropriate than Archie Leach for the embodiment of urbanity and cosmopolitan style.) Yet Woody is not exactly a normal name for anyone, even a comic, where the general trend is from ethnicity to blandness: Joseph Levitch to Jerry Lewis; David Daniel Kaminsky to Danny Kaye; Milton Berlinger to Milton Berle; Leslie Townes Hope (he was born in England) to Bob Hope; Benjamin Kubelsky to Jack Benny (after a brief interlude as Benny K. Benny). The obvious exceptions to this are the Marx Brothers—Groucho, Harpo, Chico, Gummo, and Zeppo—and it is to them that Woody's lineage goes. As with them, his first name alone provides instant recognition.

What's in a new name, however, is less significant than the new name itself. Freed, even subconsciously, from his identity since birth, a performer can grow into another, more artistically suitable persona. Yet in Woody Allen's case, initially his jokes and later his performances were so personal, so idiosyncratic that the man and his character were seemingly one. Woody Allen the stand-up comedian and film star—a plucky bungler who is more a pawn of chance and a walking compost heap of neuroses than the hipster and sex bandit he imagines himself—appears to be no different onstage or onscreen than off.

Part of the reason is simply his clothes. Charlie Chaplin had his tramp outfit; Groucho Marx, a broad greasepaint mustache and frock coat. They required specific costumes to fulfill their characters, and audiences did not expect to see them dressed that way on the street; they knew there was at least some distinction between persona and person. But Woody Allen wears the same baggy corduroy trousers and frayed sweater, the same black-rimmed glasses and sensible shoes, offstage and on. It is his idea of perfect costuming when he can get up in the morning, pull on whatever clothes he has at hand, go to the set to direct his film of the moment, and then simply step in front of the camera whenever he has a scene, generally without benefit of even a change of shirt, not to mention the addition of makeup. So while it may seem that Woody Allen and the man who plays him are one and the same, this is an instance where the apparent and the factual sleep in different beds. To fully understand either the character or the artist, it is necessary to keep them separate. This, of course, is true of many performers (Jack Benny, for instance, whose convincingly parsimonious character belied a generous private man), but few are so seamlessly welded in the eyes of their audiences.

The Woody Allen character—initially an awkward fellow of dubious skills, none of which include successfully coping with daily life, more recently a stubbornly sane misfit who persists despite his fears and neuroses—is a hilarious creation concocted from a wildly exaggerated personal basis. He is so well drawn that the thought of him brings a smile. But the filmmaker, musician, and father who is the Woody Allen of fact (it has been his legal name since the early 1960s) is as serious about the other aspects of his life as he is about his drama—and his comedy. While the character has almost no control over what happens to him, the man has almost complete control over what he does. Consider the singular deal he has had from the financiers and distributors of all his films: Providing he stays within a certain budget, he has total artistic freedom. Period. The script, the choice of actors, the direction, the editing, the music, *everything* is subject to his approval alone. It is a license no one else in films has and he does not take it lightly. He exercises that authority rigorously, confidently, and to the perfection his talent permits, often rewriting and reshooting as much as 50 percent or more of his original script. Executives at whatever company backs him (it has been Orion Pictures Corporation since 1980, but apart from one short interruption the key executives have remained the same since 1970) at first seldom saw and now never see any version of his scripts, and in fact know little about his current movie until he shows it to them when it is ready for release. Yet one would never guess that from the characters he plays. Danny Rose (to take a random example), the fiercely loyal yet constantly abandoned manager of unrated performers, and Leonard Zelig (to take another), so unsure of his own personality that he assumes the manner of whomever he is with, are as opposite to Woody Allen the artist as Daffy Duck is to Bugs Bunny. One confronts events with bravado but is generally undone; the other serenely reigns over circumstance.

Almost everyone associates Woody Allen's childhood with Brooklyn and his films with New York City. But while they are certainly the locale of his routines and stories, and although he is arguably the preeminent chronicler of American metropolitan life and mores in the late twentieth century, his influences are an amalgam of old Europe and New York.

His childhood embodied Europe far more than it did America, just as did the childhoods of millions of children of New York immigrant families. His mother's family came from Vienna at the turn of the century, his father's from Russia at about the same time. Even though both his mother, Nettie Cherry, and his father, Martin Konigsberg, were both born and raised on the Lower East Side of Manhattan in New York City, the lives they lived as children and as adults were dominated by the shtetl their parents fled but whose ways they continued to embrace.

Sarah and Leon Cherry spoke Yiddish and German and those were the first languages of Nettie, who was born November 6, 1908, and her six older brothers and sisters. The bulk of Nettie's childhood was spent in a five-story apartment building at 125 East Fourth Street, a crowded but pleasant working-class neighborhood near Second Avenue. Each floor housed several tenant families, who knew each other and whose children played together. When not doing housework or taking care of children, women often sat at the window and talked to each other across the yard. Nettie was a bright child who had a chance to go to a special school, but her mother did not want her to be different from the other children, and so she attended the neighborhood elementary school and the then all-girl Washington Irving High School on East Sixteenth Street. The Cherrys ran a small luncheonette near their home and Leon spent all day there. Sarah helped out between noon and three o'clock, the busiest part of the day; otherwise she took care of the house and family. The children came home from school for lunch and the older ones took care of the younger in the absence of their mother, a strict and effective disciplinarian but one who never hit her children. Nettie's sister Molly was the embodiment of the adage that children should be seen but not heard.

"She was quiet," Nettie recalls. "She was very quiet. She died not talking."

Leon had a seat at the synagogue he attended every Saturday, and both he and Sarah were very religious. At home, every Jewish holiday was observed, every Seder was made.

Isaac and Sarah Konigsberg were also religious but not so faithfully as the Cherrys. As with them, however, Yiddish was the primary language at home. Still, Isaac was more of the modern world than any of Allan Konigsberg's other grandparents. He dressed beautifully. He had a box at the Metropolitan Opera. He was the first Jewish salesman for a coffee company and often sailed to Europe on business. In time, he became quite successful—so successful that he sometimes sailed to Europe not on business but to attend the horse races. He came to own a fleet of taxicabs and several movie theaters in Brooklyn. He largely ignored his daughter and younger son but doted on Martin, who was born December 25, 1900; he arranged, for instance, for him to be the mascot of the Brooklyn Dodgers as a boy and he gave him a four-thousand-dollar Kissel roadster to drive in England when he was stationed there with the Navy after World War I. Then, in the stock-market crash of 1929, Isaac lost everything. His other son, Leo, who had shared in some of his wealth, was reduced to selling newspapers on street corners, but Isaac was able to make a slightly better but still meager living during the Depression in the butter-and-egg market in Brooklyn, where Martin worked with him. Yet even though he remained a spiffy dresser, a trait Martin inherited, by the time Allan came to know him Isaac was a poor man living with Sarah in a cramped and dark apartment at the back of a building on Coney Island Avenue, a noisy commercial street. Still, Allan found it fun to visit them when he was young because Sarah, a diabetic, would shake his hand when he arrived and slip him some of the sugar cubes she always had close by.

Despite Isaac's reversals, to Nettie he was always a cultured man because of his opera box. And not just to her. To Jewish families, and especially to immigrants who clung to Old World ways, the person of culture and learning was whom they respected: the doctor, the teacher, the rabbi, the lawyer, the violin player; people involved with serious work and not, as Isaac or Nettie would say, someone who wastes time with foolishness.

Martin and Nettie met at the butter-and-egg market on Greenwich Street in Brooklyn at the beginning of the Depression. Nettie, a slender redhead, worked there as a bookkeeper for one of the companies and Isaac introduced her to Martin, who bears a physical likeness to both George Raft and to former Brooklyn Dodger shortstop Pee Wee Reese but more than anything is a ringer for the French actor Fernandel. Nettie thought Isaac was a nice man and was flattered by Martin's attention. "That's what really made me go with him a lot, because he was very good to me and very attentive," she recalled years later. "He was a high-stepper. He took me to Tavern on the Green," a fancy Manhattan restaurant.

At this time Nettie and her family were living north of Manhattan in the Bronx, a borough of New York that, like Brooklyn then, was largely countryside. After she and Martin married in 1931, they took a first-floor bedroom apartment on Argyle Road in Brooklyn, at the time a respectable area with large homes. But despite the character of the neighborhood, the apartment was robbed, and so they moved to an apartment on Ocean Avenue. Soon the rest of Nettie's family, who always lived close to and worried about one another, moved to Brooklyn, all within a radius of five or six blocks—a pattern that continued throughout Allan's childhood and that generally included one aunt or another and her family sharing an apartment with his family.

It was his maternal aunt Ceil and her husband, Abe Cohen, who shared Allan's first home, a six-room apartment which comprised the upper floor of a quite small two-story, two-family frame house at 968 East Fourteenth Street, three houses in from Avenue J in the Midwood area of the Flatbush section of Brooklyn. The seven years he lived there was by far the longest he lived in any home; over the course of his childhood the Konigsbergs moved about a dozen times. In most instances they shared lodgings with Ceil and Abe or with another of Nettie's sisters, Sadie and her husband, Joe Wishnick (actually Vishnetski), a tailor who had recently emigrated from Russia. As it was, it didn't really make much difference who lived with whom, inasmuch as both sets of grandparents and many of their children lived within a few blocks of each other. During World War II, other relatives fleeing the Nazis, among them Leon Cherry's brother and his wife and their sons, arrived from Europe. They, too, were taken in or lived nearby. Nettie and her sisters and their families saw each other daily, if only to gather in the basement to clean the large burlap-sackfuls of fish that Joe lugged home several times a week from his walk to visit fishermen friends at Sheepshead Bay.

Allan's experience was not uncommon in a neighborhood where most children were second-generation Americans who more likely than not lived with both their parents and their usually thick-accented European grandparents. When as an adult he visited Vienna for the first time, his initial impression was of being back in the neighborhood of his childhood. The trolley cars, the apartments, the people sitting in chairs on the sidewalk on hot days, were all familiar sights. The culture of the coffeehouses and tea shops reminded him of the many European bakers who lived near him and of the Embassy Tea Room in Brooklyn, a Viennese-style salon with its white tile floor and strudels and pastries.

The first years after Allan's birth were financially difficult for all of the Konigsbergs. Since Isaac's loss of his businesses and fortune he and Martin had scraped by, but that was about all. Isaac's butter and egg business earned just enough for his and Sarah's necessities, but Martin couldn't support his growing family on what his little store brought in, so he tried a variety of alternatives. One was running bets upstate to the racetrack in Saratoga for some locally famous racketeers, a job he liked because they paid him well and every day and because it had a certain romance to it; but his father begged him to leave it before he became so involved with them that he could not safely quit. Over the course of Allan's childhood Martin constantly tried new ventures. One was to sell mail-order jewelry. Nettie helped him type up the many letters of solicitation he sent out. For a time they met with some success and their home was filled with containers of pearls and blue velvet boxes to keep them in. But this business petered out, too, and eventually all there was to show for it was stacks of unused velvet boxes.

There were other jobs. He worked in a poolroom, which he could have bought but thought—mistakenly, it turned out—it was not a good investment. He was also in no particular order an egg candler, a cabdriver, a bartender, a jewelry engraver, and a waiter in Sammy's Bowery Follies, a lower Manhattan restaurant that catered to tourists.

Just two people to provide for had strained the family finances, so when Allan was about a year old, Nettie went back to work as a bookkeeper. For a while, a Mrs. Wolf, who had fled Germany with Leon Cherry's brother and his wife, acted as Allan's nanny. She spoke German and thus so did he (at least for a time—Woody has no command of it today).

But for the most part Allan's day care was left to a succession of poorly educated and underskilled women who were paid by the hour and who generally lasted only a couple of weeks before quitting or being fired. An agency sent them over and often what Woody recalls as their "seedy boyfriends" came and hung around. The women's inadequacies ranged from the passive, such as letting him play alone in the street, to the criminal, such as stealing clothes, to the psychopathic. One day when Allan was three, the incumbent nanny came to him in his crib, put the covers over him, wrapped him in a bundle so he could not breathe, and said, "See? I could smother you right now and throw you out in the garbage and no one would ever know the difference." And then, as matter-of-factly as he recollected the event fifty years later, she let him go.

He never told his parents about his brush with suffocation, and after the woman freed him, he went about his normal play without apparent trauma—although his normal play as a three-year-old did not require him to ride in an elevator or go through a long tunnel, activities he avoids today whenever possible.

Not all the revolving caretakers were terrible. The occasional sweet and capable one came along, but she was usually soon lost to marriage or a steady job. Yet even when the women were nice it was hard on Allan, who cried when his mother went to work and cried even harder when at about age four she tried to send him to day camp. He wanted to be home.

Home, however, had its perils beyond maniacal nannies. Added to his misery was the nature of his parents' marriage, which he describes as "a totally contentious relationship. They did everything except exchange gunfire." The source of contention between his mother and father was anything and everything. Money was an obvious and continual problem, as Martin was free with it and Nettie was frugal. He always worked very hard at his different jobs and brought in enough to get by on. But he also was quick to spend whatever he had, whether it was on clothes for himself or to add to Allan's chestful of toys or, later, to give him money to do things. To Nettie, who kept the household together by being penurious, this was intolerable. The two were gunpowder and a match.

Allan, a constant witness to these domestic explosions, was too young to follow all their details, but it didn't really matter. The arguments were generic rather than specific: about money; about whether to move and if so, where; about Martin's clotheshorse ways; about which business scheme to pursue. The arguments had a form with limited, recurring themes, and they took place within the confines of the home.

"Their fights were never about another woman or another man, and my father never drank or anything like that," Woody says. "His only vice was to buy a lot of clothes. But every little thing escalated into a fight. If my father would put on a new shirt and my mother would cut a melon and a drop would shoot on it or something, within five minutes they were at each other with straight razors."

Many of Woody Allen's humorous pieces describe domestic strife. In one titled "Retribution," he writes: "Actually, I had a rather dim view of my family's physical appearance, likening the relatives on my mother's side to something in a petri dish. I was very hard on my family and we all constantly teased each other and fought, but were close.

Indeed, a compliment had not passed through the lips of any member during my lifetime and I suspect not since God made his covenant with Abraham."

His parents' strife seems the best explanation for Woody's temper, or rather his lack of one; he loses it only slightly more often than the sun fails to set. He virtually never raises his voice, either on the set or at home; an actor is never berated for flubbing a line for the eighth time; a technician is never yelled at for causing a reshoot. His rare outbursts at work—they happen once in several years—are almost always the result of frustration. For instance, one day he was editing a scene in *Another Woman* that begins in a shed with a boy having an argument with his father. Then the camera pans outside where his sister, now an adult, comes into frame through the screen door and talks to her brother across the years. Woody had wanted the camera to come up over the silhouette of the boy as his sister walked through fall leaves into view, but the shed was crowded with all the camera and sound equipment and it was difficult to get the appropriate angle. Woody had found the scene adequate until he tried to cut it into the film. After watching the scene a couple of times, he banged his fist on the editing machine and then buried his face in his hands. "Damn. I just want to kill myself," he said. "This is so prosaic compared to the shot I wanted to make. It should have the dreamy nature of much of the rest of the film. Now it's too late. The actor's in a play in Philadelphia and besides, there are no leaves anymore." Then within moments, he was calm again and back at work.

"Once in a while Mia and I fight but not a lot, not much," he says. "I can't do it. I don't think kids ever like to see their parents arguing. It could get terrifying or depressing. I would never argue with Mia in front of the kids. But I'm not a big arguer. It never does any good. Where my anger usually comes out is toward inanimate things. If in the morning my toaster's not working or if the refrigerator door won't close, finally I'll get angry and bang it closed. That's about it."

In a neighborhood where the daily struggle to stay afloat consumed almost every family, anxiety and arguments were the staple of many homes. As Allan grew older, the parents of some of his friends fought so bellicosely that the police had to be called in, something that never happened at his house. But the effect on a sensitive boy such as he was considerable.

Around the time he turned five, two things happened that have plainly affected his life, but how they have affected his work is less plain to see. The first is impossible even to clearly define; it was a change of attitude and personality that occurred over time and was caused by no known specific event.

"My mother always said I was a happy kid for my early years and then when I was around five, something happened, she always felt, that made me turn sour," Woody said one day while talking about his childhood. "I have no memory of any such event or anything traumatic nor could anyone offer up any traumatic event. So I don't know. I *was* a loner from an early time on. I remember other kids in class psychoanalyzing me amateurishly when I was in the sixth grade and saying, 'Well, do you notice that when he walks to school, he walks through the back alleys?' Which I did. I often went down the block and hung a left to make a shortcut. They said, 'It's because he doesn't want to be around people.' And, you know, that couldn't have been more true, though I wasn't totally conscious of it at the time. And my family was not like that. They were loud and demonstrative but I definitely have never been social. It's a paradox."

Some obvious and rather facile probable causes can be laid to his experiences with the baby-sitters and the extreme discomfort he felt from his parents yelling at each other. And there was also the mixed relationship he had with his parents. Because it was more in the custom of the time and because, too, his mother didn't know how else to cope with him, she often slapped or spanked Allan in an attempt to control him.

It is not that he was an abused child or unloved, nor that he didn't love his parents. He was just different from his family, almost from the beginning, and he was something of a problem for them to handle precisely because he was different.

"He was an extraordinary child," says his sister, Letty Aronson, who was born when he was eight and is his only sibling. She has a degree in teaching emotionally disturbed children. "He was not an average child and our entire system, whether it is the school system or whatever, is geared to the average child. So nothing worked for him."

In an interview with his mother for a work-in-progress documentary called *Two Mothers* (the other mother in the film is Maureen O'Sullivan, Mia's mother), there is this exchange between mother and son:

He: "Did you hit me?"

She: "You'll have to forgive me. I spanked you. I wasn't abusive, no. But I spanked you. . . . I hit you occasionally, yes. I spanked you occasionally."

"I remember you would hit me every day when I was a child."

Flustered: "Like what? Did I beat you?"

"No, but you were always slapping me."

"You were an active child, you spoke young. . . . You were very bright and you ran and jumped. I didn't know how to handle that type of child. You were too active and too much of a child for me. I wasn't that good to you because I was very strict, which I regret. Because if I hadn't been that strict, you might have been a more, a not so impatient . . . you might have been a—what should I say? Not better. You're a good person. But, uh, maybe softer, maybe warmer. That's the word I want to use. But it was hard for me to handle you. I was much sweeter to Letty than I was to you."

The other, more definable and probably more important event at around age five is how he came to be in Brooklyn's Public School 99, the school where he was amateurishly psychoanalyzed, and the school his father had attended. He could instead have been at the Hunter College Elementary School in Manhattan, which offered a special program for bright students. Allan scored very high on an IQ test for children about to start school and Nettie perhaps saw this as an opportunity for her son to have what she missed. But the school was a long subway ride from Brooklyn and it was too hard for her to make the two round trips a day to take him to school and to pick him up.

"Had I had the intelligence I have now," Nettie says, "I would have packed up and moved to Manhattan. But I didn't. I said, 'Well, he'll go to the neighborhood.'" And so he was enrolled at P.S. 99, a short walk from his house. (The Konigsbergs did take their children to Manhattan doctors, who were considered better—and were more expensive—than those in Brooklyn.)

"My biggest regret in retrospect is that my parents didn't live in Manhattan," Woody said one day as his chauffeur drove him back into Manhattan after touring the old neighborhood, a sentimental journey he takes every few years. (He made the tour on foot, with the car parked on side streets, to avoid ostentation.) "It's such a regret of mine. They thought they were doing the right thing and probably thought that they couldn't afford to move. In a certain sense, given who my parents were and how much money they had, it was fine to live in

Brooklyn. But the truth is, if they were a little more enlightened, I could have grown up in Manhattan in the late thirties and forties. I would have loved that. Now, of course," he added with a laugh, "the city is much more of, you'll forgive the expression, a shithole than it was then. I love it now like a boy loves a father who is, say, an alcoholic or a thief. But when I think that there were kids who grew up on Park Avenue and Fifth Avenue in the thirties and forties and had their childhood there and there was no crime to speak of, what a paradise!" He said this with no sense that his perception of Manhattan would be totally different as a result of living there. Instead of the wonderland across the river, it would have been, simply, home.

Allan Konigsberg was a boy with a watchful eye and a vivid memory. Events from elementary school, the faces of classmates, the smells and auras of places he went, remain clear and alive a half century later in Woody Allen's consciousness, almost as if they are snippets of cinema. "I paid attention to everything but the teachers," he said one day, and then added, "As I've grown older, my life has developed a more tangible continuity with my childhood than most people's. In my mind, it was only yesterday that I was standing in line to enter the school building. It's not that I just remember it like it was yesterday, I have a feeling for it. It's not ancient history in any way. I feel I'm still spinning out from that experience." One momentous part of that childhood experience was seeing Manhattan for the first time. It was the instant his love affair with the city began, and the glories of the place are in many ways seen in his films through those six-year-old eyes. New York is never dirty or decayed in a Woody Allen movie. Instead it glimmers and soars, it moves at an invigoratingly frantic pace and seems the apotheosis of cosmopolitan living. As he showed through George Gershwin's music in *Manhattan*, New York, to him, is a rhapsody.

"I first came to the city in 1941 with my father," he says, "and I was in love with it from the second I came up from the subway into Times Square. You can't believe what a thing that is to suddenly look up and see it—remember, this is before it degenerated. Every twenty feet there was a glittering marquee with a movie house. In my neighborhood there was a movie house and then three blocks later there was another and then three blocks later another, and that was a *lot*. Here, there were twenty on my right side and twenty on my left side on Broadway, and I turned onto Forty-second Street and there were twenty on this side, twenty on that side. I just couldn't believe it. There were no trash houses or porno houses. They were showing first-run films. It was all Humphrey Bogart and Clark Gable and Jimmy Cagney and, you know, papaya stands and guys with apparently stringless dancing dolls. They used to amaze me, guys working on a suitcase with those things. I never could figure out how they were done. And shooting galleries. In those days you could shoot real rifles. *I* couldn't, you had to be sixteen, but my father always used to shoot them.

"I was just *stunned* by it all. You'd come up out of the subway at Forty-second Street and walk up Broadway. At Fifty-second Street there would be Lindy's [a famous Broadway restaurant and hangout for show people, sports figures, and gangsters], then right after Lindy's, the Circle Magic Shop, which was wonderful. And there was the Brass Rail and Birdland and that restaurant right on Forty-second Street, the Cross-roads, and there was the Paramount and the Roxy. It was just absolutely astonishing. When I cut school and went to the Paramount for the first time, the movie ended and suddenly the lights went on and Duke Ellington's band came rising out of the pit playing 'Take the "A" Train.' I just couldn't believe it. It took the top of my head off.

"I not only was totally in love with Manhattan from the earliest memory, I loved every single movie that was set in New York, every movie that began high above the New York skyline and moved in. Every detective story, every romantic comedy, every movie about nightclubs in New York or penthouses. To this day, ninety-nine percent of movies that are not about the city, that take place in rural atmospheres, I rarely latch on to. They really have to be extraordinary. But I love any old film that ever begins or takes place in New York City.

"To me, people who lived in Manhattan would go from the Copa to the Latin Quarter; they'd hear jazz downtown, they'd go up to Har-lem, they'd sit at Lindy's until four in the morning. Then they'd come back home and go up in their elevators to their apartments, and their apartments were not like my apartment in Brooklyn where six million people lived together and it was small. They'd go to these apartments that were often duplexes. It was just astonishing. It was also so seductive that I've never really recovered from it. That's why I wound up with a lot of these things in my life." One of them is his duplex penthouse apartment, decorated with country furniture. A nearly 360-degree view through floor-to-ceiling wraparound windows pulls the cityscape into the rooms, making it seem an extension of the home. He made the mistake of taking a little time to consider the price after first seeing the apartment in 1970, and when he learned that someone had bought it, he immediately offered the buyer a 25 percent profit. Within a week, the place was his.

The many remembrances of movies and movie houses are not particularly surprising in someone whose work is so dominated by film. The magic of the movies is easily beguiling, especially to a very young person. To some it is even more than that. In *The Magic Lantern*, Ingmar Bergman, whom Woody Allen calls "probably the greatest film artist, all things considered, since the invention of the motion picture camera," recalls a stunning moment in his boyhood. His brother Dag had been given a cinematograph for Christmas, the only gift that Ingmar had wanted since seeing *Black Beauty* a year before. He threw a tantrum over this injustice and was sent to his room, where his grief mounted while the others enjoyed the Christmas feast. He awoke in the night and gazed at the object of his desire with its crooked chimney for the paraffin lamp and the beautiful brass-enclosed lens on a table in the room. Suddenly, he knew how to get it. He woke Dag, a military buff, and offered him in exchange the hundred tin soldiers that were his present. The deal was made. The next morning he lit the lamp, directed the beam on a wall, and loaded the ten-foot loop of film.

"A picture of a meadow appeared on the wall. Asleep in the meadow was a young woman . . . I turned the handle and the girl woke up, sat up, got slowly up, stretched her arms out, swung around and disappeared to the right. If I went on turning, she would again lie there, then make exactly the same movements all over again.

"*She was moving.*"

Allan Konigsberg had an equally revolutionary experience at an even earlier age. When he was three his mother took him to see *Snow White*. It was his first film. He sat quietly in the plush red velvet seat as the lights went down. Then the characters appeared. Allan had the same stop-breath reaction as Ingmar: They were moving! Captivated by this miracle, he ran to touch them. His mother had to pull him away from the screen.

As if his own inclinations weren't enough to catch him in the web of movies, his cousin Rita Wishnick, five years his senior, was equally ensnared. But while Allan was hooked on movies, she was hooked on movie stars.

When not living with the Konigsbergs, Rita and her parents lived a couple of blocks away, and Allan was often at their house. Of more importance, he was often in Rita's room, which was papered with colored pictures of the stars cut out of *Modern Screen* and other fan magazines. At the beginning of his moviegoing career, she taught him about the players and was his constant companion in watching their exploits. By the time he was seven, there was scarcely an actor he didn't know and he was incredulous if a kid in school had no idea who Jennifer Jones or Dennis Morgan or Caesar Romero was. It was inconceivable that these faces on the screen that were almost as familiar to him as his own in the mirror had no importance in other people's lives. Later, ten- or twelve-year-old friends would say something like "Oh, we saw this guy who is so funny, who has a mustache and a cigar and walks down low," and he would think to himself, "You must be joking. That's Groucho Marx. Did you not *know* this from when you were three years old?"

It was nice to know the stars by sight, but to him the real pleasure lay in the story on the screen. Not in a formal sense but almost by simple osmosis, he became a student of the way the films were put together. So much so that at the age of eight, while watching Tyrone Power in *The Black Swan*, the epitome of a swashbuckling pirate movie, he thought to himself, "Hey, I could do this." It was not a revelation that sent him out to find a movie camera, but it was an awareness in the back of his mind that this was a way he could tell a story. Others could do the swashbuckling.

He was able to see so many movies because there were so many movie theaters nearby—around two dozen within reasonable walking distance of home, most of them owned by the Century company. One of the nicest was the Midwood, right around the corner on Avenue J. As lost fortune had it, Isaac Konigsberg owned it before the Depression (and irony being what it is, *Annie Hall* and other Woody Allen movies would play there). Now it was a link in the Century chain, a 600-or-so-seat house with a main floor and balcony, decorated in the grand manner: red drapes, chandeliers and brass fixtures, lush red carpeting, soft velvet seats. The theater was in the middle of the block; an alley ran next to it. Three houses into the alley was the back of the Konigsberg house. As Allan walked home one day from a movie when he was about seven, he found near the theater's trash cans a strip of a half dozen frames of 35 millimeter film that had broken off the feature. It was a piece of *Four Jills in a Jeep* with Phil Silvers and Carmen Miranda. He was mesmerized by the sight of the characters as he held the celluloid up to the sunlight again and again before taking it home.

But however mesmerizing that little snippet of celluloid was, he saw something even more spellbinding later that year when Nettie took him to the Midwood to see Bob Hope and Bing Crosby in *The Road to Morocco*. As he watched the two ride on camels and sing "Like Webster's dictionary we're Morocco bound," he "knew from that moment on exactly what I wanted to do with my life." Bob Hope was a revelation. His film character is "vain, a womanizer, a coward's coward, but always brilliant," Woody said in *My Favorite Comedian*, a tribute to Hope that was shown at the 1979 New York Film Festival. "The competitive double-crossing nature of the combo and their fantastic ad-lib style with verbal interplay reached a level of graceful spontaneity rarely seen in film."

Hope's quickness, his bright, lightly delivered lines that sound conversational rather than scripted, made a lasting impression. The influence of the Bob Hope in such 1940s and 1950s films as *Monsieur Beaucaire* is evident in the early Woody Allen films but, perhaps surprisingly, only if the viewer knows to look for it. A scene where Hope makes appointments for assignations with a line of women in *Monsieur Beaucaire* is echoed in *Love and Death*. Boris is an inadvertent war hero played by Woody, who has attracted the attentions of a beautiful countess.

COUNTESS
My bedroom at midnight?

BORIS
Perfect. Will you be there too?

COUNTESS
Naturally.

BORIS
Until midnight then.

COUNTESS
(Pressing his hand to her bosom)
Midnight.

BORIS
Make it quarter to twelve.

COUNTESS
Midnight.

BORIS
But of course.

In one scene in *Sleeper*, Woody and Diane Keaton, disguised as doctors, are about to kidnap all that is left of the Leader—his nose. As they walk down the hospital corridor, Woody nervously bites Diane's fingernails while he tells her to keep calm; then as they enter the operating room where a new Leader is about to be cloned from cells of the nose, Woody taps the guard on his chest and with great bravado announces, "We're here to see the nose. I understand it's running."

"Hope was always a superschnook. He looks less like a schnook than I do, though," Woody said while making *Sleeper* in 1973. "I look more schnooky, more intellectual. But both of us have the exact same wellspring of humor. There are certain moments in his older movies when I think he's the best thing I have ever seen. It's everything I can do at times not to imitate him. It's hard to tell when I do, because I'm so unlike him physically and in tone of voice, but once you know I do it, it's absolutely unmistakable."

Allan saw all the Hope pictures as soon as they were released. For that matter, he saw nearly every film as soon as it was released. In this time before television, practically everyone went to the movies at least once a week. Barbershops and dry cleaners and other merchants had posters in their windows listing films at all the area theaters, and the Century chain sent out a blue brochure of current attractions twice a month to every home in Brooklyn. Most of the movie houses were as large and comfortable as the Midwood and they had names with a welcoming air: The Vogue, the Elm, the Triangle, and the Avalon were just a few in Allan's neighborhood. Then, a little farther away on Kings Highway, there was the really snazzy Kingsway, and on Nostrand Avenue, the equally magnificent Patio; a big fountain with goldfish in it flowed in the lobby. They were magnificent, that is, until compared with the Brooklyn Paramount and the Albee a few miles away on Flatbush Avenue. Their grandiosity, their soaring arches and sky-high ceilings, their lavish decor and sheer size were in the same league (but a little lower in the standings) as the Radio City Music Hall in Manhattan—"international palaces," Woody calls them. They were for special occasions, though.

Movie theaters became his second home. Among his favorites was the Kent, "one of the great, meaningful places of my boyhood," he says. Shortly before it was torn down, Woody shot part of *The Purple Rose of Cairo* there. "The Kent was the last outpost," he said not long afterward. "When a film played the Kent, it was the last-run theater and you'd get it for twelve cents. It was right next to a freight-train trestle, so every now and then in the movie you'd hear the freight trains rolling through. It was great. You'd see a double feature and it was those pictures that now would cost you"—he laughed—"seven dollars, and it was twelve cents. It was within a short walking distance of my house and I saw a million great movies there. You knew if a movie had not played the Kent yet, there was a stopgap before it went out of distribution."

While he attended movies more often than his friends, almost everyone Allan knew went on Saturdays, each of them held by the allure and mystery of film, each of them with different explanations for how, say, the screen caught and reflected the images. One friend said with authority that he knew of someone who threw a spitball at the screen and it burst into flame. That made sense to Allan, or at least as much sense as any other theory. But more important than understanding the mystery of the theater was simply being in it and letting the magic take over.

"I remember being the first person on line many times on a Saturday morning," Woody once said as he walked by where the Midwood no longer is. "I would be there at eleven o'clock and the theater would open at twelve. The theater would be lit up and it was amazing to be there because in those days the theater was just beautiful—the carpets and brass and everything. There wouldn't necessarily be a ton of kids at the first show like that. You'd hear a record playing first, they'd stall while people got seated and bought popcorn. Sometimes they had contests, like stock-car races on film. You'd get a number when you came in. If your car won, you went to the manager's office and claimed a prize. I won once. A box of tiddledywinks. I remember it still because it was so meaningful to me. There was always a white-haired matron in a white costume with a flashlight who tended the children's section, so your mother could bring you, put you in your seat, and go. Then four hours later you'd feel a tap on your shoulder and she'd be picking you up. And you'd say, 'I don't want to go! I don't want to go!'"

That sense of dread in facing reality after hours of pleasurable escape is "the worst experience in the world," he says. "You'd go into the theater at noon on a hot summer day, and you'd sit through *The Scarlet Pimpernel* and *The Return of the Scarlet Pimpernel* and it would be nothing but sheer magical joy, eating your chocolate-covered raisins for three or four hours. Then you would come out at three in the afternoon and leave the world of beautiful women and music and, you know, bravery or penthouses or things like that. And suddenly you would be out on Coney Island Avenue in Brooklyn and the trolleys would be passing and the sun would be blinding and there was no more air conditioning. I remember that sense of coming out into the ugly light when I walked out after *Always Leave Them Laughing* with Milton Berle and after *The Secret Life of Walter Mitty*. Any number of pictures."

Woody has tried to impart that sensation in a few of his films, but he feels he has never fully captured it. One attempt was in *The Purple Rose of Cairo*, which is largely about the difference between fantasy and reality. Apart from his dissatisfaction in conveying that specific sensation, however, it is his favorite film to date. Cecilia, played by Mia Farrow, has a brutish husband and a menial job. She escapes to the movies at every opportunity. One day the leading man on the screen turns and talks to her. ("I just met a wonderful new man," she says later. "He's fictional, but you can't have everything.") Soon he comes out of the picture and into her life, much to the annoyance of the other characters in the film, who can't go on without him. In the end, as reality demands, she is stuck with the life she has. (After Woody showed the movie to the Orion executives, one called him and politely asked if he was committed to that ending; a happy conclusion would have been worth millions more at the box office. "The ending was the reason I made the film," he answered.)

One reason Woody was unable to convey the sinking feeling that comes with reentry into the sun and the real world is that Cecilia's predicament is so terrible, and the audience is so aware of it, that the bright light of day hitting her as she exits the theater is lost. It is a subtle point and a horrible epiphany, but one better delivered if the situation is less grave—say, a child waking from a dream in which the summer is spread before him to find that it is the first day of school.

He tried again in *Crimes and Misdemeanors*, this time with humor. His entrance in the movie follows a dramatic scene between a man and his mistress that is then portrayed farcically with a film clip from the Alfred Hitchcock comedy *Mr. and Mrs. Smith*, which Woody's character (Cliff) is watching with his niece Jenny. The script reads:

CUT TO *a movie screen. A forties escapist film. It should mirror the scene we just had with Judah and Del but it's the streamline comedy version.*
CUT TO *me in audience with a fourteen-year-old niece.*
CUT TO *us exiting into the glare of the day with all its noise and horror.*

CLIFF
Oh God, sunlight—traffic—

That, anyway, is how the scene was written. It is not how it was played. He and cinematographer Sven Nykvist talked it over and they both felt that the audience wouldn't get the point; instead, they would just see the bleached and shadowed photography that results from shooting in the sunlight. (Only rarely, and then by design, does Woody shoot a scene in open sunshine.) So they decided for the audience's sake to make it rain because at least the lighting would be pretty. Even then, he reshot the scene on fifteen different occasions, each time with various changes (they walk out of a movie theater, they walk down the street; they talk with a panhandler, they talk with an ice-cream vendor; it rains, it doesn't rain); and in the end, the line went unused. "I can't get a break on this movie," he complained one day as the rain teemed on its own and the budget swelled as he tried to reshoot yet again with Jenny. "Maybe it's too realistic, or it's too atheistic—and probably it turns out there *is* a God, who doesn't want this picture made. Or certainly not at this price."

There is, Woody says, a lot of his cousin Rita as a girl in the character of Cecilia in *The Purple Rose of Cairo* (and a lot of Allan Konigsberg, too; she and Eve, the restrained and minimalist, perfectionist mother in *Interiors*, and Marion, the emotionally closed philosophy professor in *Another Woman* who at age fifty is forced to confront her past, are as close to Woody's personality as any he has created, and the three he most identifies with). Certainly he grew up in a period of contrasts similar to those Cecilia faces. It requires little perception to see the difference between two families living in six rooms on Fourteenth Street in Brooklyn and the penthouses in the movies, to understand why a movie theater might be an appealing place to spend as much time as possible.

"I grew up at a time when you would go to the movies and your basic movie was Fred Astaire or Humphrey Bogart. All those wonderful larger-than-life people," he once said. "This was such a glamorous time, as portrayed in films, and so great a contrast to life outside, that it was a pleasure to be in there and a monstrosity to be outside. My memory of it lingers: three hours of relentless sugar intake; of big apartments and white phones and characters whose biggest concern was 'Who are you going to take to the Easter parade?' You were transported to Arabia, and to Paris in the 1700s, but best of all to Manhattan, which was full of gangsters and showgirls. Afterward, as you walked out up the plush red carpet, the music would be playing to end the picture or to start the next one. Then the doors opened and you were back in the blazing light, amid the meat markets and trucks honking and people walking past. Then there was the odd hour while you waited around for dinner; or if you were lucky, there was a ball game to listen to."

In 1944 the Konigsbergs moved a few blocks away to 1216 East Twelfth Street, again to the upper floor of a two-story wooden house. It was the largest of the five homes they would have in this area of modest two-family houses bordered by nicer single-family ones. Woody stood in front of the house one day forty years after he lived there and described in detail a dozen childhood incidents. Still locked in his memory is where he was in the house when he heard radio bulletins of the deaths of two famous men: the front stoop for President Franklin D. Roosevelt; in the middle upstairs room—his bedroom—for the electrocution of Murder Incorporated gangster Louis (Lepke) Buchalter.

P.S. 99, a three-story, red-brick building rimmed by trees between Ninth and Tenth streets, was a ten- or fifteen-minute walk away. He always walked because he hated bicycles, part of what he calls "an inborn aversion to *things*. I don't like to drive a car, I don't like to ride a bike. I hate gadgets—cameras, tape recorders, airplanes. There are certain things in life that you're not just indifferent to, they're actually off-putting. If I go into a store and they're playing rock music, I want to leave. It's really bothersome to me, punishment of some sort." (He is a great fan of classical music but he has no use for almost any popular songs written after about 1950.) It's the same with mechanical objects. He can ride a bicycle, and once every few years he would ride a friend's out of necessity, but it wasn't fun and he never wanted one. He did have roller skates, and those he liked. "I was in control more. I could roller-skate to Ebbets Field, where I saw every game the Dodgers played against the Giants for years. I was a fast skater. I mean really fast. I had those heavy iron skates that you tightened with a key and I could go like a bullet in them. In a more civilized city it would be fun to get around on skates even now. But in New York you'd quickly get run over and made dead."

P.S. 99 was considered a model school but to him it was "the dread place. I hated it more than rat poison. I hated the concept of school in every way because emotionally, I wasn't prepared for readjustment." He had freedom at home—quite miraculously, considering how problematic a child he could be and how rigid parents of the Konigsbergs' class usually behaved toward children whom they wanted to rise beyond their own lives; he listened to the radio in his room and generally did what he wanted. School, however, was "the zenith of discipline and regimentation: a humorless, joyless, educationless experience provided by nasty and unpleasant teachers." Some days he walked there down Avenue L, the longer way, to postpone the inevitable. The main entrance on Ninth Street was used only by teachers and the principal, a severe woman named Eudora Fletcher who wore her hair in a tightly rolled bun. (Eudora Fletcher is the psychiatrist played by Mia Farrow in *Zelig* whose love transforms the human chameleon played by Woody Allen. He liked the name but not the person. All principals and teachers in his movies are harsh, unsympathetic characters. "Don't listen to what your schoolteachers tell you. Don't pay attention to that," Cliff tells Jenny in *Crimes and Misdemeanors*. "Just see what they look like and that's how you'll know what life is really going to be like.") On either side of the entrance was a Victory garden, where students worked as punishment for their school-day crimes and misdemeanors. There were small play yards on two other sides of the square building, and the strike zones for stickball games were painted on the walls. Allan was an excellent player who hit countless homers; the temporary reprieve of recess was the place's only saving grace. The rest of the day was regimented from the moment one arrived (and on Wednesday, which was assembly day, from the moment one got dressed: Boys were required to wear a white shirt and kelly-green tie in honor of the school colors). On clear days the first person from each class to arrive stood at a crack in the pavement three feet from the wall; the others lined up behind. Student monitors whom Woody likens to prison-camp Kapos policed the lines and teachers stood at their head. In winter they gathered in the basement, "the moment of doom coming closer, standing on line meaninglessly when it would have been more fun to dawdle and chat with friends." What for many children might be an exercise looked on in retrospect with a chuckle is, for him, an often recalled and almost Dickensian ritual:

"It was an odious task. You'd leave your house on a cold, wet winter morning despising having to go to school and leave the comforts of your little bed and your radio and the things that were so wonderful. And you'd go to the school, where all was hostility and problems, even in the first grade. You'd enter the building and line up and once you got on that line you couldn't talk. If you lined up outside in the school-yard in the warmer weather, you could speak until they told you to keep quiet for the last ten minutes or so. But inside, as soon as you came in, you had to be quiet. Then you'd line up, boys in one line, girls next to you, and there you would be with a lot of grotesque kids of which I was one. And you would have on your dreadful mackinaw or pea coat and your hat with the flaps, where you fold them out from underneath and then tie them under your chin. You'd be wet or there would be the smell of wet wool all the time. The guys would be standing in line—there would be the fat kid that you hated in front of you, and the one with his nose running behind you, and these wretched little girls in the other line. And everybody would be standing there dreading that in a few minutes you'd march up to your class and go through hours of boredom and intimidation. There are so many times even now that I think back and recall that I'd be on that line and have to go up there into the clutches of those blue-haired teachers. What an abysmal horror that was."

His memories may seem harsh and perhaps the product of an imaginative raconteur, but others in his class corroborate them. Judi Swiller Davidson, now a publicist in Los Angeles, is the daughter of a doctor who lived in the nicer part of the neighborhood, at Ocean Park-way and Avenue J. She was tall for her age, and because she ruined the symmetry of the girls' line, she was forced to her mortification to stand in the boys'. Teachers committed other, greater cruelties. Among them, both she and Woody remember, is their making fun of a boy afflicted with mongolism. Both also point out that although the students were predominantly Jewish, the teachers were for the most part Gentile, often Irish, and in some cases at least mildly anti-Semitic. It was not unknown for Gentile boys to be dismissed at the end of the day while

Jewish boys were kept behind, thus deliberately making them late for Hebrew school.

"It was the strangest thing," Woody remembers. "They were those kinds of right-wing, cross, redneck—in their case, redface—blue-haired ladies who were very strict. Like nuns in a way." He demonstrated his abhorrence of school in some predictable ways. When he first attended P.S. 99 he was placed in an accelerated class because of his high IQ, but since the strictures of the classroom did not allow him to express himself in his own way and to use his imagination in his lessons, he instead expressed himself by becoming a troublemaker. Before long, he was dropped from the class. As he grew older, his rebellious nature increased. He played hooky (and was once literally dragged by an ear up a flight of stairs into class after the female assistant principal caught him trying to flee the grounds). He failed to do his homework. He was sometimes disruptive in class and rude to the teacher, who in turn lowered his grades for his behavior. But his hostility was against the authority of the school, not his fellow students. While he got into the same schoolyard fights as everyone does, it wasn't a fistfighting neighborhood. There were wrestling matches and other conflicts, but the environment was not brutal. And he wasn't a brutal boy.

He was, however, a boy who managed to get into more than his share of trouble. His mother was called in so often to see the principal and teachers about his behavior that years later, now grown classmates who knew her from coming into the classroom would say hello to her on the street or in a shop.

The greater Midwood neighborhood was almost entirely Jewish, especially as it fanned out toward the larger, single-family homes where the doctors, lawyers, and other professionals lived. For the most part, the only differences among people there were whether they were Sephardic or Ashkenazi Jews. But as the homes became smaller and the workers nonprofessional—many had jobs in the garment industry, others drove taxis—there was some ethnic mix. On one corner of East Fifteenth Street there lived an Italian family whose son Allan was friendly with and whose apparently happy home life he envied. A policeman and his family lived across the street, and one of the Konigsbergs' next-door neighbors was another policeman. The family in the house on the other side were both Russian Jews and Communists. They shocked the neighborhood by flagrantly not observing the Jewish high holy days; a mild version of them appears in *Radio Days*. Their son was a close friend of Allan's, but they, Woody says, "were angry Russians. They had been uprooted and came to the United States and didn't like it. They were nasty sourpusses who would just sit out on the stoop of their house and chase you."

The walk to and from school down Avenue K or L was a pleasant stroll on tree-lined streets through a safe, strongly family-oriented community that had gradually overtaken large agricultural and chicken farms. Even so, in the 1930s and well into the 1940s, some homes still had chicken coops and an occasional lot was given over to vegetables. Each morning, Allan heard the rhythmic clatter of a horse-drawn milk cart as the driver guided it down the block to deliver the requisite two bottles. After work on spring and summer afternoons, people came out to water their lawns and listen to favorite radio shows or, better, broadcasts of baseball games in the great rivalry between the Brooklyn Dodgers and the New York Giants. (Allan, to everyone's horror, became a Giants fan at age eleven, mainly out of perversity; although in fairness the 1947 Giants were an exciting team—they hit 221 home runs, 51 of them by Johnny Mize—even if they did finish fourth, 13 games behind the Dodgers.) The residents were hardworking, lower-middle-class people. There was no crime to speak of, and when the people did speak, it was not in the stereotypic Brooklyn accent of "deeze" and "dem" and "doze."

As Allan turned left onto Coney Island Avenue there was a host of candy stores and a hobby shop he could stop in to spend some of the money he almost always had in his pocket, put there by his father and his aunts. Although all of them struggled financially, Allan was the only boy in an extended Jewish family and he was its cynosure. Beginning at age seven, his spinster aunts gave him twenty-five cents a week, with a nickel raise as he passed each school year. Between that and a parental allowance supplemented by finding and turning in soda bottles for the two-cent deposit and doing odd chores, such as delivering for a butcher and for a tailor, he usually managed to come up with the price of a movie ticket. Admission was eleven cents for two features and cartoons, plus a comic and a cardboard toy. (It rose gradually to twelve, then fifteen, then twenty cents without public complaint, but years later when it hit fifty-five cents for a double feature, there was outrage.)

While he attended school as seldom as he could and with no enthusiasm, he watched movies as often as he could with utmost pleasure. Until he was bar mitzvahed at thirteen, he was forced to attend

Hebrew school after classes were dismissed at public school. But on Friday afternoons, when Hebrew school was not held, or when he played hooky from it, he'd as often as not go to the Elm, the best theater for after-school shows because he could get there just in time to catch the last features children under sixteen could attend without adult accompaniment. Being late was no real impediment, however. He would just ask a stranger if he could go in with him and was always accommodated. It was often dark by the time all the films ended and he hurried home on the scary walk past a large vacant lot. Even so, he liked to be alone.

His parents had a relaxed attitude about such comings and goings. Sometimes he'd tell them he was going to the movies after school, often he would not. But he never had to hide his activities; providing there was no familial obligation, his time was his own and his parents, who trusted him, didn't care how he spent it. ("They knew I wasn't going to hold up a bank or anything.") So with the exception of going to so many movies, his afternoons were passed in usual schoolboy fashion: at the schoolyard or at a friend's house or playing on the block.

In the summertime, especially, he was amazed at how his friends had to get permission to do anything away from home. Allan simply got up, went out, and, with the exception of returning for meals, generally stayed out until his 9 p.m. curfew. If he was going to travel out of the neighborhood—say, to the Polo Grounds in northern Manhattan to watch the Giants play—he announced his intended whereabouts to his mother (his father usually was at work), who never seemed to object. In the hot summer days his continual destination was the movies, which he usually attended with a friend. This often dismayed the parents of whichever boy accompanied him, because invariably they wanted their child to play in the fresh air and sun at the beach, where, Woody says, "they could soak up all those cancer-causing rays." But if other parents did prevail, it didn't matter to Allan, who considered it a treat to go by himself. He enjoyed his own company and, as well, he enjoyed fabricating different roles and identities, generally of a larcenous nature.

One was to be a dreidel hustler. He imagined spinning the little lead top with a Hebrew letter on each of its four sides until, after a time, he was able to have the letters come up in his favor more often than not. He saw himself as a little Legs Diamond, awash in his winnings, his best dreidel in a smart carrying case that he toted from city to city on luxurious trains, his precious spinning hand perfectly manicured as he coolly played for $100,000 a game.

The first eight years of Allan's life had physical stability even if he found his home life unsettling. The family moved just once, and then only a few blocks away. But between the ages of eight and twelve his daily routine and physical surroundings were in great flux. The changes began with the birth of his sister, Letty, when he was eight. Visually there has never been any question about their relationship. Her hair is slightly redder than his, her face somewhat rounder, she is altogether pretty— and one could match them in a crowd with ease.

For all the surprise it must have been to an eight-year-old to suddenly be neither the only child nor, in effect, the baby, Woody feels that "Letty and I are just one of those things that are luck. I liked her from the moment I met her." And she says, "The big factor in my upbringing is that I had him. We were very close."

It was a big factor in his upbringing, too, and is one in his life as well. Woody's closest friends are women and his affinity for them shows in his work. The women's parts in his films are particularly meaty. (In his earliest movies he used women the way classic comedians from Chaplin to Hope had: They were objects of desire to impress, and while they fluttered the comic's heart, they led him to danger. By *Sleeper*, however, Diane Keaton was the smarter of the two characters, the aggressive one with the initiative. She was more like a heroine in a Buster Keaton film. Since *Annie Hall* his women have been strong, three-dimensional figures who dominate many films—from the title on, in cases such as *Hannah and Her Sisters* and *Alice*.) So while Woody has several male friends, his sympathies are clearly with women. "They are loyal and devoted," he has said. "They're more solid citizens. It was borne out with my sister, with whom I had a spectacular relationship." One apparent result of this is that Woody, like George Cukor, is an excellent "woman's director" who can help actresses deliver extraordinary performances.

Virtually from the time she could walk, he took Letty nearly everywhere with him and they remain close today. His interest in her was total and, he says, without jealousy (certainly he never showed any), and to all appearances, theirs was a unique case of sibling amity. Still, for all that she adores him and despite his and Mia Farrow's conviction to the contrary, Letty's training in child psychology leads her to believe her arrival was not as easy for him as it seems.

"Here you have a boy who for eight years was an only child," she says. "For good or bad, everything focused on him. Into the picture comes this baby who's a girl on top of it—and easier, more compliant, whatever. Now, I'm not saying this was conscious on his part, because clearly it wasn't. But you can deal with it in one of two ways. You can hate this person, in which case you kind of alienate yourself because obviously these people wanted another child if after eight years they've had one. Or it's a question of don't fight 'em, join 'em and give yourself that special position: 'This is my sister. I *love* my sister. This is fantastic!' And then everyone says, 'What a brother he is! Look at that! He is terrific! Did you ever see such a relationship? He is just wonderful! He is just great to her!' Thereby avoiding all the negative things that would have happened.

"Now, the fact is, he made it pay off for him. If more kids could do that in their subconscious, they would get along much better, because on account of that he was so good to me. I absolutely idolized him. There was never any conflict between us. My parents never had to say to him, 'Look at how you're treating her.' He never received negative attention for how he was with me; he was constantly praised. We developed a very good relationship that didn't have to wait as with many siblings until they're older and can sort out all that garbage. All that garbage never was. So for me, it was an enormous benefit that he never had. It took the edge off of the domination by my parents," who like many parents were inclined to overly protect a daughter from the world. Allan provided a voice of liberalism as well as a buffer. "In a sense," she says, "what I had that he didn't have was benign neglect. Basically my mother worked and my father worked and I had my brother. This worked to our benefit."

Still, Letty's relationship with her mother was closer than Allan's if only because there were established mother-daughter things for them to do: go to Manhattan to see a show on Saturday, have lunch at a Schrafft's, go shopping. Allan occasionally went to the movies with his mother, and although the films were fun, her reaction to them wasn't always pleasurable for him. After watching Roddy McDowall play a polite and enterprising young lad in *The White Cliffs of Dover*, for instance, Nettie dragged Allan by the hand up the aisle and in a loud voice asked, "Why can't you be more like Roddy McDowall?" (The two men have since met and laughed over the story.) Also, Allan didn't share his mother's interest in what she calls "a good love picture," so if only for reduced common interest he attended just a handful of movies with her, almost all before Letty was born, and fewer with his father.

There is a scene near the end of *Radio Days* where the young Woody Allen character is being chased by his father, who intends to spank him with a belt for having turned his mother's coat purple in an experiment with his new chemistry set. Moments after the father has caught him and, sitting in an easy chair with the boy over his knees, begins to strap him, an announcer breaks into the radio program playing in the background with a news bulletin about a young girl who has fallen down a well. All activity in the house stops as the family listens to the description of the attempted rescue now shown on the screen. When the film shifts back to the family living room, the boy is nestled in his father's lap, the father's arms around him as they hear this drama unfold hundreds of miles away. For a time, anyway, the family is at peace. Perhaps the fractious nature of his parents' marriage made calm time spent with them special, but whatever the reason, decades later the few movies he did see with one or both parents remain clear in Woody's memory. The few exceptions aside when his mother wished that he would emulate someone in the picture, they were very happy events. Woody saw thousands of films as a child but a handful are a special memory:

"My mother took me to see *Pinocchio* when it came out. I remember that day. I remember not being able to sleep the night before because I was so excited. They took me to see the one Irving Berlin was in, *This Is the Army*. My father loved Westerns. He took me to see the movie with all those cowboy outlaws in it, *City of Bad Men*. They were all combined—Jesse James and the Younger Brothers and the Daltons. We went to *Beau Geste*. They took me to see the one where Gary Cooper played a doctor on the island of Java, *The Story of Dr. Wassell*, and the one where Wallace Beery played a Marine who leads the people of an island against the invading Japanese, *Salute to the Marines*. My father took me to see *The Babe Ruth Story* at my insistence. I can remember them all. They were all outstanding events. The other movies I saw with friends or with my cousin Rita or by myself."

If one movie epitomized his childhood, it is *Double Indemnity*. "I love it," he says. "It has all the characteristics of the classic forties film as I respond to it. It's in black and white, it has fast badinage, it's very witty, a story from the great age. It has Edward G. Robinson and Barbara Stanwyck and Fred MacMurray and the tough voice-over. It has brilliantly written dialogue, and the perfect score by Miklos Rozsa. It's Billy Wilder's best movie—but practically anyone's best movie."

When Letty was growing up, Rita and her sister and parents shared the Konigsberg apartment in the two-family house at 1144 East Fifteenth Street. As always, other relatives were nearby and who lived with whom changed from time to time. There were Aunt Anna and Aunt Molly, there were Aunt Ceil and Uncle Abe and their two children, and there were grandparents. Allan liked the arrangement, or at least didn't dislike it; the house was a little too quiet for him during the interludes he was alone with his parents. And despite any reservations he or Letty may have had about the communal proximity of so many relatives, Nettie and Martin took pride that theirs was an open house, a haven for relatives as well as for their and their children's friends.

"They always had company, they always had people to dinner," Letty says. "We could walk in with four friends and say, 'They're staying for dinner,' and there would be enough food and nobody would say they couldn't. There were always kind of strays in terms of adults, people our parents had met or picked up who were unmarried or unhappy or unwhatever and became part of the group that would come. We once had a cleaning woman who came on Fridays. That was the night my mother would make dinner." Martin, however, usually was at work. "The cleaning woman came from Haiti and spoke some English, although not a lot. She would answer the phone and say, 'You coming tonight for dinner? Just give me your name.'"

When people did not come over, however, the family ate consecutively rather than together. Martin often worked nights, so he would have something early before he left for work. Nettie fed Letty for several years. Allan ate by himself, many nights in the basement. Occasionally it was as punishment for misbehavior, such as one offense or another at school, but usually it was simply because it offered him—an isolationist by preference—a place to be by himself and read a comic book while he ate in peace.

Between Letty's birth and the move to Fifteenth Street when Allan was twelve or thirteen, the Konigsbergs were almost constantly changing homes. In the beginning, Allan liked the variety, but not by the end.

It began with the move to an apartment for the summer in Long Beach, just beyond the eastern end of Brooklyn on Long Island. (Far Rockaway, between Brooklyn and Long Beach, is where many of the outdoor scenes in *Radio Days* were shot. It is difficult to tell one from the other.) It was no grand beach house but rather a small, unheated flat. Nor was it particularly special for them to go to the beach for the summer. It was something many people did to escape from the humid heat and the crowds of the city. But at the end of the summer of 1945, Martin and Nettie, having given up the apartment on Twelfth Street, could find no affordable place back in the neighborhood. So along with Abe and Ceil and their daughters, Jane and Marjorie (six and eight years younger than Allan), they stayed at the beach all winter and used portable electric heaters for warmth. Then when summer came, they stayed on. Allan and his cousins went to the public school nearby, a refreshing change for him from P.S. 99 because, he says, "it was easier. The kids were dumber."

"I loved living there. Spring would come to Long Beach and it was great. After school I could play down by the water and walk along the ocean by myself. I loved to do that in the gray weather." Woody's *Radio Days* narration remembering his "stormy and rainswept" neighborhood accompanies pictures of pounding seas crashing up along the shore by rows of apartments. "Then summer would come and the ocean and the bay were right at your fingertips and you'd go swimming or fishing. I had a fabulous time living in a beach community, fabulous."

After a year they moved again, this time to the other end of Long Beach, where the apartments had heat. It was yet another new elementary school and another new Hebrew school for Allan, a change that weighed on him, and it was hard on Martin, too, who had to make the long commute on the Long Island Rail Road to work in Manhattan. So there was still another move and this one, for Allan, was the worst.

Ceil and Abe took the upstairs of a three-family house in Port Chester, around twenty-five miles north of Manhattan, and the Konigsbergs moved in with them for about six months while they continued to try to find another house in Brooklyn.

"I am two with Nature," Woody Allen wrote early in his career. The twain refused to meet even in childhood and have continued on their separate ways. Now, looking out from his apartment over Central Park is about as much Nature as he can stand. He will go to Mia's country home in Connecticut but only for very limited periods.

"Woody has no tolerance for the country," she says. "Within half an hour after arriving he's walked around the lake and is ready to go home. He gets very bored. He swears he once got a tick standing by the front door. He was the only one to get one. I didn't actually *see* the offending tick. He discovered it after he went back to New York. I assume he's correct although he doesn't know much about bugs. He's been seen in a beekeeper's hat at my place when it's gnats time. He'll put it on and seriously stroll by the lake in it. Of course, he *never* goes in the lake. He wouldn't *touch* the lake. 'There are *live things* in there,' he says." (He does, however, stand at its edge to practice on his clarinet—about the only activity there for him to engage in.) Woody's avoidance of rural water extended to a scene in A *Midsummer Night's Sex Comedy* in which he and Mia fall in a lake (actually their doubles do). Rather than soak himself with lake water for the full shot of the two of them coming out, now ankle deep, he had himself doused with bottles of Evian.

So while most people would find the suburban atmosphere and sense of country in Port Chester attractive, Allan hated it for those very reasons. He abhorred seeing grass everywhere and roads almost nowhere. He detested the school. In short, he loathed everything that made Port Chester an escape from city living, which was the exact thing he yearned to escape back to. He had such a hard time that after a couple of months of unpleasantness, his parents let him move in with his maternal grandparents in Brooklyn.

Allan and his grandfather had a good relationship, and Nettie, who loved her father very much, wanted Leon's values to rub off on him. She wanted to raise a son who would please him and she hoped he could transmit his faith and his devotion to Judaism; it was important to her that Allan learn Hebrew and say the prayers because of her father. But although he attended Hebrew school as he was told to and went to the synagogue with his grandfather (Nettie went only occasionally, Martin seldom), Allan had an ecumenical view of religion. That is, he found all organized faiths equally useless.

"I was unmoved by the synagogue, I was not interested in the Seder, I was not interested in the Hebrew school, I was not interested in being Jewish," Woody says. "It just didn't mean a thing to me. I was not ashamed of it nor was I proud of it. It was a nonfactor to me. I didn't care about it. It just wasn't my field of interest. I cared about baseball, I cared about movies. To be a Jew was not something that I felt 'Oh, God, I'm so lucky.' Or 'Gee, I wish I were something else.' I certainly had no interest in being Catholic or in any of the other Gentile religions." The notion brings forth a laugh from him when he says it. "I thought those kids in Catholic school who couldn't see movies because the Legion of Decency wouldn't permit them, or who said their catechism, were silly beyond belief. I thought, 'What a waste of time.' And I felt the same thing in Hebrew school, my mind drifting out the window, not learning anything, just counting the minutes until it was over."

Now, however, he is consumed with questions of eschatology and a merciful God's existence; with questions of morality and justice when God may either not care or be absent from worldly life. Those issues are at the heart of two films made fifteen years apart: *Crimes and Misdemeanors*, in which a man has his mistress killed when she threatens to expose their affair and his financial manipulations, and, in a farcical way, *Love and Death*, in which the characters played by Woody and Diane Keaton—Boris and his (like Rita) cousin Sonia—given the opportunity to kill Napoleon, argue like two undergraduate philosophy majors over the moral rectitude of their action or inaction.

For all his questioning and agonizing, Woody Allen is a reluctant (he hopes there is a God) but pessimistic (he doubts there is) agnostic who wishes he had been born with religious faith (not to be confused with sectarian belief) and who believes that even if God is absent, it is important to lead an honest and responsible life. His observations and jokes about God and religion make him a favorite of theologians. Yet Allan Konigsberg was, he says, "amoral and impervious. When I say amoral I think of an incident with my grandfather, who was a kind and sweet man whom I liked very much. I was eleven or so and I found a counterfeit nickel on the street. It was clearly counterfeit. But I suggested fobbing it off on my grandfather, who was old and wouldn't know the difference. Now, this is an amoral act. My mother caught me later and asked, 'How could you ask for five pennies for a counterfeit nickel? That's terrible.' And I was unfazed by it. The consequences or the morality of it never crossed my mind for a second."

He attributes his attitude to his father, for it turns out he was not impervious to influence. Religious faith and tradition may not have rubbed off on him but the rough hand-to-mouth world Martin inhabited did.

"I learned all my father's streety, suspicious, tough attitudes toward everything," he said years afterward, laughing at himself. "He couldn't go for a car ride without getting into a fight with another driver. He was just difficult that way and always ready to hustle someone out of a buck. From watching him I didn't know that people ever behaved nicely toward one another." He laughed again. "Only much later did I learn that if you were in someone's house and there was five bucks lying behind the sofa, you returned it. I never knew that. It just never occurred to me. You wouldn't do that in our house. I was brought up so that by the time I was in my teens the fact that I could handle a deck of cards was already an invitation to have a dishonest life. I hustled millions of kids out of money when I was in high school, in card games, in all kinds of cheating. Dealing seconds, setting up games—I was going to be a cardsharp because it was an extension of the values I was learning. I thought that's how you dealt with the world. There was so much aggression in my house and everybody hustling, my father particularly. He would promote or hustle anything. I guess he had to to make a living." No longer. Martin and Nettie live in an apartment near Woody that he bought for them about twenty years ago. They also have a winter home in Florida, purchased by their son. "Yet even today," Woody says, "he'll do things like give a trick ball that doesn't roll straight to someone he's playing golf with for two dollars a game in Miami."

Despite his increasingly asocial outlook and habits, Allan lived comfortably enough with his grandparents in the Ethan Allen apartment house at Fifteenth Street and Avenue K for four or five months, until Nettie and Martin found the house at 1144 Fifteenth Street, right around the corner between K and L streets. Allan lived there from the age of eleven to sixteen, but by the time they moved there his outlook was set.

"You know, when I think about it, it's so clear why I'm so neurotic and I've had such a neurotic life," Woody once said while recounting his childhood moves. "Think of the number of times I changed schools and moved around, having to get acclimated to new friends and new schools and liking it or hating it—usually hating it—and then pulling up stakes and going to another place and having to get acclimated to a new Hebrew school and a new regular school and then doing that again and again.

"And of course when you moved in the neighborhood, even if you went to the same school it was an uprooting because all the kids on your block, you never saw them again. One always had two sets of friends—school friends and block friends—and they were always very distinct, well-defined groups. The kids on your block had nothing to do with your school friends because they could be any age; they could be three years younger or five years older than you and there was a hierarchy. Your school friends were all in your class and they came from twenty blocks away in both directions.

"Plus, there was my parents' totally contentious relationship all through my childhood. It's a miracle that soon they will have been married sixty-two years. They were on the verge of breaking up, I would say," he said, laughing, "every single night for the first thirty of those years. Certainly the first twenty. It was *astonishing*. So when I went to school in the morning, I never knew if I was coming home to both parents."

The house on Fifteenth Street was the site of his adolescence. It was another small, wood-frame, two-family building with four cement steps in front where Allan and his friends sat and hatched "countless schemes, most of them imaginary sexual exploits." The family again had the upstairs. There were three bedrooms. Nettie, Martin, and Letty slept in the one at the front, Rita's parents had the one at the rear, and Allan and Rita shared the middle room. Rita was in many ways like a sister to Allan and so the two of them, at opposite ends of their teens, shared the bedroom without discomfort, sheltered by familiarity and taboo.

"I had a very good relationship with her," Woody says. "She was very nice and lively and she liked me and I liked her and we constantly played cards together and had some laughs. It was like having a friend." He was old enough by the time he was eleven or twelve to be companionable to her in a casual way. They talked often and he was always asking her questions. They liked the same radio shows—*Your Hit Parade*, *Make-Believe Ballroom*, *The Jack Benny Program*, *Lux Radio Theatre*—which they listened to in their room. There were no territorial conflicts because she was five years older and had her own set of friends, and besides, she very often included Allan in her activities. Her friends in turn liked him and the boys often asked him to play ball with them. And while a twelve-year-old boy and a seventeen-year-old girl living together might in some cases be a source of physical embarrassment and sexual curiosity, it was never awkward with them, Woody says, "because she was a very close cousin and anything like that would have been unthinkable."

In *Crimes and Misdemeanors*, Judah, the character played by Martin Landau, goes back to his boyhood home in a time of emotional and moral crisis. The woman now living in the house admits the stranger who says he grew up there and lets him walk alone through the rooms. In the dining room he sees and hears a Seder peopled by his parents and relatives, and himself as a boy. It is a masterful scene in which the adults talk about murder and about faith in God, and it is the ethical heart of the movie.

It is easy for characters to ask strangers to let them in but it is not so easy for the man who writes what those characters do to ask the same question. "I'd love to go back in that house sometime," Woody said as he stood one day on the sidewalk in front of his old home. "But I have a little trepidation about going up to the door and saying, 'I lived here once,' because that's such a pushy thing to do. The woman could either recognize me and say, 'Oh, really?' and let me come in. Or she could say, 'Are you kidding?' "

A weather vane his father put on the garage is still there. As are many memories. "I could show you all the rooms where we did our various things," he continued. "Where I dyed my mother's fur coat in a chemistry experiment, as I did in *Radio Days*. My father bought me a Lionel chemistry set when I was in the hospital for allergy tests that I really didn't have to go in for. I hated it and he felt so sorry for me that as a reward he got me this forty-five-dollar set, which was a lot in those days. It was a big chest, the jumbo Lionel big deal. I loved it."

As Allan was close to Rita, so, too, was he close to his mother's sister Sadie and her husband, Joe, a good thing since he spent so much of his childhood with them. Joe was a perfect example of Old World values in a New World setting. He was a dour but likable man who was European in every way, Woody says. "He would sit around and say in a heavy accent, '*This* is not a snowstorm . . .' and was good at wrestling and things like that. European sports. Couldn't throw a ball to save his life. While he was not cultured at all, he was typically Russian in feeling and had that reverence for the Jewish religion and serious culture."

For all of his misbehavior in school and his street-wise attitude, Allan was popular, if not always on the force of his own personality then because of his associations; he was even once president of his class. He may have been a bad student but he was friendly with the bright boys in class as well as with the good-looking and popular ones. These friendships brought him into the circle of popular girls. One was Irene Weinstein, who with her equally pretty friend Stephanie Grinell had a coterie of boys who came over to play stoopball in the driveway and other games at her house after school. (At parties, they played spin the bottle.) Irene loved P.S. 99 as much as Allan hated it. Even so, in the fifth grade he hoped she would be his girlfriend, but there were just too many unconventional things about him: He had no respect for authority and did not participate in school activities; he was a little short and his features were a bit too angular; in all, he was not bad-looking, but not great-looking either. And his edges were rough. He was cute but not embraceable, not tender, even though he confided in her his unhappiness about his being punished at home and she was sympathetic. His unconventionality aside, he was well liked by Irene and her set and in return he was a loyal friend with a silly streak and a ready joke.

Still, there was the air of a loner about him that has been amplified over time. While Woody is garrulous and amusing with his closest friends, he is for the most part uncomfortable around other people. There is no laugh-a-minute ambience on his movie sets, but there is an aura of trust and some levity. Woody is particularly friendly with costume designer Jeff Kurland; the two kid each other easily. While a scene for *Oedipus Wrecks* was being readied in the apartment of the quintessential Jewish mother being visited by her son and his quintessential Wasp girlfriend, who goes into a back room to freshen up, Woody turned to him. "Is there something we can put on the bureau that she can pick up and look at, something alien to her? Like a foreskin, something she wouldn't see where she comes from." Yet for the most part he is pure business even though most of his crew have been with him for ten years or longer. And while he is loyal to them, striving to make a film a year in part because that guarantees them work, and they are loyal to him, often turning down another film to work with him, there is almost always some distance between them. He does, however, play chess between shots with a couple of the technicians (he has taken lessons from a master to improve his game), and he makes his four courtside seats for New York Knicks basketball games available to the crew when he doesn't use them. Even if he doesn't tell them directly, he is appreciative of their professional and street-wise savvy and their humor. "What a colorful crew I have," he said one day, watching as they bantered while preparing a shot. "You can't get enough of them."

Actors tend to be an intimate bunch during filming and Woody's reserve can be disconcerting to one who has not worked with him before; he is physically present to everyone but, except for specific direction, personally available to almost no one. After *Manhattan* was released,

Meryl Streep (she played Woody's ex-wife, who leaves him for another woman) said in the *Ladies' Home Journal*, "I don't think Woody Allen even remembers me. I went to see *Manhattan* and I felt like I wasn't even in it. . . . I only worked on the film for three days, and I didn't get to know Woody. Who gets to know Woody?"

Certainly not actors with lesser roles. Karen Ludwig, who played Streep's lover and whose part was filmed over a three-day period, "expected Woody to be gregarious and funny. Instead he was off in the corner reading; not only reading but reading Chekhov; and not only Chekhov but *Three Sisters*. On top of that, Meryl was doing Shakespeare in Central Park at night and also filming *Kramer vs. Kramer*. I had to contend with two inaccessible people, one of whom was supposed to be my lover." Also, as she had only her own lines, Ludwig had no idea of the film as a whole, a common practice of Woody's. (Unless actors have a lead part which requires that they have a whole script, this not only helps prevent them from investing their characters with anything more than Woody tells them, it also promotes a more natural reading of the parts. Of less importance, it also helps diminish leaks about the film's plot.) Just before *Manhattan* was released, Ludwig went to a screening with Wallace Shawn (who played Diane Keaton's ex-husband). The two "sat there holding hands, watching, having no idea where we fit in. I was astonished to see it meshed so well." It does not astonish Woody. He argues—and judging by the continually high caliber of the performances he draws from actors, argues with merit—that bonhomie is irrelevant, as are more lines than an actor has to know. He feels that he hires the best performer for a role, whom he then expects to show up and deliver the assigned dialogue with a minimum of fuss. A paradigm of his attitude and approach is what he has when he comes to the set in the morning: a corn muffin and a cup of hot water.

The childhood portrayed in *Radio Days* of a boy always living with another family along with his own, his liking that family and having many cousins and other relatives who live within walking distance, is very much Woody's own. Yet despite that childhood full of close associations, as an adult he is largely detached. Even he finds it "a contradiction how poorly socialized I am"; someone who has worked quite a bit with Woody talks about his "inability to connect." He is seen holding hands with Mia but he seldom shows others public affection, such as hugging or kissing a close friend when they greet or take leave of each other; in turn, characters in his films almost never show casual affection either. "Nobody ever did it in my family," he says with a shrug, and he finds it a show-business affectation. A rare exception was the enthusiastic hug he gave Irene Weinstein after not seeing her in nearly forty years.

Allan's athletic abilities guaranteed he was among the first chosen when sides were taken for the after-school games of football or baseball, basketball or stickball played just about every day the weather allowed, sometimes in the schoolyard, often in the street in front of the house. Fifteenth Street ran one way with very little traffic, so Allan and Arthur Miller—not the playwright but the ambidextrous stickball player who lived across from him—and other friends could throw a football or play stickball without having to leave home.

Two blocks away, however, there was an even better place to play, so they would walk up Avenue K, under the elevated tracks at Sixteenth Street, and into Wingate Field, a full-service play area that during World War II also had searchlights and an antiaircraft gun toward the Avenue L side. There was a stadium with a filigreed, art nouveau steel top and a clear area behind it where Allan and his friends would sometimes light fires and roast potatoes. The block-long grass-covered field had a baseball diamond at either end, basketball hoops against the chain-link fence on Seventeenth Street, and a track where Allan won many medals in sprint races of various lengths. In baseball, he played second base, somewhat in the manner of Nellie Fox of the Philadelphia Athletics (and, after his trade in 1950, of the Chicago White Sox. The player he came to idolize, however, was center fielder Willie Mays of the Giants). A line-drive hitter with power, too, he batted leadoff. A friend recalls that Allan was good at allowing himself to be hit by a pitch, thus getting on base, but Woody adamantly denies it. "I'd swing away all the time," he says, an action more in keeping with his personality. "What deterred me from pursuing the game was the notion of getting hit."

He also liked boxing but not fighting, which until he was thirteen was limited to neighborhood scuffles where one kid put the other in a headlock. (For several months he trained for participation in the Golden Gloves and was a good boxer, but his parents would not sign the consent form for competition and asked him to stop.) Then one day while playing football at Wingate Field with some boys he didn't know well, he had "my first taste of reality." A discussion over where to place the ball after a play turned into a disagreement over a yard or two. Allan pursued the argument unaware of how tough the boys were. Suddenly one kicked him in the groin, and as Allan doubled over and turned around, the boy brought his fist up flat into his nose, breaking it. The doctor who later tended to him thought he had been smashed with a brick.

But not all his interests were suited mainly to childhood. Magic and music—specifically New Orleans jazz—two safer pastimes he took up around thirteen, continue to be interests today and both figure prominently in his work.

Magical events both comic and dramatic occur again and again in Woody Allen's films. A small sample: A character steps off the screen in *The Purple Rose of Cairo*; a mother who steps into a Chinese box as part of a magic show has vanished when the box is opened, only to reappear in the sky, in *Oedipus Wrecks*; a philosophy professor who has led an intellectually open but an emotionally closed life confronts her past in *Another Woman*; a man who has been shot dead appears to people he loves to sum up the story and wisecrack before dancing into the sunset with the figure of death in *Love and Death*; a marauding breast terrorizes the populace in *Everything You Always Wanted to Know About Sex*; a man becomes like the person he is talking with in *Zelig*; a young boy growing up poor in Brooklyn escapes the bleakness of his home life by constantly practicing magic tricks in the play *The Floating Light Bulb*; magical herbs allow a woman to become invisible in *Alice*.

Illusions are suited to the movies. Woody's personal pleasure is in sleight of hand, something he practiced endlessly as a boy. Although he is nowhere near as diligent now, if, for instance, he has a free moment on the set or in his editing room, he will pull out a quarter and steeplechase it across the backs of his fingers, under and across his palm, and back out over the index finger, where it is picked up again by the second knuckle of his middle finger. Bills of currency are carefully folded in half and carried in a stack which he fans and piles like cards; the point is not to let the moment pass without doing something of benefit and this is an easy way to keep his fingers in shape. ("I get a sense of pleasure from it like a concert pianist putting his hands on the keys," he once said about working with cards.) Several shelves in his library at home are filled with books on magic, many of which he has had since his early teens. There are even several dozen issues of *Genii* magazine, a journal of magic he subscribed to in the early 1950s.

His interest began when someone bought him an E-Z magic set when he was ten and living in Long Beach. He was "thunderstruck. I loved everything about it: the concept; the Chinese tissue papers and the little cards with the fake backs to them; everything." He remained enamored of his magic set for a year or so but then his interest wandered. It was brought back for good when on his thirteenth birthday he was given a copy of *Illustrated Magic* by Ottokar Fischer. He still has the book, which, with the enthusiasm of a fly fisherman extolling Izaak Walton, he calls "not the best book on magic by any means because it's not basically on technique. But it's so gripping. I became obsessed with magic."

Magic was the perfect outlet for someone who liked to be alone and who is unafraid of practice. It kept him isolated from the world, and practicing magic was certainly better than doing homework. The ability and discipline to practice, practice, and practice some more is something Woody had as a young boy and has today. Dick Cavett, who grew up in Nebraska but dreamed of New York and has been a friend of Woody's for nearly thirty years, took up magic as a child, too. It is easy to suggest that magic offered escape, which of course it did to Allan, but the ends were more important than the means.

"My interest has its obvious symbolism but it's fun to those who think it's fun," Woody says. "Someone like Mia or Diane Keaton, for example, cannot see it. It would be like me running a lathe or something. It couldn't be more boring. But to someone like Dick Cavett and myself, thousands of miles apart, we were lying on our beds, slowly and luxuriously going through the magic catalogue, looking at every trick, trying to decide what to buy. I mean, should I spend my three dollars and fifty cents this Saturday on the Rope Shears or on Al Delage's Sock Trick? Everything looked so wondrous and fabulous. If you're hooked on it, you're hooked on it, and I was just completely, absolutely hooked. I had a big drawer and it was full of magic tricks and I had these books, and that was almost all I cared about."

He became proficient enough at his magic by the age of fourteen or fifteen to audition for two television shows. One was *The Magic Clown*, a Sunday-morning program presented by Bonomo's Turkish Taffy featuring a clown in a fez (Dick Du Bois was his name) who did magic tricks. On occasion the show featured amateur magicians, and Allan auditioned. His trick was an expensive classic he purchased called the Passe-Passe Bottles. The magician puts a tube over a liquor bottle and another over a shot glass of whiskey. When the tubes are removed, the bottle and glass have changed places. The tubes are replaced, and when removed again, the bottle and glass have returned to their original spots. Allan did the trick perfectly but it was a case of the right illusion for the wrong audience, which he might have realized if he had given the matter any thought. *The Magic Clown* was a kids' show, after all, and not many producers want to present a maneuver with a Seagram's 7 bottle to thirteen-year-olds on a Sunday morning.

The second occasion was as inauspicious as the first as far as getting on the program, but the experience showed Allan how effective he was as an ad-libber. He performed this time with a next-door neighbor, Jack Freed. One of their tricks was a standard called the Dove Pan, another expensive purchase. Two doves are put in a pan and covered. Then the lid is removed and popcorn has replaced the doves.

While they did the tricks well, the show's producers were not particularly taken by the duo, who were mechanically okay but lacked élan; they had no patter to accompany their routine. Instead, Allan snapped off brash, impromptu one-liners as situations arose, but this was reflexive humor, not polished material. As it did nothing to enhance the tricks, he did much better as a comedian than as a magician. For example, when he accidentally knocked some of the popcorn onto the stage, he said in his best Bob Hope voice, "Hey, we usually have stage-hands who follow us around and take care of this stuff."

"And they were laughing," Woody recalls. "But not hiring."

He did find a chance to perform at a Catskill Mountains resort when he was sixteen, one of his few public appearances. A friend from school went each summer to Weinstein's Majestic Bungalow Colony in Accord, New York, and word came down that Allan could perform there if he came up. He pestered his mother about spending a couple of weeks in the mountains, and although Weinstein's was too expensive, she soon agreed to take Letty and him to the Lakeview Bungalow Colony, about a mile down the road; for all her difficulty in handling her son and for all her own financial pressures, Nettie did her best to support his interests.

"Weinstein's was a general Jewish resort," Woody says. "There was a lake and sports and social events and movies. It was not an up-class resort, but much more upper-class than where I stayed. The Lakeview was a D level, an E level." The bungalow was really just a room in a large house with a communal bathroom, and all guests cooked their meals in a single kitchen, an accommodation known as a *kuchaleyn*, or cook-alone. "It really was a rathole of a place," he recalled while speaking with pleasure about the chance to show off his magic abilities, even if he was paid no money and even though he disdained the accommodations, which in truth weren't much. The kitchen was on the ground level and the bedroom was upstairs in another house; the bathroom was down the hall. The three slept in the same room. Allan did a couple of magic shows and spent most of the rest of his time practicing.

Weinstein's Majestic Bungalow Colony first appears as an entertainment mecca in *The Floating Light Bulb*. Then in *Broadway Danny Rose*, Danny tries to get Phil Chomsky to book one of his acts—any of his acts—into the place:

DANNY

May I say one word? Might I just interject one concept at this juncture? You're looking for somebody for Memorial Day weekend. *(Clears throat)* My blind xylophone player, okay? The man would be perfect for your room.

PHIL

Ah, forget it.

DANNY

(Gesturing wildly) What? Philly, hear me out, will you please hear me out? The man is a beautiful man. He's a, he's a fantastic individual.

PHIL

My hotel gets old Jewish people.

DANNY

Really.

PHIL

They're blind! They ain't gonna pay to see a blind guy. *(Turns away from Danny, reacting with disgust)*

DANNY

All right, all right, *(Clears throat)* so forget about that then. Phil, how 'bout, how 'bout Herbie Jayson's birds?

PHIL

Awww, come on.

DANNY

Herbie Jayson's birds.

PHIL

(Shaking his head) Nah.

DANNY

They're little birds, they peck out tunes on the piano. It's a beautiful thing.
(Phil sighs, still shaking his head, still turned away from the persistent Danny)

DANNY

All right, what about my one-legged tap dancer?
(Phil groans. He continues to shake his head)

DANNY

Take him for a weekend. My one-legged— All right, my one-armed juggler. My one-armed juggler!

PHIL

Not for my hotel!

DANNY

(Sighing) All right, what about Lou Canova, my Italian singer. He'd be great.

PHIL

Lou Canova's a dumb, fat, temperamental has-been . . . *(Pauses)* with a drinkin' problem.

DANNY

Shh, geez . . . what about, what about Eddie Clark's penguin? That's perfect . . . Eddie Clark and his penguin. Then the penguin skates on the stage dressed as a rabbi. It's hilarious. The penguin's got a beard like a—

PHIL

I'll tell ya what, Danny: Give me Sonny Chase. He's the best act you got. He's fast, he's funny.

DANNY

I don't handle Sonny anymore.

PHIL

Since when?

DANNY

Oh, it's a long story, Philly. I found, I discovered the kid, he slept on my sofa. I supported him. I don't want to bad-mouth the kid, but he's a horrible, dishonest, immoral louse. *(Clears throat)* And I say that with all due respect.

PHIL

I know, Danny. They get a little success, and then they leave you.

DANNY

That's my point! Believe me, Philly, if I had all the acts in this business that I started that made it, I'd be a rich man today.

PHIL

I'd like to help you, Danny, but Weinstein's Majestic Bungalow Colony is a classy place, and I need a classy act.

DANNY

Well, that's why I want to *(Offscreen)* show you this lady. She is the Jascha Heifetz of this instrument. She really is something. *(As Danny continues to talk, a blonde beehived woman, "the water glass virtuoso," appears onscreen. She begins to play the glasses)*

DANNY

(Continuing over the tinkling glass sounds) Never took a lesson. Self-taught. Next year, Philly, my hand to God, she's gonna be at Carnegie Hall. But you, I'll let you have her at the old price, okay? Which is anything you want to give me. Anything at all, Philly.

Allan's pleasure in being able to perform at Weinstein's was augmented by a friendship he made with a precocious and pretty ten-year-old named Marion Drayson, who, along with Allan and Letty, was one of the few children at the resort. The two struck up a mutual adoration society. Allan had such a good time, in fact, that it almost didn't matter that he was in the country. Almost. "I thought we were so far from New York that we were in Turkey," Woody continued, "and we were, what? Maybe two hours away. And while the place didn't bother me as much as Port Chester had, there were two things I definitely hated: I hated that when you walked in the daytime, the hot sun would beat down, and places were farther away than you thought. People would say, 'Oh, yeah, there's a general store a half mile down the road.' But it wasn't like walking in the city, where you could measure off perceptible distances by stores or street corners, and if you got hot, you could duck in and get a Coke and then continue. Here, you would walk and there would be nothing but sunflowers for miles. And then the thought that you needed a flashlight to walk at night"—here he rolled his eyes—"it was dead, dead black as you walked back to your bungalow from the so-called casino, where there'd been some sort of moronic activity, like bingo. But I liked performing. And I could often spend all day practicing sleight of hand. I also hung out with Marion," who became his assistant in the shows.

Among his magical feats, Allan did a rope trick and the Passe-Passe Bottles, the secrets of which Marion teasingly threatened to reveal to the world. He in turn would feign fierce anger and the two would then break up with laughter. Over forty years later, she realized that Allan Konigsberg was also Woody Allen and wrote him a letter, telling him that Allan "was very different from any kid I had ever known . . . quiet, gentle, smart, and very funny in a strange kind of way. . . . As performance time grew near, I grew increasingly nervous. He soothed my stage fright, calmed my fears, and convinced me that there was no way he could possibly go on without me as his assistant. He made me feel so important and so special that I promised to love him forever, although he never knew. . . . I have been a devoted Woody Allen fan (groupie? junkie?) all of my life, as are my husband and kids. It was only about a year ago that the connection hit me. . . . So it seems as though I kept my promise after all, although neither of us ever knew it." Woody, who normally shows little emotion over mail, was obviously pleased by the letter and remembered his time with her in great detail.

Purchased tricks such as the ropes and bottles were fun for Allan, but what really mattered was to be self-reliant, and to be entirely self-reliant one learns sleight of hand. "That's what you wanted to be," Woody says. "Not an illusionist, not a stage magician, you wanted to be a sleight-of-hand expert. Then you were complete. You showed up someplace, if there was a saltcellar, a thimble, some coins, some cards, whatever, you could work."

He worked every day, practicing the manipulation of billiard balls, coins, cards, rings, and ropes. But not those exclusively, because the purchased tricks had their own pleasures. There were pilgrimages to Irving Tannen's Circle Magic Shop in the Broadway Arcade on West Fifty-second Street in Manhattan, which instead of little boxes of easy magic had a vast cornucopia of tricks and silks and aluminum boxes.

On a gray afternoon in the fall of 1950, Allan and a friend were in the Circle Magic shop, trying to decide what to spend their few dollars on and hoping that Frank or Seymour, two of the employees they knew, might teach them some new trick or at least dazzle them with some extraordinary feat of magic beyond their adolescent abilities. As they waited at the counter in their flannel shirts, corduroys, and scuffed leather jackets, Milton Berle, the most famous comedian of the day and the man who first brought video comedy to the nation's homes (he was known as "Mr. Television"), walked in wearing a homburg, cashmere coat, and mirror-shined shoes.

Allan came over to him and said, "Henny Youngman."

Berle, playing along with the gag, looked at him and answered, "Red Skelton."

Someone in the store said Allan was a pretty fair magician. Berle picked up a deck of cards and handed them to him.

"Here, kid, do me a trick and I'll put you on the show."

"I don't usually work with cards," Allan told him, muffing a one-hand cut.

"That's okay, I don't usually work with kids," Berle said.

What Woody calls "one of the tragedies of the little moment" was his mishandling of the cards. "I could then as now snap off a one-hand cut effortlessly and for some strange reason, and it was not nerves—it happened too fast for nerves—it just didn't work at that moment. I could have done it five hundred times that day and it would have been fine. Just once in a while you muff it."

Still, he did learn something from Berle that day by watching him closely. After the missed one-hand cut Berle said, "Come here, kid." He ribboned the cards on the counter and said, "Think of a card." Allan did, and Berle took the deck, shuffled it, and asked, "What card?"

"Nine of clubs."

Then he turned over the top card and it was the nine of clubs.

"What did you use on him, Milton? Thought force?" someone in the small crowd that had gathered asked. Allan went home and figured out how Berle had ribboned the cards in such a way that the vast majority of people would have seen the nine of clubs without knowing it and then, because of the unconscious suggestion, would name it when told to think of a card. That got him involved with learning more intricate magic and other ways to force cards. Before long, he had a schoolyard reputation for his abilities with a deck of cards.

As his knowledge increased, so, too, did the occasions he misused it. His wildest scheme was to predict the winner of the college basketball National Invitational Tournament held every spring at Madison Square Garden and win a bundle of money from his schoolmates. He persuaded his neighborhood friend Elliott Mills to be his accomplice. The scam was that Allan would teach him how to use a device called a nail writer or a Swami Gimmick, which concealed a small piece of pencil lead. They would listen to the game on the radio while Allan held an envelope with the winner's name supposedly on the sheet of paper inside. At the conclusion, Elliott would take the envelope, rip it open, and exclaim, "My God, he's got it!" while using the nail writer to put in the right team. But although they practiced the trick, they never did it.

"You'll notice who was going to do the writing," Mills, who is now a professor of pharmacology at Duke University, said many years later. "I said, 'All the Italian kids will break every bone in our heads.' But his enthusiasm was contagious; after he became interested in magic, pretty soon our whole group was pulling cigarettes out of the air."

"My Sky Masterson days," Woody calls that period when he seriously wanted to be "a gambler and a cardsharp and a hustler. Another friend and I did many schemes together. We cooked up dishonest games; we bought crooked dice, and worked out signal systems for card games. We won a lot of money when we were younger, but I outgrew that." A version of that petty hustler appears as Virgil Starkwell, the bank robber who can't write a legible stickup note in *Take the Money and Run*, and a few of the kids in his neighborhood who did not outgrow youthful petit larceny ended up in trouble with the law.

Yet while Woody outgrew the worst of his childhood interests, he will never outgrow his devotion to New Orleans–style jazz. It is the perfect music for him: It hates authority; its quirky, individual style requires great discipline to play right; it is all the things that fit his own and his comic character.

In New Orleans jazz the trumpet states the melodic theme, the trombone lays out a contrapuntal bass line for the other instruments to build on, and the clarinet often rises serenely above them, weaving its own harmonies. The clarinet also has a singing quality to it, like a female voice in a chorus, and in keeping with that style, Woody's playing has a plaintive, emotional, nearly vocal tone. Drawing on its lineage from the street celebrations and funerals where it developed, New Orleans jazz is rough-hewn and slow-paced in comparison to the more common Chicago or Dixieland style, which is generally slicker and more clean-cut and which places a heavier emphasis on solos. Woody's first exposure to New Orleans jazz did not poleax him in the same way *Snow White* did when he was three and magic did at ten. It did, however, kindle an interest that quickly blazed and it is a pleasurable release for him. Although his facial expression is impassive and his eyes are fixed on the floor while he plays, he displays more feeling, more emotion, in his music than he does in any other way, at least in public. There are times in the way he loses himself in a melody when he seems almost to be caressing the notes.

He was about thirteen when a friend, one of the first of his circle to own a tape recorder, played a tape he had made of disc jockey Ted Husing's traditional jazz show on the radio. It was of a Paris concert by New Orleans–born soprano saxophonist Sidney Bechet, the legendary black musician who early in his career played with jazz pioneer Joe "King" Oliver and later with Duke Ellington, who greatly admired him. (So, too, did Swiss conductor Ernest Ansermet, who in 1919 became the first prominent classicist to publicly praise a jazz musician.) Bechet's fervent arpeggios and broad vibrato distinguish his confident, strikingly personal style. From the late 1940s until his death in 1959, he lived in Paris, where he was regarded as an artistic treasure. Many years later, Woody said to an acquaintance whom he watched buy his first Bechet record, "I'd give anything to be you and hear that for the first time." ("The second night I saw Sidney Bechet—at a concert in New York; I'd seen him before but under bad circumstances, in the place above Birdland—was the most fulfilling artistic experience of my life," Woody told Ralph Gleason of the San Francisco *Chronicle* in 1965. Many years later he added, "I went there with stupendous anticipation and he fulfilled it. Bechet was a startling musician, his ferociousness was incredible. I was struck by the intensity and total majesty of his playing.")

Allan and a group of friends became more and more interested in traditional jazz, to the point that they became experts in it. Like teenagers today who know everything about rock-and-roll or heavy-metal groups, they knew every player on every record and every bit of jazz lore and history; when one contestant on *The $64,000 Question*, a popular TV quiz show in the 1950s, took jazz as his subject, they called out all the answers as they watched. They also were entranced by *Really the Blues*, jazz clarinetist Milton "Mezz" Mezzrow's colorful account of his life, written with Bernard Wolfe (who was Leon Trotsky's personal secretary in Mexico in 1937). Mezzrow was a white Jewish man—his real surname was Mesirow—who successfully fobbed himself off as being black; he even registered in the Army as a white-skinned black (he called himself "a voluntary Negro"). Although Mezzrow was ridiculed by many of his contemporaries, to the Brooklyn jazz buffs the idea of even approximating being black, of becoming that much closer to the music they loved, was heady stuff.

For years, Allan and some of the others made weekly trips to Child's Paramount, a large, dark, subterranean club with tables and a dance floor on West Forty-third Street in Manhattan, to hear live jazz, and they were steady listeners to the radio program *Symphony Sid* from Birdland, even though the show played Thelonious Monk and Dizzy Gillespie rather than New Orleans jazz. At fifteen, he took up the clarinet. He has practiced on it daily ever since (the guilt he feels if he doesn't is too awful to bear, he says), usually playing along with recordings by Bechet or George Lewis, the quintessential New Orleans–style clarinetist whose influence can be heard clearly in his playing.

"We spent many, many, many hours doing nothing but listening to that music," Woody says. "We'd come home from school and congregate at a friend's house. Elliott Mills was one of the early people to have hi-fi equipment. I had a twelve-and-a-half-dollar phonograph that was a little suitcase kind, where you opened it and put the top up. It was still completely pleasurable. On Saturday mornings we'd listen to jazz for hours and hours. First we'd buy records at Victor's over on Kings Highway. I remember going in there and buying my first Jelly Roll Morton album, *Jelly Roll Morton and the Red Hot Peppers*, wonderful old 78 RPMs. Then I remember discovering the Jazz Record Center in New York, which was a walk-up place. That was, of course, a magical treat. And we never stopped listening, I mean obsessively to note after note. I can't tell you how obsessive it was."

It was this obsessive: Very often after school when everyone would go to Cookie's, the neighborhood joint over by the el, and have sodas and sandwiches and hang out in front and socialize and pair off for the movies or the pool hall, Allan was home hovered over the record player in his bedroom.

When he wasn't hovered over the record player, he was often hovered over an instrument. First there was the soprano saxophone, which he studied with a teacher who wore a patch over one eye, and the ukulele (he watched Arthur Godfrey for pointers); then came the clarinet, which at first he easily taught himself because of its similarity to the soprano sax. (Later, after he moved to Manhattan, he developed an interest in modern jazz and took up the vibraphone. After a few months of lessons, though, he felt he should spend his practice time on the clarinet.)

One of the regular players at Child's Paramount was clarinetist Gene Sedric, who played with Fats Waller and the Conrad Janis band, and who had the big sound typical of the era. Sedric's sound was not New Orleans jazz—it was more sophisticated—but it was in that style, and it was closer to what Allan wanted to play than to what he was playing at the time. After a couple of years of watching and listening to him with unabashed awe, the seventeen-year-old looked up his name in the phone book and called to ask if he would give him lessons.

"I'm that kid, I'm always at Child's Paramount at the first table looking up at you," he explained by way of introduction.

"Oh, yeah, yeah, yeah, yeah," Sedric said, actually remembering the white kid with red hair who sat as close to the group of black musicians as he could. "I'd have to get a couple of dollars a lesson, though."

For his two dollars, Sedric rode the subway for an hour or more from his home in the Bronx to the Avenue J station in Brooklyn. Allan met him and they walked to his family's apartment, which was now on Ocean Avenue, where Nettie made him a sandwich. Then he'd set up his clarinet and tutor his student by ear, lessons Woody remembers with pleasure:

"He would say, 'Here, say this,' and he would swing up some kind of thing. And then I'd do it and he'd say, 'No, no, no! Sing out, really sing out!' And I'd try but just couldn't hit it. He'd whale it out. You can hear him on many old Fats Waller records and he sounds wonderful. Listen to him on 'There'll Be Some Changes Made.'"

Woody still plays the soprano sax and occasionally brings it in for his Monday-night sessions with his band, the New Orleans Funeral and

Ragtime Orchestra, at Michael's Pub in Manhattan, where he has played almost weekly for nearly twenty years with most of the same musicians, only one of whom is a professional but all of whom sound as if they were. (The others include a stockbroker, a college English professor, and a worker in a radio store.) But whatever instrument he may dabble with—he can also pick around nicely on the piano—the clarinet is his enduring interest and New Orleans–style jazz his true love. He is so particular about the music and the way it should sound that he plays on a seventy-five-year-old Albert system clarinet rather than a newer one with the Boehm fingering system that was developed as the science of clarinet making evolved. An Albert system clarinet is rather unwieldy; it has a bigger sound because the horn has a bigger bore, and the fingering is more difficult to master because the spread is so much wider. Even so, it is a less sophisticated instrument; most have several open holes rather than holes that are covered with rings to compensate for pitch (as in a flute or in a Boehm system clarinet, which also has a ring at the back for the thumb and four or five keys for the right little finger). The result is that Albert system clarinets tend to play only approximately in tune, which is Woody's goal. Slight out-of-tuneness is generally a mark of authenticity; it is how his idol George Lewis and all the early great New Orleans jazz clarinetists played. (But Bechet was such a master of the naturally out-of-tune soprano sax that one of his fames was being nearly always in tune.) In an effort to get that primitive sound from all the instruments in his band, he once told trumpet player John Bucher, "Play like you're an old black man with bad false teeth."

Woody's playing is generally well rated by professionals. When he went to New Orleans in 1973 to record the soundtrack for *Sleeper* with the renowned Preservation Hall Jazz Band, Albert Burbank, probably the premier New Orleans–style clarinetist at the time, came up to congratulate him at the end of one set. (The band members, all of them but one over sixty-five years old, had little sense of the variety of music necessary in a film, as none of them were moviegoers; one recently had gone with Allan Jaffe, the band and the Hall's founder, to see *Shaft*. It was the first film he had seen since the advent of sound.) Playing next to Woody for a couple of sessions was the then eighty-three-year-old trombonist Jim Robinson, who had never heard of him. "Did anyone ever tell you you sound like my old friend George Lewis?" he asked Woody at the end of a set. "What's your name again?"

"Woody," he mumbled.
"Willard? You're real good, Willard."

If he had devoted the same interest to school as he did to music and magic and movies, Allan Konigsberg would have been a student whose grades mirrored his intellect. Then again, Woody Allen is not the first underachiever to blossom in a more personally suitable environment.

After graduation from P.S. 99 in June 1949, Allan entered Midwood High School. Located next to Brooklyn College, it has a high academic rating that is not necessarily the result of propinquity, although the proximity of a college campus has had a useful effect. Midwood was built in 1941 to help absorb the growing number of children who came with Greater New York's expansion. By the fall of 1949, however, it was filled to overflowing. Classes were divided into three sessions a day. Sophomores and juniors came from 7:30 a.m. until 1 p.m., freshmen from 1 p.m. to 6 p.m., and seniors, for the more privileged hours of 9 a.m. to 3 p.m.

For all its apparent benefits, Allan hated Midwood with the same vigor with which he hated P.S. 99. Students could take an academic, a commercial, or a general curriculum, the academic being the most demanding and the only one suitable for matriculation to college. Allan enrolled as an academic student, but he was one in name only. His mediocre grades—his average was in the low 70s—were not the result of overinvolvement in extracurricular activities, as they are for many students who ignore their schoolwork because they are consumed by sports or clubs; under his misspelled name (Alan Konisberg) in the 1953 yearbook (he was one of 702 graduated that June), where a student's activities are listed there is a large blank space. ("They should have given me two pictures," he said to a friend when the yearbook came out.) He simply found all aspects of school as uninteresting as he always had, and his one brush with a student enterprise—the school paper— convinced him he was missing nothing. The sports editor was his friend Jack Victor. In their senior year, he told the paper's faculty adviser about Allan's sending jokes to the columnists and she asked him to come in to meet her. While talking with him, she for some reason began to finger his shirt, which he did not like. So he fingered her blouse. Whereupon she threw him out of the office.

On the few occasions he might have enjoyed a class, he often found himself criticized rather than encouraged. He did well in English composition, not surprisingly, and he was often asked by the teacher to read his stories aloud to the class. But sometimes his broad talent outstripped the narrow conventions of acceptability, at least as far as Midwood defined them. One such instance was when his mother was summoned by the dean because Allan had written, according to the dean, a scandalously dirty composition.

"That was a major incident in high school," says Woody. "I was always very good in English composition and wrote a funny one, but it had a lot of sex jokes in it. They were good-taste sex jokes, though, no dirty words. They were the kind of one-liner sex jokes that you could comfortably tell on television thirty years ago. But the teacher and dean were appalled and they called my mother in."

"What do you mean by this? What do you mean by 'She has an hourglass figure and I'd like to play in the sand'?" the dean asked Allan.

Who replied, "It's a joke."

Not to the dean, who said to Nettie, "Your son ought to be seeing a psychiatrist."

The incident amuses Woody when he recalls it. "This was a very, very enlightened school; Midwood High School was exemplary. Mia is always impressed that wherever we go in the world—we'll be in high-culture places such as the European opera houses—people will come up and say something like 'Hi, I went to Midwood High School. I was a year before you.' There were these wonderful, sort of intelligent teachers there. It was a very Jewish neighborhood and there were many Jewish teachers. The school was very advanced, and yet even in that atmosphere, my little joke was considered heresy and worthy of psychiatric treatment. They were mortified, I mean *mortified* by it. My mother was stunned and embarrassed when she came to school."

The teachers' attitudes reinforced Allan's low opinion of teachers in general, and Nettie was called into school on other occasions when there was no doubt about his culpability, although it was not for his schoolroom behavior. The disruptiveness he displayed at P.S. 99 was gone. But so, often, was he.

"There are few things in life as delightful as hooky," Woody once said with the completely happy look of a man who knows a great pleasure and is about to share its secret. "To get up in the morning, early, with that horrid burden of school hanging over your head, and setting out for it, knowing you're going to get five hours of mindless, agonizing, sort of soul-deadening nothing. Then deciding suddenly with a friend that you're not going to go; that instead you're going to go buy tickets to the Dodger game, or you're going to go into New York and have breakfast at the Automat and go to the Paramount and listen to Charlie Barnet's orchestra and watch the new John Wayne movie. I mean, it's like a reprieve from the electric chair."

Allan's usual hooky partner was Michael Rose, known as Mickey, with whom he would later write *Take the Money and Run* and *Bananas*, the first two Woody Allen–directed films. Mickey lived a few miles away in the Crown Heights section of Brooklyn, closer to Manhattan and near Ebbets Field, where the Dodgers played. The two were in the same art class and quickly became friends. Their sensibilities were as perfectly matched as their physical appearances weren't: Allan was a slight five-foot-six redhead; Mickey, a muscular six-footer with dark hair. Sometimes by design, other times on the spur of the moment, they rode the subway into Manhattan and went to the movies instead of to school.

In *Take the Money and Run*, Virgil Starkwell's childhood is a continuing cycle of bullies snatching his black-framed glasses and stomping on them. Allan Konigsberg didn't wear glasses until after he finished high school, but that didn't deter bigger, meaner boys from menacing him. Because of his small size and the singularity of his red hair, he was a constant target. One day at school a bullying boy asked Allan to give him a dime a day.

"Why?" he asked.

"To protect you from your enemies."

"I have no enemies."

"You have now."

Mickey was a good friend, not only for companionship and for providing a sense that this small boy had large associates, but for advice as well. One day they were in the library when a tough Italian kid came up to Allan and challenged him to meet outside after school. Mickey knew tough Italian kids in Crown Heights—they fought with baseball bats or lifted up garbage cans and crashed them into people, the sort of thing that wasn't Allan's and Mickey's style. The only thing they wanted to do with a baseball bat was be like Willie Mays. Mickey offered Allan words to live by: "Don't meet him after school."

Instead, Mickey and Allan met after school and walked in their daily uniform of jeans, a T-shirt, and black-and-white high-topped Keds sneakers to Allan's house to pick up their bats and balls and gloves. Martin Konigsberg, Mickey recalls, "would be there watching TV in a blue suit, dozing off" before going to work. Allan and Mickey would go to Wingate Field or some other venue for a ball game, then back to Allan's house, where Nettie made them each one and a half tuna sandwiches and where his father, the snappy but indecisive dresser, would now, according to Mickey, "be in a gray suit, still dozing off."

Besides the daily pickup games, when they were fourteen Mickey and Allan played on the 70th Precinct team of the Police Athletic League. The coach was Rita's husband, Dick Weinberg, a good ballplayer who was offered a minor-league contract. It is more than forty years since they played together, but when Woody describes the team, it is as if they last played that morning. One teammate, the son of a mortician, was driven to the games at Wingate Field in a hearse, and occasionally the hearse took several players to away games. Wingate, like the Polo Grounds in Manhattan, where the New York Giants played, had a deep center field (though not the 483 feet of the cavernous Polo Grounds) and the first baseman, a Greek named Babe with an unpronounceable last name, was renowned for his ability to knock balls out over the deepest part. Woody hit his share of home runs but what he talks about with awe is Babe's ability to "really crush" the ball.

When Allan wasn't playing ball, he often was with Mickey and Elliott Mills and Jack Victor, who lived nearby. Rose still has the rosters and scorecards of a paper football game they played. All were owners of teams and their players were listed by position, college, height, and weight. When they weren't imaginary football moguls, they played Monopoly or other games at Victor's house. A favorite was dice baseball with a pair of wooden dice he owned: 1 and 1 was a ball, 6 and 1 a strike, 3 and 2 a triple, 2 and 2 a double, and so on. But the dice were worn and, like Big Julie in *Guys and Dolls* who had dice with no spots, only Victor (who is now a research psychologist and head of the grants office at Adelphi University in Garden City, New York) could tell what numbers had come up. No one at the time suspected that he might have called them as he wanted to see them rather than as how they rolled.

It was with some of this group that Allan saw his first Ingmar Bergman film, *Summer with Monika*. They had heard there was a movie with a naked woman in it showing at the Jewel, which made it a must-see film. But for Allan and Mickey, at least, what began as an adolescent expedition in voyeurism turned into a lifelong cinematic pleasure. Bergman's stark, poetic, beautifully photographed, usually black-and-white films about almost all aspects of the human condition, and about God's silence regarding it, are difficult viewing for many. For these two teenagers, however, they were thought-provoking in an unpretentious and enjoyable way.

"Seeing Bergman the first time was pleasure, just pleasure," Woody says. "Sure, we were drawn to *Summer with Monika* because we heard there was nudity, but that stopped being the reason as soon as we saw the movie. From then on we went to his films purely for enjoyment. It was never homework, never a noble endeavor or artsy or anything. We couldn't wait for them to open in our neighborhood. They were not boring, they were not abstruse or turgid. They were fun to see."

With his shock of red hair, which in keeping with the custom of the day was variously cut in a flattop or neatly combed in a pompadour at the front, Allan was often called "Red" during his childhood, although never by his friends (unless they purposely wanted to annoy him), to whom he was Al or Allan. Red was a name of derision, used on such occasions as the time he was en route to his clarinet lesson and he was beset by some toughs in the Kings Highway subway station who taunted him. But Woody has always been able to turn adversity into comedy, and years later the incident served as the basis for a very funny stand-up routine. ("He was always a target," Elliott Mills says, "but he suffered more from the girls who wouldn't date him.") Very occasionally, though, a friend not as close as Jack or Elliott used the colorful name. One time a boy told his family that he was bringing Red home that day after school. But as Red apparently had no last name, they thought he was talking about somebody's dog.

Under any name, Allan was a familiar fixture at the Rose house, but Mickey was an even greater one at the Konigsbergs'. Both families were among the first in their neighborhoods to own television sets, although the Konigsbergs didn't have one in time for the Joe Louis–Joe Walcott fight in December 1947, which Woody remembers watching at another friend's house. While he stopped boxing at his parents' request, Woody remains a dedicated observer of what A. J. Liebling euphemistically called "the Sweet Science," and before his celebrity became such that it was uncomfortable for him to attend a fight, he often went to the bouts at Madison Square Garden.

When the Roses got their TV in 1948, people came over to watch Milton Berle's show. An indication of how popular Berle was and how in thrall the viewers were to him is that Mickey's mother would pull him out of his room and away from his homework to watch the show. Not that he or Allan needed encouragement to watch Milton Berle. They were both funny and laughed a lot, and they loved funny men.

When he was eight or nine, Allan had watched his first Marx Brothers movie at the Vogue on Coney Island Avenue, and he was an immediate and great fan of theirs, as he was of W. C. Fields. (Some of Fields's meandering, singsongy, incantatory style appeared in Woody's later stand-up performances.) But Allan was inspired by more than movies. He read and reread Max Shulman, the sharp, satiric farceur whose graceful, hilarious, seemingly meringuelike prose millions of budding writers have tried with dismal and leaden results to emulate. Later he discovered the urbane and witty Robert Benchley and the incomparable S. J. Perelman, the master of elevated, rococo language, both of whom would influence him. He also listened enthusiastically to (and he and Mickey enthusiastically aped) Bob and Ray. Bob Elliott and the late Ray Goulding created thousands of perfectly oddball characters, including the Komodo Dragon Expert, broadcasting's silver-throated Wally Ballou, and the redoubtable Tippy, the Wonder Dog; they manipulated language the way Satchel Paige manipulated baseballs. ("Here is a supplementary bulletin from the Office of Fluctuation Control, Bureau of Edible Condiments; Soluble, Insoluble, and Indigestible Fats and Glutinous Derivatives, Washington, D.C. Correction of Directive 943456201, issued a while back, concerning the fixed price of groundhog meat. In the directive above-named, the quotation on groundhog meat should read 'ground hogmeat.' ")

The first writer to draw his attention to comedy, however, was George S. Kaufman. In the third grade, when he was nine, Allan's class was sent to the library to learn how to look up books. He happened to pick up a copy of plays by Kaufman and Moss Hart and opened it at random to *You Can't Take It with You*. "The scene is . . . just around the corner from Columbia University but don't go looking for it," he read, and thought to himself how funny that was. In time he read Kaufman in full and came to worship his acerbic style, so much so that he aped him in every way he could. He managed to be shy and reserved and at the same time sardonic, aloof, and uncommunicative—a pattern he would later have to reverse as part of his transformation into a successful performer. On occasion as teenagers, he and Mickey would go to stand across the street from Kaufman's house on East Ninety-fourth Street in Manhattan, not in the hope of catching a glimpse of him, but simply to silently attend to greatness. Or rather, they stood in front of what they *thought* was his house. For a period they gazed at the wrong building, and years later, one idea for the ending of *Take the Money and Run*, the quasi-documentary of the life of an inept but hopeful felon, was to have the film's producers appear and say, "Ladies and gentlemen, we've made a mistake. We've shot the wrong life. We meant to do the story of the person in the house next door."

Given a choice, Allan himself would have preferred to live in the house next door, or for that matter, because of its crowding and commotion, in almost any house other than his own—but above all if it resembled the Manhattan penthouses with grand furniture that he saw in the movies. Those seemed the apex of uptown class to a teenager who shared not only his apartment with others but his room as well.

Given a more realistic choice, Allan would have missed the Friday-night dinners at home with heaven knows who as guests in favor of attending talent night at the Flatbush Theater, one of the last great vaudeville houses, but however free his parents' rein on his activities, there was an evening curfew and the Flatbush show ended after it. He and a friend had accidentally discovered the theater one day when they were fourteen and hanging out on Flatbush Avenue. The theater showed two features, such as Abbott and Costello or Bowery Boys epics, and several cartoons. Then followed five acts of vaudeville complete with a full orchestra onstage: musical acts, tap dancers, comics, impressionists. Allan never missed a Saturday afternoon at the Flatbush from the day he discovered it until the day the vaudeville ended, when he was seventeen or eighteen. Many times he'd arrive in time for the acts, then watch the films and sit through the performances a second time. He knew every band member by name and every act so well he could repeat them, which he did. Regularly.

The lullaby of vaudeville was a natural attraction for a boy who loved magic, music, and humor and who seriously practiced them himself. Movies provided an escape into suspended disbelief, a few hours of transport from the ordinary life of Brooklyn and an imaginary springboard into the wondrous worlds on the screen. These worlds were so attractive to him that he could sit in the dark and imagine himself, if not always a part of it, at least potentially capable of having a touch of the screen world in his life; for years, for instance, Allan wanted a white telephone like the ones in the Manhattan penthouse comedies. But vaudeville was less imaginary. It was live and raucous and right in front of him. It didn't take a great leap of fantasy to see oneself performing magic tricks or telling a joke, especially if, like Allan, you practiced hard every day. So he wrote the comics' routines on the back of his Cracker Jack box and memorized them and amused both his friends and himself. Humor was a highly prized asset in his group of friends, who were themselves funny and who shared a collection of joke books.

It was his mother who may have prompted him to try to amuse strangers. "Aim high," she told him again and again.

"My parents were affectionate but harsh, not unlike other parents in the neighborhood," Woody says. "They were typical clichéd Jewish parents. You were always presumed guilty, me especially. Their attitude toward everyone was not encouraging—it was 'prove it to me' all the time. There's that old Sam Levenson joke about the kid who comes home from school and says to his mother, 'I got ninety-eight on the test.' And she says, 'Who got the other two points?' And that's exactly what it was. It was never good enough, and very 'Oh, really? You think you're so good? Okay, hotshot, show me how fast you can do that.' " Which seems approximately what his mother said when Allan told her he was thinking of becoming a joke writer.

So he did. And then, not knowing what to do with his jokes, he sent them to a cousin, Phil Wasserman, for his opinion. Wasserman was in public relations, whatever that meant; it certainly had nothing to do with anyone's life in Flatbush. But he was very encouraging. And because everything he knew about the joke business came from those he read in the newspaper gossip columns, he suggested that Allan submit them there. In so doing, Allan Konigsberg took a giant step toward crossing his personal Rubicon: the East River, which flows between Brooklyn and Manhattan.

Thus it happened that in the spring of 1952, when he was sixteen and a high school junior and when there were eight major newspapers in New York, almost all with an influential show-business and gossip columnist but none so powerful as Walter Winchell of the *Daily Mirror*, Allan Konigsberg did what the myth of show business dictates that one do first: He changed his name. Then he typed up his jokes over the signature of Woody Allen and he mailed them to one columnist or another, always with the same note: "Enclosed are some gags for your consideration and sent exclusively to you."

The first to use one of his gags was Nick Kenny, a folksy columnist for the *Mirror* who, unlike Winchell with his hard-hitting style, wrote about his vacations and listed shut-ins to whom "Cheer-up Club" readers could send letters of good wishes. But he also used jokes ("The happiest man I know has a cigarette lighter and a wife—and they both work"), and one day a friend called Allan on the phone and told him he was in Kenny's column. Since all of his friends thought Allan was funny, they were hardly surprised; making the column confirmed their belief.

Then before long, the much more powerful and widely read Earl Wilson of the New York *Post* began using his jokes regularly. The first gags appeared anonymously under the daily rubric of "Earl's Pearls" or were attributed to the nonexistent Taffy Tuttle, a showgirl/playgirl invented by Wilson and used as a humorous device.

At the end of Wilson's column on November 25, 1952, Allan Konigsberg's pseudonym made its big-time debut with a line about the Office of Price Stabilization, a World War II leftover that kept prices under control: "Woody Allen figured out what OPS prices are—Over People's Salaries." (As a point of reference, in 1952 the Copacabana, one of the biggest nightclubs in New York, charged $2.75 for dinner and had a $3.50 minimum.) Soon there was this: "Taffy Tuttle heard of a man who was a six-footer, and told Woody Allen, 'Gee, it must take him a long time to put his shoes on.' " Under the heading of "Wish I'd said that" was: " 'It's the fallen women who are usually picked up.' —Woody Allen." There was a joke about romance: "Woody Allen reports the latest Tin Pan Alley song hit: 'You Were Meant for Me—Dammit.' " And then a juvenile version of the sort of New York joke he would be famous for: "Woody Allen boasts that he just made a fortune—he was downtown auctioning off his parking space." (Juvenile is the word that perhaps best describes all these examples; but then he *was* a juvenile, and his gags matured along with him.)

There was no payment for his material, at least no monetary payment. But the publication of his jokes did offer rich possibilities. Getting into Kenny's column was a great kick because it was the first, but it was minor-league stuff. Wilson was the majors. "The *Post* was a much better place to have them because it was a livelier newspaper and Earl Wilson was a very hot thing at the time," Woody once said. "And there it was, my name in Earl Wilson's column, a column that I had read a million times before with news and gossip of people whose lives I couldn't imagine I would ever touch. But there I was. It was all I could think about. And then I started getting in all the time. It was truly heady stuff." So heady, in fact, that it is not exaggerating to say that it changed his life.

"The last year of high school, everyone was picking professions and directions to go in and I had no real vision of anything," he continued. "I had originally toyed with being a detective, being in the FBI. Mickey and I had talked about becoming pharmacists and alternating days at work so the other could go to ball games. Sometime later I thought about becoming an optometrist—that was one of my more mature thoughts. I also thought of the possibility of being a magician. Occasionally in some very spontaneous way, I thought a little bit about becoming a comedian—such as the first time I saw Bob Hope, in *The Road to Morocco* with my mother—then it would vanish off my mind and later resurface again."

Lurking in the back of his mind, too, was the notion of becoming a writer. He never thought specifically of comedy writing, but of writing in some general way. It was, after all, and despite his inattentive approach to all things scholastic, something he did well. From the seventh grade on, he was able to dash off his assigned compositions in minutes. Yet despite his offhanded attention, he was often chosen to read his papers to the class because they were invariably funny, and his classmates were an appreciative audience. As early as the first grade, he would write on such topics as what presents he'd hope to get if he were home sick in bed. And he was always able to use sophisticated and esoteric terms effectively without necessarily knowing what they meant; sometimes the teacher would go out of the room and call another teacher over and, whispering to her, point to the redhead with the gift for learned invention. So it was not without foundation that when Allan considered career choices, writing emerged as a contender. The power of comedy, too, was attractive to him, and from an early age he had the sense to use it to his advantage.

"I grew up taking great delight in comedy and making people laugh," Woody says. "I was always identifying with the comedian. It was a very painless way to get through life. Of course the comedians on the screen always had these situations prefabricated and lines written for them, but if you found yourself in real-life situations that were otherwise painful for you and you were never at a loss for a wonderful comic remark, then it was great. I was very good at that. And good to this day. I guess that's why I can be a comedy writer, because that's what comedy writers do all the time. I've done it many times on television, hosting the Johnny Carson show or something. I was good at coming up with those gliding Bob Hope one-liners. Hope was the first I saw do it. Then Danny Kaye did his version, and Abbott and Costello did theirs, and later Jerry Lewis did his. I was just able to do it. It was a big value of mine."

Broadway columnists like Wilson and Winchell, Dorothy Kilgallen, Ed Sullivan, and Louis Sobol regaled readers of their nationally syndicated columns with tidbits of celebrity gossip and wisecrackery. They and their assistants frequented the nightclubs and shows in search of information but needed help to fill their daily space. Press agents provided it. Over and above interviews in newspapers and magazines and appearances on radio and TV shows, celebrities wanted their names in the columns, so their press agents spent considerable time creating and planting items about them. A major tenet of press-agentry is to keep the client in the news, whether or not there is any news to report, and to make him sound witty, whether or not he is. This keeps the client from taking his weekly or monthly fees to another agent.

Gene Shefrin was a press agent, one of whose clients was bandleader Guy Lombardo. Lombardo seldom said anything funny, but with Shefrin's help this item appeared in Winchell's column: "Guy Lombardo says 'incompatibility' is when a man loses his income and his girlfriend loses her patability." In 1953 Shefrin worked for David Alber, a leading publicist of the day, whose office was at 654 Madison Avenue. One of the Alber office's most valued clients was Arthur Murray, the dance studio impresario. He was most valued because instead of a flat weekly or monthly fee he paid the agency every time they got his name in a column, a potentially more lucrative arrangement. This was called a "per break" basis and he paid for each break on a sliding scale based roughly on the size of a columnist's readership. So, for instance, an appearance in Winchell, the most widely read, earned a $100 payment. Sullivan or Wilson were worth $75. All were worth more if the break worked in both Murray and the studios. Shefrin was Alber's vice president and personnel man, and it was his job to find a good gag writer, not only to help keep up with the monthly clients but also to crank out all the material possible for this deep-pocketed gold mine.

At the opening night for Peggy Lee, another Alber client, at La Vie en Rose Café in Manhattan in the spring of 1953, Shefrin saw Earl

Wilson's assistant Martin Burden, who was responsible for the news and jokes that filled out the bottom of the column under the title "The Midnight Earl." He asked Burden if he could recommend a good gag writer and Burden told him about this high school kid in Brooklyn who was now being quoted so much that readers were confused; Wilson's was a celebrity column, after all, and celebrities were names people knew. Nobody knew who Woody Allen was. But his lines were so good that Wilson occasionally used some as his own and attributed others to people he owed favors. Shefrin hired the unknown celebrity.

Every day after school Allan Konigsberg, usually dressed in a sweater and brown-and-white saddle shoes, paid his nickel to ride the subway across Brooklyn and under the Manhattan Bridge to Fifth Avenue and Sixtieth Street. Then he walked down the block and past the Copacabana to the Alber office, where six or seven people worked in four or five offices in need of paint and where as Woody Allen he knocked out as many jokes as he could for three hours. He handed in three or four typewritten pages (about fifty jokes) each day and was handed back twenty dollars a week.

Alber, who in no way resembled what one might think a leading press agent should look like, was a soft-spoken, rather heavyset man in his fifties, with thinning hair and wire-rimmed glasses, who walked with a limp as the result of childhood polio. His writers were all at least twenty years younger than he and they looked upon him as a father figure; his office was by all accounts a pleasant place to work and learn the business. It was Shefrin who looked the part of a press agent: Woody calls him "a fast-talking, foulmouthed, terrific guy. I liked him very much and still do." He was in his thirties at the time and the other writers considered him, as one puts it, "a benevolent despot in the best sense of the word."

Woody's reputation preceded him. "They had heard so much about me and followed my jokes in the papers," he says. "I was this young prodigy, like Willie Mays, and like Willie Mays when he came up to the major leagues, I went 0 for 12 after I got there; I never had one hit in the papers. Then, again like Mays, whose first hit was a home run, one day I had a sudden burst of hits. It was a funny life. Those gags meant a great deal then. You were always reading in the papers how clever these celebrities were. I didn't know as a kid that other people wrote their lines. I was always picking up the paper and thinking, 'Gee, look at this.'"

His gags were funny and well used, but after a while Shefrin urged him to forgo lines about dumb women, husbands with nagging wives, or necking in the parking lot in favor of more topical material, because topical one-liners not only made the clients sound more intelligent, they were preferred by the columnists. "Read the front pages of the newspapers," Shefrin said. "I do read the front pages," Woody answered, and continued with his usual style. After a while, Shefrin began to cross out what he thought were repetitive gags Woody submitted. Every time he did, he'd hear, "But, Gene, that's *funny*."

Then one day Woody asked Alber whether he knew Bob Hope, explaining that he had written some material he thought appropriate for him. One of the lines was: "I don't have to do this for a living—I could always get rich running guided tours through Kirk Douglas's chin." It was and is a perfect Hope line; it has his rhythm and defiant mock bravado down cold. And the rest was equally topical and sharp, perfectly tailored to Hope's rapid-fire style. Alber said he knew James Saphier, Hope's manager, and sent on the monologue. Several weeks later Saphier wrote to say that Hope had read and liked the material and wanted to meet Woody when he next came to New York. The meeting never took place, but the idea that a teenager could write material good enough for Bob Hope made Shefrin cross out fewer jokes.

However great his success as a prodigy gag writer, Woody's air was always one of deference. Gag writing, after all, is not high art. "Nobody ever said, 'This kid is going to be a genius,'" says Mike Merrick, another writer, who was in his mid-twenties at the time and is now a theatrical producer. "But he was overwhelmingly likable. He was personable, he was sweet, he was curious, and we thought he was a character in a positive sense. He was the antithesis of a smart-ass. He would come in completely unassuming and never make any noise and knock out these original, funny lines for, say, Sammy Kaye. We'd read them and say, 'Sammy Kaye should be so clever.'"

Woody also sat for hours and listened enthusiastically to Merrick and Don Garrett, who had written for radio, talk about comedy. "He was full of exclamations," Merrick says, although an exclamation point is the unlikeliest piece of punctuation when Woody speaks today. "He was always saying, 'Wow!' or 'Gee!'" (Now one more commonly hears "Umm-humm," or "Really?") Often the three went out for coffee or a bite to eat at Boyd's Chemists, across the street on Madison between Sixtieth and Sixty-first, which then had a huge old-fashioned lunch counter and which Merrick calls "the Sardi's of the twenty-five-year-old press agents."

It is Merrick who is responsible for Woody's trademark black-rimmed glasses. While in college, Merrick had worked part-time as a stand-up comic. He wore black-frame glasses and a big silver identification bracelet and to Allan he was "a real Broadway guy." When at eighteen Allan had to get glasses, there was no hesitation as to what frames to buy. Merrick also helped him first perform as a stand-up comic.

Allan was seventeen and his talents included playing the soprano saxophone and doing magic tricks. He also thought he could tell jokes, at least among his friends. One night, in an effort to meet girls, he went to a Young Israel social club in the basement of a nearby synagogue on Ocean Avenue, where members of the audience performed as the evening's entertainment. A boy who knew Allan's talent was the MC and at the end of the evening he announced, "Next week, Allan will entertain us with some jokes." This came as a surprise to Allan but he decided to put aside his shyness with people he didn't know well and give it a try. The question was, what material would he use? A couple of days later at work, he told Merrick about his impending debut. Merrick had stopped performing by now but still had a loose-leaf binder with his routines in it, which he offered to loan him.

"They had a real professional air to them," Woody says. "The routines weren't like those written by amateurs, who get up and do jokes like 'It seems a [laugh] scientist and a showgirl . . .' His had a real comic's flair, like the guys you saw in those days: Phil Foster, Jack E. Leonard, all those people."

He remembers the routines still. One was about Seymour the Wonder Horse and another was about a cowboy. The dating routine had some of Woody's later style: "I'm coming home with a girl on a date and six blocks from the house, she gets her key out. (Big laugh from the audience.) Now I take her to the steps and I put my arms around her fast and she says, 'No, no, don't. I'll hate myself in the morning.' So I said, 'Sleep late.' "

He did very well. "I had a natural ability to work as a comic that I had absorbed inadvertently over the years from being a fan of comedy. I was as natural on the stage at that age as I ever would be, as I ever got in my life. It was an instinct, it was easy for me. I remember giving the material back to Mike the next day and saying, 'God, I just killed them. I just got screams.' And he said, 'Yes, it's exhilarating, isn't it?' I remember this conversation verbatim. I asked him why he quit, and he said, 'You have to want it more than anything else in the world. It's a tough scramble and you just have to want it.'"

It would be eight years until Woody wanted it more than anything else in the world. For the present, even though one of the older writers in the office said to him, "Someday you're going to look up at what you're doing and want to kill yourself," he was happy with his lot. His biggest problem was convincing his co-workers that he wasn't a mere child, a problem that was not helped when he got the mumps at seventeen and "looked just like Toulouse-Lautrec: fat face, unshaven." He called the office to say why he wouldn't be in for a couple of weeks, and when they stopped laughing, he told them they didn't have to pay him, although he'd try to write jokes from his sickbed. He was paid anyway.

"Working at Alber was a great time," Woody says, "because I was succeeding and leaving the nest. I was succeeding in a way unheard of in my environment. I thought I was in the heart of show business."

Each day after work, he took the half-hour subway ride from show business's heart back to Brooklyn's. He got off at the elevated station at Sixteenth and J, right by Wingate Field, and walked the block to home, which during his last year of high school was on the ground floor of the six-floor apartment building at Fifteenth and K where he had lived with his grandparents, who still lived there. Soon an aunt and uncle took an apartment, too. Once again the Konigsbergs lived with relatives; there were so many people in the apartment that Allan's bed was an Army cot.

He may have seen his future in Manhattan but his present was still the neighborhood. His success caused no changes in what he and his friends did: They went to the movies, ate pizzas, and listened to jazz. On weekends, they would meet at Cookie's, the café near the el station, after taking their dates to the movies, "and tell each other how we struck out." For the same reason that he liked to date girls who lived in the better homes closer to P.S. 99—because "they had softer skin"—he and his friends also often hung out in a soda shop on Kings Highway not far from the Kingsway Theater, looking for pretty girls. They "knew the best-looking girls were there because they weren't on your block."

Looking for girls was one thing. Meeting and getting them interested in him was something else. But once the prospect of sex loomed, Allan's hormones and women combined to do what twelve years of teachers couldn't: He suddenly took education, although not the education system, seriously.

"I was at an early age attracted to a certain type of woman physically," Woody said some years ago. "It's very hard to crystallize exactly the look that turned me on so much, but generally it was almost what you'd call a Jules Feiffer type of girl, the kind that appear in his cartoons with long black hair, no makeup, kind of black-clothed, leather-purse-carrying, silver earrings—almost a joke in terms of women today. But at the time I thought they were all beautiful. And I found out so frequently when I used to chase after those girls that they were almost invariably wanting to leave Brooklyn and move to Greenwich Village and study art, study music, get into literature—or blow up an office building. When I also found they weren't interested in me because I was a lowlife culturally and intellectually, I had to start trying to make some sort of effort to explore interests that they had; all I knew about was baseball. I used to take them out and they'd say, 'Where I'd really like to go tonight is to hear Andrés Segovia.' And I'd say, 'Who?' Or they'd say, 'Did you read this Faulkner novel?' And I'd say, 'I read *comic books*. I've never read a book in my life.' And so in order to keep pace, I had to read. And I found I liked what I read. It wasn't a chore for me after a while. I found I liked Faulkner and Hemingway, although not Fitzgerald so much. Then I started reading plays. The things those women read and liked led them inevitably to Nietzsche and Trotsky and Beethoven, and I had to struggle to stay alive in that kind of company."

In the fall of 1953 Allan entered New York University, not so much because he craved formal education as to please his parents. In an effort to match schooling with at least some pleasure (and because he thought it was "a dumb cinch course"), he enrolled in motion picture production. He attended the films regularly but the classes only once in a while: "I played hooky a lot in high school, but when I got to college, for*get* it. I must have skipped classes fifty percent of the time." Many days he would start out intending to go to class, but by the time the train pulled in to the NYU stop near Washington Square, the lure of midtown was too great and he rode on up to Times Square, where he walked through the theater district, browsed in the Circle Magic Shop, ate at the Automat, and went to movies.

He continued to work for Alber and now earned forty dollars a week. On those occasions when he went to class, he took the subway up to Sixtieth Street afterwards, walked the block to the office, then later went home for dinner. And on those occasions when he attended motion picture production class, he often rode uptown with an attractive woman classmate, who was a senior.

"She was a very nice person who always threatened to invite me over to her house for cake and milk," Woody once said, "but she always had the good taste not to. She thought I was quite funny. She was going to get married as soon as she graduated. 'No wife of mine is going to work. I'm afraid to be at home alone,' I told her one day. She laughed for ten minutes."

The woman lived at Sixty-second and Park, three blocks from the Alber office, and she seemed to embody everything wonderful about living in Manhattan, and everything that Allan did not have. Thirty-five years after last seeing her, Woody remembered a lot about her.

"When I was a kid and we came to our doctors on Park Avenue, it was an event. It was like coming to Monaco or something. And she was someone who grew up in those years on Park Avenue," he said, clearly envious. "What a thing to come home from school and not have to go back where I lived, but to be five minutes from Central Park and two minutes from the Plaza Hotel and ten minutes from any museum in town. So I've inflicted the city on my kids and I'm being sure to raise them in very good schools in the city. I want them to be able to come home from school and say, 'There's a matinee of Martha Graham. I want to see it.'"

At the end of his first semester in college, Allan was given a D in motion picture production, which was better than he did in beginning Spanish, which he had studied for two years in high school but managed to fail in college. He also did poorly in English, in which he wrote funny essays for humorless teachers. His papers reflected his admiration of Max Shulman, but Shulman's wise-guy style was not appropriate for freshman English papers.

Woody remembers turning in a composition in class "and catching hell for it from the teacher because he was outraged by it. He wrote on it, 'This is terrible. You can't say this. This is just plain rude.' And farther down he wrote, 'Son, are you a callow adolescent?' It was a very funny paper. But it was the first paper I ever did in college and I got an F on it. It was full of the worst kind of criticism from this professor who had never heard of Max Shulman. I remember bringing it in to the Alber office. They loved it but one of the guys said, 'Well, it's definitely not genius in the rough.' But it *was* funny."

Allan's relationships with other teachers were equally poor. In a seeming effort to understand him and set him on the proper path, one of them took him aside and in an avuncular way asked, "Now what do you do with your spare time? I bet you spend most of your time playing cards with the guys and stuff like that." Allan, who appreciated the interest and wanted to be accommodating, thought such an admission was what he wanted to hear, so he said, "Yeah, that's pretty much what I do. I play a lot of cards." Then the teacher, very reprovingly, said, "Well, you've got to do homework. You can't do that."

He simply wasn't meant to be a college student, which he freely admits. Although he enjoyed watching the films, the film course, with its lectures and in-class dissection of the movie in question, was not enjoyable at all. Then there was the requisite term paper, which he made up as he went along the night before it was due. Citing the use of drums in *Stalag 17*, he wrote about the importance of music in films. (While most films are scored by a composer, Woody almost always selects the music for his own.) He managed to get a C on the paper but he clearly wasn't a budding film scholar, at least in a professorial sense. Women and his own inquiring mind may at last have drawn him to reading books other than those with pictures in them, but the rigors of a college education dictated by syllabi and course reading lists bored him. At P.S. 99 he had been helped by tutors; at Midwood High he was warned by teachers that he would have to do better; but in college, where the educational system has no mandate to push everyone through the funnel of learning, or at least of course work, he was just thrown out as a failed student.

But not without a second chance. At the end of his first semester, he was summoned to a meeting with several deans, during which he was told he could come back for the summer course, and if he improved his grades sufficiently, he would be accepted for the fall term. The deans, however, held little hope for his ultimate success at NYU. "You are not good college material," one of them told Allan, and he added, "I think you should get psychiatric help because it doesn't look good for your getting work." When Allan told them that he in fact had a job, that he was working in show business, the dean said, "Well, if you're around other crazy people, maybe you won't stand out."

Five years later, in 1959, Woody began seeing a psychiatrist because he felt unhappy for no identifiable reason, a feeling he says he found "terrible and terrifying" and was unable to shake. He went through intensive analysis for many years and now, on his fifth doctor (there have been intermittent breaks of a year or two), goes only once a week or so, not so much for treatment as to talk with someone who has no stake in his professional life. He recognizes that highly successful people are surrounded by colleagues who want to please or agree with or even compete with them, and this is an opportunity to confer with someone who is neutral and can ask him, "Do you hear what you're saying?" He long ago abandoned the hope that analysis "would make me into a happy, contented, just-enjoying-life person" and instead likens the process to hitting with a tennis pro once a week: a useful exercise. It has never been connected with his work—"I've never had a problem working in my darkest hours"—nor has it provided him insight into it. Yet because of his long experience, analysts and jokes about analysts are common in Woody's films, and several of his stand-up routines revolved around them. ("I was in analysis. You should know that about me. I was in group analysis when I was younger, because I couldn't afford private. I was captain of the latent paranoid softball team. We used to play all the neurotics on Sunday mornings. The nail biters against the bed wetters. If you've never seen neurotics play softball, it's pretty funny. I used to steal second base, then feel guilty and go back.") Despite his long commitment to the analytic process and its beneficial aspects, his view of it is ultimately pessimistic.

"It's worth it if you can see an end to it," he said rather prophetically in 1973. "But with me, it's like Cole Porter's leg—that endless series of doctors who treated him after his horse fell on it. It's like someone saying to you, 'Well, we're going to try to work together and you must have faith, but we can't guarantee anything and there may be a lot of operations.' Porter went to doctors for twenty-five years and they worked and worked on his leg—and finally they amputated it. I feel the same thing."

After being bounced from NYU and "in an effort to keep my mother from opening her wrists," Allan enrolled in a night course on motion picture production at the City College of New York. It was "a total disaster. They had a dreadful film course compared to NYU's. They had no idea what they were doing. You'd meet in the basement and the teachers had nothing planned." He didn't last the term.

He continued to work for Alber in the afternoons, and he thought seriously about becoming a playwright. Each week he took a class from Lajos Egri, a charismatic Hungarian who taught in an office on Columbus Circle. He liked Egri but felt the rest of the class was "a half dozen real losers—some fat housewife, a salesman. There was no one in the class under forty-five years old and nobody knew what they were doing, but Egri was good. It helped give me a sense that I was doing something. It helped my morale. I still think his *The Art of Dramatic Writing* is the most stimulating and best book on the subject ever written, and I have them all. I find it better than any of the others I'm supposed to like. Nobody can really teach you, but there are certain things they can make you aware of when you watch a play or read a play. You can see that something is lacking or that the conflict jumps and isn't a gradual buildup."

Egri's class, though, took up only two hours a week. The rest of the time Allan spent "scrounging around trying to find out what I could do to be a writer or playwright." He and Mickey Rose once looked into acting lessons. They went to a brownstone on Manhattan's West Side and were ushered into a dark room, where the almost invisible acting teacher sat at the other end of the room and spoke with them, presumably listening to their voices to see what they needed. What they needed was not available from that teacher. Mickey never returned. Allan lasted one week.

He thought, too, that maybe he could be a film director. And to appease his parents, he looked for some way he could get back into school. There was a studio on the East Side where one could take lessons in still photography, and he enrolled because he was told that one of the hardest things to become is a film director and that a class in photography might help. But once enrolled—there is a pattern here—he never attended.

These rather makeshift activities did not overshadow his primary talent, however. Allan may have been an unsuccessful student, but he was a very successful comedy writer. By the spring of 1954 he had branched out into radio as well and was writing bits for Peter Lind Hayes and other performers. Still, his parents wished he were in school, so that summer he took one last stab at college. He enrolled in the NYU summer session and took motion picture production and English again. He raised his grade in the former from a D to a C minus but the latter was a lost cause. There was no room in academic composition classes for jokes and satire. He wrote an interpretation of Ernest Hemingway's "The Killers" that he read to the class and got huge laughs. It also got an F. At the age of eighteen, he was out of college for good.

He continued to live at home for the next several months. Martin, perhaps afraid that his son would be relegated to a succession of jobs as he had been, frequently asked him one of the most basic of fatherly questions: When do you intend to get a real job? His mother occasionally asked, too. But the fact is, Allan was earning a substantial amount of money, certainly more than they earned at his age. So while they might question his choice of work, they couldn't argue with his evident success.

However well Allan's professional life was moving along, his dating life was not unlike that of many boys his age, which is to say it was minimally better than nonexistent. His tendency to be a loner did not help either; he belonged to no clubs or fraternities, which serve as a means for mixing. Then the girls his age whom he met or was introduced to on blind dates always wanted to date older boys. And while he might have been able to overcome those problems if he had been socially inclined, he was an ingoing rather than an outgoing person.

He was outgoing enough, however, to agree to play his soprano sax as part of a trio at the social club where he did the stand-up routines. His friend Elliott Mills was the drummer but Allan had never met the piano player before the first rehearsal. Her name was Harlene Rosen and she was recommended by a girlfriend of hers whom Allan had dated a couple of times. Harlene was an attractive, dark-haired student at nearby James Madison High School two years younger than Allan, with the physical look that he loved. The song they played was a Dixieland standard, "I Found a New Baby." So did Allan. He stopped dating the friend and soon, for the first time, he had a steady girl.

In time, of course, he would of all things prove to be something of a sex symbol to a perhaps surprisingly large number of women; a book whose contents catalogue dreams women have had about him was published some years ago. Woody Allen plays a hapless, scrawny, and not very handsome character, and to assist the artifice he has made his screen self unattractive insofar as customary good looks go. Yet despite that, or maybe because of it, something quite attractive comes across. Because his looks are unthreatening to both men and women, he is able to present their foibles and fears in a way the audience can both laugh at and identify with. In fact, however, Woody Allen is actually a wiry, well-proportioned, athletic man with muscular arms, even if at 128 pounds he is a little underweight. W. C. Fields once said of Charlie Chaplin, "The guy is a goddam ballet dancer," and others could say it of Woody: He is graceful, smart, and appreciated by women of great beauty, who sense the magnetism of his intelligence and the strength of his personality, which is unveiled to people with whom he is comfortable. The Clark Gables of the film world may have won the heroine's heart in reel life, but in real life the boy who lost himself in celluloid fantasy has become a man with achievements beyond any scriptwriter's imagination.

As with any success story that starts with humble beginnings, there is a prodigious divergence from the path of reasonable expectation that Allan Konigsberg took on his way to becoming Woody Allen. Among the most unlikely aspects of it is his eleven-year-long relationship with Mia Farrow. It was a vast understatement when he said that the best-looking girls weren't on his block; one of the best-looking of all wasn't in his time zone, or even realistically in his universe. The daughter of the actress Maureen O'Sullivan and the director John Farrow; at twenty-one the wife of Frank Sinatra; Mia grew up in a world—the theatrical communities in Beverly Hills, Spain, and England—that Allan knew only from Rita's wall and the movie screen. To Rita, as with most fans, those communities were inhabited not by people but by mythological creatures whom one could adore but not conceivably touch. That those creatures were for the most part born and raised in modest circumstances did not provide any sense of affinity. Yet a good number of those stars Rita so adored have against all odds touched her cousin's life. He has directed some in movies. Others have become friends. Even the greatest heartthrob of her adolescence has played a peripheral role.

"I remember Rita as a young girl, as the whole country was at the time, just awestruck at Frank Sinatra in the shrieking way people were at the Beatles," Woody once said. "He was just the end-all of all there was. He was at the pinnacle of the glamorous world, I mean movies and records and radio, and he was simply a god, just simply a god. And deservedly so. The thought that in any configuration my dreary little life would somehow connect with his even tangentially was laughable. Here I was this wretched little four-year-old, living in a tiny little flat in Brooklyn with no one in my family in any remote way in show business or really achieving anything, everybody struggling at these low-class jobs like driving cabs to make ends meet. If someone had said to Rita that the mother of my children would be the ex-wife of this illustrious man, it's so unfathomable that she would have thought they were from Mars."

It would have been even more unfathomable if someone had told Rita that her little cousin would evolve into Woody Allen: world-renowned writer, stand-up comic, screenwriter, actor, director, and, according to *New York Times* film critic Vincent Canby, "America's most authentic, most serious, most consistent film auteur." Woody himself is aware of the unlikeliness of it all. Shortly after he began shooting *Crimes and Misdemeanors* in January 1989, he said, "It's an amazing thing when I think back on the awful days in that little school, and coming home and sitting at the oilcloth-covered table, that one day I would actually be in a movie with Charles Boyer [*Casino Royale*] or direct Van Johnson [*The Purple Rose of Cairo*] or take Jane of *Tarzan* fame to dinner because she's the grandmother of my kids. It's so unimaginable to me, and I guess you can say in a certain way that I get the full value of appreciation of all that's happened. Such an astonishing fact has retained its power to amaze me. Sometimes when I look in the mirror I'll see myself back there and I'll say, 'You're Allan Konigsberg from Brooklyn. Shouldn't you be eating in the basement?' "

Part
Two

The Heart of Show Business

Show business is dog eat dog. It's worse than dog eat dog. It's
dog doesn't return other dog's phone calls.

—CRIMES AND MISDEMEANORS

One of the smallest leaves on the Konigsberg-Cherry family tree was a man named Abe whose father's sister was married to Nettie's brother Paul. But however close-knit the family was, this was a pretty unraveled end and Allan had never met him. Then Nettie, who herself barely knew him, realized he might be of help to her seventeen-year-old gag writer. After all, the man knew something about jokes, having been head writer on the radio show *Duffy's Tavern* and the librettist of *Guys and Dolls*.

"Why don't you just drop in on him?" Nettie said to Allan, who favored white buckskin shoes now that he was making a living, however modest, with jokes.

"Just drop by? Just like that?" he said, incredulous that someone might do such a thing.

"Sure. You don't have to call. Aunt Anna knows his address."

So one day in 1954 Allan got off the subway by the Beresford apartment building at the corner of Eighty-first Street and Central Park West in Manhattan and said to the doorman, with all the nonchalance in the world because his mother had told him this was a perfectly correct thing to do, "Abe Burrows, please." He was sent up in the elevator and arrived at the door just as Burrows was leaving.

"I'm Allan and we're related," he said to Burrows. "I'm Nettie's son."

Burrows put off his departure and graciously invited his tenuous relative in.

"I write some jokes and they've been getting into Earl Wilson's column and I'd love to be a writer and I was wondering if you could help me out," Allan said in a burst. Then he handed Burrows two pages with about thirty jokes on them, which he had little choice but to read. But what began as an exercise in polite behavior changed quickly to enthusiasm. "Wow! His stuff was dazzling," Burrows wrote in his autobiography, *Honest, Abe*. He excused himself from Allan and went in to see his wife. " 'I have just read a couple of pages of . . . jokes, none of which I could ever have thought of,' " he told her. "That's generally my egotistical test for comedy writers."

Burrows wrote letters recommending Allan as a writer to friends, among them Sid Caesar, Phil Silvers, and Peter Lind Hayes, and Hayes, who did a radio show with his wife, Mary Healy, immediately wrote out a check for fifty dollars for some of the gags Burrows included and asked Allan for more. Burrows, meanwhile, took a continuing interest in his uncle's nephew by marriage and on a couple of occasions invited him over to talk about his ambitions.

"I want so much to be a television writer," Allan told him. Burrows was aghast.

"You don't want to be a television writer your whole *life*, do you? That's not your ultimate goal?"

"Of course. Why not?"

"You should think of the theater," Burrows said. "If you have the talent and you want to write comic dialogue you should think of the theater."

"Well, maybe the *movies*," Allan ventured. "Don't all the guys in the theater want to get into the movies?"

"No, it's just the opposite! A screenwriter is nothing, just an anonymous name whose work is butchered. All the screenwriters in California would love to get a play on Broadway."

And so he started reading plays and going to the theater. He found that the playwrights he enjoyed the most were the dramatic ones: Tennessee Williams, Arthur Miller, Henrik Ibsen, Anton Chekhov, Maxwell Anderson, Robert Sherwood. Occasionally he would be knocked out by a comedy such as Garson Kanin's *Born Yesterday* but for the most part he was drawn to drama and was unimpressed by many of the supposedly great writers of stage comedies. He didn't much like George Bernard Shaw (although he thinks *Pygmalion* is the best comedy ever written) and he hated Shakespeare's comedies; he found them—and still finds them—"dumb and bumpkin-oriented and aimed at the groundlings." He appreciates the power of the dramas but it is Shakespeare's writing in all his plays that most appeals to him. It is "beautiful and superior to the other writers of his era and to writers since. The speech is so magnificent, so gorgeous, that you're overcome by it. Often you sit through the plays only because the language is so elevated."

His immersion into the performing arts steeped him in the variety of entertainment and philosophical inquiry that came with the Beat generation. Soon he had steady company, too, in Harlene Rosen, who perfectly fit his bill of what a woman should look like and like to do.

"We went to poetry readings and we went to concerts given in one room on the sixth floor by one piano player," Woody says. "There'd be five rows of people in a little garret somewhere on the Lower East Side, listening in the dark to a piano player. And we went, naturally, to a meeting or two on aesthetic realism, the silly philosophy stuff that they still have going downtown, surprisingly. We went to all those kinds of things: every single Off-Broadway play; every single Off-Off-Broadway play—but at that time those were [Eugene O'Neill's] *The Iceman Cometh* with Jason Robards, and Edward Albee, and [Samuel Beckett's] *Krapp's Last Tape*."

The excitement of the art world opening to him was doubled by the excitement of having someone to explore it with. Woody and Harlene grew up less than two miles apart but their circumstances could scarcely have been more different, at least in Brooklyn. Julius and Judy Rosen were a happily married couple, younger than the Konigsbergs, and they owned a very comfortable single-family home; to Martin and Nettie, they lived in unbelievable luxury. He owned a shoe store that did well enough for them to keep a boat in the basin at the shore. She was part of a Great Books class that met every week. He was a good amateur trumpet player and Allan often joined father and daughter to play as a trio. Harlene also had a song fake book and could transpose music so Allan could play his clarinet in such accommodating keys as B flat. On other occasions Elliott Mills or Mickey Rose would play drums and Jack Victor would join in on a comb and waxed paper. For the first time, the jazz fanatics had a real group.

The show-business world was also opening to Woody and he wanted to have an agent, not only to help him find work but to handle the deals for all the work he was getting. Sol Leon, a William Morris agent, liked Woody and his talent and arranged for Woody to meet Herb Shriner's manager. Shriner was the host of *Two for the Money*, a very popular comedy and quiz show simulcast on TV and radio. The manager liked Woody's material and he was hired to supply gags for Shriner's monologue. Apart from Leon, however, the William Morris agents were unimpressed, and Woody's hope of being represented by the agency soon soured. "They never returned my phone calls and they treated me as a nobody and a kid, for the most part," he says. Leon took no commission for the help with Shriner, so Woody sent a bottle of champagne each to him and to his secretary in thanks.

Woody worked at home or took the train to the home of Shriner's head writer, Roy Kammerman, in suburban Larchmont, where they arranged the monologue. Woody was happy with the work but unassuming as to his position. The show had a live audience, and early in his employment, the producer saw Woody and Harlene standing on line with the ticket holders to get in to see it. "*You* don't need tickets to see the show," the producer told him, laughing, as he took them backstage.

When he was eighteen, Woody got himself a manager. Harvey Meltzer, who worked in the garment industry, lived near the Konigsbergs; Woody knew his brother Zachary from Midwood High. Meltzer wanted to be in show business, not the clothing business, and he thought he would make a good manager for Woody, whom he was convinced was going to be a great writer. So he asked Woody if he could represent him. Woody liked Harvey and "thought he was a pretty big deal then," although in fact Meltzer was about as far from the William Morris office as Santiago is from Nome.

One of the premises of *The Floating Light Bulb* is that a mother realizes her husband is about to leave her and she pins her hopes for the future on her magician son, a teenage amateur who practices by the hour but will never make it. She forces him to audition before a neighbor in the building who talks a great game of show-business connections but in reality is little better connected to show business than his TV set. When the play ran at Lincoln Center in New York, Bea Arthur and Jack Weston captured the poignancy of the characters but also made them hilarious.

It was, of course, not exactly that way with Woody. His parents weren't splitting up, at least physically; he did not audition for Meltzer, who handled him as a writer; and he seemed clearly headed for success. But the story is an example of how Allan Konigsberg's childhood twists itself into different shapes in Woody Allen's work. Joining with Meltzer was also the worst business deal Woody ever made. At eighteen he signed a five-year contract that paid Meltzer a commission on a sliding scale that slid the wrong way: the more Woody made, the greater Meltzer's percentage, which worked out to be between 30 and 35 percent.

The forty dollars a week Woody was making with David Alber was not included in the agreement. He still knocked out as many jokes as he could every day (he estimates that he wrote 20,000 in his two-plus years there), and he occasionally used his head in other ways. One of the Alber clients was Parker Brothers, the board-game manufacturer. Alber doubled his fees by having his celebrities pose playing Monopoly or some other Parker game. But for verisimilitude, the celebrity needed to be playing with someone, the back of whose head would unobtrusively (no balding, no irregular shapes to catch the viewer's eye) help compose the picture, which consisted mainly of the game board and the celebrity's face. The back of Woody's head made a perfect "someone."

But by 1955 Alber's client list had dwindled as celebrities got less and less mileage from being attached to a gag in the columns. One Friday afternoon when Woody walked into Gene Shefrin's office to hand in his daily copy and get his weekly check, Shefrin asked him to close the door.

"Woody," he fumbled, "I hate to do this, but business isn't good and, as you know, we no longer have many clients who want jokes in the columns. So, no reflection on your abilities, but we have to let you go."

"Oh, okay," Woody said, startled. "But . . ."

"I'm sorry. No buts. We have to do this. However, because you've been with us over two years, I've added two weeks' severance pay."

"But you don't have to . . ."

"No, I don't, but I want to. I've added eighty dollars to your check. Don't argue, just take it."

He took the check and stared at it as Shefrin tried to console him with the usual "you're young and you've got a lot of time to build your career" boilerplate. When Shefrin finished, Woody said, "What I was going to tell you, Gene, is that I was going to quit today. I've been hired by NBC as part of their new writers' development program. I start there on Monday at a hundred sixty-nine a week. But I really appreciate the extra eighty dollars. Thanks."

Meltzer had heard of the new NBC program to find and develop young writers and proposed Woody to them. The program was headed by Tad Danielewski, who had an eye for fresh talent. Danielewski had worked at NBC but left for CBS to become a director on *Omnibus*. He became disenchanted with his new home after the producers there turned down a show by a then unknown young writer from Ohio, Rod Serling. Danielewski introduced Serling to NBC, which took his show

Patterns on the spot, and followed him soon after. He saw every night-club act, every play, every TV show, looking for new writers.

One day a piece of yellow legal-sized paper with jokes scribbled on it appeared on his desk. "Our submissions were usually very elegant, typed between covers," says Danielewski, now a professor in the drama department at the University of Southern California. "This was slightly greasy and slightly chewed up and in pencil. Most of the material was one-liners; the longest may have been three lines. A lot were wife jokes. Even so, I was conquered immediately. I didn't know Woody but I said, 'This must be either a very old man or a very young one because he seems to either not care or not know yet how to move in these highfalutin circles.' I was struck, for lack of a better word, by his directness. It was as if someone had decided to tell the truth through jokes—not some philosophical inquiry into the essence of being, but extremely personal snippets of information."

Danielewski became Woody's champion with the others on the selection committee. After several interviews and meetings Danielewski said to the others, "Let's hire him. He may not amount to much but he's already sold a lot of jokes and he's young, that's the attractive part. He's so young that it might be the key to the program." It was because of his youth that he was finally chosen to be one of the half dozen in the program. (At nineteen he was several years younger than anyone else; because he was a minor, Nettie had to sign the contract for him.) He was proof NBC meant it when they said they wanted to develop young people.

For all its good intentions, the writers' development program lacked clout and therefore never really flourished. Television popularity is tenuous at best and performers want proven creative forces behind them. Producers and stars, told that these young but unestablished talents were available to them, were "totally pessimistic about the program," Danielewski says. "Especially the comics. They thought it was some weird thing Pat Weaver [the head of NBC television at the time and the creator of the *Today* and *Tonight* shows] was trying to do." But a few new comics such as Jonathan Winters and Kaye Ballard took at least some of the help available to them, and *Tonight* show host Jack Paar was supportive, too.

How well or poorly the program was received made no difference to Woody. He was happy just to have the opportunity to write sketches and monologues and be paid for learning. The idea was that everyone would turn in one piece a week and Les Colodny, an agent turned writer, would pass judgment on them. Sometimes Danielewski would assign pieces that were for no particular comic but were rather an exercise for the writer's imagination. No one stood over the writers and made them turn things in, however. If one wasn't already motivated to make the best of the opportunity, he could find real work. So there were people who took the money and did no writing and three months later were dropped from the program. And there were others like Woody.

"I was such a little digger ant," he says. "I wrote and wrote and wrote. It was a big deal to me."

"Woody's material was different when it was not constricted by the personality of a great performer and I thought it showed originality," Danielewski says. And presaging some critics of such films as *Another Woman* and *Interiors*, he adds, "But some people thought it wasn't funny, that it was a little too serious, or too attenuated, or too fancy, or too naïve. It was always too something. I guessed that what Woody needed was more exposure to the important or dangerous or highly energetic people in life. My dream for Woody was and still is that he would get interested in the power games of this world, because with his freshness and courage he could perhaps illuminate some of those dark corners. Now in retrospect I realize he was not interested in that and he went the other way, the way of Ibsen and Strindberg and Bergman, into the interior world."

But first he went to Hollywood. One of the few shows willing to take a chance with developing writers was *The Colgate Comedy Hour* (which became *The Colgate Variety Hour* in January 1956). Les Colodny found a head writer for it in Danny Simon, the older brother of the playwright Neil Simon. When he was fifteen, Neil was briefly Danny's protégé, then, after Neil was in the Army, the two wrote together for nine years. They had recently split up and Danny was looking for "writers whose jokes stemmed from the human condition rather than from gags written for a laugh alone." Colodny called him to tout one of the participants in the writers' development program.

"I've got a young kid I want you to meet," he told Simon. But when he said how young the kid was, the response was predictable.

"He seems so young. What kind of experience does he have with life to write about it?"

"Just read this guy's material," Colodny asked Simon. And he did. Simon's response was similar to Abe Burrows's.

"Les, I think this kid is my next brother."

"I don't know how many pages there were from this kid just out of high school," Simon recalls. "I don't even think the jokes were typed out. I think they were just on lined paper, written with his geography notes. But when I read the jokes, the sense of humor was what I was looking for. Not that it was like Neil, because they were completely unalike. Neil's jokes came from Neil; Woody's jokes came from Woody. But they were rooted in some kind of inner feeling rather than just being joke jokes."

By this time Woody and Harlene were talking about marriage, and they were engaged in January 1956. He was reluctant to leave her, but going to Hollywood for a few months to get a start on his career was too good to pass up. Soon after their engagement, he flew to California and checked into the now defunct Hollywood Hawaiian Motel at the intersection of Yucca and Grace streets, where the *Colgate Variety Hour* writing staff was billeted. One of the writers on the show was Milt Rosen (no relation to Harlene). He was paying $290 a month for a one-bedroom suite while making $300 a week and supporting his family back in New York. Les Colodny offered him a deal: If he would share his room with the twenty-year-old from New York, the writers' development program would pick up the tab. Rosen gratefully accepted and his new roommate arrived almost immediately.

"Woody had George S. Kaufman hair, like a mad Russian," Rosen said in 1973. "His first words were: 'Tennessee Williams is the greatest writer who ever lived.' Then he went out and bought a pair of shoes at some schlock store for six cents, and almost immediately he had blisters.

" 'I'll buy you a new pair,' I told him.

" 'No,' he said, 'I bought them and I have to wear them.'

"I think his real purpose in coming out was to work for Bob Hope. He spent his first day looking for Jimmy Saphier, Hope's manager. Then he called up a guy he had met years ago at a party and they agreed to meet at Hollywood and Vine. They each got there on time, but they were diagonally across the street from each other. They stood there for weeks before they realized where the other was. Finally they got together and they decided to pick up girls. His friend was growing a beard and his face itched, and Woody was limping from the new shoes. He came home about twelve-thirty in the morning and said they had struck out, because 'between his scratching and my limping, no one wanted to stop.' "

Woody immediately became the favorite of all the writers; he was smart and pleasant and young enough not to pose any sort of threat. Also, he was the only one who wasn't married. It was like having a younger brother around. But when the others went out with their wives in the evening, Woody was lonely. He often phoned Harlene but he wrote even more often.

"He wrote her five letters a day, each twenty-five pages long," Rosen said. "He got so he was describing what was in the refrigerator. I mean, how much can you say in a day?"

When Woody wasn't writing to Harlene, he was writing to Jack Victor, as he did soon after his arrival:

We have much to talk about but I can't give it all to you in a letter. Let me just say that I know I'm finally in the heart of Hollywood. Yesterday on the street I passed Richard Loo.

It's sunny and warm and the houses are pink and white against clean streets. It's an honor system town with few traffic lights and there's nobody at the newsstands on the corners as they depend on you to pay for your paper and stop for pedestrians—rather than the New York method of stealing everything not nailed down and taking direct aim at the elderly.

I eat at the Brown Derby and run all over town. . . . I've befriended all the writers staying at my magnificent hotel (in which I have a suite with bar, kitchen, two rooms, pool), particularly Danny Simon (of Danny and Doc Simon). . . .

This is a real resort type land. Pastel and Oz-like.

I love it but I'm very alone.

The sketch on Sunday. . . . the 12th—the beach sketch—is Danny Simon's and mine. Mostly his but then he makes 1800 a wk. He's head writer and as good luck would have it, my best friend out here. . . . Write. Give me Jerry's home and college address. Write air mail. To Woody Allen—hotel address on envelope.

Hope to see you soon,
Al

The Colgate show had its offices in an old building at the corner of Hollywood Boulevard and Vine Street, the sort of ancient structure that has sliding iron gates on the elevators. Almost all of the eight writers were from New York because Simon felt there weren't enough good

TV writers yet in Hollywood. The feeling was that Hollywood writers wrote radio jokes, designed to play on the ear rather than the eye.

Be that as it may, a line of Woody's Rosen remembered is strictly for the ear. He and Simon and Woody were writing a sketch for Fred MacMurray. A girl is on her first date and her parents are waiting for her to return. They are worried. "There's too much laxity in this house," Rosen wrote as the father's line. Which should have been the joke, although with just an odd word it was not much of one. Woody added, "From now on, there's going to be a lot more strictity," as a better, but not particularly funny tag. It is a line whose modest success depends entirely on its delivery, a style of writing typical of Sid Caesar's shows.

Woody was a popular writing partner with both Simon and Rosen, and as Simon hoped, he found in him the partner he lost when he and Neil split up. It had not been an easy search. In fact, he had given up looking for someone who shared his sensibility that a joke not only has to be funny, it also has to contribute to the story.

"I really had the confidence that Neil would be one of the great writers of the world," says Simon. "I felt that way because of the original jokes he came up with. Most of the other writers I met or worked with until that time wrote the kind of jokes that sounded as if a professional joke writer had made them up. They rarely came from truth and reality. And then I met Woody, and when I read his jokes there was something in them that made me feel, here was another completely original comedy mind. Woody was far above most of the other writers I worked with but he didn't know much about construction. He took to teaching, though. I loved him like my brother, except I was afraid we might split up also."

Although they worked together less than a year, Woody has said on several occasions, "Everything I learned about comedy writing I learned from Danny Simon." Simon did not teach Woody Allen how to be funny; what joke to write is not teachable, but where to think of a joke is. And Simon did that. Woody learned how to use jokes to build characters.

"He turned my professional career around completely," Woody says. "I was a writer basically of jokes, not knowing if they were good jokes really or not so good jokes. And this was a guy who read them and said, 'These are great. If you didn't do anything but write jokes, you'd make a very big living in this business.' But in writing sketches I was theoretically a step up from writing jokes. And sketches are theoretically a prelude to writing for the theater, because at least you get your feet wet writing for actors. In Neil's case, it was exactly that. And in my case, too, it was a jump-off spot.

"Danny drilled into me in the toughest way—also, he was very nice—what to do and what not to do when writing. He taught me what's great about a great joke is the straight line. The straight line is what makes one guy's joke better than another guy's joke, because an unforced straight line leads you to a bigger payoff. A forced straight line triggers the audience a little bit. You don't do a straight line just because it leads to a punch line. You do a straight line because it's the correct line at the time and *then* you make the joke off it; then the joke is good."

He also learned that "*every* writer has trouble with beginnings, that the beginning *is* the hardest part. And once you get going it *does* get a little easier, and you *can't* just do a joke that doesn't keep the plot moving just because it's a good joke. Now, later in life you wind up breaking those rules, but you break them in the same way an abstract artist does, who learns all the rules and then doesn't draw representationally; once you know what you're doing, you break those rules consciously, not mistakenly."

Simon may have been something of a martinet but his toughness gave Woody a ruthless sense of what really is funny and what isn't. "One of the many things he instilled in me, because *he* had it, was an unyielding self-confidence, an unyielding sense in your own convictions, and I've never lost it," Woody says. "So everyone in town could be saying that the sketches on a particular show were funny, but if he said they weren't funny, he couldn't be swayed. And when he thought something *was* funny and somebody screwed it up, he would not lose confidence but show you how to do it so it worked. He'd say, 'Of course it's not funny. But if you do it *this* way,' acting it out, 'it is funny.' "

Simon taught Woody to act out sketches as they're written. "If it's actable in the room, then most likely it's actable on the stage," he told him. He also drilled in the notion that the purpose of a first draft is simply to get a rough idea of the sketch's possibilities. Then the work begins: "That's why God invented the word 'rewrite.' "

As course material for this seminar Danny had Woody work with him on some sketches he and Neil had written some years before at Camp Tamiment, a then popular summer resort a couple of hours' drive west of New York City in Pennsylvania's Pocono Mountains, whose owners hired some of the best New York writers and performers to create a new show each week for their 1,000 guests. Woody did not know he was doing this at the time, but since the material was already proven, Danny and Woody could set to work on a premise and then Danny could help Woody bring it to its successful form; it was a quick way to show him how to construct a sketch without spending the two or three days it would take to develop a new one.

Simon also taught him to question every premise. "And *then* what?" is a recurring theme of his, one that Woody has learned to use. Many of his films start off as one thing, run into And Then What?, and are put into a drawer while he goes on to another idea. For instance, after he had the initial idea for *The Purple Rose of Cairo*, he says he heard Danny Simon's voice in his mind saying, "Great. An actor in a movie comes down off the screen. *Then what?* You only have half a premise." As he couldn't figure out what then, he put away the fifty pages he had written and spent months trying to write what eventually became—several years and several quite different versions later—*Another Woman*, which in turn had been started and put away. Only later, after he came up with the idea that both the actor who played the character *and* the character who comes off the screen had to fall for the same woman, could he complete *Purple Rose*.

After a month or so in Los Angeles, Woody called Harlene and asked her to come out so they could be married. The other writers on the show couldn't believe it.

"What, are you crazy?" Simon said. "What do you mean, you're getting married?"

"Well, all you guys, at the end of the night you all go up with your wives to your room and I've got nobody to go to the movies with."

"That's no reason to get married!"

"Then give me a better one," Simon says he answered. "I want to see *Casablanca* Saturday night."

But that and other reasons—among them that they were in love—were good enough for Woody. While he awaited Harlene's arrival, the other writers tried to make sure he was sexually prepared for the future. ("It's hard to believe how ignorant some of us were sexually," Elliott Mills recalls. "Before Woody married Harlene, I walked around Wingate Field with him, explaining what a clitoris is. I drew a picture in the dirt, the blind leading the blind.") Simon was the ringleader of their genuinely affectionate, predictably crude, fraternity-like pranks. Woody, he says, "was like a toy." But these were comedy writers, after all; jokes were the basis of their lives and they wanted to have some fun with this event. They just neglected to remember that Woody was a comedy writer, too.

"Are you a virgin?" Simon asked Woody as they all sat around and talked one night.

"No, no, no. I'm not a virgin," he said, but in such a nervous way as to convince them that he was.

There was a prostitute who worked out of the motel and Simon said, "Fellas, let's get him fixed up."

"A hooker?" Woody asked, wide-eyed. "Oh. How much does she charge?"

The plan was it would be the other writers' treat (although she was never engaged), but to play him along, Simon told him the price.

"Oh, wow," Woody said, reaching for his wallet and looking into it. "Do you think she'll take a traveler's check?" He did this so believably that to this day Simon and the others aren't sure if he had reversed the put-on or not.

"Do you really know what a woman's body is like?" Simon continued, figuring if he became as outrageous as possible he could squeeze more fun out of the situation.

"Oh, sure. Sure."

"Then you understand that a woman's two breasts are like a man's testicles, right? That a woman's left breast hangs lower than her right, just like a man's testicles?"

"Oh, yeah. I know that." But the way Woody said it, Simon still wasn't sure that in putting Woody on, he himself hadn't fallen off. Simon thought that the joke had such promise, however, that he continued, leading Woody along a line of physiology that ended with women having four vaginal compartments, each for a different purpose. Woody hesitatingly allowed that he was aware of this, but when pressed by Simon to name them he answered with a wave of the hand and a confident "Don't worry, I know. I know."

Thirty years later, after *The Purple Rose of Cairo* was released in 1985, Simon sent Woody a note congratulating him on the film. In response, Woody wrote in thanks: "Your approbation still carries more weight with me than almost anyone else's." The letter closed: "Finally about the vaginal compartments. I have located two but have not yet found the other two."

Woody was twenty, Harlene seventeen, when they were married by a rabbi on March 15, 1956, at the Hollywood Hawaiian Motel. In a timeless gesture, Simon and Rosen short-sheeted their bed, but the newlyweds had the good sense to honeymoon elsewhere.

I pause in the insipid scramble for wealth, power and riches to write you [Woody wrote to Jack Victor shortly after the wedding]. If my mother hasn't already told you . . . I'm married. . . .

Give your ego a gold star: I miss you a great deal and especially miss the subtle windings of our intellects. In a world of pseudo bigwigs and phonies, I'd really like to be back home with you debating the relative merits of Muggsy Spanier and Wingy Manone.

I met [Bob] Hope and [his manager Jimmy] Saphier and may work for Bob. He has that certain small town idiom in his speech and when someone mentioned a fact to him, he said (with his grin and in wonderment), "No kidding, is that the awful truth?" I broke up inside.

Funny thing dept: I saw [The] Rose Tattoo (twice so far) and marveled over [Anna] Magnani. I saw Dick the III with Olivier and flipped too. Nobody here of all the so-called "artistes" mentioned anything but you did in your letter and it was so refreshing to know you still have close friends who are moved by something that really tries.

I shan't be here too much longer but it will be a few months before I hit New York. . . . Hollywood is a rural village that would bore you stiff in no time. Pray you, avoid it.

I have been corresponding with Abe Burrows and after a look at movies and TV from about as inside as I've ever gotten, I can agree with him about why the stage, with its lack of censorship, its intelligence and depth, is the only medium to eventually wind up in. . . .

Working for Bob Hope on assignment [he wrote in his next letter]. Must do sketch for Bob and Kathryn Grayson. Ah so.

Will either send you the following items or bring them home whenst I arrive: An Academy directory, giving the names of all the actors and actresses in Hollywood—we will have a mound of chuckles identifying many faces we've enjoyed repeatedly but never could name. . . . —a two-sided 78 record of me playing "A Closer Walk with Thee"—and one other too numerous to mention. Meanwhile, I'm working hard, reading a lot, and learning—. I miss you, however, because there are so few of us left. Malicious Jews who, as Perelman says, would rather fight than eat and vice versa.

Right now my humble wife (she walks five paces behind me at all times) is brewing coffee. It will no doubt taste like chicken. I can't figure it out. Everything she makes tastes like chicken. . . .

Love . . .
Write . . .

The first couple of months of adjustment to marriage was difficult for both Harlene and Woody. The romance of dating suddenly became the reality of everyday life with the same person. Woody confided to Jack that they argued almost every day, and added that soon after the wedding he was "seized with a selfish horror" that caused him to wonder if getting married had been a great mistake. But he and Harlene also had fun. They made a couple of records of themselves playing, and nearly every afternoon they went to a record store where, in the custom of the time, they could sit in a soundproof room and listen to as many recordings as they liked. Harlene, who was also close to Jack, wrote him that as they were on their honeymoon, her husband allowed her to sneak in a Gershwin record between those of George Lewis and Sidney Bechet. They harangued Jack to date and constantly sent him likely prospects. Woody added reading assignments:

Things here are OK, but as I wrote, I miss the magnificent interplay of our combined sensibilities—dragging all those who can possibly be superior down with contrived slander and back-biting. . . .

Harlene and I have decided to launch a campaign to get you married. (Clearly I'm happy as a husband except for the time spent out of bed.)

I'm reading heavily [he wrote in his next letter]. Ibsen— O'Neill—D. H. Lawrence. Do yourself a favor. I guarantee you'll have the greatest time. Take out the following O'Neill plays, prob-ably found in one volume, and read: *Desire Under the Elms— Dynamo—The Hairy Ape*. All three are such unusual plays. . . .

You'll also see the mood of the kind of thing that I'm interested in writing. You'll notice that my ideas although lacking in craft and a coherent point of view lean always to what I can only call a poetic mood built from existential horror, insanity and death. . . .

Both sets of parents had the usual trepidations over the marriage but, perhaps surprisingly, it was Woody's parents who raised the greatest objections. Harlene's parents wanted to be sure that she really was ready to marry so young, but once they were convinced, they quickly gave their blessing, although Judy Rosen did fly out to Los Angeles after the wedding and took a room at the Hollywood Hawaiian for a while. Martin and Nettie, however, were hurt by its suddenness and their not being there, and they wondered whether their son could handle the financial burden of marriage.

About the latter, they needn't have worried. After *The Colgate Variety Hour* folded in May 1956, Woody and Harlene went back to New York via Las Vegas ("to gamble") and New Orleans ("to hear jazz, visit with George Lewis over on St. Philip St. and case the town," he wrote Victor, although they in fact did not get to New Orleans. Woody's first trip there came many years later, with Diane Keaton). Once home, they lived briefly with Harlene's parents before taking an apartment at 110 East Sixty-first Street. That fall, Harlene entered Hunter College to study philosophy. Woody was in steady demand to supply a few jokes or a whole monologue to comedians; the going rate was $100 for a minute's worth of material. Simon also hired him to do a little work on a show he was writing, and from time to time would make other offers; a television writer's life then as well as now was often a revolving series of two weeks on a show that was then canceled.

"Danny would call me from a phone booth when he was in town, it was always very secretive," Woody says. "He'd say, 'Meet me at this coffee shop, I have to talk to you about something.' So I'd go off in the pouring rain to see him and he'd say, 'I have a great thing for you to work on. I can't get you much money but I can get you a tiny bit. I could use your help.' I was thrilled."

Simon also recommended him to Tamiment, and the summer of 1956 was the first of three consecutive ones he spent there. The pay was not much—about $150 a week—but the experience of doing a new show every week and the exposures to New York agents and producers were invaluable.

The People's Educational Camp Society, as Tamiment was originally known, was founded in 1921 near Stroudsburg, Pennsylvania, as a summer retreat for socialists and their families. Set beside a lake on forested and unspoiled land, it flourished as an idealistic, and ideal, retreat for ten or fifteen years. By the mid-1930s, however, it had turned into an ordinary summer resort where young single men and women came to meet and, with luck, find some temporary romance for, in the mid-1950s, about $90 a week with all included except the bar. Between the end of June and Labor Day, 1,000 came at a time, mainly from New York, Philadelphia, and Washington, D.C. For the most part, they were white, middle-class, and Jewish. Most were young professionals in their twenties and thirties, lawyers, salesmen, secretaries, and other business people out to have a good time. Tamiment did not have the religious character or ethnicity that there was at the resorts in the Catskill Mountains north of New York; Tamiment guests were more assimilated and the jokes they heard were Broadway jokes, not Jewish jokes.

Unlike most resorts, Tamiment was not built as a hotel. There were only a few central buildings—a dining room where eight or ten sat at each table, a hall for dancing and socializing built out over the lake, and a 1,200-seat theater. Guests stayed in cabins set among giant trees. Some cabins were deluxe and had their own baths; all housed two or four people. There were tennis courts, canoes, rowboats, and, later, a Robert Trent Jones–designed golf course. Signs of the socialist past were hard to find. One of the few was a bust behind the tennis courts of Morris Hillquit, a renowned New York socialist politician who died in 1933.

The accommodations were not nearly so nice for the help, however, who lived three or four to a room in "seamy old row cabins, like the Bates Motel," as one former staff member puts it, with shared bathrooms between them. When Woody arrived the first time with Harlene, there was no accommodation for her. He was assigned a cabin with a comic and another fellow, but instead rented at his own expense what he calls "a crummy room in a boarding house over a hash fry place" so he and Harlene could be together. That used up most of the money he made and required him to arrange for rides to and from the resort, but it didn't matter. His writing was an immediate hit.

The shows at Tamiment were not nice little summer theater-in-a-barn productions. Every week there was an original musical show with freshly designed, constructed, and painted scenery. The theater had wings and flies and a big backstage. The 1,200 seats were comfortably spaced in a nicely raked auditorium. The summer staff included a pit conductor, a resident composer, an orchestra, an arranger, and rehearsal pianists; dancers classical and modern; a lead male and female singer; two top banana comics; and two writers. Agents from William Morris and MCA came to the last show of the season. For writers an added benefit besides the practice of doing one or two sketches and monologues and a new live show every week was that at the end of the summer they had accumulated a dozen new sketches to offer for sale.

The roster of talent who worked there in the forties and fifties is stunning: Danny Kaye, Sid Caesar, Imogene Coca, Carl Reiner, Mel Brooks, Neil Simon, Danny Simon, Dorothy Loudon, Sylvia Miles, Jack Cassidy, Mel Tolkin, Lucille Kallen, and Sylvia Fine (Danny Kaye's wife and a principal writer for him) are just a few. Until a couple of summers before Woody came, the shows had been produced for many years by Max Liebman, a theatrical wizard who recognized Caesar's talent when he directed him in the Coast Guard show *Tars and Spars* in World War II and worked with him afterward. He took Caesar and Coca to Tamiment, and then in 1949 fashioned the *Admiral Broadway Revue* around them. The show was so popular that the television manufacturer sponsor didn't have enough product to sell to would-be new viewers. In turn, the *Revue* became *Your Show of Shows*, which ran from 1950 to 1954 and, with its ability to combine slapstick with satire, was as good a comedy presentation as has ever been on the air. The young and sophisticated viewers who made the show popular were much the same as those who a decade later were similarly drawn to Woody Allen.

Liebman may have been gone but his influence remained. His replacement, a man with the unfortunate name of Moe Hack, wanted the eight- to twelve-minute sketches that Caesar and Coca did so well on TV and had done at Tamiment. Woody was a natural at them. His first one had a group of people at someone's house for dinner. Afterward, for the evening's entertainment, they call up people at random, speak inanely into the phone, and hang up. On one call they get an answering machine and the host leaves a stupid message. As it happens, the answering machine is his boss's. The boss, out for the evening and finding himself in the neighborhood, unexpectedly stops by the host's house. He borrows the phone to pick up his messages and gets the idiotic chatter. The host, hearing his voice blare into his boss's ear, realizes he can't speak or he'll be recognized as the message leaver.

Meanwhile the boss is saying, "I know that voice from somewhere. Some moron . . ."

It was a typical TV sketch for the times, as was another, called "Opening Night," in which a playwright goes with his family to the theater. He has written the play completely realistically about events in his own life. The family members are at first thrilled to be with their genius relative. Their enthusiasm gradually disintegrates as they see themselves depicted, and by the end they hate him.

But then Woody began doing atypical, surreal sketches. One took place at Cape Canaveral, where a just launched rocket goes off course and heads for New York City. "Hello . . . Look, Mayor," the general says on the telephone, explaining to the angry official that the missile's path is irreversible, "try not to be a baby about this. . . ."

In another sketch, called "Psychological Warfare," adversaries meet on the battlefield and fight against one another with weapons aimed at the mind rather than the body, such as one creeping up behind another and whispering, "You're short. You're too short, and you're unloved."

Performances were Saturday and Sunday nights. On Monday, the cast got the material for the next show and rehearsed through Wednesday. On Thursday there was a run-through in the theater. Friday was more rehearsal and technical adjustments.

The unyielding self-confidence that Danny Simon instilled in Woody was evident his first week. He was at rehearsals of his material Monday through Wednesday but skipped the run-through on Thursday, to the astonishment of everyone else.

"I don't have to go to the run-through. I know that it works," he told anyone who asked why he didn't go. It was not a wholly popular stance.

"Let me tell you something," a dancer who was married to the choreographer said. "The several other sketches in the show are going just fine. Everybody's laughing at them. But your thing . . ." She shrugged.

"Well, you're wrong," he answered quietly. He knew that the sketch was rigorously written and that the audience would laugh at it. And indeed on Saturday night, they did.

Woody's material was so popular that the next year he was given whatever he wanted, including a cabin where he and Harlene could live and, after a short battle, the right to direct his sketches. The two comics in the summer of 1957 were Milt Kamen and Len Maxwell. Maxwell was crazy about Woody, and Woody was warm in return; each made the other laugh. Maxwell is a tall, stout man with a thousand voices, many of which can be heard in TV and radio ads. The two looked like Mutt and Jeff, and their friendship was interesting in that, as a comedian, Maxwell was all the things Woody would reject; by his own estimation, Maxwell was "more of the spread-collar, white-on-white comic, a little loud. I believed in entertainment, in singing and dancing. Woody actually had to sit down and explain to me why Mort Sahl changed the face of comedy from the humor of broadness to the humor of statement."

They had watched him on Eddie Fisher's show on television and Woody had roared at Sahl's material. After Sahl finished, Woody turned and said, "Well, Maxwell, what do you think?" And he said, "Gee, I don't know. As a performer, I feel sort of cheated."

"By nature?" Woody asked, not skipping a beat.

"Woody's really a paradox," Maxwell says. "When I first met him, he was tiny and I used to make jokes about his height and his thinness and I used to call him a dart, a redheaded dart, which I don't think he liked very much. And then he got out on a baseball field with the busboys from Tamiment, these huge guys. They're looking at Woody with disdain, and the first pitch, he knocks it over the handball courts. You know how there's a lot of noise in a game? When he did that, everything stopped. I tried to get him to change his name to Heywood because I thought he would be such a great writer, like George S. Kaufman. I wrote the name on the inside of his cabin. I said to him, 'You can't be Woody. A Woody does not write great Broadway plays. A George S. Kaufman, yes. A Maxwell Anderson, yes. But a Woody?' "

Woody wrote with a manual Olympia typewriter and, Maxwell says, "when he typed it sounded like a buzz saw, because he was that fast a typist. And as he was typing, if you were standing over his shoulder—which he could stand for about a minute and a half at most—jokes were pouring out, really good jokes. I was aghast." Maxwell wrote some material with Woody and was impressed by his generous response to someone else's ideas. "Woody was thrilled when I came up with something. He just jumped on it and made me feel elated. I thought of the punch line to one sketch and he ran around the room laughing hysterically." On one occasion, because of a printer's error, the weekly program failed to list Maxwell as co-author with Woody on a sketch.

So before the performance, Woody and Harlene handwrote his credit in over 1,000 playbills.

Maxwell also played in all of Woody's sketches. "As a director, Woody was very definitive, very precise," he says, in explaining how he wanted his sketches played. But once he did that, he let the players work out their performances. "He gave us our head; after giving us his he gave us ours. He wouldn't say another word until the dress rehearsal Saturday morning. The thing I always remember about Woody with performers is that he was so damn smart about comedy. He knew. And the other guys, the other directors and writers, they were off on Pluto somewhere."

Apart from a copy of "Opening Night" recently discovered at Tamiment, none of the sketches Woody wrote exist on paper, but they still play in Maxwell's mind. There was the prune Danish sketch: "It only had the words 'prune Danish.' Milt Kamen and Evelyn Russell were lovers and I was the husband who came in and discovered them together. Milt and Evelyn are sitting at a little table with a candle on it. Very romantic. He grabs her hand and kisses it and he says, amorously, 'Prune Danish.' And she says, coquettishly, 'Oh, prune Danish.' And so on, substituting what people would say. Then I come in and see them and say, apoplectically, 'P-p-p-p-rune Danish?' And she tries to explain, and so on."

There was the Groucho Marx sketch: "Milt Kamen and I were two guys looking to score one evening. We're standing out on the apron and I say, 'Gee, we're supposed to go to a party. I wonder where it is.' And then the curtain parts and there's a sign that says 'Party.' And Milt says, 'Hey, here's a sign that says "Party," this must be it.' And the stage is empty. There is furniture but no people. So I say, 'If this is the party, where are the people?' And then the first woman came on. She came out beautifully gowned, in high heels—except she had a cigar and glasses and heavy eyebrows and a mustache. And she looked at us and said, in a Groucho voice, 'Yeah, this is wonderful. I'll go tell the other girls you're here.' And then Milt looked at me and I looked at Milt.

"The bad thing about that sketch was that it had only one laugh, which began when it started and finished when the sketch ended. We couldn't get our lines out. We had to shriek. Because all these gorgeous girls came out dressed as Groucho Marx. And they're all beautifully gowned. They're all dancers. You can imagine the figures on these women. And they were doing the whole Groucho bit. We were screaming and the audience was on the floor. You couldn't do anything.

"He resolved the sketch at the end by having them all do Jimmy Durante. But it didn't matter because the laughter was so great. Woody always said, 'The best ending for a sketch? When you say in Durante's voice, "Oh, no!" and follow it by humming "Hooray for Hollywood." ' "

There was the Albert Schweitzer sketch: "I played Schweitzer. Bob Dishy played my assistant. He came over and said, 'Dr. Schweitzer, Dr. Schweitzer, you've been pacing all night long. You're obviously very upset. You haven't slept. I'm your assistant. I care about you. I want to know what's on your mind.'

"And I said, in an old, slow, accented voice, 'Vell, I have been sinking it over, and I vant to become a ventriloquist.'

"And he said excitedly, 'Dr. Schweitzer, you're my hero.' He tries to be a ventriloquist himself. 'Tell me if my lips move.'

"It went on and on. And then the assistant said, 'Dr. Schweitzer, there's a call for you.'

" 'A call?'

" 'Yes, it's long-distance, it's from America.'

" 'All right, give me zuh phone. Hello? Who is dis? Who? Paul Winchell! Paul Winchell, you're the greatest man in the world! I love you and Jerry Mahoney!' [Winchell was a ventriloquist and Mahoney his dummy.]

"And then at the end Eleanor Roosevelt came on. Actually it was Cardinal Brancusi but we did it again with Eleanor Roosevelt. She said, 'Dr. Schweitzer? I'd like to award you this prize. But first . . . pick a card, any card.' "

There was the prison sketch: "My name was Boom-Boom, the MC:

"[In mug's voice] 'Good evenin, all you fellow menaces to society, warden, and screws—nyah [snaps thumb from under front teeth]. To-night, instead of the usual prison variety show, the warden and I have decided we're going to present the annual prison vaudeville show, which will be followed immediately by the annual prison riot. You're all invited to attend. Thank you. By the way, the warden is very happy tonight because his daughter just got engaged and married one of the guys in here who was doin life. The only thing he is upset about is they eloped. . . .

" 'And for the end of the evenin's festivities, wadda ya say we all sing a little "Heart o' My Heart." Okay, all you cons, here we go. [Starts singing] "Heart of my heart, I love that melody . . ." [Then, interrupting] *Murderers only!* "Heart of my heart brings back a memory . . ." [Interrupting again] *Assault with a deadly weapon!'*

"And Woody was on the floor. It ended with: ' "That gang will say heart of my . . ." *Rape!* . . . "heart of my heart." ' "

Finally, there was the publicist sketch:

"Milt Kamen played Marlon Brando and Evelyn Russell played a starlet. I played her publicist, who could never get her into the papers. The whole sketch was about the frustration of not being able to get her name in the papers. At the end of the sketch, I said, 'I know how to get your name in the papers. I've finally figured it out.' And I was supposed to reach inside my jacket and pull out a gun and shoot her. And I forgot the gun. I'm onstage in front of a thousand people and I don't have the gun. And I said, 'I know how to get your name in the papers.' I looked around, flummoxed. 'Oh, boy, do I know how to get your name in the papers.' I looked around again, still stalling. And I heard one laugh coming from the back of the theater. It was Woody. Everybody was frozen on the stage for what seemed like an eternity and then I said, 'Yes, you know how I'll get your name in the papers? Like this!' And I choked her.

"Woody told me afterward that when he realized that I forgot the gun, he ran up to his cabin to get Harlene to bring her down to the theater to show her what I had done. As if it had been frozen in time. And that showed me the purity of how he just liked what he was doing. That was the sum, the substance, and the totality of it. Nothing else meant anything. Just the joy of what he was doing. That's why I quit comedy, because I couldn't equal that. He was just marvelous. Short but marvelous."

Woody had a spectacular season at Tamiment and would have one again the next year. But after his third summer he decided against returning again because he didn't want to spend his life in summer theater. He had come to see that there are certain people who devote themselves to it to the exclusion of working the rest of the year. That was fine for some people, but it wasn't what he wanted to do.

What he wanted to do was write for Sid Caesar, but that is like saying he wanted to eat. There wasn't a comedy writer alive in the 1950s who didn't want to write for Caesar. Caesar was a comic incarnate. He acted every laugh. He completely became whatever he played, from a poor schnook of a husband at a country club to a Japanese movie star, which is what set him apart from other comedians; rather than play the same character in different situations, he played hundreds of characters differently. He invented language that sounded exactly like that of whatever country it was supposedly spoken in, except it was total and hysterical gibberish. Like Milton Berle, he was big—over six feet tall—but his elastic face and body emoted like that of an acrobatic opera star, and every nuance, which an audience for a stage performer would miss, was there for all his viewers to see in that wonder of television, the close-up. He was, simply, dazzling. Moreover, Caesar's spectacular abilities were enhanced by the dearth of comedy from character on television. Shows at the time were almost all situational, and the situations were invariably the same, only fitted to a specific show—different versions of the jealous husband, the wife's old boyfriend or the husband's old girlfriend, minding a pet for a friend or perhaps finding a stray animal and bringing it home. Caesar was breathtakingly unique.

On Saturday nights, every writer (and almost every person with a television set) stopped what he was doing to watch the Caesar show. (From 1954 to 1957 it was called *Caesar's Hour*.) Then at work on Monday, and probably before, he'd talk about the show with other writers. "Writing for Caesar," Woody says, "was the highest thing you could aspire to—at least as a TV comedy writer. The Presidency was above that."

Woody came near to writing for *Caesar's Hour* in the spring of 1957. Danny Simon had spoken to Caesar about Woody, but the show had its full complement of writers and had therefore used up its budget. Caesar offered Woody work but not at the rate guaranteed by the Writer's Guild agreement with the networks. The guild would not allow him to take the job. "I was heartbroken," he says.

But then Milt Kamen, who was Caesar's stand-in, went to Tamiment in 1958.

"There's this guy who should be writing for you," Kamen told Caesar after he returned. "I worked with him during the summer. He's great and does your kind of stuff."

After a year during which Caesar had no regularly scheduled show but did specials, in the fall of 1958 *Sid Caesar Invites You* aired Sunday nights on ABC. He also was signed to do a couple of specials on NBC, where he had spent most of his career.

One of Caesar's writers for the specials was Larry Gelbart, himself something of a prodigy. He had written for *Duffy's Tavern* as a teenager and then for the heralded *Your Show of Shows*, and he has such other credits as *A Funny Thing Happened on the Way to the Forum*, the adaptation for TV of *M°A°S°H*, and most of the scripts for its first several years, and the recent Broadway hit *City of Angels*.

He is only a few years older than Woody, so when Kamen brought Woody into the room where Gelbart and Caesar were working on a sketch and announced, "I've got the young Larry Gelbart with me," Gelbart pointed to himself and said, "The young Larry Gelbart is *here*." Then he and Caesar went back to work. Woody sat quietly, listening to them for a while, then said, "We could try this if you want," making a suggestion. From time to time he made others, none of which Caesar acknowledged. After another hour or so Caesar said to Gelbart, "Well, it's five o'clock. See you tomorrow." Then he turned and spoke to Woody for the first time.

"You. You're hired," he said with a grandiose wave of the hand.

"I'm hired?" Woody asked Gelbart as the two left after Caesar had gone.

"Sure you are. What's the worst that could happen? Would you work for the minimum?"

"Sure."

"Then of course you'll be hired."

The *Chevy Show* that Gelbart and Woody wrote was broadcast on November 2, 1958, on NBC. It celebrated ten years on TV for Caesar and won a Sylvania Award as the year's best television comedy.

The first part of the hour-long show was a parody of *Playhouse 90*, the live-broadcast ninety-minute dramatic show on CBS during the so-called Golden Age of television. *Playhouse 90* was hosted by well-known actors. Along with the commercial breaks between acts, it was standard for the host to plug the upcoming show that he would star in, so audiences saw TV's version of coming attractions. It could get confusing.

Caesar's guests were Art Carney and Shirley MacLaine. For the show, the three glamorous stars they played were named Rock Garden, Chuck Steak, and Rhonda Corner. Their show was called *Hothouse 9D*. The first sketch takes place in an English manor house.

The lord, whose first and much beloved wife, Cecily, has recently died, brings home a new American wife. Before the happy couple enter, the house staff complain bitterly about the idea of a new mistress, for to everyone who knew her, Cecily was irreplaceable. Caesar then opens the front door and a billow of fog engulfs the set. He introduces his new wife, who is coldly greeted. Trying to comfort her, Caesar explains, "I hated you when I met you. Everybody does. That's because you're a hard person to love, my dear. But that's only because you're something special."

Sweetly: "Am I as special as Cecily?"

Maniacally enraged: "Don't ever mention Cecily's name in the house or I'll . . ."

"END of ACT I" came on the blackened screen. Then Caesar, Carney, and MacLaine appeared in regular dress, each explaining that they were a host of this week's show, which made him or her the star of the next week's show, or of one after that, or of one that had already aired.

The second act of the drama came on. Still in the living room, MacLaine is about to sit down.

Caesar (angrily): "Don't sit in that chair. Cecily used to sit in that chair. It's like sitting on her memory." MacLaine moves across the room to another one. He says, "Don't sit in that chair. She used to put her feet on that chair when she sat in [pointing to first] *that* chair. She was a very long girl."

MacLaine puts a hand on his head and says, "Please get a hold of yourself."

"Don't touch my hair. Cecily gave me that hair."

"John, please."

"Don't call me John. She called me John."

"I . . ."

"Don't call yourself I. You're not I. You're not supposed to call yourself I. She was I and she will never be you and she was she and that's it!"

"But, darling, I wouldn't rob you of her. She was she and you were you . . ."

"You have no right to be you! What right have you to be you? She was you and she was I and we were we and we were . . . wow!"

MacLaine flees as the screen goes black.

Art Carney, playing the host, came on to show "Act Two of the play three weeks from tonight, an original repeat of a drama presented by our alternate sponsor who brings you next week's show on an every-other-week basis, and who is this week's co-sponsor but in three weeks will be the regular alternative sponsor."

The production, a parody of Tennessee Williams's *Cat on a Hot Tin Roof*, was called *The Hot Tin Cat*.

The scene is a run-down cotton farm in the South. Carney comes out on the farmhouse porch with a bandage on his thumb that makes it nine inches long and three thick. MacLaine is sitting in a chair. Carney says, "My eyes have seen too much and my head won't turn off the picture. Things in me cry out to be written." He holds up his thumb and looks at it sadly. "How can I write with this? I want to write about the one paramount, most overwhelming, most wonderful love of my life—me!"

Caesar, dressed as a Big Daddy figure, comes out. "Always talking about yourself, self, self. I hate selfishosity. I hate selfishosity. And you, you want to be a writer? What are you going to write poems about? Eh? Why, there's more poetry in cotton than in any ordinary words. Why, you plant cotton and then it grows with rain and the sun and you stand on top of a hill and you look down and you see buds of cotton opening up and you see cotton, and that's the real true poetry of cotton— cash. Cold cash. That's poetry."

The sketch ends with Caesar, who is now settled in a wicker chair, saying pompously, "Just so you have dignity. If you don't have dignity, you don't got nothing." He gets up to make a dramatic exit but is stuck in the chair. After a moment, he walks off-camera with it attached to his bottom.

The show's final segment was *Teentime*, with Carney as a Dick Clark–type host ("Your MC for the rest of your life") of a record-and-dance show for teenagers. "We're going to play the top thousand records this afternoon," he tells his enthusiasts. He then touts a concert he is promoting, featuring such groups as "The Tin Ears" and "The Sisters Karamazov" and introduces the day's new song: "Your Love Drove a Stake Through My Heart."

Carney asks if it is the birthday of anyone in the audience. Caesar, a boy with a greasy pompadour haircut from Sal Mineo High, raises his hand.

"What are you going to do when you get out of school?" Carney asks him.

"Anything that doesn't mess my hair."

Carney gives him an album of the Top 20 hits and tickets to his concert and to his new movie.

"Thanks."

"That'll be three ninety-eight," Carney says after a beat. Caesar fumbles for some money; Carney gives him two cents change. Then he says grandly, "On account of it's your birthday, what tune would you like to hear?"

Caesar, looking at him in awe, says, "Anything you want to play is okay with us, Johnny. Whatever you tell us to buy, we buy it. We watch your television program every day. We listen to you on the radio. We buy your records, we listen to your records. We go to your concerts, we do anything you want us to do because you're the only one who understands us, you know what I mean? You're the only one who understands us."

"Thank you," Carney says, trying to stop the increasingly manic Caesar. But he will not be deterred.

"You're the only one we can look to," he goes on, grabbing Carney. "After all, we just dance and jump to this music, you know, and listen to you. That's all we got." He turns to the camera and pauses. His face changes from mania to doubt. "I mean, is this it? Is this our life? Jumping around to this dopey music and listening to you?" He looks increasingly desperate as the camera slowly zooms in, framing his face. "I mean, look, we need help. Anybody out there. We need help!"

For all the success the show had, it also had the problems inherent to television. One of the greatest then as now is that the sponsors have considerable control over what is aired. An axiom of the medium is that a show must attract the greatest audience at the expense of offense to the fewest viewers. As tame as the satire on *The Chevy Show* might seem, it was a fight to keep the sketches intact. There were lines in *Teentime*—such as "Thanks for coming here instead of doing your homework" and "Here's a record I get an awful lot of money for playing"—that met with trouble.

As Gelbart recalled many years afterward, "The sponsors came in with cross faces and said, 'We can't offend teenagers,' because, I don't know, they steal a lot of Chevys, I guess. They just went page by page and said, 'This is too controversial and this is wrong and this is too strong.'"

However hard sponsors are to deal with, comedians can be harder. They rely on writers to keep them at their funniest, they pay them very well, and yet, no doubt because in part some resent needing writers, they are often abusive toward their staffs. They demand that writers sharpen the idiosyncrasies that make their comic character distinctive, yet at the same time they depersonalize those who make them unique.

In return, comedy writers refer to their work as "feeding the monster"—the character of the comedian—and speak of the need to "housebreak" a comic so he respects a writer's individuality.

"A comedian is not your garden-variety-type person," says Gelbart, who has written for nearly every major one in the past forty years. "Given years of success and power, he's going to get more and more bizarre. Jackie Gleason moved whole networks to other parts of the Union because he wanted to broadcast from there." Gleason lived in Miami, from where many of his shows were broadcast. "They have more power than is really good for them and they don't hesitate to use it. A lot of them have the feeling that for the money they're paying, you should stay the extra minute after work, or the whole night."

Depersonalization, however, is not limited just to comedians. Producers have a generic view of writers as well, and not only because most comedy shows have a large group of contributors, as Gelbart explains. "Years ago, Norman Panama and Mel Frank were a writing team at MGM. One day Mel Frank was walking alone and [producer] Arthur Freed passed him. 'Hello, boys,' he said."

Because the group writing of shows does not allow for one writer to fashion a whole piece, almost all comedy writers dream of breaking out on their own into plays or films. A few succeed, such as Neil Simon and Gelbart and Mel Brooks, who also wrote for Sid Caesar. It did not take Woody long to learn that Abe Burrows was right when he described the lowly status of TV writers. (An old Hollywood joke tells of a dumb starlet who, thinking she can advance her career, goes to bed with a writer.) Even more, he realized that as long as a writer is writing for someone else, he is writing in that person's voice and not his own.

"Writing for people, you're a paid hack," Woody says. "That's what I was and what I could do to this day. You go in and ask them, 'What do you want?'—and then do it. If I was going to write something for Jackie Gleason or Art Carney, what I need to do is dictated because of the established character."

Worse still was writing material for less well-known stand-up comedians, the people who bought material by the minute. "Anonymous nightclub comics who had no personality and never would have," Woody calls them. They delivered jokes, they didn't build a character. And jokes without character make second-rate comedy.

Recalling the dozens of comics he wrote for, Woody once said, "They'd ask, 'What should I talk about? What's my attitude? Should I get out there and be angry? Should I be a nebbish? Should I make phone calls to my mother?' I could never answer that. There *is* no answer, but at the time I didn't know that. The good comics establish a personality, like Bob Hope, then get guys to feed that monster."

Woody wrote a scene in *Annie Hall* that perfectly combines his feelings with his early experience and distills them through his comic sensibility. Johnny Haymer, who played the comic, is one of the stand-ups to whom Woody provided material. He also was a Tamiment comic Woody's first summer there. (The film version is slightly different from this excerpt from the script, which reads better.)

CUT TO: *INTERIOR, OFFICE*

A typical old-fashioned theatrical agency in a Broadway office building. Autographed 8½ × 11's plaster the sloppy room. The agent, chewing a cigar, sits behind his desk talking to one of his clients, a comedian, who stands with his hands in his pockets. A 21-year-old Alvy [played by Woody] *sits stiffly in a chair nearby watching.*

AGENT

This guy is naturally funny. I think he can write for you.

COMIC

(*Buttoning his jacket*) Yeah, yeah. Hey, kid, he tells me you're really good. Well, lemme explain a little bit how I work. You know, you can tell right off the bat that I don't look like a funny guy— like some of the guys that come out. You know, right away they're gonna tell yuh their stories, you're gonna fall down, but I gotta be really talented. Material's gotta be sensational for me 'cause I work, you know, with very, very . . . come on, I'm kinda classy, you know what I mean? Lemme explain. For instance, I open with an opening song. A musical start like (*Ad-lib singing*) and I walk out (*Ad-lib singing*),

> The place looks wonderful from here!
> You folks look wonderful from here!
> And seein' you there with a smile on your face
> Makes me shout, This must be the place!

Then I stop right in the middle and then I open with some jokes. Now, that's where I need you, right there. For instance, like I say, "Hey, I just got back from Canada. You know, they speak a lotta French up there. The only word to remember is Jean d'Arc—means the light's out in the bathroom!" (*He laughs. Seated Alvy looks up smiling*) "Oh, I met a big lumberjack . . ."

ALVY'S VOICE
(*To himself*) Jesus, this guy's pathetic.

COMIC
(*Overlapping above speech*) . . . big fellow, six-twelve . . .

ALVY'S VOICE
(*To himself while the comic continues his routine*) Look at him mincing around, like he thinks he's real cute. You want to throw up. If only I had the nerve to do my own jokes. I don't know how much longer I can keep this smile frozen on my face. I'm in the wrong business, I know it.

COMIC
(*Overlapping above speech*) And he's married to Marie. Sometimes they argue. One day they have an argument. He runs out of the cabin into the canoe and he's rowing away from Marie. Oh, he's mad at Marie. She runs out and says, "Chéri, come back. I love you."

(*He makes rowing motion*) "Get out of here, I'm never coming back to you. I'm through with you, Marie."

"But what will I do with the washing machine?"

"Give it to your father."

"What will I do with the television?"

"Give it to your mother."

(*Comic reaches end of his routine, walks up close to Alvy, sticking his chest out like breasts*)

"But, chéri, what will I do with these?"

(*Rowing back toward her*) "Oh, Marie, sometimes you make me so mad."

(*Laughing*) Oh, they scream at that. You think you can write me a French bit like that with a lot of jokes in it?

Apart from the problems of writing for someone else's character and dealing with sponsors is the quite separate problem of writing something that lasts.

"TV is a one-shot deal. It's also a small screen, so it's harder to be really effective," Woody has said, explaining why he has chosen film as his most common vehicle of expression. "Somebody who is terrific on radio or television is like a Renaissance painter who worked on sand. You have to pick a medium that has some staying power. Stage is fun, but the most exciting way for me personally to accumulate a body of work with substance to it is through film. It has a chance to grow with time. Plus, I always thought TV has a tendency to hurt your drawing power in films, that exposure makes you kind of familiar, but people like Eddie Murphy disprove that. Still, if people can see one of my movies every year or year and a half, that's nice. They make a commitment to come and see you. On TV, you're in the house for free and they can switch the dials back and forth."

Despite his generally negative feelings about working in TV, Woody has long supported public television. In December 1971 he donated his services as writer and director and was paid the minimum scale of $135 to act in a political satire of the Nixon administration for the Public Broadcasting Service (PBS). It was originally titled *The Woody Allen Comedy Special* but later was changed to *The Politics of Woody Allen*. The title, however, was immaterial: The program was never shown. "The commercial networks offer you no freedom at all," Woody explained when he agreed to do the show. PBS offered freedom but ultimately withdrew it. Privately, PBS felt the program was potentially too offensive to the administration at a time when they were the subject of intense criticism from conservatives and their funding was under consideration. Publicly, they said that the portrayal of presidential candidates (Richard Nixon, Hubert Humphrey, and George Wallace) would mean that equal time would have to be granted if the candidates asked for it. The show was replaced by one featuring comedian Pat Paulsen, a bona fide candidate for president in the New Hampshire primary. No one asked for equal time.

Woody's intention was to make a "little funny documentary" about all the branches of the administration. (Films of this type demonstrate the importance of realism in comedy.) Had Lyndon Johnson or John Kennedy still been president, he said, the show would have satirized them. As it was, the show centered around a Henry Kissinger–like character named Harvey Wallinger, played by Woody.

"Nineteen sixty-eight, an election year, and the United States is swept by turmoil at home and abroad," the narrator begins as newsreel footage of various 1968 scenes appears. "Men vie for the presidency, the highest elected office in the world with the exception of the Pope, although the president does not get to wear a red suit. . . . The Democratic party turns to Hubert Humphrey, a man of style and grace [Humphrey, dressed in academic robes, stumbles]. While Humphrey publicly sides with the Johnson war policies, in private he has his own opinion. [Probably making the second part of a point, Humphrey instead appears to be making a commonly used finger gesture for indicating displeasure.] The Republicans choose a man of force and magnitude—of personal charisma and a profound grasp of major issues—but that man refuses the nomination and they settle for Richard Nixon."

On it went in this vein. Of Wallinger a politician says: "Nobody goes in to see the president without going through Harvey Wallinger. If you want something done, you've got to be in good with Harvey. If Mrs. Nixon wants to kiss her husband, she has to kiss Harvey first." And regarding Wallinger's life as the capital's most eligible bachelor, Sister Mary Elizabeth Smith says, "He's an unbelievable swinger, a freak."

"Harvey Wallinger continues to do his job," the narrator concludes. "Some may criticize him, others may praise him, but everyone—will forget him."

Had Woody agreed to cut the scenes of Sister Mary Elizabeth Smith, Humphrey's hand gesture, and one where Wallinger discloses that "Dick is out of the country a lot and sometimes Pat calls up and asks me to come over, but I say no," the show would probably have been aired.

"It was an honest disagreement," he said during the controversy over the show's cancellation. "They honestly felt the material should be cut and I honestly felt that it shouldn't. Everybody who saw it thought it was in enormously bad taste. It *was* in bad taste, there was no question about it. It's hard to say anything about that administration that wouldn't be in bad taste. And so they decided not to air it because they felt that if the United States saw the show it would impair the morals of the country and turn the general population into a violent people. I thought it was an innocuous and perhaps an insulting show. Undoubtedly it lacked great political depth and insight, but it was a sometimes amusing half hour. Those people who were against the administration would have loved it, and those who were for the administration would have written me off as a crackpot. It was all so silly. It wasn't Jonathan Swift.

If the show had gone on as scheduled, it would have passed unnoticed."

Which is why Woody makes films.

In the late 1950s and early 1960s, however, he was reasonably content writing for television. One of the shows he worked on was produced by Max Liebman, who was responsible for bringing Caesar to TV. Liebman was a Viennese impresario. He was a great producer, with a matching ego. He was showered with awards for the Caesar show and others he produced, which he kept in his office in the back of the City Center building in Manhattan. When Woody came in for his first interview, Liebman was sitting behind a desk nearly as big as most rooms. On the desk were perhaps thirty-five statuettes—Emmys, Peabody Awards, and so forth. Woody looked at them and said, "Gee, Max. I didn't know you played tennis." Liebman was not amused. He told the insolent kid to leave.

"Max was brilliant but he had no sense of humor," says Coleman Jacoby, who wrote for him and later wrote with Woody. "He knew what was funny but was totally unfunny himself. There are people like that."

For all his lack of humor, Liebman could spot a funny writer, and he soon hired Woody to work on a show for Buddy Hackett. Liebman, in a rare miscalculation, was convinced that Hackett was another Charlie Chaplin. He felt Hackett combined that same pathos and brilliance as a comic that made Chaplin so wonderful and he designed a show called *Stanley*, in which Hackett ran a cigarette stand in a hotel lobby, to showcase him. But *Stanley* stayed on the wrong side of the fine line between pathos and bathos. Even with Danny Simon coming in to try to rescue the show after a few disastrous weeks, it was beyond salvation. Everything backfired. Carol Burnett was brought in to be Stanley's girlfriend; after the first week, she was in greater demand than he was. According to Woody, "Liebman was too strong a personality and too wrongheaded about what was going on."

By 1960 Woody was in such demand that he was making $1,700 a week writing for *The Garry Moore Show*—eighty-five times as much as he had made seven years earlier, when he started working for David Alber. But even though he was at the height of the profession and was earning top dollar for his services, he was itching to get out of television. He did his work for Moore, but he spent more and more of the time supposedly in Moore's employ writing a play and other projects for himself. The other writers knew this and many of them resented it, in part because they felt Woody wasn't doing all he could for the show and in part because they wished they could break out of TV, too, but they lacked the nerve to risk giving up such a lovely weekly paycheck. To use Fred Allen's description of working in radio, television writing was a golden treadmill.

Jacoby, who was one of the writers responsible for *You'll Never Get Rich*, the comedy starring Phil Silvers as Sergeant Bilko, was also a writer on the Garry Moore program. Friday was the day the writers and actors on the show sat down to read the script aloud.

"Woody always had a wisecrack," Jacoby recalls. "He was trying to say things to make people pay attention to him. He was a soft-spoken, very kindly person. But he always had a crack and would saunter out of the room, throwing something like 'I've seen funnier jokes on a Wheaties box top' over his shoulder. He also used to say 'It needs work' a lot. I'm surprised he didn't get mugged. After one reading, he got up and in his best George S. Kaufman voice said, 'Well, boys, I might as well tell you. I'm not putting any money on this one.' And then he snapped off Kaufman's trademark two-finger salute. Guys were furious, except for me and another writer, Carroll Moore. He laughed like hell." (The snappy bon mot was another Kaufman trademark; for instance, the telegram to his father about a summer-stock theater in Troy, New York: "Last Supper and original cast wouldn't draw in this house.")

Woody lasted only a year on the Moore show before he was fired for lack of interest—not the show's in him but his in it. The producers expected the writers to come to work every morning, an expectation Woody found distressingly like school and which he fulfilled about as often as he had gone to class. It was his final job as a TV writer. In the past few years the team of Mike Nichols and Elaine May had burst onto the comedy scene literally overnight. Woody loved their intelligent humor. But while he was a huge fan of theirs, it was Mort Sahl, who came onstage in a sweater and with a newspaper under his arm and talked about the world as he saw it, who won Woody's heart and mind. Woody saw Sahl and came to realize that he, too, might be able to be a stand-up comedian. In between the hours he worked for Garry Moore—and sometimes during those hours—he had written a mono- logue for himself and had begun to perform.

Part
Three

Ladies and Gentlemen,
Woody Allen!

I think I will review for you some of the outstanding features
of my private life and put them in perspective.

> —a Woody Allen monologue

On a cold and windy day beneath a threatening sky in October 1972, Woody Allen sat in his suite in Caesars Palace in Las Vegas and worked on a German Expressionist comedy (the paradigm of an oxymoron) called *Death*, one of three one-act plays he was writing. When he occasionally glanced out the window overlooking the hotel's fountains and its gigantic marquee with his and Harry Belafonte's names on it, his view was filtered through latticed blocks reminiscent of a turquoise-cement mosque, and it offered all the awesome splendor one might expect from looking through brick at neon. But work rather than scenery was the reason for his stay and he was gratefully near the end of a two-week run as a stand-up comedian, the last engagement he was committed to by a contract signed in 1965 that originally paid him $50,000 for two weeks of performances. In fact, he was gratefully near the end of a six-week, six-city tour, his first since 1968. His salary—it was now $85,000 for the two weeks—was low by 1972 standards and a pittance by today's, which is why although for most people Las Vegas is a neon oasis dedicated to greed and bad taste, for headline entertainers it is a brightly lit Get Out of Jail Free card. Still, Woody had no regrets that he was turning his back on fat paydays. This tour was a coda to the eight years in the 1960s when the focus of his career was his comedy act. The couple of remaining performances at Caesars Palace plus a weekend each in San Francisco and Los Angeles would be his last as a stand-up. From now on, he would devote himself almost entirely to making movies.

He was not ungrateful for his salary, however. He hadn't made any money for over a year, even though he had completed two films in ten months—*Play It Again, Sam* and *Everything You Always Wanted to Know About Sex (But Were Afraid to Ask)*—and would begin *Sleeper* in the spring. Woody takes the minimum salary required by the Writers,

Directors, and Actors guilds to write, direct, and perform in his films and in return he has a percentage of their gross receipts. His 10 percent of *Play It Again, Sam* would bring him over a million dollars and his 20 percent of *Everything You Always Wanted to Know About Sex* would bring at least twice that, but none of that money would come in right away. His performance fees aside, the redeeming grace of Las Vegas for him was that he always did a great deal of writing there. After his shows he gambled for low stakes for a couple of hours, and sometimes he would deal blackjack for a while, often making sure the customers won by looking at the card he was going to deal himself. If it was a winner, he'd bury it in the deck with no objections from the management, who were thrilled to have a star mixing with the customers. But that and dinner and an occasional show of another performer's were the extent of his distractions. The rest of the time, he worked.

"Nothing you do here can affect your career in any way," he said before going down for the eight o'clock show, the first of the evening's two performances in the Circus Maximus, where 1,200 people paid fifteen dollars for dinner and an hour and a half of entertainment.

Half the hotel's guests had come for the National Sash and Door Jobbers' annual convention and, like all conventioneers, they were ready for a good time, packing the long tables that ran in rows on the Circus Maximus floor and the plushly padded, tiered booths that rose in the back of the hall. The full house was a smaller audience than those Woody had played to in Chicago the week before; the 2,000 or so for each show there were good crowds but not great. Despite his popularity as a performer on the stage and in films, his drawing power as a stand-up was never that of, say, Bill Cosby.

Elsewhere on the tour, Woody was the headliner, but in Las Vegas it was Belafonte. He had already been booked when Woody found he could fit in his appearance, and Woody had no objection to being second. In fact, he liked it because the responsibility of drawing crowds is on the top name, and "because billing makes absolutely no difference." (Billing in Woody's films is often alphabetical, a generally no-lose proposition for him because Allen is usually the first name. But not always. For instance, Carolyn Aaron and Alan Alda precede him in the cast credits for *Crimes and Misdemeanors*.)

The slightly odd nature of this booking was not particularly different from Woody's previous bookings in Las Vegas. Nothing about his engagements was ever standard. He was, for instance, the first comic to work Las Vegas in street clothes rather than a tuxedo, which he refused to wear from his first appearance on; he thought tuxedos silly, on the one hand, and on the other, his refusal was a manifestation of his stubbornness in the face of authority. (It also brought him attention.) The hotel's managers had assumed he would follow custom and were shocked when he appeared for the first time in the wings in a corduroy suit. As he was moments away from going onstage, there was little they could do but stare at him in disbelief. But after he went out and got huge laughs, there was nothing they wanted to do other than watch him bring down the house, and they forgot about his clothes.

A more difficult problem in negotiating his contract as a headliner was the amount of time he would spend onstage. The hotel expected an hour. Woody felt that forty-five minutes of continually great material was enough. So when he first performed there, the singer would first do three or four numbers, then introduce Woody, who would come out and kill the audience for forty-five minutes. Then the singer returned to finish his or her numbers, by which time Woody was off having dinner. He loved everything about the arrangement. And so, too, did the house before long. They came to realize that a shorter show of high quality left the audience just as happy, if not happier, and that it got them back out onto the gambling floor earlier. To bring players to the gaming tables, after all, is why they put on the show.

During his early years as a performer, Woody was very nervous all day before going onstage, and the last few minutes were excruciating for him. There was a period when, in an effort to overcome that anxiety, he imagined himself a prizefighter in the moments before he went on; he shadowboxed in the wings while awaiting his introduction, reminding himself that he'd have to pace himself, that he'd have to counter a bad round with a better one, and that most of all, he'd have to knock out the audience to win. But by this point in his career he had overcome the dread. As the audience ate their dinner he sat comfortably just offstage in his dressing room, which, decorated in wild purples and brilliant greens, looked like some mad Henri Rousseau painting. He passed the time by doing card tricks and he talked about trying to catch Milton Berle's show while he was in town.

"I find Berle hysterically funny. He's one of the few people I've gone to see in years. There is a certain kind of broadness one associates with television presentations like the old *Milton Berle Show*, as opposed to, say, a much tighter kind of thing like Nichols and May or Sid Caesar.

Caesar does a sketch about a Japanese movie, it looks like a Japanese movie. It's very realistic and consequently funny. Milton belongs to that school of comedy that's very broad, and of course he's the best of that school. If he does a Japanese movie, he comes in with two teeth hanging down and it's very funny, but for Milton exclusively. Most of the TV shows had all the stupid broadness of the Berle show without the genius that he had. At least when Milton's in women's clothes, he's hysterical. He's a guy whose delight in dressing up in women's clothes and blacking teeth out is so spectacular that you're overwhelmed by it." (In *Broadway Danny Rose*, Berle appears as Cinderella, wearing a blond wig and a long white gown, riding on a float in the Macy's Thanksgiving Day parade.)

At eight o'clock the lights went down and a voice announced, "Ladies and gentlemen, Woody Allen!" To warm applause, Woody, wearing a pair of brown-and-white saddle shoes, beige corduroy trousers, a blue shirt with a button-down collar open at the neck, and a dark brown checked tweed coat (which anyone with a head for such minutiae would remember from the film *Play It Again, Sam*), walked quickly onstage, waving to the audience. He grabbed the microphone with his right hand and flung out the cord with his left, something he did almost constantly throughout the show. He also constantly moved about, which made him appear nervous and a little ill at ease. He was a wispy, sparrowlike figure; his long red curly hair trailed over his collar; black-rimmed glasses encircled his large eyes and set off a seemingly confused face. He looked lost.

He wasn't.

"I think I will review for you some of the outstanding features of my private life and put them in perspective. Then we'll have a brief question-and-answer period and evaluate them," he told the audience.

The material was not new. Most of it was written between 1962 and 1968, constructed from ideas and lines he jotted down on scraps of napkins, bits of paper, and backs of matchbook covers as they came to him and then tossed in a drawer. When he worked on the act, he laid the litter out on the floor of his apartment and walked around in it like a gardener in his vegetable patch, picking what was ripe. (When Norma Lee Clark, his secretary of twenty-five years, came to work for him, he brought her a suitcase full of paper scraps and asked her to type them out. They filled two hundred pages.) To prepare for these shows Woody had listened over and over to the three record albums made from some of his performances to reremember the routines. The audiences didn't mind the old material. Most of them, in fact, had never heard any of Woody's act before and were not familiar with him until the mid-sixties, when he began to appear in films.

Everyone in the Circus Maximus laughed right away, which is what they came to do. Woody told them about his growing up in Brooklyn; about organizing the workers in his father's store, going on strike, and driving him out of business; about a cousin who sells mutual funds and whose wife has orgasmic insurance ("If her husband fails to satisfy her sexually, Mutual of Omaha has to pay her every month"); about his traumatic childhood ("I was breast-fed from falsies"); and about his sexual prowess ("On my wedding night my wife stopped in the middle of everything and gave me a standing ovation").

The jokes were what he calls "verbal cartoons." They have a surreal, fantastic quality to them, but even so they are somehow believable, when Woody describes them, as events that could happen, if only to him; his jokes work so well because he delivers them as if they were problems in his life. No matter how fantastic what he says is, he makes it sound real. And then, because he's believable, he's funny. While most of the material in his act was a kind of long narrative, there were little throwaways interspersed, such as one about a girl he met in Europe who ran away to Venice, became a streetwalker, and drowned.

A little more than halfway through the act he stopped and pulled out a pocket watch. "Pardon me a moment while I check the time," he said. "They're pretty punctilious about time here and I can hear the band padding in behind me." He looked at the watch and held it up, as if all 1,200 people could see it. "I don't know if you can see this, but it's a very handsome watch." He brought it down and looked closely at it. "Has marble inlay," he continued, still looking at it. "Makes me look Italian." He paused. "My grandfather, on his deathbed, sold me this watch."

If the audience believed for a moment that he really did have to check the time, they knew now that they'd been had. What they didn't know was that the line gave him a chance to see how he really was doing against time. He was supposed to do forty-five minutes; that joke should have come at about twenty-eight minutes into the act. If it came before, he'd have to stretch the rest of the material as much as he could while protecting the laughs. He was right on schedule. He put the watch away and soon told the audience:

"I was kidnapped once. I was standing in front of my schoolyard and a black sedan pulls up and two guys get out and they say to me, do I want to go away with them to a land where everybody is fairies and elves and I can have all the comic books I want, and chocolate buttons, and wax lips, you know. And I said yes. And I got into the car with them, 'cause I figured, what the hell, I was home anyhow that weekend from college.

"And they drive me off and they send a ransom note to my parents. And my father has bad reading habits. So he got into bed that night with the ransom note and he fell asleep. Meanwhile, they take me to New Jersey bound and gagged. And my parents finally realize that I'm kidnapped and they snap into action immediately: They rent out my room.

"The ransom note says for my father to leave a thousand dollars in a hollow tree in New Jersey. He has no trouble raising the thousand dollars, but he gets a hernia carrying the hollow tree.

"The FBI surround the house. 'Throw the kid out,' they say, 'give us your guns, and come out with your hands up.'

"The kidnappers say, 'We'll throw the kid out, but let us keep our guns and get to our car.'

"The FBI say, 'Throw the kid out, we'll let you get to your car but give us your guns.'

"The kidnappers say, 'We'll throw the kid out, but let us keep our guns, we don't need to get to our car.'

"The FBI say, 'Keep the kid . . .' Wait a minute, I've screwed this up.

"The FBI decide to lob in tear gas. But they don't have tear gas. So several of the agents put on the death scene from *Camille*. Tear-stricken, my abductors give themselves up. They're sentenced to fifteen years on a chain gang and they escape, twelve of them chained together at the ankle, getting by the guards posing as an immense charm bracelet.

"Here's a story you're not going to believe," he went on as the applause died down. "I shot a moose once. I was hunting in upstate New York and I shot a moose. And I strap him onto the fender of my car, and I'm driving home along the West Side Highway. But what I didn't realize was that the bullet did not penetrate the moose. It just creased his scalp, knocking him unconscious. And I'm driving through the Holland Tunnel and the moose wakes up. So I'm driving with a live moose on my fender and the moose is signaling for a turn. And there's a law in New York State against driving with a conscious moose on your fender, Tuesdays, Thursdays, and Saturdays. And I'm very panicky.

"And then it hits me—some friends of mine are having a costume party. I'll go. I'll take the moose. I'll ditch him at the party. It won't be my responsibility. So I drive up to the party and I knock on the door. The moose is next to me. My host comes to the door. I say, 'Hello, you know the Solomons.' We enter. The moose mingles. Did very well. Scored. Some guy was trying to sell him insurance for an hour and a half.

"Twelve o'clock comes, they give out the prizes for the best costume of the night. First prize goes to the Berkowitzes, a married couple dressed as a moose. The moose comes in second. The moose is furious! He and the Berkowitzes lock antlers in the living room. They knock each other unconscious.

"Now, I figure, here's my chance. I grab the moose, strap him on my fender, and shoot back to the woods. But I've got the Berkowitzes. So I'm driving along with two Jewish people on my fender. And there's a law in New York State, Tuesday, Thursday, and especially Saturday . . .

"The following morning, the Berkowitzes wake up in the woods in a moose suit. Mr. Berkowitz is shot, stuffed, and mounted at the New York Athletic Club. And the joke is on them, 'cause it's restricted."

The audience was convulsed with laughter for the last three-quarters of the story, and Woody was about to quit. But first he told them, "I came home one night some months ago and I went to the closet in my bedroom and a moth ate my sports jacket. He was lying there on the floor, nauseous. It's a yellow-and-green sports jacket. Little fat moth lying there groaning, part of the sleeve hanging out of his mouth. I gave him two plain brown socks. I said, 'Eat one now, eat one in half an hour.' "

Finally he said that he was going to go and get dinner. He pulled a room key from his pocket and looked at it a second. "I was walking around the casino yesterday and I saw a really beautiful girl. I dropped my room key in her pocketbook. Twenty minutes later I went up to my room—and my typewriter was gone. Good night."

Onstage he had appeared just as the audience had come to expect: nervous, a little forgetful, a small man beset by huge obstacles. Nothing could have been further from the truth. There was a moment's nervousness just before he walked onstage but it vanished even before the first laugh. The pacing about, the flicking of the microphone cord, the seeming momentary forgetting of a line, the apparently spontaneous taking off of his glasses and rubbing his eyes while delivering a punch line, were all part of the act. He knew where he was and exactly what he was doing at every moment. Every good comic does. They have done their routines hundreds of times, polishing them until they sound new with every performance. That kind of knowledge of the material can have its drawbacks, Woody said after coming offstage.

"Sometimes I catch myself just going by rote, looking down at a girl in the audience, thinking about the show I'm going to after I'm done. When I first started, if I did a show for three hundred people and another show three hours later where some of them might be there, I was ashamed to use the same material. It takes about a year to write a new act, so I don't mind doing this now. I never improvised onstage until the last year and a half of performing, and then I started asking for questions from the audience because I found, simply, that my standards for material are very high, and it's very hard for me to get a lot of time, so I really condense it. I'll write hours of material and wind up with thirty-five minutes that are really funny, where the jokes keep ripping off each other. I found I was always short-timed and I started asking for questions from the audience. As it turned out, the questions were the best part of my act because the material couldn't stand up against reality." (He was asked on one of his TV specials on which Billy Graham was a guest to name his greatest sin: "I once had impure thoughts about Art Linkletter.") "So now I think I could go out there and very nicely do a show that is almost all questions with occasional material because of the situation. They accept me. Acceptance is more important for a comedian than for other performers. They laugh at me all the time. I don't have to prove anything. They think things are funny even if they're not that funny."

An audience that has accepted a comedian will also laugh at jokes they don't understand. One time when Bob Hope performed in England in the early 1950s, the punch line to a joke was the word "motel," and when Hope said "motel" everyone duly laughed. But Larry Gelbart, then one of Hope's writers, asked the woman next to him backstage if anyone knew what a motel was. "No," she said, and explained that the audience laughed "because they know it's the end of the joke and they know he's funny."

"One of the most popular routines I did was getting robbed and mugged in my lobby," Woody continued. ("When I lived in my apartment in the brownstone building in New York, we were constantly getting robbed all the time. It was a very big feature of the neighborhood. Guys would break in and steal. And my apartment was robbed about four times in two years. It really got to be a bad thing. I didn't know what to do. So finally I put on my door a little blue-and-white sticker that said 'We gave.' I figured that would end it brilliantly, but it didn't. . . . Then some friends said there is an ad in the back of *Esquire* magazine where you can send away for a fountain pen that shoots tear gas. It's a real fountain pen and it secretes a gaseous, billowy cloud. A really great pen. Seven and a half dollars. I send away. It comes in the mail two weeks later in a plain brown wrapper. I unscrew it. I put in the tear gas cartridges. I clip it in my breast pocket. I go out. A long time ago, this was. Some friends in my neighborhood had a surprise autopsy. And I'm invited. I'm coming home by myself. It's two o'clock in the morning and it's pitch black and I'm all alone. And standing in my lobby is a Neanderthal man. With the eyebrow ridges and the hairy knuckles. He had just learned to walk erect that morning, I think. He came right to my house in search of the secret of fire. A tree swinger in the lobby at two o'clock in the morning. A mouth breather looking at me. I took my watch out and I dangled it in front of him—they're mollified by shiny objects. He ate it. Under pressure, I backed off and I pulled out my tear gas pen and I pressed the trigger and some ink trickled on my shirt. So I made a mental note to call *Esquire* and tell them. I'm standing in the lobby, two o'clock in the morning, with a product of a broken home, I had a fountain pen in my hand. I tried writing on him with it. He came to me and he started to tap-dance on my windpipe. Quickly I lapsed into the old Navajo Indian trick of screaming and begging.")

"There are routines and there's talk," Woody said. "I prefer talk. The kidnapping thing is a routine. Of all the routines the moose thing is probably most popular. It was a happy accident. It's not long, only about two and a half minutes, so it's hard to get bored in it. It has a beginning, a middle, and an end. It goes uphill; I was able to wring twist after twist after twist out of it till the end, so it keeps going and doesn't die. And it doesn't depend on jokes. It gets the audience involved in this premise, this concept, and they go with it."

It took time, however, to condense the material and decide what to keep in the act, because sometimes what turns out to be the funniest doesn't begin that way. One of Woody's most successful routines was about the damaged-pet shop and the ant: "I couldn't get a dog because it was too much. And they finally opened up in my neighborhood in Flatbush a damaged-pet shop. You could get a bent pussycat if you wanted; a straight camel. I got a dog that stuttered. The cats would give him a tough time and he would go b-b-b-b-b-b-bow wow."

"I was home in my apartment and I was walking around working out these jokes that I was going to use that night at the Village Gate," he explained. "One was that I always wanted a dog but my parents were too poor and so they bought me an ant, and I called it Spot. And I thought, God, that's so funny to me. And I did it that night and it got nothing. I did it the next night and it got nothing and I dropped it from my act. Then about ten months later I came across it in my notes and again I thought how funny it is. So I used it and this time it started to jell. It became one of the biggest laugh-getters I ever did. I have no idea why those things happen. I can only surmise that you have to give the material a fair shake at the time and you have to deliver it with confidence."

Contrary to the perceived wisdom among comics that new material should be tried out at such non-prime times as the late shows on Tuesday or Wednesday to contain any damage, Woody always tried his out on the fullest houses. "It's hard enough to go over with your *best* stuff on a rainy Tuesday," he said, "so I'd always try to break in new material in Vegas or someplace like that. The hardest thing is to do it with confidence, to do the new stuff like it's your old stuff. I get out there and bludgeon them to death with my old stuff. I just know how to say it. But if you're tentative with new stuff you screw yourself out of laughs left and right. It's like offering up a loser. You've got to offer it up as though it's a winner."

The night at the Blue Angel in Manhattan in 1954 when he heard Mort Sahl for the first time, Woody was overwhelmed by what he saw and heard. The gossamer way Sahl laid down his lines, his relaxed presence but energetic material, made him realize that a nightclub comic could be different and score anyway. Still, he had no immediate thoughts of becoming a stand-up comedian. He had enjoyed his performance of Mike Merrick's material at the social club in Brooklyn a year or two before but there was never a sense that he might write some for himself. Now he was just moving up from being a gag writer for newspaper columnists and all he wanted was to be a writer of material for others to perform. Later Sahl would inspire him to become a comic, but if anything, seeing and hearing Sahl that first time drove him further away from the notion because "I was just so discouraged by how great he was that, for maybe a year or two, I felt played out, that there was nowhere to go."

Sahl and Lenny Bruce were the Lewis and Clark of comedy in the 1950s. They pushed out the frontiers of possibilities of American humor in much the same way that John Osborne and other "angry young men" redefined the British theater around the same time. In the years following World War II there was a great jump in America's sophistication, in part because of the GI Bill that put millions of ex-soldiers through college. The standard comedy that had worked so well for so long, in which jokes were almost interchangeable among co-medians (if only because they were written by many of the same anon-ymous writers and sold to the nearest buyer), did not become any less funny; the audience simply became smarter. New ideas and fresh faces were welcome; individual and unique performers who wrote from their own hearts and with their own vision became more valued. Perhaps because of the reality the war forced upon people, realistic comedy, comedy of substance, was sought out rather than thought odd. In a broad sense, the outrageous and absurd finality that the atomic age augured helped bring out an appreciation for the outrageous and the absurd in comedy, one of the truest mirrors of a society. The revolution of the later 1960s had its seed in performers like Bruce and Sahl, who saw the hypocrisy and profanity of modern life, and were the first to stand up and say, among other things, that government was not nec-essarily the friend of the people it supposedly served.

When Sahl began performing shortly after his graduation in June 1950 from the University of Southern California (his B.S. in city man-agement is perhaps an inappropriate major for most comedians, but not necessarily for Sahl, whose stock-in-trade is the mismanagement of the world), comics got laughs from lines about women's underwear. They sang and danced with a bunch of chorus girls between jokes that were devoid of character, and they dressed in suits or tuxedos, as if they were businessmen or waiters.

One of the more popular comics of the time was Jack Carter, the star of *The Saturday Night Revue* on NBC, sponsored by the Campbell Soup Company. Here is how one show in 1950 opened:

Announcer's voice: "And here he is, that man of Campbell's Soup television, Jack Carter."

Elevator doors open; Carter comes out. "Thank you. Good evening, ladies and gentlemen. Welcome once again to our little show. I want you tonight to meet once again the lovely girls that watch our elevator doors. Are you girls happy working for me and Campbell's Soup?"

In unison: "Oh yes."

"There's a couple of smart chickens who use their noodles. Ho-ho.

"But I do want to welcome you here tonight. We've got another brand-new show this week. We're going to have a lot of fun. I know that you're going to love this show because we've got singers that are going to sing a lot, dancers that are going to dance a lot, and showgirls that are going to . . . I know you're going to enjoy the show tonight and I do want to get underway and tell you all to relax because things have been so hectic lately. I've been reading in the newspapers that they're investigating crime in the district attorney's office and they've put the police force on the [frying] pan, and it's murder. I've noticed now that all the mounted police are walking. Have you noticed that? Sure, they're afraid to be seen putting anything on a horse. So I . . . [Laughter from audience.] . . . I think that was a clever one, wasn't it? [Applause.]

"The sporting news is in the world today. I was so excited about the World Series. Of course I went to the game. I went with my sponsor, Mr. Campbell. He gave me a box. Of course I had to take the cans out first . . . I was sitting in asparagus all day. When I got to Yankee Stadium, wow, when I walked in the crowd cheered, they screamed, they yelled. You can ask [President Harry] Truman. He was right next to me."

Sahl was the antithesis of such humor. His act is about "the dilemma of metropolitan man drowning in the surroundings he himself fashioned," Jonathan Miller once said. But what was truly revolutionary about Sahl was not only the substantive nature of his material but the casual manner in which he delivered it. His is bare-bones comedy, the truth stated simply and gracefully without benefit of dancers, songs, or foils. He is strictly a verbal comedian who gets all his laughs from the subtlety and wit of his delivery and none of them from physical funniness. (That subtlety makes it difficult to do complete justice to his material on the printed page, where, however well it comes across, a reader who is not familiar with Sahl's voice and delivery is short-changed.)

Sahl appeared onstage in a sweater and open-necked shirt, a rolled newspaper under his arm, and in a staccato voice that could be like a machine gun, he spoke his piece about what he perceived as the incongruities of the world. His subjects were politics, corporations, psychiatry, women, smoking, jazz, sports cars, philosophy—hundreds of daily items of popular and slightly esoteric culture that a college-educated audience immediately latched on to as they were filtered through a personality that was as hip as they hoped to be.

One of his earliest and most famous jokes was a long story about Senator Joseph McCarthy, whose rabid anti-Communism was still in swing and who was still a fearful enough figure so that nightclub comics did not commonly make fun of him. "Senator McCarthy does not question what you say so much as your right to say it," Sahl said, and went on to point out the difference between the Eisenhower jacket, which had a lot of "multi-directional zippers," and the McCarthy jacket. "The McCarthy jacket is just like the Eisenhower jacket, except that it has an extra zipper to go across the mouth." And on the subject of fervid anti-Communism he said, "For a while, every time the Russians threw an American in jail, the Un-American Activities Committee would retaliate by throwing an American in jail, too."

Another routine was about a group of college students trying to hold up the Fairmont Hotel in San Francisco; they plan to use the money to live in the hotel for the rest of their lives. The cashier they are demanding the money from is also a college student.

"Give us the money and act normal," they say.

"First you must define your terms," the cashier tells them. "What is normal?" And so on.

Sahl joked that when someone told him he had a Christlike image of himself, he answered, "If you're going to identify, *identify*." Woody loved that line. (In *Manhattan* when Michael Murphy tells him, "You think you're God," he says, "I gotta model myself after *someone!*") Other favorites were Sahl's description of a sixteen-year-old girl in Greenwich Village, dressed in a short skirt and long earrings, who says that "Western religion has failed me"; Richard Nixon's answer to the questioner who asks if he was born in a log cabin: "That was Abraham Lincoln. I was born in a manger"; and the account of the newscaster in San Francisco covering the end of the world. He describes the terrible events, then switches back to the anchorman, who says he is in New York, "where the world ended three hours ago."

"He was the best thing I ever saw. He was like Charlie Parker in jazz," Woody said many years ago. "There was a need for a revolution, everybody was ready for the revolution, but some guy had to come along who could perform the revolution and be great. Mort was the one. He was like the tip of the iceberg. Underneath were all the other people who came along: Lenny Bruce, Nichols and May, all the Second City players. I'm not saying that these people wouldn't have happened anyway, but Mort was the vanguard of the group that had an enormous renaissance of nightclub comedy that ended not long after Bill Cosby and I came along. He totally restructured comedy. His jokes are laid down with such guile. He changed the rhythm of the jokes. He had different content, surely, but the revolution was in the way he laid the jokes down."

Sahl, of course, did not set out to start a revolution, which began in 1953 with his first steady engagement, at the "hungry i" in San Francisco, a basement nightclub that held eighty-three people. "It wasn't exactly nobility that got me going," he said in 1973. "I was twenty-six. I was working on a novel and introducing things for a theater group. I was out of the service, I was out of work, and I was out of gas. I was really angry that anybody told me [that my kind of humor] couldn't be done. It became an end in itself. There's no problem that there will be a guy that comes along. The problem is in building a constituency."

Sahl had been living and performing on the fringe of the University of California campus in Berkeley, often sleeping on the window seat of the apartment shared by three women he knew. "My girlfriend was in Berkeley, I was starving there," he explained, "and she said, 'Why don't you try out at the "hungry i"?' Then she said something very wise: 'If they understand you, you're home free; and if they don't, they'll pretend that it's whimsical humor.' Which is really a veiled attack on phony intellectuals that was quite prophetic. So what I did was ask for an audition and they gave me one, of one night. And I packed the house with students. I loaded it. And I had them laugh. And like any tutored group, it lacked spontaneity. I got up and said hello and they laughed."

Enrico Banducci, who ran the "hungry i," was not taken in by Sahl's audience packing. He hired him, really, on the strength of the two McCarthy jokes. Then came the evolution of Sahl's act.

"Banducci hired me for seventy-five dollars to fill in for a singer named Dorothy Baker for a week. I thought I was really home free. Then I got up onstage on Monday night without my audience. Dead. People started throwing pennies onstage, peanuts. I was shaken. That's how the newspaper was born in my act. I wrote my key lines on paper and stapled them in the newspaper, because the silence would make me forget my lines. Then I'd say, 'I see in the paper . . .' but under the harsh lights I couldn't read my own writing. And every once in a while I would digress because I had no discipline. And when I digressed, I got my first laugh."

Jazz musicians such as Stan Kenton and Dave Brubeck, with whom Sahl appeared, appreciated his act for the flights he took. But the free-form, jazzlike nature of Sahl's act contrasts with the deliberate scripting of Woody's. Where they are similar is in how they adjusted their embryonic acts until the audiences accepted them as real people. A comedian doesn't define his character, audiences do by what they accept.

"I took off my coat at Banducci's urging. I took off my tie," Sahl recalled. "And then it occurred to me, you mustn't look like any member of the society you're criticizing. What could I be? I was twenty-six. I went out and got myself a pair of blue denims and a blue sweater and a white button-down shirt open at the neck: graduate student. Which I was. And I went out there and I did it and it worked. It let the audience relax."

With his farraginous material Sahl is like a precocious student who hasn't focused on his major, an incipient failure as a Ph.D. who is no threat to anyone. He doesn't talk about the mechanics of gene splicing, he makes no great dissections of literature; rather, he speaks with intelligence on daily events and lets the apparent truths he uncovers make them funny. Here, for instance, is how he imagined the comments of the three leading contenders for the 1960 Democratic presidential nomination on their arrival in Los Angeles for the convention:

John F. Kennedy: "I am here to accept the nomination."

Lyndon B. Johnson: "I am a candidate, but I can't be here because I have to run the country."

Adlai E. Stevenson: "I am not a candidate and I'm not here."

Twenty-eight years later, he described another presidential candidate with his usual innuendo and deprecation: "Jesse Jackson . . . The *Reverend* Jesse Jackson . . . A man of the cloth . . . *Cashmere.*"

There is little difference between Sahl onstage and off; in each instance he exudes free-flowing energy, sensitivity, and outrage, even down to the near bark of a laugh that punctuates his speech. But because his act depends on his audience being familiar with such diverse and occasionally vaguely esoteric subjects, many people in and out of show business perceive him as an intellectual. (Bob Hope once introduced him at the Academy Awards: "Here he is, the favorite of nuclear physicists everywhere.") They are wrong. Sahl is an obviously intelligent man and certainly, as Robert Rice wrote in *The New Yorker* in 1960, "the first entertainer in years who contrived to smuggle his brains past a velvet rope." But he is not an intellectual. He skillfully slips his audience into the know by first laying out the factual premise—the great straight line Danny Simon taught Woody about—and then laying in the joke, because the audience can't laugh at the joke without knowing the facts. Everyone else did jokes based on common knowledge. Sahl was really the first comedian to do verbally what S. J. Perelman did in the leads of his stories: He explained the runway he was on before he took off.

"I submit to you I've been called an intellectual more times than you can count," Sahl said. "I was a sort of C student in college. To me an intellectual is someone like Bertrand Russell or Robert Oppenheimer or Albert Einstein. I'm not an intellectual. It shines great light on show business that I would be called an intellectual. After all, I *quote* intellectuals. Fifty years ago I would have been a reporter with some promise on a newspaper, maybe."

Woody, too, has been called an intellectual comedian and it is as wrong a label for him as it is for Sahl. "People have always thought of me as an intellectual comedian, and I'm not," he said during his engagement in Las Vegas (proof enough right there). "I'm a one-liner comic like Bob Hope and Henny Youngman. I do the wife jokes. I make faces. I'm a comedian in the classic style." But with a different veneer. (One of Woody's first *New Yorker* pieces was "My Philosophy," a send-up of Kierkegaard, Spinoza, Hume, et al. It begins: "The development of my philosophy came about as follows: My wife, inviting me to sample her very first soufflé, accidentally dropped a spoonful of it on my foot, fracturing several small bones . . .")

What makes Woody different and original is his personality and outlook. Like Sahl, he made intellectual references and esoteric comments in his act ("I took all the abstract philosophy courses in college, like Truth and Beauty, and Advanced Truth and Beauty, and Intermediate Truth, Introduction to God, Death 101. I was thrown out of NYU my freshman year. I cheated on my metaphysics final. I looked within the soul of the boy sitting next to me"), but they are not that far removed from his ability as a grade-schooler to use sophisticated material without necessarily understanding it. His act encompassed all the standard fare: ex-wives, pets, family members. He just presented them in a very idiosyncratic, original, surreal way.

"People reacted to Sahl just as they did to every great turn of art," Woody said. "He had all the symptoms of every modern development of art. He was suddenly this great genius that appeared. He himself was a great funny man. They didn't know that the art was inborn in him, in his intonation. People would say, 'I don't like him, he doesn't do anything, he's not funny. I do that all the time; I sit at home and talk and nobody pays me. *He's* not doing any comedy.' It was just the kind of thing where you could see art critics saying years ago, 'Who are these terrible *impressionist* painters?' "

However disheartening Woody initially found Sahl's brilliance in terms of his own performing, as he continued to watch him over the next year or two on Broadway and on television, Woody began to feel that Sahl's manner of expression required the sort of personal equipment that he, too, had. The onetime wiseacre who sat in the movies and made witty commentary to his friends looked at Sahl and eventually thought, "Hey, maybe I could be a comedian."

In many ways, he had already been one for years. He was demonstrably funny among people who knew him and his early success at joke writing was proof of his talent. His identifying with the comedian as a youngster had developed his humor as a defense against an uncomfortable and often painful childhood. Still, for all his success at deflecting discomfort with a quick ad-lib, he never thought of being a comic like Hope or Kaye or any of the others until Sahl showed him how to combine intelligence and character in a way he could be comfortable.

His biggest obstacle was his shyness around people he did not know. He seldom said anything in any school class other than English, and the only reason he spoke there was that the teacher had him read his compositions aloud. But then once he did speak and got laughs, his shyness receded and he spoke more and more often, to more and more laughter. He did this to such a degree that there were really two Allan Konigsbergs at Midwood High. There was the shy boy who in most instances said nothing and whom hardly anyone recognized. And there was the Allan Konigsberg with Woody Allen bursting out of him who showed his brilliance to pockets of people. So even though, judging by the evidence, he was the funniest student at Midwood, he was not voted class comedian; someone named Mike Brill, who was well known, won that distinction. But Woody says he finished second, to his amazement, because those few who were aware of his talent knew how good it was. "I don't know how I was considered at all," he adds. "I was so out of it in high school."

Yet for all his intentions to be strictly a writer and for all his shyness around strangers, there was a Walter Mitty-ish character in him who desperately wanted to perform. As early as the fourth or fifth grade, he and a friend would volunteer to entertain at the Friday-night Cub Scout meetings at P.S. 99. His friend did all right, but Allan was pathetic.

"The scoutmaster would say, 'Okay, you want to entertain us, what do you do?' And I didn't know," Woody remembers.

"I'd say, 'Well, I do imitations.'

" 'Okay, great. Who?'

" 'Well, name somebody. I don't know who to name.'

" 'Okay, do you do Jimmy Durante?'

" 'No.' Meanwhile, the whole audience is looking at me."

His ambivalence reached a peak when as a freshman at Midwood he saw the then yearly student variety show. The late Morty Gunty, a well-known Borscht Belt comic and a Midwood graduate, was the MC and entertained a little between acts: A girl did the Dorothy Parker monologue of waiting for the phone call for a date; a boy did card tricks; others sang; and so on. In *Broadway Danny Rose* Gunty is one of the comics whose table conversation is like a Greek chorus.

Woody was overwhelmed by the possibilities of it all. "I came away with stars in my eyes," he says. "I thought it was the greatest thing I had ever seen. I just wanted to be a comedian in the worst way. I wanted to be on the next variety show and I bought every joke book I could and started to make routines, culling jokes. It never occurred to me to write them at that young age. I did everything I possibly could. I wrote a song parody for myself. It was such heady stuff, it was so glamorous. I was knocked out by it. As it turned out, there was never another variety show in all my years at Midwood. If there had been, I would have been just frozen with fear and I doubt I could have done anything. But all I thought about afterward was: When is the next variety show? Can I get on it? Mercifully, there wasn't another."

It was in situations where he didn't really have time to think about what he would do that he came out of his shell. The Milton Berle encounter at the Circle Magic Shop was one such instance. Had he known Berle was going to be in the store, he would not have been relaxed enough to jump into bantering with him as he did. Another was the time he fought a much larger boy in the Midwood cafeteria. The boy took the chair one of his friends was using and Woody told him to return it: "The boy socked me and I just socked him back and the fight was on. Had the guy come up to me and said, 'Hey, kid, come here,' I might have thought about it a little bit and not done it. But it was on me so quickly that I had no time. I was thrust into it immediately."

"I was thrust into it immediately" are the operative words. Performers are not thrust in immediately. They know all day that they are going on that night, and all the next day, and all the next. Even Woody's performance of Mike Merrick's material came about in a semi-instantaneous way when he was volunteered without his knowledge to regale his peers with some jokes at the Young Israel social club. His performance was in essence the same as the teacher calling on him to read his composition. He was propelled by an external force that could overcome his own inertia. It was not until his mid-twenties that he learned to overcome it himself.

He was fortunate that the nightclubs of the time were undergoing a revolution, just as was the comedy they presented, because their relaxed and informal atmosphere provided the perfect environment for him to grow. In the late 1950s, Greenwich Village (about two miles south of Times Square and midtown Manhattan) was a collection of affordable, low-rise apartment buildings and brownstone houses with the New York University campus in the middle. There was a European cast to the area. Small coffeehouses such as the Figaro and the Reggio abounded in blocks comprised primarily of working-class Italians. On West Third Street there were several traditional, formal nightclubs with a band and chorus line and singers—the style of entertainment since Prohibition. There were also strip joints, and drag clubs with transvestites and female impersonators. That area, called the West Third Street Strip, catered more to tourists than to locals, and one had more than somewhat of a chance of being fleeced. The uptown tony establishments such as the Stork Club and the Copacabana were places where people went to be seen and become items for the gossip and social pages; these, on the other hand, were places not to be seen.

Bleecker and Thompson and Macdougal were sleepy streets in the heart of the Village where folk musicians such as Pete Seeger and Odetta and the Weavers, and Beat writers such as Jack Kerouac and Allen Ginsberg, hung out in the coffeehouses. As they attracted others, new places where people could just sit and talk opened, such as the Rienzi and the Manzini. On Macdougal Street, there was the Café Caricature, where artists drew caricatures and sipped coffee. This was a period of intense social ferment as America pulled out of the McCarthy era. Music was changing dramatically: The experiments in free-form jazz by John Coltrane and Eric Dolphy and Charlie Mingus, among others, were revamping that style; folk music went from the prairie style of Woody Guthrie to, eventually, the urban contemporary style of Bob Dylan; comedy began its renaissance with Mort Sahl and Lenny Bruce; and people even dressed differently, replacing coats and ties with jeans and work shirts.

Of course, this was happening not only in New York but also in other large cities such as Chicago and San Francisco. In fact, the Village Gate was in part modeled after the Gate of Horn in Chicago, whose slogan was: "A nightclub for people who hate nightclubs." When Art D'Lugoff started the Village Gate in 1958, the building he took over at the corner of Bleecker and Thompson streets was the largest flophouse in the city; it had cubicles for 1,400 derelicts to sleep off their ravages. Within a few years, the quiet, generally Italian-American neighborhood and quasi-bohemian enclave metamorphosed into an entertainment area. Max Gordon ran the Village Vanguard, and Fred Weintraub opened the Bitter End on Bleecker Street in 1960. Between those clubs, many coffeehouses sprang up. The Village's development is an example of how art and business often go hand in hand.

"Because of its reputation, people gravitated down to the Village culturally, musically, and artistically," D'Lugoff says. He is a pleasant, bearded man who sums up the period this way: "We enjoyed it, made a living, and got laid. People would be coming from Brooklyn and Queens. They wanted to exchange their lives or enrich their lives, they didn't want to be just sitting in Brooklyn or Queens. Of course, tourists came along, but it was a place where people went to school, went to NYU, and met with curious onlookers. There was still room to maneuver because you could get apartments relatively cheaply and businesses could be opened up. Where I settled was a rather reasonable place because no one else wanted to go there and I got a decent price for a big space. There was a tradition of coffee shops from the old country that continued. Midtown had nothing like it. The area was ripe for something to happen culturally and the business could support itself. Folk music was self-contained; there was not a big expensive group to pay. Where else in Manhattan could you get space to put on a show and have a place for people to sit and drink coffee all afternoon for fifty cents, which was considered highway robbery. I remember Mike Wallace interviewed me in the early sixties and his big beef was: 'How can you charge fifty cents or seventy-five cents for a cup of coffee?' I said, 'We're renting them our space for a long time. It's not like Forty-second Street, where they come and go.'"

On the next-to-last of the dozen days Woody reshot Cliff's (Woody's) first scene with his niece Jenny outside the Bleecker Street Cinema for *Crimes and Misdemeanors*, he looked across the way to where the Bitter End still stands. When he performed there, the club could hold about 140 people, who sat in old church pews and for their one-dollar cover charge—it eventually went up to two-fifty—drank coffee or seltzer which cooled in ice in flowerpots on the tables. There was no liquor and therefore no rowdy behavior. The bare-brick-wall backdrop for the acts that is so common in clubs today was first used at the Bitter End. There were shows at 9:30 and 11:30 p.m. weekdays, and a third show on weekends, featuring performers such as Judy Collins, Theodore Bikel, and Peter, Paul, and Mary. It was show business at its most relaxed. "There was no real talk about money. It was not a money club," says Weintraub, who went on to produce films (*Woodstock* is one) and was for a time a member of the Warner Brothers board of directors and the studio's vice president of creative services. "There was a kind of camaraderie. Nobody was really making it but everyone was pulling for everyone else." Between shows, Weintraub and various managers sat outside on whatever cars were parked at the curb and talked about new acts.

During the time Woody performed there, he became very friendly with Weintraub. The two of them and Hilda "Cash Register" Pollack, the club's cashier, who, according to Weintraub, was so bright that she seems to have passed the New York bar exam not long after she learned how to write, lived in the East Seventies. They were all in psychoanalysis, and before their appointments they often would meet at Stark's restaurant, then on Madison Avenue at Seventy-eighth Street. One day they decided to switch dreams and see what their analysts had to say.

"Fred, they're going to institutionalize you in a week," Woody said when they met after their sessions.

"Hilda, you're a genius," Weintraub told her.

"Woody," she said, "you're gay."

It was raining hard on this day's attempt to get the scene the way Woody wanted it. As he stood in the theater, looking through the rain at the Bitter End, he said, "I came down by cab for my shows, got off at the corner of Bleecker and La Guardia Place, and walked in. I'd be surprised to see a long line waiting to get in—not all that often," he added. "Freddy gave me my money wrapped in a rubber band. José Greco or other flamenco dancers were sometimes on my bill. The Simon Sisters, too. I went to the Dugout a couple of doors down to eat and get a drink. Always soda. I never drank in those days." (For a period of a few years in the late seventies and early eighties, Woody became entranced with fine French red wines, the only time in his life he drank. He stopped after getting an ulcer.) "I used to walk around the block again and again between shows with Bill Cosby. One of us would be at the Bitter End, the other at the Village Gate. We'd say, 'I have to be back on in twenty minutes.' 'I have to be back on in an hour.' He was nice. Now twenty-five years later he's giving a hundred million dollars to colleges and I'm . . ." Woody let out a little laugh and waited for the rain to lessen a bit so he could try the shot yet again.

The sweetest Woody Allen movie—although they all have an edge to them—is *Broadway Danny Rose*. Part Damon Runyon, part show business, it is all about loyalty. Danny Rose, a failed Catskills comic who "did all the old jokes . . . he stole from everybody," believes in his clients, who include a one-legged tap dancer, a stuttering ventriloquist, a blind xylophone player, and a virtuoso of making music from variously filled water glasses (all, incidentally, real acts). He believes without reservation in their talents and he believes with undying faith that, given the proper break, they will be stars. He lends them money, he lets them sleep on his sofa, and they return his loyalty—at least until they get a little success and a more powerful manager shows interest in them. Then they brush off Danny like dandruff.

Jack Rollins isn't Danny Rose. For one thing, he has never gathered all his clients together on Thanksgiving Day and prepared them frozen turkey TV dinners. But in all the important details, he could be Danny. His office in the early 1950s was a tiny room at the top of the Plaza Hotel, one of a row of cubicles that once were maids' bedrooms. When he met his future partner, Charles H. Joffe, in 1952, Rollins had one client, a former short-order cook by the name of Harry Belafonte, for whom he had fashioned an act. It was not that Rollins could convince only Belafonte to sign with him (actually it was Belafonte who persuaded Rollins to abandon his unsuccessful attempts to be a theatrical producer and become his manager). Rather, he turned down other performers because he felt he had to concentrate all his efforts on Belafonte's development and promotion, and he was devoted to him. When warned early in his career about becoming emotionally involved with his clients, Rollins said it was the only way he could do his job: "I have to work with people who fulfill me emotionally." He also believed he would be eventually fulfilled professionally. Belafonte, Rollins was convinced, was going to be, to use his term, "an industry." Still, Rollins had much to overcome. No matter how talented his client was, hotels, like most other public places, were segregated and that made it difficult for him to work in many instances and impossible in many more. Even in the few hotels where blacks could perform, they couldn't stay.

Rollins (born Jack Rabinowitz in 1914 and raised in Brooklyn) is a tall, slender man with a wide smile who seems to have perpetual bags under his eyes and a cigar perpetually in his hand. He has the appearance of someone who spends a lot of time playing poker and the horses, and his is a case of appearances being what they seem. He also has an eye and ear for talent. Besides Woody, Belafonte, and Nichols and May, other performers he has found and helped develop include Robin Williams, David Letterman, and Billy Crystal.

Crystal is an example of Rollins's faith. He knew Crystal was immensely talented; it just took a few years for people to realize how right he was. In the interim, Rollins's faith never wavered and he ensured that Crystal's never did either. With Belafonte, Rollins spent every day trying to book his unheard-of star-to-be. One of his many stops was the offices of MCA, the then powerful talent agency that was disbanded after a U.S. government antitrust action in 1962. (Music Corporation of America, which also owned Universal Studios, had to choose whether to be producers or agents.) Charlie Joffe, who was born in 1930 and also grew up in Brooklyn, was a junior agent not long out of Syracuse University, where he got his start in the business end of show business by booking student performers into local clubs after a brief, unsuccessful fling in the show end as the singer in a Dean Martin and Jerry Lewis type of act. Joffe watched with both interest and amusement as Rollins came up to the office every day and walked up and down the halls extolling the talent of a black folksinger who in those days couldn't work in Florida and couldn't work in Las Vegas, among most other places. Yet Rollins would repeatedly proclaim "This man is an industry!" to people who had never heard of folk music and whose idea of a colored performer was Eddie Cantor in blackface.

"I had never seen anybody in my life with such dedication to one cause," Joffe says. "It totally floored me, particularly because every agent would laugh at him behind his back. They made fun of him. They thought he was a jerk. How could he believe this guy was an industry when he couldn't even get him a job? Well, the facts followed." Belafonte started a calypso music boom. Then he left Rollins for another, better-known manager.

Joffe was fired from MCA not long after he began work there and Rollins called on friends to give him a job. But it entailed booking bands, something despite his college experience he knew nothing about, and before long he was again out of work as well as out of money, usually eating dinner with Jack and his wife, Jane. By 1953 Rollins's clients included singer Felicia Sanders, impressionist Will Jordan, and actor Tom Poston, and he hired Joffe, if only so he could buy his own dinners. Joffe has learned his business well. Robin Williams calls him "the Beast" in affectionate tribute to his ability to stand up to studio and network moneymen and make almost unbelievably lucrative deals for his clients. It was Joffe's negotiating abilities that got Woody his total-control and percentage-of-the-gross deals. He is only slightly bigger than Woody, and for all his ferocity in contract talks, he is otherwise a friendly, easygoing, bespectacled man, given, like Rollins, to the pleasure of cigars.

Rollins and Joffe are unique in a business that often stresses getting the most money in the least time for a performer—and for his manager. They don't take more than 15 percent, they don't charge their clients expenses, they don't bill for commission—and for all their eventual success (they and the two partners they had in the 1980s grossed several million dollars a year, not counting the 15 percent of Woody's income going to only Rollins and Joffe), they didn't make much money for a long time.

"Our guiding line was never, ever the amount of money that could be made," Rollins has said. "It was the challenge of developing someone who we felt was worthwhile to develop. Now, we also got to know after a while that this eventually will reflect in money. If you develop someone properly, people will come to you offering more money than you ever

Above: Woody Allen's parents, Martin and Nettie Konigsberg, circa 1930. *Left:* Woody Allen, nee Allan Konigsberg, 1937.

Above: Isaac Konigsberg,
Allan's paternal grandfather.
Right: Allan, age eight,
and his sister, Letty, 1944.

Above: Playing a Boehm system clarinet—a rarity for him—circa 1952. *Left:* Circa 1956. "Boy genius without the genius" is how Woody describes the photograph. "Note the silver ring with black onyx, the wristwatch—and the arrogance."

Below: Doing his stand-up act at the Bitter End, circa 1964.

Top: With managers Charles Joffe
(left) and Jack Rollins, 1974. *Above:*
Hosting *The Tonight Show,* 1967, with
Ursula Andress and Jerry Lewis.

Audiences tend to
think that Woody
Allen's character
has a single look,
but he is different
in nearly every film.
Above: With Romy
Schneider in *What's
New, Pussycat?*
Right: In costume
while directing a
scene from *Zelig*.

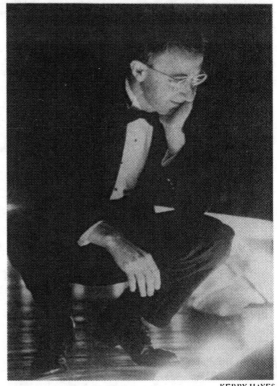

Left: As Howard Prince in *The Front. Below:* As Ike Davis in *Manhattan.*

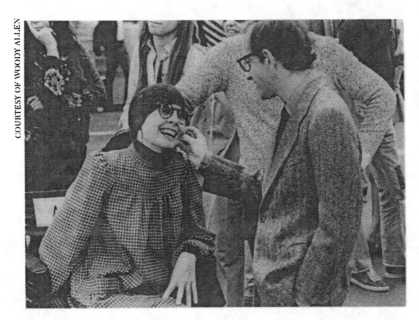

Diane Keaton on a visit to the set
while Woody was acting in *The Front*.

dreamed to please use your act. But that came later. The big thing was the challenge to develop what we saw that other people didn't, because that was the *fun*."

"It took Jack three years to knock out what he used to call my MCA agent wise-guyness," says Joffe. "When a performer came to us, we'd ask what his aspirations were. If he said, 'I want to be rich and famous,' he wasn't for us. They had to be about their work."

Neither Rollins nor Joffe thinks that a manager can be any better than his client. "I believe a manager is as much a hero as his client is good," Rollins says. "It's the clients who make the manager. We don't suffer the delusion that we can make silk purses out of sows' ears. And there are certain silk purses that we don't want. The people we have are people who we feel can do their part of the work as we see it, who are self-starters. We can help, we can guide, we can kick ass once in a while, but the client is the guy, he has to have the creative ability. He may need a little help in extracting from himself the best that he can do, but he has to have the seeds to be able to do it." For that reason, they have never taken on a comedian who bought material from joke writers.

In *Broadway Danny Rose*, a group of comedians sit around a table at the Carnegie Delicatessen. They tell stories and make jokes and gossip, and they constitute a clever device for Woody's telling of what amounts to a cinematic shaggy-dog story. He did not have to make up the device, however. During the 1950s, tables like that were the staple of the Carnegie and the Stage Deli and, especially, Lindy's, which had three tables where comics and their agents and managers gathered. One was the comics' table, where Milton Berle sat at the head. Another table was for underling agents. The third was for managers. Rollins and Joffe went every night at a time when they were barely making enough to cover their meals. Still, Rollins would often grab the check for the table, not only out of generosity but also to put up a good front.

One night as the other managers at the table were going on at length about the television shows their clients were getting and other high-paying successes coming their way, Rollins turned to Joffe and said with an utterly straight face, "Did you hear from the factory today?"

"Sure, they called about three o'clock," Joffe told him.

"What's the news?"

"Nothing great, but the order they got yesterday was sensational." Suddenly the other managers stopped talking.

"What factory?" one asked.

Rollins smiled. "You didn't think we were making our living with what we're handling in show business, did you?"

"Well, of course," the others answered.

"We have a factory in Canada," Rollins told them.

The others were amazed. "A factory? What kind of factory?"

Rollins took off one of his shoes and put it on the table. "Heels. That's our business, heels. We have a machine that puts heels on without nails. That's where we're making our money." It was the mid-1980s before Joffe told the last manager that the story was a hoax.

By the late 1950s, Rollins and Joffe were doing much better. With a partner named Larry Tucker, they booked acts into a basement room turned nightclub at the Duane Hotel on Madison Avenue at Thirty-seventh Street. It was called the Den at the Duane and they put unknown acts in there for a month or six weeks to let them try to build a reputation. They were the first to bring Lenny Bruce to New York. The closing act on his bill was Nichols and May. On their second night, Joffe says, "the world broke open for them. They did one television show [*Omnibus*] and that night there were lines around the block. Milton Berle came three times and couldn't get in."

Len Maxwell was a friend of Joffe's, and after he worked with Woody at Tamiment in the summer of 1957, he talked often to Rollins and Joffe about the twenty-one-year-old he was convinced was "this generation's George S. Kaufman" and "the most brilliant joke writer" he had seen. He talked often as well to Woody about the managers of Nichols and May, whose act Woody admired and for whom he wanted to write.

Maxwell spent a lot of time with Woody and Harlene after their summer together at Tamiment. She was studying philosophy at Hunter College in Manhattan and Woody read along with her to keep up. ("She used to engage me in a philosophical argument which proved I didn't exist," went a line in one of his stand-up routines.) After a lifetime of averting his mind from schooling, he now was intellectually ravenous. He arranged for a tutor from Columbia University to help him with a sort of at-home version of a Great Books course. Beginning with the pre-Socratics, then moving through Plato, Aristotle, Dante, Thomas More, and up to James Joyce, Woody and Harlene read a book a week and discussed it with the teacher. That autodidactic process continues today; depending on a given period's interest, his bedside table is piled with books on semantics and linguistics, or poetry, even the Bible. He read philosophy for years and still returns to it. His eclecticism, he finds, has its pluses but is more of a drawback. His quest for a rounded education has left some surprising gaps in customary knowledge because his reading follows no syllabus. (The grammar in his writing is idiosyncratic; when he gave Saul Bellow lines to read in *Zelig*, Bellow politely asked, "It's all right if I change this, isn't it? Because it's grammatically incorrect to say this as it is.") Woody is well aware of his shortcomings: "In talking with me for a while, if you hit on six of the subjects I've taught myself about, you'd think I'm literate. But then suddenly you hit something—it can be a very simple thing—that every college kid knows and because I'm self-taught, it's a gap in my learning."

His penchant for philosophy might seem odd, but maybe anyone named Konigsberg is susceptible to it, because the city of Königsberg (now Kaliningrad, on the Baltic Sea in a remote area, in the former East Prussia, annexed to the Soviet Union in 1945) was the home of Immanuel Kant, the great thinker of the Enlightenment, who taught in the university there in the last half of the eighteenth century. Because of Kant's influence in all German-speaking universities, Königsberg was a shrine of philosophy.

Now, no known relative of Woody's studied under Kant, or for that matter even dined with him. And Kant and his followers and ideas certainly were not the topics of conversation in Allan Konigsberg's home life as a boy. Most likely no one in his neighborhood, beginning with his parents, ever heard of them. (His father left school in the fourth grade, his mother stopped after high school.) But his European and Russian lineage is an integral part of Woody Allen's psyche and creativity. It is the clearest sign of where he comes from as well as of where he is coming from. The quest for a philosophical model to explain a metaphysical order, the search for a proof of God, and the problems inherent in the existential dilemma of man not only are a part of Woody's heritage but are also his daily preoccupation.

So although Kant may be a little sober and uncharismatic for his intellectual taste, the zeitgeist of Königsberg is reflected in the more romantic minds he likes: Fyodor Dostoevski, with his Russian sense of guilt and quest for absolutes; Albert Camus, who felt that human life was absurd but also felt that one should work to make it better; Søren Kierkegaard, who based his system on faith, knowledge, thought, and reality; and Nikolai Berdyaev, the Russian Christian existentialist. For a man who sharpened his mind on comic books and grew into one of the funniest people on earth, these may be strange heroes and even stranger influences. But there they are, and they have engendered in Woody a certain awe for, and even envy of, intellectuals and higher learning that sometimes crops up in his films. For instance, Marion Post is a philosophy professor in *Another Woman*. Which is not to say that Woody is an intellectual slouch. Along with such artists as Martha Graham, Jerome Robbins, and Frank Capra, he is one of ten honorary members of the American Academy and Institute of Arts and Letters, "persons of great distinction in the creative arts whose work does not easily qualify them for membership in the departments of art, literature or music." Woody was elected in 1987 to replace Orson Welles.

He also has great fun torpedoing the intelligentsia (a line in *Stardust Memories*: "Intellectuals are like the Mafia. They only kill their own"), while at the same time making his point that people today unfortunately place "importance on media experience, not life experience." In *Annie Hall*, Alvy (Woody) says to his wife, Robin: "I'm so tired of spending evenings making fake insights with people who work for *Dysentery*."

"*Commentary*."

"Oh, really? I heard that *Commentary* and *Dissent* merged and formed *Dysentery*."

And in *Love and Death*, he has a quick romp through the novels of Dostoevski, who had a sentence of death commuted as he stood before a firing squad. In the movie, Boris (Woody), who is to be shot the next day, has a conversation with his father.

BORIS

I have no fear of the gallows.

FATHER

No?

BORIS

No. Why should I? They're gonna shoot me.

FATHER

Remember that nice boy next door, Raskolnikov?

BORIS

Yeah.

FATHER

He killed his landlady!

BORIS

No! What a nasty story.

FATHER

Bobick told me. He heard it from one of the Karamazov brothers.

BORIS

My God, he must have been possessed!

FATHER

Well, he was a raw youth.

BORIS

If you ask me, he was an idiot.

FATHER

And *he* acted insulted and injured.

BORIS

I hear he was a gambler.

FATHER

Funny, he could have been your double.

BORIS

Really, how novel.

All this made Woody and Maxwell's a rather offbeat friendship. Maxwell was an old-fashioned comic, a tummler, whereas Woody was evolving into something unique. As part of his continuing education, every afternoon at four o'clock Woody walked the four blocks from his apartment at 4 East Seventy-eighth Street to the Metropolitan Museum of Art and spent half an hour studying a different exhibit. His choice for viewing was sequential rather than random and so eventually, by doing his thirty minutes each day, he studied the whole museum.

For all the differences between them, Maxwell loved Woody and Harlene's company. He found Harlene "lovely. Very sweet, very nice. Woody wrote a sketch once that Milt Kamen did," Maxwell said one day, his voice suddenly becoming that of an elderly Eastern European Jew: "Rorschach was one of the most brilliant men in the world, but he didn't quite know how to tie his shoelaces." His voice became a New Yorker's again. "And that's the way he once described Harlene to me. I went to have dinner with them before they moved from 310 West Seventy-fifth Street, a house that Arthur Conan Doyle once had. They had a one-room thing. We had a steak dinner and the peas were cold. Woody was eating away, perfectly happily. So I said, 'Harlene, these peas are not cooked.' And she looked at the can and said, 'Yes, they are.' "

Woody wrote for a wide variety of people from 1956 through 1958 during the nine months a year he was not at Tamiment. It was a good living but not a notable one. "I had little stints doing monologues on *The Tonight Show* with various hosts I can't remember, and writing material for various nightclub comics you've never heard of," is his summary. The work paid well, though, and Woody's reputation grew, but the biggest boost to his career came about through Maxwell's determination that he have proper management. Woody, however, refused to consider a change in managers until the end of his five-year contract with Meltzer. Fortunately it was about to expire. Meltzer's only real contribution over the span of the contract was to get Woody into the NBC program and some work on Pat Boone's TV show. The two were never a good match. Woody was shy and understated, Meltzer was flamboyant and pushy. As sincere as Meltzer may have been in wanting to help Woody, his vision was focused by his association with the clothing industry. His managerial services ran to such advice as "Writing jokes is like doing piecework in the garment district. What you write, you get paid for." After weeks of badgering Woody to go with him to meet Rollins and Joffe, Maxwell finally simply announced one day over lunch, "We're going." Woody's shyness always made it hard for him to meet people, so, as in a scene from a cartoon, Maxwell dragged him into the new Rollins and Joffe office at 200 West Fifty-seventh Street.

Woody quietly asked if he might write some routines for Nichols and May. After Rollins told him that they wrote all their own material, Woody asked if he might read aloud a sketch he had written. As always happened, the moment he began to enact his writing, his shyness evaporated. Rollins and Joffe were entirely captured by him. They not only liked Woody, they found his material completely original. Yet Woody delivered his lines in such an understated way that he was at first puzzled by the laughter he generated. Rollins and Joffe each says that he thought to himself, "If only he could stand up and do this stuff himself." But they said nothing because Woody had told them he was not interested in being a performer. Instead, he asked if they would manage him as a writer.

"Well, we don't manage writers, we manage performers," Rollins said. "We don't know much about writers or how to manage them or where to bring their stuff." Woody persisted and asked if they would consider starting with him as a writer. Rollins said that if he was willing to spend six months with them, all three would then decide if they could do Woody any good. They hoped that they could because, Rollins says, he and Joffe "found his material was so powerful, so funny. We knew there was real quality there." They shook hands on the deal and that handshake is the only binder they have. Rollins and Joffe have since negotiated millions of dollars' worth of contracts on Woody's behalf with others, but no written contract exists among themselves. Woody thanked them and asked if he could make some calls. After he had left, Rollins found three dimes placed discreetly by the phone.

As it turned out, Rollins and Joffe were as good at handling a writer as they were at managing a performer. They arranged a number of jobs for him, among them a TV special he wrote for Art Carney and *The Garry Moore Show*. But the more time they spent with Woody, the more certain they were that he ought to be performing his material, not writing it for others. One night after dinner at Jack and Jane Rollins's house, Woody read a routine with a premise that *The New York Times*, which, with a brief exception in the early 1900s, has never run comic strips, began to do so. Joffe was also there and all three roared at the material. Woody was just naturally funny. After coming to know him, Rollins and Joffe were now sure he could learn how to turn his assets into an act, and they asked him to consider becoming a performer. Simply performing, however, was not their goal. Rollins and Joffe envisioned Woody, as Rollins puts it, "as the first triple-threat man since Orson Welles": someone who could write, perform, and direct his own material. As Woody was already known within the business as a great comedy writer, the best path to that end, they felt, was for him to make a name as a stand-up. Once the public knew and appreciated him, he could go on from there.

Woody is nothing if he is not deliberate. Decisions may take a while to be made, but once his mind is made up to do something, he devotes all his effort to it. "Well, I've thought about it," he told Rollins and Joffe after a few days, "and if you fellows think I ought to try performing, I'll write an act and I'll try it." He spent a few months writing one, and, because of his association with Rollins, in October 1960 he was given a one-night audition at the Blue Angel, following comedian Shelley Berman's last show on a Sunday night. It was a great break for him. The Blue Angel was like the Palace in the days of vaudeville, *the* hall to play. But where the Palace was a huge theater, the Blue Angel was a low-ceilinged, smoke-filled room. Every big agent in town joined the audience seated at tiny round tables in front of the pocket-sized stage to watch each new act. Berman introduced Woody kindly, saying that he was a young television writer who wanted to perform his own material, and that he was funny. He was true to his word; the audience laughed from the beginning. Actually, they laughed too much for Woody. Their response was so good that he drew back into his shell. After the first wave of acceptance, he became quieter and quieter over the twenty-five or thirty minutes of his act. To Larry Gelbart, with whom he was then writing a TV special and who had come to see him, he sounded a little "like Elaine May in drag." Still, despite what Woody recognizes was a psychological problem, he was a success, and job offers came in on the strength of his performance. But Rollins, who knew that despite Woody's favorable inaugural performance he was not yet ready for wide exposure, turned them all down. What Woody needed was to perform regularly in a low-risk environment to develop into a seasoned comic, and Rollins had just the spot in mind.

The Upstairs at the Duplex in Greenwich Village was a second-story room slightly bigger than a cupcake. Tables and chairs for about fifty people were bunched together and ended at the performer's feet. An average weeknight audience was eight to ten people. It was the perfect place for Woody to learn the art of stand-up comedy and to refine material, because his exposure was minimal and he had a chance to work two shows a night, six days a week; it was a small-scale version of the Improvisation and other comedy clubs today. Even so, getting a small crowd in an otherwise empty room to laugh is hard for the best of comics. For someone just starting out, it was horrifying. Not that Woody always presented his material in the best way to get laughs. There were times when it seemed he had no idea of how to stand in front of an audience. Mort Sahl sat on a stool, so Woody thought he could just stand still. He looked like a post. His nervousness, which generally evaporated when he began to perform, sometimes resurfaced. When it did, if he didn't stand still, he wound the microphone cord around his head, or scratched, or put his hands all over his face as if he was trying to shield himself. His delivery would lack affect and his pacing became uneven. These audiences were not as easy as the one he had played to at the social club as a teenager, and he was not as relaxed in his delivery with strangers as he was when he read his material to classmates or to Rollins and Joffe.

While for the most part his material was very like that which he did in Las Vegas in 1972—some of it was essentially unchanged—his delivery sabotaged it when he spoke too fast, or he spoke too softly, or he spoke to the back of the hall, but he didn't speak to the audience. Moreover, he stubbornly included jokes with esoteric punch lines that he loved but that most audiences would not get. One was about a girl he dated who had a tattoo that read, "Bird Lives." Jazz aficionados got the reference to the late saxophonist Charlie Parker, but audiences for a comic aren't always made up of jazz aficionados. "You do lines that only dogs can hear," Joffe told him time and again. "You can't do that. You have to make them palatable for an audience to understand your references." Woody finally added the phrase "tattooed on the inner surface of her thigh," and the idea of the tattoo's location got the laugh. Still, Woody never hesitates to use parochial references in his films that only a small minority of the audience will get, so long as he thinks they are good lines. In *Sleeper*, Miles Monroe (Woody) is the proprietor of the Happy Carrot health-food store. He goes into the hospital for a gallbladder operation, is cryogenically frozen, and then is defrosted two hundred years later. A doctor explains to Miles what happened to civilization as he knew it: "According to history, over a hundred years ago a man by the name of Albert Shanker got hold of a nuclear warhead." Shanker was the strident head of the United Federation of Teachers in New York but was unknown to the rest of the country. New York audiences roared at the line; all others were mystified. (Woody has since regretted using the line because "although objectively it's a wonderful joke and it works beautifully, it's too harsh on him. There are many things about him I like.") And in *Crimes and Misdemeanors*, Halley (Mia Farrow) says of Cliff's brother-in-law Lester (Alan Alda):

"He's a natural phenomenon."

"So's acid rain."

"Boy, you really don't like him."

"I love him like a brother—David Greenglass," Cliff answers, using a phrase that was a favorite of New York liberals in the 1950s. Greenglass was the brother of Ethel Rosenberg, who with her husband, Julius, was executed in 1953 for passing U.S. atomic secrets to the Russians. Greenglass, who supplied them with the information, turned prosecution witness and got off with fifteen years in prison.

Either Rollins or Joffe went with Woody every time he performed. Often both would go, and sometimes Jack would swing by in his station wagon to pick up Woody for the drive downtown. The first couple of months he worked at the Upstairs at the Duplex, Woody earned no money; Rollins's attitude was this was how a young comic paid his dues. And while it may seem the perfect Danny Rose booking—working for free in front of ten people—in return Woody was given the chance to perform regularly, something every new stand-up needs and few get. Because of Nichols and May, Rollins was considered the best manager of comic talent, and when he came to club owners with Woody, they were ready to give someone Rollins believed in a chance. It was a chance worth every penny he wasn't paid.

Though it was a marvelous opportunity, it was an agonizing period for Woody. He had such anxiety prior to performing that it was a good thing Rollins or Joffe was with him; sometimes they literally had to push him onstage. Jan Wallman, who ran the club and introduced the performers (there were three acts: a musical group, a comic, and a singer), sometimes had to talk Woody into going out for his turn as they stood backstage—a cul-de-sac about the size of a table—waiting to go on. "There were many times Woody and I stood back there and he shook like a leaf," she remembers. She is several inches taller and some pounds heavier than Woody. "That little body would be quivering and I would be holding him. He came up to about here on me"—she pointed to her shoulders. "I'd pat him on the back and say, 'Come on, you're going to be great.' Then I would introduce him and wonder if he was going to come out. Once he was out there, though, he was fine. He really was a breakthrough comedian. No one used first-person conversational material like he did. He would paint a whole picture before you knew you were laughing." Later on, when he began to get bookings at uptown places like the Bon Soir and the Blue Angel, he once said to her, "What am I going to do next week when you're not there backstage?" She hugged him and said, "Just put it in your head that I am."

At age twenty-four Woody was starting to do what most successful comics had started doing in their teens. It would turn out that in performing, as in everything else he studied, he was a fast learner; within two years he became an established comic. But two years pass very slowly when night after night brings no discernible improvement. At least that's how Woody saw it. Rollins and Joffe saw progress and understood how much he had to learn, and they remained confident in his ultimate success. In between his two evening performances, Woody usually paced around outside whichever club he was working in, often unhappy (or "not gruntled," as he once said) about the previous performance. One evening after Woody had bombed in the first show, Rollins asked, "What's wrong?"

"They're fighting me," Woody said, but the essence of his complaint was: "They don't know what's funny."

"If they're fighting you, they're not going to like you and nothing you can do will please them," Rollins told him. "But once they like you, you're home free; they will laugh at your jokes. Can you come out twenty times and do it not for them but for yourself? You know what's funny." On another occasion he told Woody, "Just do what I say and don't worry. In two years you'll be a great comedian."

"Why?" Woody asked. "What makes me any different than any of those guys on *The Ed Sullivan Show*?"

"Just don't think about it," Rollins answered.

Woody's whole intent at that time was to be another Mort Sahl, but Rollins, who could see what would happen if Woody would let the audience like him, pointed out the difference between Woody and Sahl, and also between Woody and comedians like Jonathan Winters. They're popular, Rollins said, but they will not be big stars. They have what he called "a shrill brilliance": They come out and do their material and go off. Yet however much the audience laughs, no person is accessible behind them. Woody's material was all about the person behind it.

"I always thought the material alone mattered, but I was wrong," Woody says. "I thought of myself as a writer and when I was onstage all I could think about was wanting to get through the performance and go home. I wasn't liking the audience and I turned it around because I was petrified. Yet there was no reason the audience wouldn't like me; they had paid to see me. It came from very complex psychological feelings I couldn't begin to understand. But then I went onstage with a better attitude and I learned that until you want to be there and luxuriate in the performance and want to stay on longer, you won't do a good show. Jack was so important to me. He's one of the four most important people to my career. Danny Simon is another, for teaching me the fundamentals of how to construct sketches and, even more, for the psychological boost of having someone that accomplished believe in me. The third is Arthur Krim [the former head of United Artists and now of Orion Pictures, who has always given Woody free rein over his work]. And the other is [*New York Times* film critic] Vincent Canby, whose review of *Take the Money and Run* turned it around. [The film opened in only one theater, the 68th Street Playhouse. A second was added after the film broke the ticket sales record.] My three-picture deal with United Artists followed that. He's also been enormously supportive over the years and that has been very meaningful to me."

Nobody tape-recorded Woody's early performances, but Rollins and Joffe listened attentively and every night after he finished they would go to the Stage or the Carnegie Delicatessen and rehash the act, pointing out lines that needed work or stage mannerisms that needed attention. At about 3 a.m. the day's work was done and Woody went home to sleep before having to face it all again the next day.

Of all the people in the audience at the Blue Angel for Woody's first performance, the one whose opinion mattered the most was Herbert Jacobi, who owned the club and who was among the first to recognize the talents of Jonathan Winters, Harry Belafonte, Eartha Kitt, Lenny Bruce, and Nichols and May. Jacobi was a large man with a dark visage who sounded as if he were the voice of Dracula. People called him "the Prince of Darkness" but his was a case of mistaken identity. "He looked like he wanted to bury you but he came to praise you," Woody says. He praised Woody from his first appearance on and a year or so after the audition he booked Woody for a couple of weeks as part of a long-term agreement. Woody's performing abilities were still a little raw, however, and one night after his set a customer went up to Jacobi and said, "Herbert, this kid stinks. This kid is the worst. He's garbage. What are you going to do about it?"

"Oh," Jacobi told him evenly in his Transylvanian tone, "I've already signed him to a three-year deal, where he comes back four times a year at a raise in salary."

The man was dumbfounded. "What are you talking about? That kid is terrible. The audience hates him."

Jacobi smiled and said, "Ah, but you see, the audience is wrong."

. . .

Many times during the writing or shooting of a film, Woody will despair of ever getting a particular line or scene to play the way he envisioned it. Then once he has given up all hope of getting it right, he will usually find a way. The process, however, requires that he first be convinced of defeat before victory can win out. But however discouraged he is at those moments when he believes that he will have to settle for something only close to what he wants, it is fair to say he has never been more discouraged than he was during his first two years as a stand-up comic. He had given up $1,700 a week in salary to work first for nothing and then for $75 or $100 a week, doing two and sometimes three shows a night, six nights a week, to small and often uncomprehending audiences. He came home in the middle of night after night, spent from the effort of trying to make people laugh. Even when he did well, there was no surcease, because whenever the audience applauded, it embarrassed him; he would cover his ears as they clapped at the end of his set, a phenomenon perhaps explained by Oscar Wilde: "In this world there are only two tragedies. One is not getting what one wants, and the other is getting it."

"It's the same as when people ask for an autograph," Woody has said. "I don't really know the cause. It could be that I had a childhood desire for applause and recognition that was so strong that it embarrassed me, and therefore applause and recognition embarrass me."

It was a hard time for Harlene, too. Her belief in Woody was as total as Rollins's and Joffe's, but her aspirations for him seemed even higher than his own. She believed he had the talent to be a great writer, not just a great comedy writer. When she saw him turn his back on a steadily improving career that was earning him top dollar while in his early twenties, and in its place pursue a line of work in which every night he was emotionally beaten up by strangers, she was convinced becoming a stand-up comic was an unworthy ambition. Combined with that, their marriage was shaky. They were young people growing in different ways.

One night Rollins drove Harlene and Woody home after she had attended Woody's shows and they had gone with Jack and Jane to the Stage Delicatessen to review the evening's work. Harlene had said virtually nothing the whole night. Then, once back at their apartment, she suddenly burst into the middle of a conversation between Woody and Jack.

"What are you doing to my husband?" Rollins recalls her screaming at him. "You're cheapening his gifts. Here's a man who's a brilliant writer and you want to turn him into a cheap comic."

Woody had his doubts, too. On many nights, he just died onstage. As Rollins says, "He knew zero about the art of performing and bringing the material on a nice silver platter to the audience. He was successful with a segment of the audience that had the brainpower to know what was there. But he didn't help himself because he didn't know anything about pacing his material, or stopping for laughs." On other nights when his routines didn't go well, he would race through them and get offstage, not bothering about the laughs. (He did that even at the end of his career, although by then he was accomplished at working an audience. But if they weren't going to come for the ride, he finished as fast as he could.) "He was arrogant and hostile," Joffe says. "If the audience didn't get it, he had no patience. But the pain in those first years was terrible."

There were dozens of times he said he thought he should quit. "Do you fellas still think I should continue?" he would ask Rollins and Joffe. "We thought so," Rollins once said, "but neither of us had to get up there and take the brickbats, he was the one. He was the shyest person by nature I've ever seen. A normal person doing what he was trying to do started at fifteen or sixteen, and he had the inclination to perform. Woody had none of that. He lived in a sanitized atmosphere with his typewriter. And now we're asking him to do it. Because we think, we *think* that he has something funny to say."

"Because we think he's an industry," Joffe added with a laugh.

"We said to him," Rollins continued, " 'Woody, it's easy for us to tell you that there's something unique and funny about you as a persona. Easy, because we don't have to get up on that floor. Hard for you because you've started so late in life. You're a hothouse comedian. We sort of pushed you into it. So it's easy for us to say, "Stick with it." But it's your decision to make. All we can tell you is that if you're asking us "Should I quit now?" we're not ready to say that, because you haven't given it enough time yet.' "

Each time Woody thought it over, and each time he decided to continue. Then one night after months of this, he sat down with Rollins and Joffe at the Stage Deli and said, "Look, let's be serious. This is crazy. It's killing me. I'm throwing up, I'm sick, I shouldn't be doing this. I know I can make a big career as a writer. We've tried it with me as a stand-up and I'm not good. I can't handle this anymore."

Rollins had heard all the complaining he could take. "Woody," he said, "we can't force a man to live an unhappy life, so if you want to quit, it's over."

Woody was stunned. He left Rollins and Joffe at about 3 a.m., and at 5 a.m. he was on the phone to Joffe, who is close to him in age and who grew up a few blocks away from him in Brooklyn; in business, he is Woody's brother to Rollins's father.

"Did Jack really mean that?" Joffe recalls him asking. "Did he say that because he doesn't have faith in me, or because he thinks I'm a quitter?"

"Woody," Joffe told him, "it came from only one place. Both of us feel that it's just too hard for you and therefore not worth it to all of us to keep you in this pain. And Jack meant it. I want to cry, if you ask me."

"I can't believe it," Woody said. "We've had this discussion ten times and Jack's always said to go on. He really meant I should quit, didn't he? I was in total shock after he said it. He's really ready to let me stop."

"Yes," Joffe said.

The next morning, Woody came to the office and said, "Let's keep trying. If you fellows think it's too short and I need more time, and it's worth taking more time, I'll give it six months more."

Woody's friends talk about his courage, not only in the beginning of his career when he had to overcome his anticipatory stage fright, but throughout his career when he has stretched himself to make pictures he wants to make rather than simply make ones that fit into his perceived mold. Woody's response is: "I wanted to perform. I was encouraged by bookings and people around me and I felt it was wrong to give in to the fear. I mean, I gave in to the fear but it was wrong to not perform on account of it." But not giving in to fear and real courage are two separate things for him. In *Manhattan*, Ike Davis says, "Talent is luck. The most important thing in the world is courage." As Woody wrote and speaks Ike's sentiments, it is not surprising that he subscribes to them.

"Talent is absolutely luck," he said one day while talking about his early fear of performing. "And no question that the most important thing in the world is courage. People worship talent and it's so ridiculous. Talent is something you're born with, like Kareem [Abdul-Jabbar] is born tall. That's why so many talented people are shitheels. But courage is everything because life is harsh and cruel. I believe it completely. The two things that I wish are that I had courage, which I don't feel I have, and that I was born with religious faith. Those two things would be great. I'd probably need less courage if I was born with religious faith. But if I was born with those two things, I'd be very far along in the game.

"You can't mistake courage for show-business courage. That's like being a comedy genius. There's a difference between being a comedy genius and a genius. There's the kind of courage where people on talk shows extol genius and courage. Genius for them is, you know, a guy who's got six sitcoms going at the same time, and courage is always 'He went on with just two days' rehearsal.' The stakes are embarrassment in those cases.

"Artistic courage is no big deal because life and death and bodily injury are not at stake. Courage is where you work for the underground in the war. Going onstage is not really courage, that's sort of childish courage. The proper response to my fears is: 'What are you making such a fuss for, jerk? Go out onstage and do it or stop complaining and go home and get another job.'

"My fear that I wouldn't have courage under the right circumstances always humiliates me when I'm alone with myself," he continued. "I cannot think of an act that I've done that required courage of any significance. Anytime that I've thought I might have a serious illness I was always reduced to sniveling, petrified anxiety. And I hope I never have to show courage. I hope I'm never passing a situation where two guys with knives are threatening a little old lady and my choice is to intervene or not, because I would be paralyzed."

Whatever courage it took, Rollins and Joffe agree that Woody's decision to give performing an additional six months was the turning point in his career. "There was a very strange thing going on during this period," Joffe says. "He was really as bad a performer as you could know. The world had never seen such a scared person. But through it, the jokes were so brilliant that he was successful."

There is much learned writing about Jews and humor: that Jews have been strangers in whatever land they live; that because Jews are outsiders, their separateness is the wellspring for Jewish comedy and Jewish comedians; that humor is not only a way to retaliate against prejudice by having the laugh on yourself before others have it on you, it is also a way to bridge the chasm between Jews and Gentiles. And there are many good examples of comedians who prove this point. Myron Cohen and Henny Youngman are two. Woody Allen is not one.

Woody is an outsider all right—or at least, like almost every performer breaking in, he was when he began performing. Now, with the exception of Steven Spielberg, he is the most inside of filmmakers. The difference between them is that Spielberg is at the core of the Hollywood establishment, while Woody, who possesses much of his power, does so from the core of the singular counter-establishment he has created apart from Hollywood.

And he is a Jew, as people are quick to point out and as if it mattered more than it does. Freud wrote, "I am a Jew, and it always seemed to me not only shameful but downright senseless to deny it," meaning at least in part that he was a Jew because everybody reminded him he was a Jew. Woody does not deny it either, and everybody reminds him he is a Jew, but his Jewishness as an artist is more the result of external identification than it is the source of his humor. He uses Jewish references that are specific, not generic. They may have been the signposts in his neighborhood, but under different circumstances of birth they could just as easily have been those of a lower-middle-class Irish Catholic in Boston who saw prettier women and a more interesting life across the river and set out to get there.

Woody Allen is not Sam Levenson telling jokes about Jewish life, the underlying basis of which is the permanent outsiderhood of Jews—a type of humor that with its idiom and dialect celebrates an insular world. The tension and humor in Woody's work come from the anxiety produced in him by his wanting what he doesn't have and by the discomfort the world inflicts on him for being the things he is. Woody's persona as a stand-up and through his early films was that of a baseball-loving, lascivious guy who thought he was Bob Hope. And his travails and foibles are not ethnic, they're universal. They're the same as Charlie Chaplin's pretensions and Hope's thinking he is a ladies' man. The three are little men, common men, who see themselves as big and special, and within that is the conflict and the joke.

Woody's stand-up material may appear at first glance to have been classic Jewish humor—he was superficially the self-deprecating schlemiel with a wife who, while he was in the bathtub, "would walk right in whenever she felt like it and sink my boats." But layered on top of that was the brilliance of a comedian who was as comfortable with Plato or French literature as he was with schtick, and who slipped characters with such names as Guy de Maupassant Rabinowitz into his routines. Whether this made him an intellectual comedian is immaterial. What matters is that it demonstrated that he was not an intellectually timid comedian mired in his own past; he was clearly a writer and a performer who was willing to grow beyond expected bounds. Traditional Jewish humor may have been the base of Woody's act, but it was really just the most convenient foundation. What he built on that base transcends ethnicity. While *Take the Money and Run* and *Bananas*, the first two films he wrote and directed, have much evidence of a Jewish sensibility (such as Woody taking cake as a gift when invited to dinner at the palace of the dictator in *Bananas*), by his third film, 1972's *Everything You Always Wanted to Know About Sex*, segments such as the lush Italian movie parody are without a trace of what is considered Jewish comedy. And while *Love and Death* and *Annie Hall* draw on the hapless guy who can't get the girl, a staple of Jewish humor, that poor fellow belongs to other cultures, too, and is evident from Charlie Chaplin to Benny Hill. By the time Woody made *Stardust Memories* in 1980, there was no way to tell solely by the film the heritage of its maker (although Sandy Bates, Woody's character, did attend Hebrew school as a child). Since then his movies have had a universality that draws on a wide variety of humor from and about almost all races, creeds, and colors without prejudice toward national origin.

Woody Allen as a young comic was like the ad in the late 1960s for a bread sold in New York. Posters showed a Chinese man happily holding a sandwich, and the copy read, "You don't have to be Jewish to love Levy's real Jewish rye." You also did not have to be Jewish to love Woody Allen. More specifically, *he* did not have to be Jewish. That he was was incidental. What mattered was the conflict between where he came from and where he was going. When he described his parents and neighborhood as being from "the heart of the Old World, their values are God and carpeting," that perception mirrored anybody who was embarrassed by how unhip his parents were, and that was any person with cultural and intellectual ambitions and pretensions who wanted to move from his figurative Brooklyn to a figurative Manhattan. It just happened that in Woody's case his ethic was Jewish and his journey was an easily identifiable one. His problems were those of any second- or third-generation American, for whom ethnicity is as much a passkey for getting into the artistic or intellectual world as it is awkward baggage from the old country, the prototypical old country being Brooklyn. In his autobiography, *Making It*, Norman Podhoretz writes that "one of the longest journeys in the world is the journey from Brooklyn to Manhattan—or at least from certain neighborhoods of Brooklyn to certain parts of Manhattan." But in fact Brooklyn is anywhere one leaves his family behind—it is the black and white of Dorothy's Kansas; and Manhattan is wherever he flowers in new and more fertile soil—it is the Technicolor of Oz.

After Woody straightened out his delivery and let the audience into his act, and thus into himself so they could like him, an audience flocked to him. Manhattan was filled with young people making the same journey as he, and so were such other cities as Chicago and San Francisco and St. Louis and Washington, D.C., and Los Angeles, all of which Woody performed in once he was established in New York. But one didn't have to identify with specific migrations to enjoy Woody. All that was required to enjoy him was a working set of ears. He was, in a word, funny; and he was funny for the only reason that matters in comedy: He made people laugh. As he would say, that is more profound than you think.

One of his earliest and biggest fans was Jack Benny, which shows among other things that Woody's comedy cut across generational lines. "He's one of the most amazing men I've ever known," Benny said in 1973. "It's very tough to use the word 'genius,' because it gets thrown around so much. I've used it on Noël Coward. Maybe George M. Cohan. Ed Wynn at one time. Al Jolson, of course, who was the world's greatest entertainer. But I don't know anyone who is as clever and funny and has the knowledge of what to do in his writing and acting as Woody. No one compares with him. I used to say these things about Ed Wynn. My wife wouldn't sit next to me when I watched him because I made a fool of myself. Now I sit alone and scream at Woody Allen."

While Benny never claimed to be a theoretician of comedy, he could define in five sentences what he did and what Woody does as a comedian: "The only way I can explain what I do, and it would be in a way comparable to what Woody Allen does, is that I play on the faults and frailties of man. I think I'm a big lover, and I'm not. You play up to people, you don't play down to people. Don't ever go for the laugh. The laugh should be there."

. . .

Woody made three friends around the time he began performing who helped him through the tedious, discouraging process. One was Louise Lasser, a Brandeis University political science major who dropped out midway through her senior year to be a singer in New York, where she was raised. She was an outrageously funny and beautiful strawberry blonde who, when she was twenty-one, looked not unlike Liv Ullmann. (And also not unlike Mia Farrow. Louise used to receive notes from friends with pictures of Mia, pointing out the likeness; even Mia's children find early pictures of them similar.) She became, in more or less this order, one of Woody's best friends (they shared the struggle of new performers and occasionally appeared together in cabarets), Woody's wife (they were married on Groundhog Day, as they liked to point out, 1966), his ex-wife ("We didn't think the marriage would work even before we got married. But we had been together for about six years and there was the possibility that the act of getting married might have some psychological effect," Woody says. They were divorced in 1969), an actress (she played in *Bananas* and *Everything You Always Wanted to Know About Sex* and was the star of the TV series *Mary Hartman, Mary Hartman*), and one of his best friends ("She's really in a class by herself").

Woody and Harlene were married for nearly seven years but they decided after about four that the marriage was going nowhere. Woody moved out in the spring of 1961, about a year after she graduated from Hunter College. They were divorced in 1962 and have not seen each other in more than twenty-five years. "It was partially my fault we got divorced," went part of one of his routines. "I had a tendency to place my wife under a pedestal." In 1967, after no prior public objection to Woody's ex-wife jokes, Harlene sued him and NBC—he had done several of the jokes on *The Tonight Show*—for $1 million "for holding her up to scorn and ridicule." They settled out of court. "Today, we would have just lived together. We were both young," Woody says of their marriage. He places the blame for the lawsuit on a lawyer who he feels talked her into it as a way to make money for himself. In the letter to Woody outlining the case against him, the lawyer wrote that Woody heaped abuse on Harlene by referring to her as Quasimodo, "a well-known hunchback in literature," and that his saying, "My wife cooked her first dinner for me. I choked on a bone in the chocolate pudding," was patently false since Harlene didn't make chocolate pudding. A judge issued a temporary cease-and-desist order against Woody and Johnny Carson, host of *The Tonight Show*, but eventually Woody resumed telling some of the jokes. *Time* said of the suit that Woody "defames no one more scandalously than he does himself."

Just as Harlene and Woody helped each other to break out of the orbit of their parents, Louise made Woody a citizen of New York, a city she was born to and knew in the best way. She was raised on Fifth Avenue, she attended Fieldston, an excellent and exclusive private school, and her father, S. J. Lasser, had a distinguished career (he wrote the second most famous income tax assistance book and is always confused with J. K. Lasser, who wrote the most popular manual and is no relation). In sum, she had all the things that Woody wished he could have had as he grew up.

"I became a human being with Louise," Woody says. "She made a major, lasting contribution to my life. The years with her were the time I made the transition from writer to comedian. Before that I was just someone who had lived in Brooklyn and moved into New York and didn't know anybody besides my wife. With Louise I assumed citizenship of Manhattan. We had friends. She was someone who put me in touch with living in the city as a person, not as someone who is trying to make his way."

Woody and Louise met through a friend of his who was in the last stages of dating her. They were also near neighbors. Woody and Harlene lived then on East Seventy-eighth Street and Louise was living with her parents in their apartment four blocks down Fifth Avenue, between Seventy-third and Seventy-fourth streets. Soon after they were introduced, Woody called her and asked, "Want to go for a walk or something? Want to buy a record?" She did and he walked down to 923 Fifth Avenue, where the doorman looked at this twenty-four-year-old in a zipper jacket and in need of a shave and said, "You're going to have to wait down here, sir. We'll call her and she'll come down." Their courtship took place in all the museums, in most of the movie houses, and in many of the restaurants in Manhattan, as well as in nearly every cranny of Central Park.

Harlene and Louise could scarcely have been more dissimilar. "Harlene was a very nice, very stable, very sweet neighborhood girl who became very educated," Woody says. "She was a philosophy major, she learned German, she played classical piano; now she paints. She became a very formidable person. Louise was really and truly a wonderful, sensational person, but she was crazy as a loon. She was one of those persons where you get two good weeks and two bad weeks a month, but the two weeks are so worth it. Then after a while you're down to two good *days* a month. Even the two days are almost worth it because two good days a month with Louise were better than a good year with most other people. It was like [Arthur Miller's] *After the Fall*. When I read some of the dialogue of that, I swear I thought to myself, 'God, I've heard Louise say these lines.' But she was extraordinary. All my friends and family remember her in the most affectionate way. I think I used some of this in Charlotte Rampling's character in *Stardust Memories*."

Woody's second new friend of this time was Dick Cavett, a recent Yale graduate, a former *Time* magazine copy boy, and, when they met, a newly hired joke writer for Jack Paar, whom Paar sent "to check out this comedian I'd heard about who was writing for Sid Caesar when he was six and had decided to do an act." Woody's effect on Cavett was like Sahl's effect on Woody: "I remember when I heard about Woody I just loved the idea of what he was doing, because it seemed suddenly to ring like a bell, like maybe if this works then that's what I'll do. When I called Woody to tell him I was coming to his show, Harlene [this was before they split up] told me that he was out for a walk. I even liked the sound of that. I said, 'Yeah, that's what you'd do if you were converting from a writer to a performer.' " It's something Woody continues to do every day.

According to Woody, when Cavett went to see him a subsequent time at the Bitter End in June 1961, "it was during the period when you would hear people filing out and saying, 'Gee, the guitar player was great, but that comedian.' " But Cavett wasn't one of them. "The minute I walked in that night, the sound of the material was so high; I couldn't believe that he could go on so well for twenty minutes with this level of wonderful stuff. I had never heard this level of comedy, one thing after another, in anybody except, maybe, Mort Sahl, in a very different way. There wasn't one routine he did that wouldn't have been the highlight of any comedian's act. Yet some of the audience were talking. They were a nightclub audience who had come to hear the noise act. I wanted to say, 'You idiots! Listen to this! Am I the only one who knows this is a great, great talent here?' "

After Woody's set the two chatted a while and then went back to

Woody's apartment to continue. Cavett was taken with the posters on the walls: for the Sidney Bechet memorial concert at Carnegie Hall; for an Erroll Garner concert, also at Carnegie Hall; and for *From A to Z*, a 1960 two-act revue with Hermione Gingold that included Woody's "Psychological Warfare" and Groucho sketches from Tamiment. (Among other contributors were Fred Ebb, Herbert Farjeon, Miss Gingold, and Mary Rodgers.) The show, which opened April 20, 1960, at the Plymouth Theatre to poor reviews and closed after twenty-one performances, was Woody's Broadway debut.

Cavett, too, was a fan of George S. Kaufman, who had died two days before; he tried without success to convince Woody to go with him to the funeral the next day. Woody generally avoids encountering heroes of his even when they're alive. "They're polite and say how much they like your work, you're polite and say how much you like theirs," he says. "It's always disappointing." (After he met Groucho Marx, Woody said, "He seemed like one of my Jewish uncles." The two remained friendly admirers, however. "Now here's a funny man," Groucho said one day as Woody arrived to see him during a visit to New York. When Groucho invited him to his seventy-fifth birthday party in Beverly Hills, Woody, who had work in New York, cabled, "Sorry I can't attend your 75th birthday, but I expect you to be at mine." But there are exceptions to not attending to dead heroes. When jazz pianist and composer Thelonious Monk lay in a funeral parlor on Third Avenue in 1982, Woody, who was driving up the street with Mia, suddenly said to her, "Let's go in here." They got out of the car and quickly paid their respects as Monk's friends and family looked on in surprise. Mia, who had been seeing Woody for a couple of years, chalked up the event as "one of the strange corners of him I was still learning about.")

Soon Cavett and Lasser signed with Rollins and Joffe. After Woody and Harlene split up, Cavett spent much time with Louise and Woody. Woody, who was playing billiards daily then, took Cavett with him. "It was kind of fun hanging around those billiard clubs late at night. Woody had just started to appear on TV and a certain number of mug types would come over and say, 'Hey, Woody, out playing games, ain't you?'

"One night we went downtown in the rain to a movie. I think he had worn his first hat that day. I had an extra one, a Russian shako-shaped thing that I pulled out of the closet. As we walked, he said, 'This is great. You put on a hat and it doesn't feel like it's raining.' " (Now Woody commonly wears what he called years ago "my disguise hat. It cuts out fifty percent of my recognition, and my act cuts out the other fifty percent.") "A truck had wheeled around the corner and a huge box of tomatoes fell off. Across the street was a billboard with a face on it where a building had been torn down. The strangest image I have of me and Woody is the two of us pitching tomatoes at this face on that sign on a dark rainy night downtown. I was also impressed by what a marvelous arm he had. I felt like a real nancy boy when later I threw the ball around in Central Park with him."

Woody was then also playing high-stakes poker with a number of friends, among them Coleman Jacoby and Ken Roberts, the radio announcer and father of Tony Roberts, who has appeared in two of Woody's plays on Broadway and in several of his films. Woody was a serious player and did well. Among other things, he bought with his winnings a painting by Oskar Kokoschka that hangs in his apartment. While filming *Casino Royale* in London in 1966 his poker take paid for an Emil Nolde watercolor and a Kokoschka drawing; German Expressionism remains one of his preferred schools of painting. When Woody lost, it was graciously and with some humor. He once wrote a check to Ken Roberts, and in the memo space at the bottom he noted, "For heart transplant."

In November 1962, about two years after he began to perform, Woody got his first big review. Arthur Gelb wrote in *The New York Times* that he was "the most refreshing comic to emerge in many months. . . . He is a Chaplinesque victim with an S. J. Perelman sense of the bizarre and a Mort Sahl delivery despite the fact that he steers clear of topical material." In a period when nearly every comic made reference to or imitated John F. Kennedy, Gelb noted that "for a wonder, [he] eschews any references to the President and his family." The next day, NBC's Chet Huntley and David Brinkley, two of the top television newsmen of the time, read the review on the air. In early 1963, *Time* gave him a rave review, and not long afterward *Variety* said, "By way of runaway hits this season . . . nightclubs have Woody Allen . . . the brightest talent on the cerebral comedy scene since Sahl's ascendency." Jack O'Brien of the New York *Journal-American* called Woody "the best young American new-wave comedian. . . . He cracks a marvelous modern wit which, unlike Mort [Sahl]'s wit, which needs a target and too often smacks of cruelty, is aimed straight at himself, his own pintsized physical ineffectiveness, his owlish face and what he maintains is his special disaster-prone capability for hilarious social and physical indignities. . . . He deserves deeper classification as a humorist, not just a wit."

The comments proved that Woody had achieved Rollins's first goal for him: Audiences saw him as a person, and they liked what they saw. That person, of course, was far more an invention than a reality but he was utterly believable. One reason was that he was partially a product of the audience.

"My character was assigned to me by my audience," Woody told the New York *World-Telegram & Sun* in November 1963. "They laughed more at certain things. Naturally, I used more of those things. And the critics helped assign me a character, too. They would write about me and describe me as a certain type. So I put more material in the act that would fit that type."

"All good comedians are men that we relate to," he told William Zinsser in *The Saturday Evening Post* in 1964. "America is involved in the life of Jack Benny and Bob Hope. Put them in any standard comic situation—say, a roomful of pretty girls—and you know how they're going to react. . . . If people come away relating to me as a person, rather than just enjoying my jokes; if they come away wanting to hear me again, no matter what I might talk about, then I'm succeeding."

Soon Woody was an established comedian and in demand across the country, or at least at one club in each of several metropolitan areas. (By 1964, his salary was $5,000 a week and he was headlining in Earl Wilson's column, ten years after anonymously writing jokes for it.) The out-of-New York circuit was Mister Kelly's in Chicago, the Crystal Palace in St. Louis, the Shadows in Washington, D.C., the "hungry i" in San Francisco, and the Troubador and the Crescendo in Los Angeles, clubs whose clientele was likely to appreciate Woody's stories about "an authentic, ethnic folksinger who still had the leg shackle on," and a girl he met at NYU whose favorite form of recreation was "listening to Marcel Marceau LPs" (she also introduced him, he said, to "a pseudo-post-impressionist artist" who attempted to cut off his ear with an electric razor). But however established Woody had become and however sympathetic the audiences were, he was not yet a constant hit. "Cavett:" he wrote from San Francisco. "A fast note to explode the myth of the 'hungry i.' The allegedly hip audiences that nurtured Sahl, Berman, Nichols and May have vanished and gone over the horizon. I can't see any difference between this and a Lions Club audience in the Midwest."

But then, Woody had never played to a Lions Club audience in the Midwest.

He did, however, play before a group of Chevrolet dealers in New Jersey soon after he started. "Some agent booked him and he got a thousand dollars," Charlie Joffe says. "He was the only performer in a room full of men. I was in the back. He went through his entire act and never got a laugh. The only laugh I heard was when he looked back and laughed at me. I was just standing there, mortified. Not a single laugh. Nobody had heard of him, nobody cared that he was there. It was painful. But that didn't disturb him as much as great applause."

It was at one of his first bookings at Mister Kelly's in Chicago that Woody met Jean Doumanian, a former model and current producer who is probably his closest friend. After the show one night, she and her then husband, John, who was in the record business (and who often crops up in small roles in Woody's movies), were at O'Connell's coffee shop, the show-business hangout across the street from the cabaret. Nancy Wilson, one of Doumanian's singers, was on the bill with Woody. Rollins and Joffe, who were not going to stay through the whole engagement, fell into conversation with John and Jean. "He's alone," Rollins said of Woody. "Would you just watch out for him?" They did. They even arranged dancing lessons for him so he could learn such then current steps as the Swim and the Monkey.

"He was in his wrap-the-cord-around-his-neck phase," Jean recalls. "He always hated his performance and I always gave him my honest opinion. But what was amazing was to shortly see him go from that guy to someone who could completely mesmerize an audience. He was and is always a joy to be with. He's extremely intelligent and he's whimsical; he has such an incredible way of looking at things that's so on the money and so hilariously funny."

Apart from his relationship with his sister, Letty, Woody's companionship with Jean has been the longest steady friendship of his life. They have never been romantically involved but regardless of marriages or steady relationships they converse on the phone almost daily (they also share an answering service) and see each other often. They also travel together from time to time, which can create special problems. In Paris on one occasion Woody affected a disguise in an attempt to keep fans at bay. While Jean and her companion Jacqui Safra checked them into the Hotel Crillon, Woody lingered in the lobby wearing dark glasses, a hat, and a false mustache. American Secret Service agents guarding Richard Nixon, himself a guest, became suspicious of this man so clearly in disguise and kept him under close watch. The three moved to another hotel but his camouflage was in vain. On the steps of the Opéra later that day, two German tourists stopped him. "Are you Woody Allen?" they asked. One of Mia's first gifts to him was a mustache comb.

Woody generally kept to himself on the road and had little to do with other acts on his bill, although folksinger Judy Henske was an exception. He and the tall, full-voiced, attractive woman became close friends. He liked her for many reasons, one of which was that "she always got the jokes. You could never get a reference by her. Whether it was Proust or Joyce, she knew it. She was very bright. Once as a joke I looked for the driest, most unromantic book to give her, so I got something like *Pennsylvania Real Estate Laws*, one of those books that you buy in a bin for a quarter. And she read it. She'd read anything that came her way. She was from Chippewa Falls, Wisconsin—that's where I got the name for Annie Hall's hometown. Keaton always reminded me of her." But whatever his friendships on tour, Jean and John Doumanian were the only out-of-town substitutes for Rollins and Joffe. Joffe especially. For besides going to his performances every night in New York, Joffe was Woody's almost constant companion when he was on the road, which was four or five months a year. They ate together, played poker together, and chased women together for about eight years. (Joffe was so devoted a manager that on their wedding night he took his wife to Woody's performances at the Duplex, she still in her bridal dress. "The Stage Deli gave us a salami when we came in with Woody after the show," he once recalled with a huge laugh. "Was I a putz, or what?") On one occasion, however, Woody went alone to St. Louis to play the Crystal Palace, owned and run by Jay Landesman. Woody wrote to Rollins and Joffe and their secretary, Estelle Baroff, to tell them how good a time he was having:

Dear Jack, Charlie, and Estelle:
      I don't know how it happened but this morning I woke up and found myself in St. Louis, Missouri. With sedate aplomb I fled screaming to the airport where two dynamically juxtaposed southern bullies prevented me from boarding my flight because of a well placed phone call from a man named Jay Landesman who seems to have an incredible amount of influence locally stemming from the fact he has me under contract.

It has also been made quite apparent to me that the disobeying of a nightclub owner's orders while out of town comes under the heading of mutiny and is punishable by hanging from ten to twenty years. (It's a long time to hang.) The thought is constantly upon me here (in what to me is the Deep South) that chain-gangs are still abided and the slightest offense on my part could provide ample reason for Governor Meyner (to me all governors outside of New York are called Governor Meyner [Robert B. Meyner was governor of New Jersey from 1954 to 1962]) to shackle me to some full-throated Big Sam type and see to it that I never see the inside of a Max's Special [sandwich] again.

And so I pass my time prudently reticent in the confines of my luxurious no-room apartment trying to keep the mirror from steaming up from the air conditioner. The nightclub by the way is a study in anti-matter and turns in on itself. Rococo balconies abound in every drawer and magnificent stained glass windows give one the feeling of being in the actual Crystal Palace. The French have been here, one realizes, and they have left. . . .

Admittedly, however, the gaslight section of town is something to be seen. Unfortunately the civil officials are in the process of dismantling the gas lamps and changing over to sealed vans. I happen to enjoy this creative, Greenwich Village–like part of town and have managed to befriend a local artist who is doing enormous things with Silly Putty. He has some interesting abstract, nonobjective items that the museum is quite agog about. He says that he will let them go for a song and while I feel he displays great skill and depth, I frankly can't sing that well.

My one salvation is the opera. There is none anywhere. Not much else save that if I can manage to tie my bed sheets together effectively I plan to be home soon. I look forward to seeing you all again if only from behind. Meanwhile I peek in the mail every day to see if my own personal lobotomy has arrived. Until the fall I remain good naturedly your vapid little patsy. Don't go to pot on my commissions.

Please excuse the penmanship as I am writing this in the bathtub. [The letter was typed.]

Woody Allen

Woody endured the unpleasantness of the road because he knew it was the only way to establish himself as a comedian. But that was only his immediate, not his long-term goal. Around this time he drew up a list of what he wanted to do in his career, which was to end up as the writer and director of (but not the actor in) original dramatic films. The question was, how could he accomplish that? He knew nobody was going to give him a million dollars (then the going price for a movie) to do a serious film at this point. What seemed the best way was to first gain a reputation, then write scripts for others to direct, and eventually work himself into a position where he could write and direct his own material. This mid-twenties plan was a more refined version of the one he made when he was sixteen or seventeen and had not yet been introduced to the films of Luis Buñuel and Ingmar Bergman and thus had no desire to make serious movies. Instead, Abe Burrows's advice about the theater had impressed him and the more plays he read and saw, the surer he was that he wanted to write dramatic plays for Broadway. Yet his means of advancement was also his greatest impediment. He had such a flair for comedy that even as a teenager he was immediately hired as a writer; later he had relatively quick success as a performer. Then when he began to make movies, they were so funny that before long *Time* had him on its cover, proclaiming him a "Comic Genius." In a way, he was too successful for his own good. He created such an original comic outlook and voice that any subsequent attempt at drama jarred the sensibilities of many in his audience. "I succeeded at my second choice, and I was happy to succeed at it," he has said, "but it was not what I ultimately wanted to do."

In the fall of 1987, Woody stood across from the Duplex waiting to make a shot for *Another Woman* and said, "I'm very happy with how this film is going. I think I have a chance with it, that people will respond to it. I got my foot in the door with *Interiors*, and *September* [which was about to be released] should get it in a little further. Of course, I may get my ass kicked and so it would be the next one or the one after that that works. But right now, I see this as the culmination of a journey that I thought might take ten years but has taken about twenty-five." As things turned out, the film was not the success he hoped for. The critical and financial success of *Crimes and Misdemeanors* moved him a little bit along, but it is not the entirely dramatic film without him in it he seeks to make. An added problem for him as a dramatist is that he has not had the luxury of gradual development he had as a young writer of comedy. With his success in other areas, he can't make gradual progress in a new field: He must create full-blown dramatic successes to be taken seriously. His solemn films are judged against his comedies, not against themselves, and so there is little tolerance for interesting failures or provocative near misses; neither is there broad credit for successes.

When Woody went to Los Angeles in the fall of 1963 on one of his performance tours, Cavett also happened to be there writing for Jerry Lewis, who had a two-hour live show on NBC ("Live being an anagram for vile," Cavett says). The two friends spent much of their free time together. One day they rented either a big black or a big pink Cadillac (the color varies from telling to retelling) to drive to Santa Barbara, about ninety miles up the coast, and have a lobster dinner at a highly touted restaurant by the water. It was a trip better recalled than experienced. Woody, who is not much of a driver, sheared off a piece of roadway cliffside, and the restaurant was closed. From then on, they kept their excursions local. On a Sunday morning they walked around Beverly Hills, two tourists looking for the stars' homes. They found the house where W. C. Fields had lived, and they searched out Jack Benny's on Roxbury Drive. As they passed by they imagined Benny and his wife, Mary Livingstone, and Eddie Anderson, who played Rochester, putting together that night's show. They knew that wasn't really happening, but years of listening to the show on the radio had given them a mental picture of Beverly Hills and the Benny household that in many ways was more real than what they were seeing.

For dinners, they went often to Trader Vic's, where drinks came with paper umbrellas in them and the Chinese food had a vague Oceania cast. "One evening," Cavett recalls, "Woody said, 'I can't imagine that life could be long enough for me to do the number of projects I have in mind.' I remember thinking, 'God, I can't think of a *joke* until they give me a subject. I don't have *any* projects in mind.' What stunned me as I sat over oysters casino Chinese style is that he had more than one thing in his mind, that he had his life planned out."

He still has. In the summer of 1988, twenty-five years, eighteen films of his own, and three produced plays later, Woody talked in detail about a dozen new movie ideas. Then he outlined a few more and spoke in general about some plays and at least one novel, all of which occupy his thoughts from time to time. He would have gone on to others but he was in a hurry to play with his three-year-old daughter, Dylan, about the only person on earth who can tell him what to do and have him jump to do it.

One reason Woody is so prolific is that, like almost every great artist, he is a prolific recycler of his life. His ideas, he says, all have some autobiographical content in that they spring from "a germ of experience" that he turns and augments. While acknowledging the breadth of Woody's imagination, Charlie Joffe thinks there is more than a germ of reality in his work. "He denies a lot of truths in his life. *Radio Days* was easy to admit was autobiographical because he was six in it." And Mia adds, "I think everyone in Woody's life plays roles and replays them in different contexts. Some of *Hannah* was drawn from my family, and I guess other sisters Woody has known, like Diane Keaton and her sisters. It's kind of nice. No one was upset in my family, anyway."

Cavett took in Woody's shows on that Los Angeles visit, and between sets they hung out together. Sometimes he was the only one laughing at Woody's material, which upset them both: "One night, after about twelve gems in a row had gone by unrecognized by the audience, who sat there stupidly blinking at the lights, Woody just came to a complete stop. There was an awful long moment when nobody knew if he was going to continue or not. Then he said, 'If I were giving prizes for the worst audience I've ever seen, you'd win it.'"

Woody's hostility to the audience that night and on other occasions, such as one show at the "hungry i" when he turned his back to a rude crowd and started talking to the brick wall, shows the paradox about him. The shy Brooklyn boy who had trouble with girls, the man who virtually never raises his voice in anger and who nearly had to be led by the hand to the stage when he began to perform, the entertainer who covered his ears at the Bitter End if there was applause when he left the stage, is enormously self-confident about his talent.

He is also enormously alienated from other people. Some years after their divorce Louise Lasser said, "The worst thing in the world could happen to him and he would go in that room and write," and Woody himself admits, "I could get bad news and still sit down at the typewriter. Maybe it's because I'm depressed so often that I'm drawn to writers like Kafka and Dostoevski and to a filmmaker like Bergman. I think I have all the symptoms and problems that their characters are occupied with: an obsession with death, an obsession with God or the lack of God, the question of why are we here. Almost all of my work is autobiographical—exaggerated but true. I'm not social. I don't get an enormous input from the rest of the world. I wish I could get out but I can't."

He said that in 1972. It is in large measure still accurate but there are important exceptions: He is regarded by his close friends as being exceptionally loyal, kind, and thoughtful, and his generosity is legendary among them. For all his obsessions, he is not a brooder at a dinner party with people he trusts; rather, he is open and amusing. What is most likely the root of his disassociation is a line that appeared in an early draft of *Another Woman*: "She feels so deeply that the only choice is to deny feelings or be overwhelmed by them." It is a condition echoed by Tennessee Williams's answer to a reporter who asked him his definition of happiness: "Insensitivity, I guess."

Again in an early draft of *Another Woman*, Marion, who has just turned fifty, sees a pregnant woman and flashes back to the abortion she had when she was much younger. "I liked the idea of a child," she says, "but the personal aspect of it was too much." Woody became a father at fifty and her early ambivalence is not just coincidental to his own. "It's no accomplishment to have kids," he often used to say. "Any fool can do it." Then he met Mia Farrow, who had seven children. André Previn was the natural father of the three oldest, all boys—Matthew and Sascha, who are fraternal twins, and Fletcher. Then they adopted Lark and Daisy, both Vietnamese orphan girls, and Soon-Yi, an orphaned Korean girl. After their divorce, she adopted a two-year-old orphaned Korean boy with cerebral palsy and named him Misha Amadeus Farrow. A few months later Woody took Mia to a Knicks-76ers basketball game, and they enjoyed watching Philadelphia's Moses Malone. "Woody pointed out," says Mia, "that it was a lovely name." Not long after, Misha became Moses. As her relationship with Woody strengthened, he assumed paternity for him. Then, in 1985, Mia adopted another child, a newborn American girl, whom she named Dylan O'Sullivan Farrow. At first, Woody thought Mia "had enough kids, with enough encroachments on our time. When she brought Dylan off the plane, I didn't have much response at first. I didn't want it to interrupt my schedule. But after three or four days, an attachment forms. Six months down the line, I found myself jumping out of cabs stuck in traffic and running to the apartment to get an extra five minutes with the baby."

In *Manhattan*, Ike (Woody) lies on his couch and dictates into a tape recorder a list of meaningful things. "Well, all right, why is life worth living?" (It is a question he asks in another form in *Hannah and Her Sisters*.) "That's a very good question. Well, there are certain things I guess that make it worthwhile. Uh, like what? Okay. Um, for me, oh,

I would say . . . what, Groucho Marx to name one thing . . . uh, and Willie Mays, and, ummm, the second movement of the Jupiter Symphony, and ummm . . . Louie Armstrong's recording of 'Potatohead Blues' . . . um, Swedish movies, naturally . . . *Sentimental Education* by Flaubert . . . uh, Marlon Brando, Frank Sinatra . . . umm, those incredible apples and pears by Cézanne . . . uh, the crabs at Sam Wo's. . . ." It is entirely Woody's personal list; Ike is just his spokesman.

Shortly after the film was released, Woody received a letter from a woman who was astounded that Ike's child was not part of the list. At the time, her complaint was read by unseeing eyes. "I used to think, 'I've got big plans for myself. I don't have time for kids,' " he told an acquaintance in 1987 who himself had just become a father. "Only after being around Mia have I seen that children are so meaningful to people in helping to define their lives. I wouldn't have thought about it by myself. Now it seems that woman made a damning charge. Once you have a child, it is so powerful an experience, it's impossible not to put it first. It eclipses others by far. It's a bigger kick getting a laugh from the baby than it is from a whole audience. I find I'm always doing things to get that laugh because it is so gratifying. I thrust my face in rapidly toward hers, make foolish incomprehensible sounds, things that in the past I thought others were making such asses of themselves doing. There's a whole world out there that for fifty years I was not interested in remotely." (A line in an early draft of *Another Woman* read, "I was past fifty now and it was time to leave certain notions behind." Just before he turned fifty-three Woody said, "I put all I felt about turning fifty into Marion. It took me at least a year to get over it.")

His devotion to Dylan, who was then not quite two, was such that he carried a rubber pacifier in his pocket wherever he went so as to always have one at hand. One day in the spring of 1987, he had lunch at *The New York Times* with several of the top editors to talk about his support of the campaign to halt colorization of black-and-white films and to otherwise not alter a director's work without the director's consent. While talking about Dylan a few days after the lunch, he pulled the pacifier out of his pocket. He looked at it a moment and then with a little smile said, "I remember sitting at that lunch with all these accomplished journalists in business suits and hoping that they don't frisk me and find it."

That fall, Mia brought Dylan along when she came to shoot her costume tests for *Another Woman*, which would begin filming a few days later. Dylan, who had recently turned two, was already a veteran of two films. Woody was thrilled to see her and expected that once again she would come often to the set during filming. But instead of placidly ignoring the bustle of the crew as she had as an infant, Dylan behaved as any normal two-year-old would at the sight of so many strangers making a fuss over her: She burst into tears. After various attempts at solace failed, Mia took her home, to Woody's great disappointment. As they left, assistant director Tom Reilly came over to him.

"You couldn't expect her to sit on sets forever," he said. Woody shrugged.

"Well, at least until she's eighteen."

He behaved toward Satchel O'Sullivan Farrow, their son to whom Mia gave birth in 1987, with the same face thrusting and foolish incomprehensible sounds. The forename is in honor of Satchel Paige, a hero of Woody's, and they decided on Farrow because they didn't want one child named Allen amidst two Farrows and six Previns. (When Woody told his mother Mia was pregnant she asked, "By you?" "This after seven years!" he said in a rare exclamation. "It gave me pause. 'I guess so,' I told her.")

"I can't imagine a more committed father than Woody," Mia says. "When we first got Dylan, I did feel he would be a warm and loving father. That happens to ninety-eight percent of the people who have children; why should he be an exception? But I was not prepared for the degree to which it happened to him. I can see that the children make him really happy, and that's not found easily in life, especially for Woody." Yet despite—and in part because of—the influence of the children, he remains in most other ways as alienated and as pessimistic as ever. "The kids clarify for me and vivify my worst feelings and apprehensions and perceptions about life," he says. "You really get some sense of what a horror show it is when in my case you look at those two sweet, innocent kids who have no negative ax to grind and yet for whom the negative possibilities are myriad—disease, muggers, kidnappers. It just heightens my perception of the world as a fearful, dreadful place." The theme of alienation runs through his nightclub material and his films. In *Sleeper* he plays an alien in a world two hundred years from now, a man on the lam much like Virgil is in *Take the Money and Run*; in *Crimes and Misdemeanors* his character is both honest and unrespected; in *Broadway Danny Rose* he is a decent, hardworking man who is the butt of his colleagues' jokes; in other films he is a misfit.

It is not that he worries that people are out to get him. That is a minor, almost trivial issue—although he has been subject to the mania of cranks who hound celebrities and is appropriately uncomfortable when an apparent fan reaches into a purse or bag; who knows whether he—or she—will pull out an autograph book or a pistol? In his play *Death*, in which a murderer on the loose is in fact Death, the enemy is bigger and more complex than simple humanity. Yet however impersonal the force, he takes it very personally. "It's very important to realize that we're up against an evil, insidious, hostile universe. It'll make you ill and age you and kill you. And there's somebody—or something—out there who for some irrational, unexplainable reason is killing us. The only questions of real interest are the ultimate questions, otherwise who cares about anything else."

On the other hand, dealing with those ultimate questions all the time can drive one nuts, so Woody purposely puts distractions in the way. "An idea for a short story," Ike says in *Manhattan* just before making up his list of meaningful things, "about people in Manhattan who are constantly creating these real, uh, unnecessary neurotic problems for themselves, 'cause it keeps them from dealing with, uh, more unsolvable, terrifying problems about, uh, the universe." Woody's neuroses may include his need to occupy his mind with work so as to avoid the larger issues—a famous line of his is: "I don't want to achieve immortality through my work. I want to achieve it through not dying." But as with most of his neuroses, he puts this one to his best advantage. He assigns himself mental tasks throughout the day with the intent that not a moment will pass without his mind being occupied and therefore insulated from the dilemma of eschatology. If he is going to ride six floors in an elevator or walk sixty blocks around New York, he mentally raises an issue to consider for the duration of the trip. It could be a scriptwriting problem or a contemplation of the next day's work, but whatever it is, by design it will keep him occupied with thoughts over which he can exert control, and by effect it enables him to work at a prodigious pace. "He's fertile and compulsive," his friend Tony Roberts says. "Not a bad combination."

"Why not opt for a sensual life instead of a life of grueling work?" Woody said one day in an egalitarian consideration of ultimate disposition. "When you're at heaven's gate, the guy who has spent all his time chasing and catching women and has a sybaritic life gets in, and you get in, too. The only reason I can think of not to is, it's another form of denial of death. You delude yourself that there's a reason to lead a meaningful life, a productive life of work and struggle and perfection of one's profession or art. But the truth is, you could be spending that time indulging yourself—assuming you can afford it—because you both wind up in the same place."

These feelings gave substance to his work as it developed and continues to do so, and they explain in part his constantly making different kinds of films rather than assured successes along the lines of *Annie Hall* and *Hannah and Her Sisters*. As assured success holds no allure for him, his desire is to make whatever film interests him the most at the time, whether it is a comedy or a drama. "I'm obeying nobody but my artistic muse," he says. "The experience is doing the project; the critical and commercial responses are not terribly relevant. Doing the idea and expressing yourself, maintaining your own criteria, is. People I spend my time and life with have like minds. We have our own feelings—whether adored or reviled—and we stick with our own judgment. If I don't like something, it doesn't matter how many awards it's won. It's important to keep your own criteria and not defer to the trends of the marketplace."

His concerns and apprehensions have led him to make films such as *Stardust Memories* and *Crimes and Misdemeanors* that he knows have "a grousing quality about them," but the grousing is not personal, as is often thought. Rather, "I'm just complaining about the human condition." In addition, he has developed a reputation as a recluse, "never going anywhere and never participating in anything" (although he publicly supports a number of causes for artists' rights and a more liberal social policy). He allows that his reputation is in part earned. "I'm not really a recluse, although every time you see pictures of me in the newspapers, I'm always shielding myself from paparazzi or suing somebody. I hope that somewhere along the line it will be perceived that I'm not really a personal malcontent, or that my ambition or my pretensions—which I freely admit to—are not to gain power. I only want to make something that will entertain people, and I'm stretching myself to do it."

He also believes that if he were simply to make out-and-out comedies again and again, audiences would soon tire of them despite the accepted wisdom that they wouldn't. "People go to see you because they expect you to be a certain way," he said after making *Sleeper* in 1973. "But after four or five films they suddenly say, 'That's the same old stuff.' You have to present a moving target. If you hold still long enough, someone will get you."

His terrifying feelings about the problems of the universe aside, Woody is genuinely leery of strangers. He walks purposefully and with his eyes averted from others on the street. If cornered he will graciously sign an autograph but does what he can to avoid being stopped. On the other hand, he enjoys the perks that fame offers: He gets a reservation easily at any restaurant he chooses and good seats at sporting and other events. It is common to see him at a front table in trendy Manhattan restaurants in clear view of other patrons, which raises the question of whether he secretly enjoys his prominence. The probable answer is, few on earth wouldn't—although he could do without interruptions from strangers. One benefit of a front table is its proximity to the door, which enables him to make a hasty entrance and exit without having to go through a crowd. (Not all of his customary tables are at the front, however.) As with many stars, he finds it nice to be known, but only from afar. He relishes his privacy and would rather pick the occasions he presents himself to the public. Surprise exposure only makes him nervous.

Once, during an engagement in Las Vegas, he was invited by two performers via their manager to come to their show. Although when he accepted he had asked the manager to make sure he would not be introduced from the stage, during their last number the performers stopped and, as a spotlight burned its way across the floor toward Woody's table, they said how nice it was to have him there. By the time the spotlight hit him, Woody's face was ashen and his hands were trembling. Had there been space enough and time, he would have succeeded in his effort to slide under the table, which he began to do as soon as he realized what was afoot.

Woody, however, has not hesitated to catch other people off guard. In 1963 he did several guest parts on *Candid Camera*, a show he is still "irresistibly drawn to" because of its spontaneity. In one prank, he played a bookstore clerk who gives away the plot of mysteries to buyers as he takes their money. One woman was so upset that she tried to run out of the store before he could tell her the denouement of the second book she was purchasing. For another show, he was someone determined to give a cabdriver exactly a ten percent tip on a forty-cent fare. When the driver says he doesn't have six cents change, Woody says, "All right, make it fifteen percent," and asks for four cents. The bits were wonderfully funny, if sometimes painful to watch, especially the look of horror on the face of the woman being told yet another plot against her will.

His favorite of all his *Candid Camera* episodes is the one in which he dressed in a dark suit and set himself up in a very severe, businesslike office. One by one he brought in public stenographers, whom he seated beside his desk. After explaining that his regular steno was ill, he then dictated the most unbusinesslike letter he could think of. After a few lines the steno would discreetly make a puzzled face. The more he dictated, the funnier the response. The reaction of one was priceless.

" 'You walk in beauty like the night,' comma, quotation mark wrote the poet, colon: And he must have—dash been thinking of you. Period. New paragraph," Woody dictated in closing the letter.

"Until we meet again my love know this: colon. I love you! Exclamation point. I must have you!! Two exclamation points. You are everything to me!!! Three exclamation points. The world revolves around you? Question mark."

"After 'revolves around you'?" asked the befuddled steno.

"Yes. I love you. I love you. What should I remain?"

"*You're* writing the letter," the steno said. Then, with less exasperation, "I'm sorry, I never expected to take a letter like this."

"Do you think it's a funny letter?" Woody asked.

"It's not funny if that's the way you feel about someone but I would think you would sit down and write a letter like this yourself."

"But I composed it."

"But you're not going to typewrite a love letter, are you? If it's not a love letter, what is it?"

"It *is* a love letter."

"You're going to typewrite a love letter to someone?"

"It's an electric typewriter."

Not believing her ears: "That's not the point! What, it's an electric typewriter? That's not personal . . ."

"Could you read it back?"

"I certainly can."

"With punctuation, please."

The steno gave him a double take. "Dearest beloved darling, comma, I cannot live without you anymore; semicolon. I need you more than I have ever needed anybody (parenthesis. And when I say anybody, I mean *anybody*. Close parenthesis). Quote: 'You walk in beauty like the night' end quote, wrote the poet and he must have—dash been thinking of you.

"New paragraph. I A) need you B) want you C) miss you. It is my fondest wish . . . dot dot dot, that you A) love me B) need me C) miss me. Kindly check any two. Until we meet again, my love, know this: colon. I love you! Exclamation point. I must have you!! Two exclamation points. You are everything to me!!! Three exclamation points. The world revolves around you? Question mark. I remain . . ."

"Your humble servant?"

"No, no, no, no."

He paused a moment, then said, "Take another letter. Mr. Allen Funt."

"Allen!"

"You know Allen Funt?"

"Candid Camera!"

Woody smiled, then dictated, "Dear Allen. Once again we have put a secretary on television without her knowing it. Her reactions were priceless." They were indeed. No actress, however great, could have done the scene any better.

"I dictated about fifteen love letters to an anonymous name," Woody told Funt after the segment. "Susan something or other. And on the way home, when it was over, I began to miss Susan."

"The degrading things I had to do when I started," Woody said after he watched a tape of the show in 1989, although he did snicker with pleasure a couple of times. "But they're funny. Funny in the context of the show. I did the show for pure career advancement. Now I'm trying to do Dostoevski," he added with a laugh, "trying to live down this shit."

But the show and the only three ads he has done (for Smirnoff vodka in the early sixties, for Foster Grant sunglasses—"Who's the man behind the Foster Grants?" was the line for a series of ads with celebrities—and one a few years later for Arrow shirts that appeared only in copies of *Time* magazine sent to subscribers in college) served their purpose. Woody was trying to make his name, and Jack Rollins's philosophy was that he should make himself known to the public in any way possible. The ads paid little or no money but he did receive a rack of shirts, and many cases of vodka—which he served at the first New Year's Eve party he gave with Louise Lasser. (Woody also worked an embellished version of the vodka deal into his act: "I did a vodka ad.

A big vodka company wanted a prestige ad. And they wanted to get Noël Coward but he was not available. He had acquired the rights to *My Fair Lady* and he was removing the music and lyrics and turning it back into *Pygmalion*. And they tried to get Laurence Olivier. Haleloke [the sprightly ukulele player on Arthur Godfrey's TV show]. They finally got me. I'll tell you how they got my name. It was on a list in Eichmann's pocket when they picked him up. And I'm sitting home, watching television. It was a special version of *Peter Pan*, starring Kate Smith. They were having trouble flying her. The chains kept breaking. And the phone rings and a voice on the other end says, 'How would you like to be this year's vodka man?' And I said, 'No. I'm an artist. I do not do commercials. I don't pander. I don't drink vodka. If I did, I wouldn't drink your vodka.' He said, 'Too bad. It pays fifty thousand dollars.' I said, 'Hold on. I'll put Mr. Allen on the phone.' ") Fostering recognition was the goal and Smirnoff took billboards all over the country, which is just what Rollins wanted. "Don't be fooled by success in New York," he told Woody. "It takes a long time to seep in." Woody appreciated what the ads did for his recognition but, with the exception of appearing in a non-product-advertising campaign for a Japanese conglomerate several years ago, which he did mainly for the promotional benefits in Japan it offered, he has declined to do any others.

"I'm reluctant to do ads only because I think it will undermine my credibility in some way," he says. "I mean for me to suddenly be seen selling I-don't-know-what on television . . . I've had the full range of offers. I've been offered institutional products, and I've also been offered mayonnaise. I don't know, I'd have a very tough time if they came to me with a really breathtaking sum of money. I really don't know what I'd do. I probably wouldn't do it because once you do, you can't buy your name back." Judging by his response to offers so far, the sum would have to be breathtaking indeed. Some years ago Charlie Joffe told him about an ad a company wanted him for that would take only a day or two to shoot. Woody said no.

"It pays a million dollars," Joffe told him.

"I already have one of those," Woody answered. More recently, he has turned down an offer of $5 million.

He did not, however, turn down any television shows when he was a stand-up. He appeared in comedy specials, went on Jack Paar's show, did stints on *Hootenanny*, was a guest or guest host dozens of times on *The Tonight Show*, and had two specials of his own. He also went a couple of rounds with a boxing kangaroo and sang "Little Sir

Echo" with a talking dog. And of course he was on that most famous variety program of all, TV's answer to vaudeville, *The Ed Sullivan Show*. On one occasion as Woody walked offstage after he finished his monologue, he told Sullivan in his best Bob Hope wise-guy voice, "You do a great job." That he managed to get a second booking was surprising because during the dress rehearsal the morning of his first appearance in the mid-1960s, Sullivan became furious over his use of the joke with "orgasmic insurance" in it; this was a time when even "pregnant" could not be used on the air. Woody intended to use another routine on the show and used this one so he wouldn't have to recite the routine twice in one day and his performance would therefore be fresher. Sullivan did not know this. When Woody finished, Sullivan, in front of the cast and crew, berated him for his perceived lewdness, threatened to throw him off the show, and accused him of practically single-handedly being responsible for the moral decay of the country. ("Attitudes like yours are why kids are burning their draft cards," were among his declarations.) Woody thought briefly of telling Sullivan what to do with his complaints but decided that would be self-indulgent. Instead, he said he was sorry. It was the right response, for Sullivan obviously soon realized he had overreacted. "When the storm abated, from that day on I had no better ally in show business," Woody says. "He had me to dinner, he plugged me in his column, and had me on the show all the time."

Woody refuses to watch any of his movies once he has readied them for release. His feeling is that he will only see things that need correcting or that could be done better, and if he is flipping his TV dial and happens across one of his films—they play on TV constantly—he turns past as fast as he can. But while he has no videocassettes of his films at home, he does have some tapes of himself performing, and during the filming of *Crimes and Misdemeanors* he was persuaded to comment on some as he watched. It was not a happy experience for him. In one of his first appearances on Jack Paar's show, Paar introduced him by saying, "An Indiana humorist wrote a wonderful line about somebody else one time that applies, I think, to our friend Woody Allen. He would have said, 'Woody Allen looks like the kind of guy who would come up on the stage if a magician asked him to.' " There was a big laugh from the audience.

Woody, dressed in a corduroy suit and a dark tie, had lots of movement and was working hard. He told the audience that "I was going with a girl at that time and we were going to get married and there was a religious conflict. She was an atheist and I was an agnostic. We didn't know which religion not to bring the children up in."

"I'm doing all those things that I hate in people on those shows," Woody said as he watched and listened to another routine about being a TV writer. "I'm a little kindly disposed toward myself because it's me, but if this was another guy, I'd"—he snapped his fingers—"change the channel. I'm milking. I never liked this routine, but I was turning out so much material in those days. It's leaden." He listened to the NYU routine and about cheating on his metaphysics exam. "The one inspired joke in this entire thing got no laugh at all: 'I looked into the soul of the boy sitting next to me.' It just went"—he snapped his fingers again—"right past them." He watched a while longer, obviously not gruntled. "I definitely favor a firing squad. I mean, you know, it doesn't have to be the agonizing death I'd wish on most other people I saw doing this. But it's definitely deserving of a firing squad. I'm no better than any bad comic, any pushy comic. I'm pushy. I think I'm cuter than I am.

"I hate what I stand for," he continued. "All those stupid girl-chasing jokes and sex jokes and, you know, self-deprecating stuff. It's repugnant to me now. At the time it was probably just easy laughter. And I probably felt more like a child at the time and accepted those roles. I feel if I were to come out in front of an audience now, I'd come out as an equal to them and talk to them as an adult. But in those days I was currying favor. All that bullshit about being short and unloved. It would be easy for me to do this kind of work now. I would talk more as an adult to people. I'd still try to be funny but I would never do the same kind of material. I would not posture myself as someone who couldn't get women or someone who is short and unloved."

The best host and the best show for Woody were Johnny Carson and *The Tonight Show*, which was then broadcast from New York. Carson is unparalleled at feeding guests setups that sound like casual conversation but allow them to use whatever material they've prepared for the show. Still, it is not an easy thing to deliver set material in a conversational tone and Carson appreciates Woody's ability to put the show to his best use. "Woody is one of the few people who could do set routines and make it look like stream of consciousness," Carson says. "His selection of words and his timing are a part of his genius."

The 1965 New Year's Eve show is a good example of how the two worked together. Now as Woody watched a shot during that show of the throng in Times Square waiting for the ball to drop signaling the new year, he said of the crowd and noise, "I think of our soundtrack in *Radio Days*, when we did this outside soundtrack up on the roof in the studio. Horns honking. Doesn't this sound great?" He was smiling. Then, after the new year had come, Woody came on the show. As he watched himself, the smile vanished.

"I'm fantastically excited," he told Carson. "I've been waiting all year long and when twelve midnight comes, I'm going to go crazy."

CARSON: I hate to be the first one to tell you, but about fifteen minutes ago was the start of the new year.
W: [Sadly] It's over, right?
C: It's over.
W: [Straight] I spent New Year's, for the first time in my life, together. [Bolder, like acceptance speech] And it's touching in a way and I'd like to thank the many fans and friends who share with me tonight the welcoming in of 1966, in which I'm looking forward to a year of some sorrow and some sighs, some slow moments and some delicate moments. [Taking hand of pretty woman next to him.]
C: Are these some of your resolutions? It's only fifteen minutes into the new year.
W: Let's not be sentimental. Yes, I had some champagne for dinner.
C: Remember two years ago we had champagne here on the set? And that was the last year we had it.
W: People still ask me if I was drunk two years ago on New Year's Eve, and I was not drunk. I was pleasantly high, and [he slipped in a prepared joke] I went home after the show and jumped naked into a vat of cold Roosevelt dimes. [Big laugh.] That's how I get my kicks.
C: What do you normally do on New Year's? Are you one of those people who go to parties or go to a nightclub?
W: Last year, New Year's, let me think. I was in Paris when we did *What's New, Pussycat?* and I was writhing in my hotel room with agony New Year's Eve. I couldn't get a date for New Year's Eve. I was living in Paris for about four months and the only French word that I could manage to say was *potage*, which means soup. I used to accost strange women on the street and say *"po-*

tage!," you know, and if the girl was Jewish she would make it for me.

c: You were around some beautiful women there.

w: Oh, can I tell you something?

c: Sure.

w: You know I'm a connoisseur from beautiful women. That's my thing in life. ["See, he's led me into my material here," Woody said appreciatively. "You'd meet in the afternoon with his talent coordinator and work out the questions."] And the great woman of the world to me was always [Brigitte] Bardot. I always felt that she was without a doubt the greatest thing in the world. And Sophia Loren I liked. I was not crazy about Sophia Loren, but I'm having an operation and that's going to be changed. And also Julie Christie, the girl who starred in *Darling*, I also felt was spectacularly beautiful. And I never met any of them or anything but in the last ten days I met all three of them. Can you believe that? I was at a party with Bardot and I had lunch with Sophia and I was out listening to jazz with Julie Christie one evening. Want to hear about it? [The story was true, except for being at the party with Bardot.]

c: Yes, yes.

w: Well, nothing happened.

c: Tall girl or short girl? I'm living vicariously now.

w: Well, Bardot I found good. Good quality, basic good quality. All thirty-two teeth. Poised. And Loren I found a little tall for my taste. She was a little too what you call *zaftig*. [A big laugh from the audience.] I don't know what kind of word it is. I guess it's Jewish. It means abundantly conceived. [Another big laugh, including Carson.]

c: I think that nails it pretty good.

w: And I had a fabulous time. I had known Sophia's husband, Carlo Ponti. I hate to drop names like this but I'm going to. [Laughter.] And he wanted me to write a film. We were talking about it. Originally the talk was [that the film would star] Sophia Loren and Marcello Mastroianni. And I had lunch with Loren and I suggested that in place of Mastroianni, that since I had appeared in *What's New, Pussycat?* [the audience tittered]—and it *was* a love story as opposed to a comedy—that I ought to play opposite her in the film. And, uh, she laughed. [A bigger laugh.] She laughed for about an hour and a half. Then she made a funny Italian gesture of some sort.

c: And that was the end of the lunch.

w: Yes. She moved the check over to my side of the table.

"My acting is not bad but what I'm doing is nauseating," Woody said glumly as he watched the tape. "I thought I performed it well. It looks like I'm thinking. I could have rattled that story off like a shot."

c: I never know whether you're telling me the truth or making this stuff up, like about the girls. Are you lying or is this for real?

w: That was true. I am a compulsive liar, though. I will not hesitate to lie to prove my point. I had a bad childhood and I lied to compensate for it. My parents did not want me. That's true. They put a live teddy bear in my crib.

"It's bad rehearsed material," Woody said, watching himself say, "When I was a kid I used to identify with Superman. I felt Superman and I had many traits in common because he used to go into phone booths all the time and remove his clothing." He shook his head. "The jokes are not about anything and they're not very good, more often than not."

On the tape, Woody got up from his seat beside Carson and continued his material. As Woody watched, he said, "See, it looks like I'm standing up onstage now, I'm no longer like a human being." It was a routine that ended with his saying:

I'm on the BMT subway going out to Brooklyn, and I'm coming to the Avenue J station and I look out on the platform and I see Hermina Jaffe being molested. She's five years old but a swinger. She had an overbite. The biggest overbite in Brooklyn. She'd eat a piece of toast and finish the outer edge first. The train pulls up and the doors open and I leap out on the platform. I put on my cape. She's being attacked by Guy de Maupassant Rabinowitz, one of the worst kids in Brooklyn. In the [1944] Roosevelt-Dewey election, his parents voted for Hitler. . . . [A rumor in Woody's neighborhood during the campaign was that if elected, Dewey was going to have the Jews sterilized.]

c: You had a fascinating childhood.

w: Can I tell one other quick story?

c: [Laughing] We've got a minute or so.

w: I was once, listen to this, terrorized as an adolescent on the

BMT. I was on my way to an amateur musical festival. I come from a semi-musical family. My father used to play the tuba. He tried to play "The Flight of the Bumblebee." He blew his liver out through the horn. [Big laugh.] And I'm on the train and these twelve hoods come up, really hairy-knuckle types. . . . And they start cursing and screaming and tearing up the seats. I just looked down. I continued to read *Heidi*. And the leader grabs me by my tongue and he lifts me up quickly and he snaps his knee up violently. And I did one of the greatest imitations of Lily Pons you've ever seen. I hit an L over high C. I was late for the music contest. I came in third. I won two weeks at interfaith camp, where I was sadistically beaten by boys of all races and creeds. [The routine was inspired by teenaged Allan's being menaced in the Kings Highway subway station.]

"When I'm not in my stand-up mode, when I'm sitting down on a panel or something, I'm less loathsome," Woody said with a bit of a laugh. "Less mannered. It's mannered in the form of every comic when I'm doing my stand-up. But it's so patently material. In those days it was a little less obvious as material. It's disgusting now. It doesn't hold up well at all. It's not about anything. I'm just a tummler, a guy up there making jokes. Probably the only good thing I can say about it, because I hate it, is that there was a certain amount of attention paid to telling the story to the audience and telling it to Johnny at the same time. A certain amount of acting went into it that was effective at the time. But better that these things are never seen by anybody because they're not a very flattering record of anything I did—or what I did then was pretty terrible most of the time."

The only performance he praised even faintly was at the opening of the London Playboy Club in 1966. Woody came on wearing a jacket and a tie. He took the mike from its stand and swung the cord out. "This is what I looked like in clubs," he said as he watched. Onscreen, he talked about his jacket. "It came with an extra button inside," he told the audience. "I didn't know what the button was for. They told me that if you lose a button, you take the button from the inside and sew it onto the outside and you have a button. I had the jacket two weeks and just my luck, I lost from the outside of the jacket, a buttonhole."

Then he told them about a time he was in the South and was invited to a party. As it was Halloween, he thought he'd go as a ghost.

So I take a sheet off the bed and I throw it over my head. I go to the party. You have to get the picture. I'm walking down the street in a Deep Southern town and I have a white sheet over my head. And a car pulls up and three guys with white sheets say, "Get in." So I figure they're guys going to the party. I get in the car, and I see we're not going to the party, and I tell them.

They say, "Well, we have to go pick up the Grand Dragon."

All of a sudden, it hits me. Down South. White sheets. Grand Dragon. I put two and two together. I figure, there's a guy going to the party dressed as a dragon.

All of a sudden, a big guy enters the car and I'm sitting there between four Klansmen. Four big-armed men. And the door is locked. I'm petrified. I'm trying to pass, desperately. I'm saying, "You-all" and "Grits." I must have said "Grits" fifty times. They'd ask me a question and I'd say, "Oh, grits. Grits." Then the leader— you could tell he's the leader because he's the one wearing contour sheets . . .

They drive me to an empty field and I gave myself away, because they asked for donations and everybody there gave cash. When they came to me, I said, "I pledge fifty dollars."

They took my hood off and threw a rope around my neck. Suddenly my life passed before my eyes. I saw myself as a kid again. In Kansas. Goin' to school. Swimmin' in the swimmin' hole. Fishin'. Fryin' up a mess o' catfish. Goin' down to the general store. Gettin' a piece of gingham for Emmy Lou.

I realize, it's not my life. They're going to hang me in two minutes and the wrong life is passing before me.

So I spoke to them. I was really eloquent. I said, "Fellas, this country can't survive unless we love one another, regardless of race, creed, or color." And they were so moved by my words, not only did they cut me down and let me go, but that night I sold two thousand dollars' worth of Israel bonds.

As the audience laughed and applauded on the tape, Woody said, "I'm a little better here because I don't think I'm as cute. I was marginally less loathsome. It had a certain energy. All that fooling around with cords and stuff is fake. And you'll notice in almost every movie at least once I'll do this," he said, taking off his glasses and rubbing his eyes. "It distracts you from the crudeness of the material. It doesn't sound so much like a joke. One of the things about Bob Hope that I always liked was that he could go through a picture and it sounds like a man conversing, yet he's getting those one-liners in."

Woody's feelings about his stand-up material came as a surprise to him. "I was absolutely convinced that as the years went by, if all else failed, I would always be able to listen to the records of my nightclub act and think, 'That was very good stuff.' But it sounds pretty terrible to me when I listen to it. I sound pretty repulsive and obnoxious and it just doesn't sound like anything to me. And I'm not being falsely modest here. I'm just trying to be honest about it." (Mia Farrow once said, "I don't think I would have fallen for that kind of hip *guy*. It's not at all the Woody I know. I can imagine him with his family in Brooklyn, but when he showed me some tapes from his early shows I said, 'Is that really you?' ")

However terrible the material sounded to Woody, it is, of course, brilliantly funny. The standard he judges himself by is higher than anyone else's, but that is not really the point of his complaint. He will, if pressed, agree that his act was funny. What he finds disappointing about it is seeing it in retrospect; he is like anyone who has moved on in his life and is suddenly confronted with a past that no longer fits. A 1964 photo spread in *Life* of him sitting in the bathtub while his "wife" sinks his toy boats does not complement the serious filmmaker he now is, nor does a 1964 *Esquire* cover story of his advice on how to survive college. ("It isn't my fault my grades slipped. My roommate tried to commit suicide and I used up all my energy trying to help him gain a better mental attitude, sir.") He has turned down offers to compile a videotape of his best stand-up performances because "I hate it," he says. While he adds that he would do the tape if he liked the material, he declines in part because he is acutely aware of how different he is now from that comedian working the audience for laughs. The self-imposed force that has impelled his career is the notion that he must always move ahead, to present, as he says, a moving target. Thus he has avoided turning out laugh-a-minute comedies one after the other primarily because he loves the challenge of stretching himself to—and occasionally beyond—his abilities. ("An interesting failure" is how he described *Interiors*, a film that gets better with each viewing, shortly after making it.) He also knows that presenting the public with the same thing year after year is like being in jewel-filled quicksand: The riches are great but after a while, you can't get out.

Instead he is accumulating a body of diverse work, which gives him some hope that in retrospect all his films will be worthy of appreciation to one degree or another. It is not an ill-founded wish. *Another Woman*, which did very moderate business, will likely stay around. If it follows the course of *Interiors*, which was not particularly well received, over time it will draw support from critics and audiences who see it now because they like other Allen films. Many seeing it for the first time will find they like it. And others, who at first disliked it, will find they have revised their opinion.

Shortly after the release of *Another Woman*, Woody said, "I think because I'm an individual filmmaker and have made so many films—and, I hope, will continue to—that, not to be presumptuous about this, a hundred years from now there will still be times during the year when they show all of them. I would think even the ones that were not popular when they came out will have supportive interest to the more popular ones, because I think at the minimum, there are things in all of these pictures that are worth seeing.

"There's a problem in self-definition and public perception of me. I'm an art-film maker, but not really. I had years of doing commercial comedies, although they were never really commercial. Pictures like *Take the Money and Run* and *Bananas* were forerunners of movies like *Airplane*—although they didn't make a fiftieth of what *Airplane* made. First there was a perception of me as a comedian doing those comic films, and then it changed to someone making upgraded commercial films like *Annie Hall* and *Manhattan*. And as I've tried to branch off and make more offbeat films, I've put myself in the area of kind of doing art films—but they're not perceived as art films because I'm a local person, I'm an American, and I've been known for years as a commercial entity. So they're not seen as being [François] Truffaut films or foreign films or [Luis] Buñuel films, yet they really don't have much more commercial appeal than that.

"What I should be doing is either just funny commercial films, comedies and political satires that everyone looks forward to and loves and laughs at, or art films. But I'm sort of in the middle. *Purple Rose* and *Zelig* and *Radio Days* are examples of films that are not popular, yet they're not so esoteric that they're art films exactly. They just fall into an odd category. If they're art films they should be made for very little money and shown in twelve cities. But mine are shown in a hundred, or however many.

"I've changed over the years. I didn't follow the logical path that I was heading for. Theoretically, at this stage in my life what I could be making, and probably a lot of people feel I should be making, is one American comedy every year. When I make a comedy, it's funny and commercial and probably more literate than most current comedies. But I deliberately wanted to go in a different direction. So instead of growing in terms of popularity, I was relatively high and then dropped down tremendously—not that it was ever *high*; this was always on a low scale on the chart. So of course if a picture comes out like *Hannah*, which gets tremendous reviews all over, it does pretty decent business— for me. That means it does only forty percent of what a movie like *Cocktail* will do and twenty-five percent of what a movie like *Big* will do. Still, if I made those at Orion all the time, they'd all be getting rich. But as long as I'm fooling around with, you know, a black-and-white film like *Danny Rose*, or *Purple Rose* with a very downbeat ending to it, or *Zelig*, which is a specialized taste, I'm not going to have huge hits."

Many critics make the point that the secret ambition of every jester is to play drama; one newspaper story on him ended, "Woody Allen doesn't want to play Hamlet. He wants to be Ingmar Bergman." It irks Woody that he is so readily pigeonholed. "I can never bear seeing a headline like 'Woody Dying to Be Taken Seriously,'" he continued. "It misses the point entirely. I don't *want* to be taken seriously. I *have* been taken seriously. The comic films are taken quite seriously—too seriously. It isn't that. Certain ideas occur to me that are not comic and that's the long and the short of it. I don't sit home wanting to play Hamlet or wanting to be taken seriously. I just want to feel free to create any kind of work that occurs to me and do my best on it."

After all, even though he established himself first as a comedian, he is an artist in the middle of his career whose work is continuously evolving. For audiences to complain that Woody is not producing a comedy each time is rather like complaining to Picasso that he never should have stopped using mostly blue.

Among the guests at the New Year's Eve party Woody threw in 1976 was S. J. Perelman. (*Everyone* in the stellar alphabet was there: the M's included Arthur Miller, Bette Midler, and Norman Mailer.) An acquaintance of Woody's mentioned to Perelman how much Woody admired him and, when he began to write, how hard he had worked to write like him.

"You have no idea how hard *I* have worked to write like myself," Perelman answered with a not altogether happy laugh.

Perelman's predicament resonated with Woody when he was told the story, as did James Thurber's behavior at a birthday party some years earlier for Larry Adler, the harmonica wizard. As the evening wound down a number of guests performed—George London, the opera singer, sang; Adler, who is also an accomplished pianist, played. After Adler finished, Thurber stood up and walked over to the piano, a tumbler full of scotch in one hand.

"Jamie, sit down," his wife called out.

"No, I want to say something," Thurber said. By now the room was quiet as everyone watched him. "I love music," he went on, his voice rising. "I've always loved music. I always wanted to be a musician. But what am I?" he shouted as he slapped the piano. "Nothing but a god [slap] damned [slap] humorist!"

No matter how harshly he criticizes his stand-up act now, Woody is quick to admit that it "was perfectly fine commercially in terms of getting my career launched." As well he should. Just as Rollins and Joffe envisioned, Woody's career as a stand-up led directly to his career in films. His constant concern, however, is that he not wind up an esteemed elderly gentleman who slaps a piano in regret for not at least trying to do all he wanted.

Part
Four

Hold the Dolce Vita, S'il Vous Plaît

PHILOSOPHY I: Everyone from Plato to Camus is read, and the following topics are covered:

Ethics: The categorical imperative, and six ways to make it work for you.

Aesthetics: Is art the mirror of life, or what?

Epistemology: Is knowledge knowable? If not, how do we know this?

The Absurd: Why existence is often considered silly, particularly for men who wear brown-and-white shoes. Manyness and oneness are studied as they relate to otherness. (Students achieving oneness will move ahead to twoness.)

—SPRING BULLETIN, first published in *The New Yorker*

A couple in the audience for Woody's performance at the Blue Angel one night in 1964 was Shirley MacLaine and a conservatively dressed man in his late fifties wearing a dark suit and quiet tie. While MacLaine laughed uproariously, he sat with all the sobriety of his clothes. He looked rather like Clark Gable but his name was Charles K. Feldman, and although he listened to the surreal, intelligent jokes and routines that had the audience convulsed, what he heard was a cash register ringing. Feldman was a film producer and he needed a writer to turn a frothy comedy about a successful Don Juan called *Lot's Wife*, by the Czech writer Ladislaus Bus-Fekete, into a contemporary comedy that could co-star someone like Capucine, who happened to be Feldman's girlfriend. He had bought the story rights several years earlier for Cary Grant and had since commissioned several versions of the script, one of them by I. A. L. Diamond, a master of farce, but none were to his liking. As MacLaine and the audience laughed on and on, Feldman became convinced that Woody was the answer to his lingering problem even though he had no experience with films. Watching him, Feldman realized that Woody "appealed to a modern audience," he said after the picture was made. "I felt if he could reach them through a microphone, he could do it via a screenplay." The next day he sent his emissary, a photographer–producer–graphics designer–general show-business wonder named Sam Shaw, to deal with Rollins and Joffe, perhaps the only two people in show business Shaw did not know. Feldman told Shaw he could offer up to $60,000 for Woody's services.

Shaw went to the Rollins and Joffe office, which was then one newspaper-scattered room on West Fifty-seventh Street. (They have since moved down the street to a tastefully and expensively furnished multi-large-room duplex with nothing scattered anywhere.) Dressed in tennis shoes and old pants and with a bunch of newspapers under his arm, Shaw wandered into the office and went over to Charlie Joffe, who figured him for one of the crazies off the street.

"How much do you want for your boy Allen to write a movie script?" Shaw asked.

Never being one to ignore a possible good deal, even from a crazy, Joffe told him, "Thirty-five thousand dollars," one of the few times he has ever undersold a client. (Joffe may not have gotten all the money for Woody that was available, but at least he chose the right deal. Woody had also been asked to act in *The Bedford Incident*, which took place on a Navy destroyer; the part was eventually played by Wally Cox.)

"Fair enough," Shaw said. "Feldman will be in touch with you."

("A representative of Charles K. Feldman . . . called on my managers," Woody wrote in the New York *Herald Tribune* when the film was released in 1965, "and offered them six figures for my services. After much haggling they picked one and a deal was made. . . . I have several ideas, most notably a suspense thriller based on the use of iambic pentameter by the metaphysical poets. Feldman was not overly responsive to the notion at first, but I think I can convince him. Here is a chance to contribute true art to a usually sterile medium.")

A few days later, Feldman was in fact in touch, and they agreed that not only would Woody write the script but he would also have a part in the film (and be paid more money); not a bad deal for a relatively unknown twenty-eight-year-old stand-up. And not a bad deal for Feldman either, who was right about Woody being the answer to his problem. *Lot's Wife* became *What's New, Pussycat?*, Feldman made millions of dollars on it (it became the biggest-grossing comedy to that time), and Woody had instant credibility as a screenwriter and actor, even though his script was massacred by Feldman and the experience was joyless for him. After making three films on his own, he said of *Pussycat*: "If they had let me make it, I could have made it twice as funny and half as successful." Which sums up the most important of the many differences between Woody and Feldman—and just about anyone else in the film business: Woody, then as now, wanted artistic successes; Feldman wanted commercial successes.

Hollywood was invented for people like Feldman. A lawyer turned agent turned producer, he had, according to a friend, "the soul of a gambler." As an agent he had about three hundred clients, among them: John Wayne, Gary Cooper, Richard Burton, Kirk Douglas, Greta Garbo, Marlene Dietrich, and Marilyn Monroe. He did unheard-of things for someone who expected to make a living in show business—he married Louis B. Mayer's girlfriend, Jean Howard, which led to Mayer's exerting influence to have him barred from many studios; on the other hand, he was the only agent with whom Darryl F. Zanuck, Twentieth Century–Fox's head of production, dealt personally. And he made unheard-of deals: He got Irene Dunne $150,000 for one film, *Magnificent Obsession*, at a time when she had been making $60,000 a year under her studio contract, and he did the same for Claudette Colbert, whose studio salary was $2,500 a week, for *It Happened One Night*. He raised John Wayne's fee to $750,000 plus a percentage of the profit (Feldman claimed he was the first agent to get a piece of the take for his stars). He was also the first agent to make package deals (which are now as common as agents in Hollywood), bringing script, star, and director (usually clients of his) to a studio which agrees to finance and distribute the film (although he did not take fees from clients in pictures he produced).

Until his death in 1968 at the age of sixty-three, Feldman lived the way one imagines the stereotypical producer would live. He had homes in, among other places, Beverly Hills, the French Riviera, New York, Rome, London, and Paris (but he once said, "When it comes to properties, I'd rather buy a story than a house any day"). He was called variously "the King Midas of Celluloid" and "the Caliph of Camp," which pretty well encompasses the breadth of his films: They ranged from *A Streetcar Named Desire* and *The Glass Menagerie* to *The Seven Year Itch* and *The Group* to *Pussycat* and his last film, *Casino Royale*.

Feldman was a devoted believer in the star system and the high salaries stars command. "No one ever heard of Aly Khan until he married Rita Hayworth," he once said, "and no one ever heard of Prince Rainier until he married Grace Kelly." Feldman was magnanimous toward stars who served his pictures well; he was so pleased by Peter Sellers's help and cooperation during the filming of *Pussycat* that as a thank-you he gave him a new Rolls-Royce. He was, as well, generous to people of talent who were, as the saying goes, between jobs. He had never read anything by Katherine Anne Porter until Sam Shaw gave him a collection of her stories and mentioned she could use some work. He became an instant fan; her stories made him cry, and when he saw Porter he told her, "You write with your balls." She was incensed. "I write with my clitoris," she snapped.

"Charlie was generous, the kind of guy you could go to when you needed a favor," Woody said a few years after finishing *Pussycat*, "but he was crap to work for. Yet I have an enormous affection for him. When you see those other big-time producers, they were so cheesy and drippy. Charlie was charming and funny. He would go over to the baccarat table and lose a hundred thousand dollars the way you'd lose your Zippo lighter. I wasn't happy with *Pussycat*. It was clearly a star vehicle. But I think small and Charlie Feldman thought big. Consequently, he was a multimillionaire when he died and I gotta work Vegas."

Feldman and Woody had trouble almost from the start. Woody was told what the Diamond script was about, but he never read it because he doesn't read scripts given to him, in part because he thinks they will be of no help and in part because he doesn't want to be influenced by them. Feldman's advice was that he "write something where we can all go to Paris and chase girls." Which is essentially what he wrote and then read aloud to Feldman and Warren Beatty, who was a sort of surrogate son to Feldman and was supposed to star in the film. Woody's first version no longer exists but it contained, he says, "a million great jokes. But you could see right away that Feldman came from the old school of Hollywood. I had named the lead female character Becky, a Jewish name. He didn't like it. And when she met the lead male, who was supposed to be Warren, she had confident dialogue; she would say, 'Well, you know, I'm gorgeous and I'm great-looking.' Charlie couldn't countenance that because it was immodest and against the cliché of what the heroine would say." Then there were the film references that peppered the script, famous lines Woody remembered from dozens of movies; one was the last words of *I Am a Fugitive from a Chain Gang*. When Beatty asked the heroine how she will live after they break up, she replied: "I steal."

Beatty, who was a fan of Woody's and had come a few times to see his act at the Bitter End and the Blue Angel, didn't mind the references so much but he did think that Woody's initially minor part was funnier than his. Also, "Woody couldn't quite grasp what was funny about a compulsive, successful Don Juan," Beatty said in 1974. So Woody wrote another version, very different from the first. Feldman liked it enough to go ahead with the film, which at this point lacked a title. Beatty provided it. He was living at Feldman's house in Beverly Hills, always on the phone to one beautiful woman or another. His usual greeting was: "What's new, Pussycat?" Feldman, it is said, heard him once and cried out, "Title!"

"In the original script," Beatty said, "Woody's part might have appeared on six pages. His first rewrite, the part went to twelve or fifteen pages and it was funny. Then it went to twenty or thirty pages. By the time we got to what Woody thought was an acceptable rewrite, his part was almost half the script. Mine was almost as large but not quite as good."

There are several versions of the changes the script went through, but no matter which version, it is certain that what appeared on the screen was only remotely connected to what Woody wrote. *Where* he wrote it was all over Europe. The preproduction was an exercise in how not to make a film, or at least a film on budget. First Woody and Joffe and Feldman and his staff were in London for six weeks. While there Woody got the news ("I was fiftieth to get any news") that Feldman was about to lose Beatty to another picture and so had sent the script to Peter O'Toole. Then Feldman thought he had a good deal to make the picture in Rome, so they went to Rome for six weeks. All the while Woody tried to persuade him to make it in Paris because it had, he said, "a Gallic flavor." Feldman's reply, according to Woody, was: "Aah, you can change it to Rome, Rome is the place"; a script to Feldman was something that could be changed like a shirt. Months dragged by and Woody became more testy, arguing with Feldman about the changes and the locale and threatening to leave the project. Joffe, meanwhile, tried to keep peace between them by counseling Woody that he had to accommodate Feldman because, as he pointed out, it isn't every day that a comic at the Blue Angel suddenly finds himself as the sole author of and with a part in what was shaping up as the biggest comedy of the year. He urged Woody that rather than be temperamental and run off, he instead try to see what he could gain from this opportunity. It was good advice. Apart from the aggravation of the work, among the things he gained was exposure to Europe at a level no one in his neighborhood in Brooklyn could even imagine, and it was at the very least luxurious and interesting, even if he was simply present more than he was a participant. He had drinks with Darryl Zanuck on the Via Veneto, then dinner with Peter O'Toole, or William Holden, or Jules Dassin. There were lavish parties and gorgeous women. Money was disposed of as easily as script pages. For a time, Feldman put Woody and Joffe up in the South of France. (Feldman always had a string of attractive women whom he paid to be available to friends and associates working on the film. One night in Cap d'Antibes he invited Woody to join his party.

When he came, Feldman introduced him to one of the ladies and explained that she would be his escort for the evening. Woody took one look at her and blanched. She reminded him of one of his aunts. That was the end of the night for him.) Later Feldman told them to take a week off and go to Florence at his expense. "It was absolutely incredible," Woody recalled a few years later. "Capucine would call me up on a weekend and say, not romantically, 'I have nothing to do. Shall I take you around Paris?' I found myself yanked suddenly into this *dolce vita* role."

For Paris is where the film, which had grown from a small comedy into a big picture—its budget was around $4 million, an astronomical figure for the time—was finally made. It was a big picture with a big budget because in the end it was filled with big stars: Peter Sellers at the height of his career; O'Toole, who had just appeared in *Lawrence of Arabia* and *Becket*; Ursula Andress, who had made a hit in the James Bond picture *Dr. No*; Romy Schneider; Paula Prentiss.

Woody loved Paris, even though he did not speak French or particularly care for the language at the time. "I learned more Italian in several weeks than I'll know French for the whole trip," he wrote to Richard O'Brien, whom Jack Rollins has called "the greatest press agent in the world." O'Brien, Woody's only press agent until 1984, orchestrated his wide coverage by papers, magazines, radio, and TV, and has long contributed jokes to him. "It's a rough language and I'm not wild about the sound of it." (He has since learned to speak it well.) Still, he managed quite nicely. "I posed with some of the nude lovelies at the Crazy Horse for publicity and spent quite an hour and a half in there chatting with them," he wrote O'Brien. "The fact that I don't understand a word of it didn't matter. I just nodded my head, smiled, and kept looking." (Woody's character has a job as the backstage dresser who helps the girls get into their stockings, garter belts, and G-strings at a striptease club. "How much is the salary?" Peter O'Toole asks. "Twenty francs," Woody says. "Not much," says O'Toole. Woody shrugs. "It's all I can afford.")

"Tracked down a boyhood idol, Claude Luter, who carries on jazz in the Bechet tradition and is superb," he continued. "I go see him constantly where he plays at a joint called the Slow Club. They really play authentic for young white men and their influences are clearly the great Negro originators whom they have great respect for, not disdain as so many modern players do. I posed for pictures with him." Finding Luter helped ease Woody's disappointment over missing two other heroes. "I wanted to go to France my whole life to hear both Sidney Bechet and [jazz pianist] Bud Powell. Bechet died a few years ago and Powell left for New York when I arrived [he died in 1966]." Woody did, however, happen to meet Samuel Beckett in a café; he later called the meeting the one exciting moment he had during the six months he was in Paris. He also had a cultural picnic, visiting buildings and cathedrals and revisiting the Louvre often, studying its collections as systematically as he had those at the Metropolitan Museum in New York. But not all the great sights were inanimate. "Going into a movie I walked past Bardot!" he wrote. "She was gorgeous. I turned what Charlie Joffe later described as kitchen white and steam started coming out of my ears. Black stockings, blonde braids. What a face! I followed her for a while and finally was cautioned by a gendarme for being a suspicious figure. I wonder if I'll ever meet her and if she could ever love a short man with red hair and my name?"

He did not have to ogle all blond movie stars from afar, however. Woody stayed at the Hotel George V along with several others in the film. One was Peter Sellers, who was married to Britt Ekland. Woody on several occasions had been told he and Sellers looked alike. "It astounds me," he wrote, "because we're not alike [but] Britt said it was weird when I walked into the room where she was reading, for a split second she thought I was her husband and even said, 'Peter?' I posed with him before her and she felt it was strange but finally decided I looked even more like Stan Laurel." (He is also often told that he looks a lot like Alec Guinness.)

As he had been by the writers for *The Colgate Variety Hour* ten years earlier, Woody was more or less adopted by the cast of *Pussycat*. O'Toole came back one day with a sweater he bought for him. The only trouble with it was that O'Toole, who is several sizes larger than Woody, had bought it to fit himself. And besides Capucine, Paula Prentiss took him around town. Still, Woody was, as ever, happy being alone, using free time to work on a play (it eventually became *Don't Drink the Water*) for Max Gordon, the legendary Broadway producer of such hits as *Design for Living, Born Yesterday*, and *My Sister Eileen*. Woody's prosaic loner habits earned him a reputation as an eccentric: He practiced on his clarinet every day unaccompanied in his hotel room; it was rumored he didn't tip the hotel staff because service was included in the price of the room (actually, he is a lavish tipper like his father and one of his heroes: "The only thing Jean-Paul Sartre and I have in common is that we're both overtippers"); and he ate the identical dinner in the same restaurant (La Boccador) every night for six months—the soup du jour, fillet of sole, and crème caramel. (The same neurosis that makes him leery of change and had him stick for months to the same dinner also contributes beneficially to his associations and friendships. Woody is extraordinarily loyal to those he has become close to, and to the artisans and technicians on his film crew who have proved themselves capable. Personally, once he finds something or someone he likes, he is loath to deviate from it or him or her. Artistically, however, he is the reverse: Repetition is avoided, not embraced.)

Woody's "gloom and cynicism" didn't allow him to get involved with the social life around the movie as much as he could have. He didn't like being away from home for so long. He wouldn't eat European meat because he had heard he shouldn't, so Louise Lasser and United Artists were sending him steaks. Plus, he says, "they were mangling my movie—I didn't like that. I didn't like going out every night socializing. So it wasn't a positive experience for me. I felt I was among philistines for the most part."

Even in Europe his services as a comic were in constant demand. He flew to London to do shows for both American and English television and performed at a rally at the Eiffel Tower that Americans Abroad sponsored for President Lyndon Johnson's campaign. "I opened by saying, 'Good evening, ladies and gentlemen, this is my first tower,'" he wrote O'Brien. "I'm one of the few comics who can look at that structure in a movie and say, 'I played that room.'"

(Woody was invited—along with Rudolf Nureyev, Johnny Carson, and Carol Channing, among others—to perform at Johnson's inaugural in 1965 and a few months later to dinner at the White House, an offer he felt he could not refuse even though it was for him alone and not for Louise, whom he was dating. "Now I wouldn't think of going under those circumstances," he says. "Mia was invited to the Reagan White House but they didn't invite me. She turned it down for many reasons but one reason was, you can't do that.

("But they didn't know about Louise and they just sent me an invitation to dinner. I took the shuttle and planned to fly back home that night. I didn't want to fly in a tuxedo, so I changed into mine in the bathroom at the Washington National Airport and stuck my clothes in a locker. I went to the White House and like all dinners that I go to and all party invitations I accept, I was the first one there. About ten minutes later Richard Rodgers came in and he threw his arms around me. I didn't even know him but he knew of me and of course I knew who he was. And he said, 'God, if only our grandparents could see us!' This was Richard Rodgers at the tail end of one of the most illustrious careers and he was so stupefied. And I was thinking the same thing.

("Then famous people started filing in. The next one was Jimmy Durante. When Johnson came down for dinner—they served filet mignon but I was surprised; it tasted like institution food—there was a small military band playing 'Hail to the Chief' or some such thing. I thought, 'That's amazing that this guy gets played to through his meal every night.' It was a wonderful evening. You had a feeling it was right out of *Gone With the Wind*, because here we were slightly South, and because it was a warm night they had opened the garden and hung it with lanterns for dancing. Later, one of the Johnson daughters came over to me. She had read in the newspapers that I had said I was going to the White House for dinner and maybe I should bring some cake or something. She thought it was funny. And then her mother said to me, 'We all thought you wore a wig,' because my hair in those days was silly.

("I so wanted to impress Louise at that time because she was my girlfriend that I asked if I could make a phone call. They showed me into a little private room with a phone. I wanted to say, 'Hi, I'm calling from the White House.' But she wasn't in. It was so annoying.")

The commotion over *Pussycat* brought Woody attention in other areas. Offers to direct a Broadway play, adapt books for films, and act in others poured in—"all legitimate and big projects," he wrote O'Brien. But Jack Rollins's advice was that he refuse anything that was not a script for him or an interesting original he might write. Still, there was one part of his career that disappointed him. Colpix Records had released an album of his nightclub act, and although it made the bestseller charts, Woody initially found the sales mystifyingly low. "I cannot for the life of me understand the failure of my record album to go big," he complained to O'Brien shortly after it was released. "(Did I mention that I have heard that the copy I sent to [English critic] Ken[neth] Tynan delights him and he plays it for all his friends?) It will be issued in London any day now and the advance copies have been greatly appreciated. The reporter from the London *Express* is coming here to interview me this week.

"I should have a greater following than my record sales indicate as I have done worse so far than any other reasonable name comic. Comics less exposed on TV have sold much more (the first [Bob] Newhart album, Mel Brooks, etc.). Comics exposed far more often on TV have also sold more ([Shelley] Berman, Nichols and May, Jonathan [Winters]). More Jewish comics have sold more (Mel Brooks, Shelley Berman). . . . Also Negro comics. . . . I know the album's funny because it's all the stuff I got my start with plus some and when it's played here in London, people love it, so I can't figure it out. My sales have been awful. . . . It's not that I'm too intellectual either because I'm not and besides, Mort Sahl and Nichols and May at their most cerebral wipe out my sales too. The mystery is that audiences laugh at me, my price goes up, my career is moving but no one buys my album???" (His complaints aside, the album finally outsold those of Newhart, Cosby, and Berman that year and was the number five comedy album of 1964. Parody-song writer Allan Sherman's was number one.) "I'm anxious to do another one," he wrote at the end of his next letter to O'Brien, "just to see, is it my voice, the record company, a family curse?" He closed with an arresting observation and a fervent plea: "I have now played two straight weeks of love scenes with Romy Schneider and I'm bruised like it was Sonny Liston. Pray my work remains undiluted and uncut and the film pays off."

Whatever his disappointment over his record sales and the misuse of his work on the film, United Artists, *Pussycat*'s backer and distributor, realized they had a hot property in Woody and strove to keep him happy. They bought him a clarinet to keep him relaxed during shooting, which he considered a nice gesture but a lousy instrument, and piled his room with Hershey bars, of which he was then a constant eater; "literally hundreds lie about my room," he wrote O'Brien. "[And] I have been sent salamis from friends in the U.S. They decorate the French antique door knobs of my room hanging down."

However nice the United Artists executives were to Woody, he knew they were not going to back him in his arguments with Feldman, which grew worse as filming went on. The heart of his trouble with Feldman was the same as it was with television: He didn't like what people were doing to his material—one of the reasons he became a performer. Now, having finally broken through as a comedian, he was back in the quagmire he had pulled himself out of four years earlier and he resented it. But resent it as he might, he was powerless to change his circumstances. He was not a film star, he was not a proven film writer, he had never directed anything, nor had he produced anything. The fact that he quite probably could have made a better film was immaterial. What mattered was that he was, as he said, "a flea compared to the others. They were at the zenith of their popularity and I was a total nonentity." And while fleas can bite and irritate, eventually they get squashed.

For a while, Feldman was able to keep Woody writing good material by telling him to write something for himself; then he would often give the scene to Sellers or O'Toole. But that bothered Woody less than Feldman's overproduction. "Everything they did was big and jazzy," Woody said afterward. "They couldn't do anything small."

The plot of *What's New, Pussycat?* runs something like this: A psychiatrist named Fritz Fassbinder (Peter Sellers), whose marriage is in trouble, has a patient named Michael James (Peter O'Toole), the features editor of a fashion magazine, who wants only to be faithful to and to marry Carol Werner (Romy Schneider), a Berlitz teacher, who is his jealous, but patient fiancée of many years and to whom he has been faithless with most of the women in Europe. Three luscious and seductive ones he has somehow missed—named Renée, Liz, and Rita (Capucine, Paula Prentiss, and Ursula Andress)—work independently to gain his favor. With the help of weakness of the flesh and such quirks of fate as a stalled elevator and a parachute being blown off course so that its passenger lands in a moving car, they succeed, but only momentarily. In the end, love triumphs and the marriage takes place.

There are two subplots. One involves Fassbinder's obsession with trying to do but once what James cannot help but do and the constant pre-coitus interruptus by his Wagnerian wife, "the creature that ate Europe." The other details the Woody Allen-ish stumblings of Victor Shakapopolis (Woody), whose love life appears terminal before it has even begun. The film featured an ad-libbed cameo role by Richard Burton, who had just filmed *Becket* with O'Toole; he walks up to him in a bar and says, "Don't you know me from someplace?" Woody was told of the new scene after it was filmed. "It was so cute, you want to vomit," he says. "They're both great actors but the problem was people thinking garbage was funny."

The pace is breakneck: Third persons stumbling into harmless interludes make them Compromising Situations; jealous wives chase wayward husbands; jealous husbands chase wayward wives; jealous lovers chase jealous lovers; would-be wayward husbands/wives/lovers are caught before the fact, almost always without the élan this sort of farce requires. There are chase scenes through apartments and streets; interrupted suicides (Sellers wraps himself in a Norwegian flag and prepares to float into the Seine in a rowboat and immolate himself Viking-funeral style—the scene got the film banned in Norway, where the Viking funeral lobby apparently packs a lot of clout); more chase scenes down country roads and through hotel rooms; a penultimate scene that gathers the whole cast at a country inn where they all run down corridors and hide in closets, cedar chests, laundry hampers, and under beds. The final chase scene is on a go-cart track. (One imagines Georges Feydeau turning over in his armoire.)

"It's like the Milton Berle shows without his genius, the way Feldman produced it," Woody said afterward. Instead of showing an ordinary psychiatrist's house and a conventional psychiatrist's marital problems, the opening scene shows a strange castlelike art nouveau house. Seen from afar, two small figures chase each other around. Shouts are heard; bodies appear at windows, on balconies, in turrets; the camera moves to Sellers in a pageboy wig and red velvet Little Lord Fauntleroy suit having at it with his gargantuan wife. The interior of the elevator in which O'Toole and Capucine are trapped is more splendidly decorated than a presidential suite. The jumpsuit Ursula Andress wears when she parachutes into O'Toole's car is made of snakeskin.

In a scene where Schneider and O'Toole declare their mutual love in dialogue purposely out of a bad romantic movie, Woody's script called for a small "Author's Message" to flash on and off at the bottom of the screen. Feldman argued that it was unnecessary; Woody told him that without it, it would just be a dull, flat love scene. In this instance, Woody finally prevailed, but it was a Pyrrhic victory. Instead of small letters, Feldman had it done in the rococo title design of the picture, and so it is overfancy. But Woody conceded that "the film wasn't factory-made. It wasn't Doris Day."

However overproduced it is, *Pussycat* is funny to many people and it made the point Feldman was gambling on. "There's a great new audience today," he said in the hyperbolic style of a natural promoter. "The young adults of the world who think young, do things the young way, and live in a young manner. I make my films for a particular audience. Disney films like *Mary Poppins* are directed specifically to the overall family audience. My films are made for a more specific contemporary audience. They're directed toward the same people you'll find at the baseball and football games, the ones who throng the discotheques, who wear mad fashions and keep beat to a different drummer." Fortunately for him, Feldman never had to make his living on his words, but his ideas found their audience.

And that audience also found a new star in Woody Allen, even if he didn't feel like a star when the film was being made. If his lines weren't always given to Sellers or O'Toole, the camera was virtually always on them. When Sellers is about to commit suicide, Woody comes down to the quay and, without paying attention to him, sets up a picnic for one, complete with champagne. His trip to Valhalla interrupted, Sellers angrily asks Woody what he's doing there. Woody explains that he always comes there on his birthday (it was, coincidentally, his twenty-ninth birthday the day they filmed it, a freezing December 1). Sellers does a little slapstick and then gives up the suicide. But an even funnier scene between the two of them was passed by in favor of getting all the possible footage of Sellers. Woody "kept doing the best I could. Not that I could have done better than him, he was very strong and good. But I could have contributed something."

Woody's hostility grew. "One night at rushes I told Feldman to fuck off. The Feldman contingent was there and other foreign people were hanging around; I don't know who they were: English people, French people, international money. They would be watching my gags, guys who had no relation in the world to film, and saying, 'Oh, I don't think that's funny,' or 'I think what should happen is he should be more crazy in that scene.' It's pretty hard to see rushes anyway. You work hard all day, and you're hungry, then you see your face on the screen at seven o'clock at night and you're not as funny as you thought you were. It was a nightmarish experience in many ways. I kept making nasty remarks to the point where Feldman spoke to Charlie Joffe and said, 'Can't you get your guy to stop digging me like that? It's hurting my feelings.' "

"If Woody's hurting your feelings, you're crucifying him," Joffe told Feldman. "You're being influenced by a bunch of people who don't know anything about comedy."

"Feldman was always an unruffled gentleman," Woody says of the episode. "I was beneath disdain. My outburst just slid right off him. Probably he'd been cursed out so often that it was not a bothersome moment to him."

Finally, about halfway through shooting, Woody and Joffe had had enough. Joffe told Feldman that Woody was through making changes and that if Feldman wanted he could take Woody's name off as screenwriter. Subsequent changes were made by practically everyone connected with the film.

For all their arguments, Woody feels Feldman "liked me and treated me well. He was a genius," or at least a certain kind of genius who could get films made. "I've seen him on one phone to Peter Sellers, on a second phone to United Artists, and on a third to the Italian government, saying, 'I can get Peter Sellers, maybe, to do this picture,' then picking up the phone to United Artists and telling them, 'I've got to have another two hundred thousand dollars to get Peter Sellers,' and the Italian government saying, 'You can shoot the picture but you have to have this certain deal,' and then Sellers saying, 'I won't work in Italy,' and it went on and on. He was a big-time charming con man and I never trusted him on anything for a second. He was just an out-and-out, hundred-times-over proven liar to me. I worked with him knowing that. I wish he were alive, though; not just because I wish he were alive, but I'd love him to see I was able to get into my own films. He started me and I think he would like them."

Woody was not the only one to get his start from Feldman, or the only novice he smothered. He hired a truckload of young, talented, and innovative unknowns for *Pussycat*: Clive Donner, who had just directed *Nothing But the Best* and *The Caretaker* but whose experience was mainly in English TV; Burt Bacharach, who wrote the title song, and Tom Jones, who sang it; Mia Fonssagrives and Vicky Tiel, two nineteen-year-old designers fresh out of design school in the United States, who were all the rage in Paris; and Dick Williams, who did the titles. Yet while Feldman had a tremendous flair for seeking out and gambling on new talent, he did not have the sense to give his people their heads. That Woody in the end was credited as the sole writer was a rarity for Feldman, who, like many producers, thought nothing of taking the work of three—or six—writers and blending it together.

"I think Charlie sensed that there was a certain kind of comedy I knew and that it was hard to find other people to do it," is Woody's assessment of why, despite their bickering, Feldman never brought another writer in.

What's New, Pussycat? opened in June 1965 to generally unenthusiastic, even hostile, reviews. Bosley Crowther, the *New York Times* critic, wrote:

Woody Allen, the nightclub comedian, is formally charged with the minor offense of having written what is alleged to be the screenplay of *What's New, Pussycat?* But Mr. Allen can deny it, if he wants to, and he is bound to be believed. He can simply state that no one in his right mind could have written this excuse for a script. . . . The idea is neurotic and unwholesome, it lacks wit, and the actors slamming through it are not true humorists.

Kate Cameron in the New York *Daily News* agreed, saying the film was "wholly lacking in good taste." But Andrew Sarris of *The Village Voice* called it "the best picture of the year thus far, and by far the funniest comedy."

Pussycat was booked into two New York theaters for a six-week run, but audiences loved the film and word of mouth kept them coming and packing the houses. Feldman's untapped audience had found its faucet and the $17 million that poured in established a record for a comedy.

More surprising than the money was the attention Woody was given. People who loved the movie were happy to give him credit for the script, even though he would rather have not accepted it. People who hated it were, like Crowther, ready to forgive and forget; they still liked him. Woody was invited onto talk shows and featured in newspaper and magazine stories. In part because he was in America and the major stars were not, he received more exposure and publicity than anyone else connected with the film, and he became its chief pitchman. "I thought the best thing about it was the title song," he said once on *The Tonight Show*, "but it's too bad that they didn't let me do it because I wrote a terrific song." Whereupon he sang over and over, to his own horrible melody, "What's new, Pussycat? What's new, Pussycat? What's new, Pussycat?"—an act funny in the performance if not in the reading.

About his contribution to the film, Woody says, "I was not in a position to tell the public, 'It's not my fault, this is not what I would make as a picture.' It was the whole approach to filmmaking that I hate and I've since demonstrated that it isn't my kind of film. But I've never had anything as profitable. *Pussycat* was just born to work. There was no way they could screw it up; try as they might, they couldn't. It was one of those things where the chemicals accidentally flow right."

Woody plugged the film on the good advice of Joffe, who felt that no matter what happened, the movie was an enormous success and it was self-serving to be associated with it. And in the end, it was. It was also a source of new material for his stand-up act. Of his success, he said in an interview with John S. Wilson of *The New York Times*, "I fail with a better class of women now, but my problems are the same. I'm just as ashamed to do everything. I'm just as afraid of getting robbed, beaten, or attacked."

One woman of good class he didn't fail with was Louise Lasser. On February 2, 1966, he gave his parents, who adored Louise, a couple of hours' notice of the event but not an invitation to the marriage ceremony performed that evening by a New York State Supreme Court justice in the Lasser home at 155 East Fiftieth Street. Five people were there, not counting the principals: Louise's parents, plus Mickey Rose and his wife, Judy, and Jean Doumanian, who doubled as witnesses. That night—there was a huge snowstorm—Woody did two shows at the Royal Box at the Americana Hotel, where he was in the middle of an engagement (their honeymoon was at the Plaza Hotel, where he was living between apartments). Her parents' wedding present to them was a projector so they could watch movies at home.

Woody's parents were more informed about the wedding than most of Woody's and Louise's friends. Woody was then creating dialogue to accompany the action of a Japanese James Bond–type movie entitled *Kizino Kizi*. Others involved in the project were Mickey Rose, Len Maxwell, and Frank Buxton, as well as Louise. Characters had such names as Phil Moskowitz, Lovable Rogue; the Cobra Man; and Wing Fat. Maxwell created voices for the last two plus some others. The plot they made up revolved around the hunt for an egg-salad recipe and the finished product was *What's Up, Tiger Lily?* On the morning of February 3, Maxwell and the others read in the gossip columns that Woody and Louise had married the day before. They arrived as usual at 9 a.m. at the studio that producer Henry Saperstein had rented, but Woody and Louise were not there. After a while, Woody arrived alone to predictable commotion from his friends. Maxwell asked where Louise was.

"Maxwell," he says Woody told him, "she is probably on the way to my bank with a fucking wheelbarrow."

"Louise was so funny," Maxwell adds. "She bit his fingernails. She saved him a lot of work. Actually, though, I don't think he said 'fucking.' He once had a line that went: 'I met my ex-wife in a restaurant and, being a roué, I wafted gingerly over to her and said, "How about going back and making love one more time?" And she said, "Over my dead body." And I said, "I don't know why not. That's the way we always used to do it." ' Anybody who can write 'I wafted gingerly over to her' doesn't need to say 'fucking.' "

None of *Tiger Lily* was scripted out. Before moving to a studio to do the voice-overs, Woody rented a room at the Stanhope Hotel on Fifth Avenue, set up a projector, and ran the film several times. Everyone just said whatever came into their minds as the scenes played. "If Woody liked it, he put it in," Maxwell says. "How I knew things were funny is that Woody would roar. I never knew anyone who liked to laugh as much as Woody, including at the stuff he wrote himself."

Woody did not hesitate to argue with Saperstein when he tried— and eventually succeeded—to make them finish the film before Woody felt it was done. He never hesitates when it comes to defending his work. But even correcting a stranger in a restaurant was then and is now another matter. One day Woody and Louise and Maxwell and two others went to Lindy's for lunch. Woody ordered scrambled eggs and bacon. What the waitress brought was eggs sunnyside up and ham. But he refused to say anything about it, and ate them rather than complain.

Of Woody's marriage to Louise, Dick Cavett said some years ago that they "have always gotten along well; solemnizing it didn't seem to make much difference." They moved into a six-large-room duplex apartment in a brownstone on East Seventy-ninth Street (Cavett lives there now) and lived, in Louise's words, "like two kids in a castle. We left all the decisions about the house to the housekeeper." One room had an antique billiard table in it that Woody had found upstate near Jack and Jane Rollins's country place for a couple of hundred dollars; it took up so much of the room that a short cue was needed to make shots from one side. Another room was wood-paneled and, as Cavett describes it, "looked like the Athenaeum Club" except that it was never furnished. At one point it held a jukebox and an electric organ and a pile of cartons. "You had a sense of," Cavett said, " 'Oh, you haven't moved in yet.' It was one of the handsomest closets I've seen. The rest of the house was nicely decorated." Part of the decoration was a large collection of magic paraphernalia.

What Woody collected professionally in the months after *Pussycat*'s release was opportunities to work: He was paid $66,000 to do *Tiger Lily*; David Merrick agreed to produce his play *Don't Drink the Water* on Broadway; ABC asked him to do a TV special; movie roles were offered, and so were film scripts to write. One was to turn *Don Quixote, U.S.A.*, a satirical book by Richard Powell about a naïve American Peace Corpsman in a Caribbean country ruled by a dictator, into a comedy for Robert Morse. The film was to be produced by Metro-Goldwyn-Mayer, who also negotiated with Woody for him to be the director. Woody called in Mickey Rose and in two weeks they wrote about forty pages at Woody's apartment. They had such fun writing the broad jokes that made up the story they tentatively called *El Weirdo* that they decided to show it to Morse and his producer to see if they liked it. They didn't. Eventually it became *Bananas* but for the time being it was put away. Woody and Mickey then began work on *Take the Money and Run*. Mickey, who had been writing for *The Tonight Show* but was recently fired (in the tradition of writers for the show, he would be hired and fired many more times), went each day to the Plaza Hotel, where Woody was staying (he and Louise were not yet married) while his apartment was being renovated. Woody already had the story in narrative form, and in three weeks the two of them turned it into a script, Woody typing away as they worked out the jokes.

"There was outright laughter sometimes as we worked," Rose remembers. "Those silly jokes when we were describing Virgil Stark-well's gang: Wanted for killing, and dancing with his mailman."

Then of all the jobs available to him, Woody took what might seem an odd one: He accepted Feldman's offer to appear in a James Bond spoof called *Casino Royale*, and he flew off to London in the early spring of 1966 for what was supposed to be six weeks of work. In the end he and Charlie Joffe were there six months, during which time they lived well on their expense money and played a lot of poker with other show-business people in town, and Woody enriched his traditional jazz record collection with albums impossible to find in the United States. He also had tea with the dean of Westminster Abbey, a fan who had both his record albums and "thinks I'm a riot," Woody wrote to Richard O'Brien:

> *Casino* is a madhouse. I haven't begun filming yet but saw the sets for my scenes. They are the height of bad pop art expensive vulgarity. Saw rushes and am dubious to put it mildly, but probably film will coin a mint. (Not money, just a single peppermint.) I play the villain (okay to give that out) and also James Bond's bastard nephew (not all right to give that out) and my part changes every

day as new stars fall in. [His part included being billed as the tallest dwarf in the world.]

I bought some jazz records over here for Sophia Loren because she's interested and I wanted to get her on to something good. Like the sofa. Have not spoken with Julie Christie yet regarding a book someone proposed would make a good film for her and me. Doubt if she'd be interested but you never know. A chance to play opposite me comes once in a lifetime. . . .

Bought a record player and am inundated with discs purchased to sublimate my sexual drive. Doing a lot of gambling for some reason. I'm the only man in the world who gets dealt a five card poker hand with no two suits the same. Having a very big, fine English tailor make me some corduroy suits, speaking of suits, and it's funny because he's used to working only on fine tweeds. Still, should he put a clothes-pin on his nose when he measures me? Of course, I haven't changed my pants, jacket, or sweater since I got here. I would like it emphasized and made quite clear that I am not a writer of *Casino*. I'm adding a few ad-lib jokes to my own part but that's all. In fact (off the record) we demanded a letter saying my name cannot appear on screen as writer. This because everyone who contributed a comma is demanding his name *on* the film and the writers' list looks like Terry Southern, Ben Hecht, Michael Sayers, Frank Buxton, Mickey Rose, Peter Sellers, Val Guest, Wolf Mankowitz, etc. [Billy Wilder, John Huston, and Joseph Heller were among the others who shared the screenplay credit.] . . .

Weather is lousy [he concluded in another letter]. I'm working on material for myself. Charlie is working on girls for himself. Neither of us has made much progress but of the two, his stuff is funnier.

> Regards to the entire office—
> That wolf in sheep's clothing—
>
> Woody Allen

Along the line, he was invited to a benefit where he was introduced to Queen Elizabeth. Unsure of what to say, he settled on "How do you do? Are you enjoying your power?" A photo of the occasion shows him in white tie and tails flanked by Raquel Welch and Ursula Andress, who is shaking the Queen's hand. "The girls look great, but I look like a magician," he said of it some years later. The highlight of the period for Woody seems to have been the purchase in June 1966 of the "merely beautiful" Emil Nolde watercolor with his poker winnings as a surprise for Louise. "He has long been a favorite of mine [he wrote to O'Brien] and they exhibited him with some Klees this week. The Klees were too expensive but I did barely manage to scrape together the dough to pick up what I felt was one of the more charming Noldes. His watercolors at this particular exhibit were better than his oils." But that was about all that made him happy. He had learned well Jack Rollins's lesson about the importance of the person emerging through the character and that good writing alone wasn't enough to make a comedian come through. Sadly for him, the makers of *Casino* hadn't:

I am still waiting to shoot and will begin finally tomorrow [he wrote O'Brien]. I think the film stinks as does my role. There is no involvement or story or importance to any of it. It is silly like an old Berle sketch as opposed to a fine Nichols and May sketch. There is no seriousness or maturity of approach. It is unfunny burlesque. All I can hope for is to get some ad-lib laughs and try and benefit from the exposure which will probably outdo my Smirnoff ads in sheer impact if such a thing is possible. I think it's impossible to "score" in a film unless the audience is involved in one's role. Julie Christie could score in *Darling* or [Alan] Arkin in [*The*] *Russians* [*Are Coming, The Russians Are Coming*] or [Steve] McQueen in *The Great Escape* because not only did they do fine jobs but because the audience cared about the fictional characters they were portraying and their predicaments within the tale. . . . The audience would have responded emotionally well to many performers in those good roles. Add to that, that in each case the above performances were also superb. In contrast, I think that anyone playing my role in *Casino Royale* has nothing going for him. The audience couldn't care less and the part lives and dies joke by joke. The jokes, incidentally, are basically the dying kind. In my own film *Take the Money*, when I set up a situation like [Virgil's] breaking from prison and not being told the break had been called off, or running chained together with six convicts, I've set up a strong enough comic situation for it to actually work on laughs alone. But those are hard to come by. In *Casino* it's like a bad fashion show and they could just as well have Bob Hope emcee it as me.

In the fifteen years since he had begun to write professionally, Woody progressed chromatically up an inverted pyramid: first jokes for newspaper columnists, then jokes for radio personalities; sketches for television performers, then routines for comics. It was a step-by-step, one-at-a-time progression. Now suddenly he was doing almost everything simultaneously: performing his own routines; doing his own TV specials; writing films for others; acting in films he'd written. He was also a contributor to *The New Yorker*, the showcase magazine for virtually every significant American writer of humor in the past sixty years, and a nearly produced Broadway playwright.

His first *New Yorker* piece, published in 1966, was "The Gossage-Vardebedian Papers," a series of increasingly hostile letters between two men playing a game of chess by mail—although, judging by the positions of the pieces on each man's board, not the same game—both of whom are convinced that the other is deranged. In the polite way of the magazine, the editors asked if Woody was willing to rewrite the ending. "Willing" understated his readiness. "I would have been willing to turn the ending into an aquafoil," he said a few years afterward, so eager was he to appear in the magazine. His original ending no longer exists, but in light of the new one he gave them, it hardly matters:

Gossage:
Bishop to queen five. Checkmate.
Sorry the competition proved too much for you, but if it's any consolation, several local chess masters have, upon observing my technique, flipped out. Should you want a rematch, I suggest we try Scrabble, a relatively new interest of mine, and one that I might conceivably not run away with so easily.
Vardebedian

Vardebedian:
Rook to knight eight. Checkmate.
Rather than torment you with the further details of my mate, as I believe you are basically a decent man (one day, some form of therapy will bear me out), I accept your invitation to Scrabble

in good spirits. Get out your set. Since you played white in chess and thereby enjoyed the advantage of the first move (had I known your limitations, I would have spotted you more), I shall make the first play. The seven letters I have just turned up are O, A, E, J, N, R, and Z—an unpromising jumble that should guarantee, even to the most suspicious, the integrity of my draw. Fortunately, however, an extensive vocabulary, coupled with a penchant for esoterica, has enabled me to bring etymological order out of what, to one less literate, might seem a mishmash. My first word is "ZANJERO." Look it up. Now lay it out, horizontally, the E resting on the center square. Count carefully, not overlooking the double word score for an opening move and the fifty-point bonus for my use of all seven letters. The score is now 116–0.

Your move.

Gossage

S. J. Perelman was the master of insulting letter exchanges and his influence on Woody is evident. Of all the writers of humorous prose, Perelman's is by far the most distinctive and the most often imitated. (But everyone learns from someone. Perelman once said that some of the models for his style were Stephen Leacock, George Ade, Ring Lardner, and H. L. Mencken.) His prose is a dense thicket of jokes on the way to jokes on the way to sentences on the way to paragraphs that are funny. He made an art of names. In one sentence there are "Gossip Gabrilowitsch, the Polish pianist; Downey Couch, the Irish tenor; Frank Falkovsky, the Jewish prowler; and myself, Clay Modeling." There were Urban Sprawl, the architect, and Candide Yam, the Chinese secretary; Howells & Imprecation, lawyers, and Moe Juste, the French grammarian. The rococo style—the names; the sentence structure; the esoteric, even exotic, vocabulary; the leads that have nothing to do with the story for the first several paragraphs—is his and his alone.

"Perelman is so utterly unique and complex," Woody has said. "You can't be influenced a little by him. You have to go so deeply that it shows all over the place. You can't write something that's a little Perelmanesque, just as you can't play a little bit like Erroll Garner. There are so many points that are recognizable." Woody's earliest stories were pure Perelman, and what he did to pull away from Perelman's influence was to simplify his style—and thereby write more like Robert Benchley. The works of both evoke outright laughter, but where Perelman is hilarious in a complex way, Benchley is broad and simple;

whereas Perelman is a punch in the eye, Benchley is a soufflé (in the introduction to one of his books, Benchley is called "the world's least embittered satirist"). In the most general way, Perelman is dyspeptic, specific, and personal (one collection of his pieces is entitled *The Rising Gorge*; a title to one story is "Garnish Your Face with Parsley and Serve"), while Benchley and Woody are bemused, generic, and impersonal. (Benchley wrote "Opera Synopses: Some Sample Outlines of Grand Opera Plots for Home Study"; Woody, "A Guide to Some of the Lesser Ballets.")

Comical names are an integral part of a comic story, and Woody's choices for characters, he says, were modeled more after Benchley than Perelman (with Perelman and Benchley, and to a lesser degree Woody, even a slight knowledge of Yiddish adds to their funniness). The cast of "Opera Synopses" includes Strudel, God of Rain; Schmalz, God of Light Drizzle; Immerglück, Goddess of the Six Primary Colors; and Ludwig Das Eiweiss, the Knight of the Iron Duck. Benchley created Dickensian figures (George, Lillian, and Baby Lester Gummidge); tradesmen (Abbamonte and Frinchini, shoe repairers); and corporations (the Frivolity Mitten Co.). Woody has invented Europeans (Fears Hoffnung, Horst Wasserman, and Gunther Eisenbud); mafiosi (Thomas "the Butcher" Covello, Albert "the Logical Positivist" Corillo, Little Petey "Big Petey" Ross, and Kid Lipsky); the chess masters Gossage and Vardebedian; and the intrepid Kaiser Lupowitz, a private eye who could have been named by Perelman. There is a chorus of characters in his play *God* inspired, no doubt, by the *Physicians' Desk Reference*—Trichinosis, Hepatitis, and Diabetes; and Everywriter's publisher: Venal and Sons.

Prose writing is akin to musical composition in the importance of balance and harmony, of style—what E. B. White referred to as "the sound [a writer's] words make on paper." Careful phraseology and the juxtaposition of words make the difference between a passage that reads like a broad river gently flowing or a child skipping left and right, left and right, up the block, and one that seems like railway cars that slam-slam and jerk when the engine starts too fast and make a lot of noise. Jokes are akin to poetry in that the balance must be closer than in prose; the canvas is less broad and one wrong word—even one wrong syllable—can ruin the laugh. (In "Peter Quince at the Clavier," Wallace Stevens took White one step further: "Music is feeling, then, not sound.")

"In jokes, in actual one-liners, there's something succinct," Woody said one day. "In a very compressed way, you express a thought or feeling and it's dependent on balancing the words. Now, you don't do this consciously. For example"—he paused and mumbled to himself, thinking of a line—" 'It's not that I'm afraid of dying, I just don't want to be there when it happens.' In a compressed way it expresses something. If you use one word more or less it's not as good. Maybe if I experimented I could find a better way to do it, but basically that seemed the right way when I thought of it. You do that instinctively; you don't count it out, or anything like that. This is what poets do. They're not working their meters by the numbers, they're feeling."

Woody has gone through several periods of intensive poetry reading over the past twenty years. Considering his ability to capture American culture, it is not surprising that he is drawn to poets with a particularly American idiom, such as Carl Sandburg and Walt Whitman; William Carlos Williams and Robert Frost; Emily Dickinson and E. E. Cummings. ("I like that stuff that oozes American images and speech; it always sounds very pretty to me.") He also likes T. S. Eliot, whom he calls "the great city poet." William Butler Yeats he finds simply "astonishing." Woody was in his thirties, however, before he took poetry seriously. It was after he developed an appreciation for modern art and he was able to use one to understand the other.

"Years ago, I thought modern art is like you give a guy a piece of paper or a canvas and he slops paint on it and says, 'Yeah, that's what de Kooning's doing and Kandinsky's doing. I could do ten of these a day.' He doesn't get it. You want to say to him, 'That's not what they're doing. You're just splotching paint, but they're not.' That's how I was with poetry. The more I study and learn about it, the greater still I find Yeats. He handles the language like Shakespeare. I think that had I been better educated, I could write poetry, because a writer of comedy has some of that equipment to begin with. You're dealing with nuance and meter and ear, and one syllable off in something I write in prose ruins the laugh. Sometimes an editor will correct something in a story I've written and I'll say, 'Can't you see that if you add just that one syllable, the whole joke is ruined?' "

A succession of his syllables where no joke is ruined: "It began one day last January when I was standing in McGinnis' Bar on Broadway, engulfing a slab of the world's richest cheesecake and suffering the guilty, cholesterolish hallucination that I could hear my aorta congealing into a hockey puck. Standing next to me was a nerve-shattering blonde, who waxed and waned under a black chemise with enough provocation to induce lycanthropy in a Boy Scout."

Except "like everybody else, I would have liked to have written the Russian novels," Woody has no envy of other writers: "I've never thought of wanting to have written something else." He alternates Benchley and Perelman as his favorite comic writer and enjoys reading others he finds naturally funny: novelist Peter DeVries and essayists Russell Baker, Art Buchwald, and Fran Lebowitz; he is, he says, amazed at how the essayists especially can be so funny so often. Of contemporary writers, however, he puts Saul Bellow "at the very top of achievement in terms of comic writing. In *Humboldt's Gift*, for instance, the wit is so cascading and so wonderful, it reminds me of the feeling I got when I first saw Mort Sahl: that endless invention of great wit and great comic notions one after the other."

Between 1966 and 1980, Woody published more than fifty comic pieces, mostly in *The New Yorker*, although a handful appeared in *The Kenyon Review* and other magazines. They parodied a broad range of subjects. A random but representative sample: "Notes from the Overfed (after reading Dostoevski and the new *Weight Watchers* magazine on the same plane trip)"; "Selections from the Allen Notebooks" ("Should I marry W? Not if she won't tell me the other letters in her name"); "The Discovery and Use of the Fake Ink Blot"; "A Look at Organized Crime" ("The Cosa Nostra is structured like any government or large corporation—or group of gangsters, for that matter. At the top is the *capo di tutti capi*, or boss of all bosses. Meetings are held at his house, and he is responsible for supplying cold cuts and ice cubes. Failure to do so means instant death. [Death, incidentally, is one of the worst things that can happen to a Cosa Nostra member, and many prefer simply to pay a fine]").

"If the Impressionists Had Been Dentists (A Fantasy Exploring the Transposition of Temperament)" is a series of letters from Vincent van Gogh to his brother. It begins:

Dear Theo,

Will life ever treat me decently? I am wracked by despair! My head is pounding! Mrs. Sol Schwimmer is suing me because I made her bridge as I felt it and not to fit her ridiculous mouth! That's right! I can't work to order like a common tradesman! I decided her bridge should be enormous and billowing, with wild, explosive teeth flaring up in every direction like fire! Now she is upset because it won't fit in her mouth! She is so bourgeois and stupid, I want to smash her! I tried forcing the false plate in but it sticks out like a star burst chandelier. Still, I find it beautiful. She claims she can't chew! What do I care whether she can chew or not! Theo, I can't go on like this much longer! I asked Cézanne if he would share an office with me, but he is old and infirm and unable to hold the instruments and they must be tied to his wrists but then he lacks accuracy and once inside a mouth, he knocks out more teeth than he saves. What to do?

Vincent

A story entitled "The Early Essays" updates a popular seventeenth-century literary form, with a note of introduction fit for a college textbook:

Following are a few of the early essays of Woody Allen. There are no late essays, because he ran out of observations. Perhaps as Allen grows older, he will understand more of life and set it down, and then retire to his bedroom and remain there indefinitely. Like the essays of Bacon, Allen's are brief and full of practical wisdom, although space does not permit the inclusion of his most profound statement, "Looking at the Bright Side."

On Seeing a Tree in Summer

Of all the wonders of nature, a tree in summer is perhaps the most remarkable, with the possible exception of a moose singing "Embraceable You" in spats. Consider the leaves, so green and leafy (if not, something is wrong). Behold how the branches reach up to heaven as if to say, "Though I am only a branch, still I would love to collect Social Security."

During the last half of the 1960s, Woody turned out dozens of pieces for *The New Yorker*. On average, each took seven or eight days to write. Often the idea came while he was filming, so he would work three or four weekends on it, usually rising before 8 a.m. (if only from the habit of needing to be up early during shooting). He likes to write and finds the chance to spend a day at home doing it a treat: "It's the most pleasurable part even of a film," he says, adding, "Tennessee

Williams said, 'It's a pain in the neck to put plays on. It would be nice to just write them and throw them in a drawer.' That's how I feel."

An idea may take years to mature, however, and it is often the idea rather than the finished piece that is stuck in a drawer. Woody tried ten times over a period of seven years to work out "Fabrizio's Criticism and Response," a restaurant review with angry letters of criticism from readers in the manner of a particularly high-minded academic journal, before one day it fell together for him. Another story idea that took years to jell before it was quickly written is "The Kugelmass Episode." In it, a college professor, bored with his second wife, desirous of an exciting affair, is told by the Great Persky, a magician, that "you can meet any woman created by the world's best writers." He picks Emma Bovary and is transported via Persky's wondrous but cheap-looking, badly lacquered Chinese cabinet to Yonville, where she greets him invitingly "in the same fine English translation as in the paperback" and says, "I've always dreamed that some mysterious stranger would appear and rescue me from the monotony of this crass rural existence." The affair deepens as Kugelmass goes back and forth in time (always returning to chapters where there is no competition from other men) so as, in one instance, not to miss meeting his wife at Bloomingdale's. Meanwhile, "students in various classrooms across the country were saying to their teachers, 'Who is this character on page 100? A bald Jew is kissing Madame Bovary?' " " 'I cannot get my mind around this,' a Stanford professor said" when Persky brings Emma to New York. " 'First a strange character named Kugelmass, and now she's gone from the book. Well, I guess the mark of a classic is that you can read it a thousand times and always find something new.' " The story ends unhappily for the lovers, as all relationships based on unrealistic expectations must, and particularly sadly for poor Kugelmass. Hoping for better luck with the Monkey in *Portnoy's Complaint*, he steps into Persky's cabinet, which bursts into flames while transporting him. Rather than *Portnoy's Complaint*, Kugelmass is instead projected into *Remedial Spanish*, where he is left "running for his life over a barren, rocky terrain as the word *tener* ('to have')—a large and hairy irregular verb—raced after him on its spindly legs."

Woody writes his prose pieces in a tiny and meticulous hand on a legal pad while lying on his bed, the pencil and his nose pressed to the pad as he puts words in, takes words out, and rearranges what he's written with a series of arrows, cross-outs, and margin notes. Once in a while he'll laugh over a line as it comes to him "because it's a surprise to me as it emerges," and think, "Wait until people read this, it's so funny"—and often that is the line his editors don't think quite comes off and is cut from the piece. Every couple of hours he takes a break to practice on his clarinet or go for a walk and then returns to work. While the stretches of work and breaks are similar to how he writes a screenplay, writing dialogue and writing prose are distinctly different to him.

"Every word is meaningful in prose," he says. "When you're writing dialogue, you could almost say it, act it out, and then quickly get it down on a typewriter. If I act it differently the next minute, I just put another sentence down. In most cases it will be just as good because what's interesting in a film is behavior and words don't mean as much. So I can go into a film with a scene I have written for, say, Diane Keaton or for Mia, and we can look at it and completely change it as long as we get the sense of behavior." (His outlines for a movie rarely fill a single page. "I don't have to write it down after I've thought of it. I write 'Alvy meets Annie. Romantic flashback to when they met.' I'll write eight of those and by the time I get to the ninth, I'll have lost interest because I know it so well.")

The key to Woody's creativity is his intense discipline. He refuses to be ensnared by the traps that many writers fall into, which "turn out to be an excuse not to do the unpleasant thing of getting up in the morning and being alone all day." He constantly sets himself a problem to work on and incorporates a change in venue if he is stuck. "Any momentary change stimulates a fresh burst of energy," he says, so if he's working badly in one room, he goes into another. After Abe Burrows told him that Robert Sherwood walked the streets, writing in his mind and speaking the lines as they came to him, that was a favorite aid for Woody until he started to be recognized so often it broke his concentration. Now he paces back and forth on the terrace that sweeps around his apartment, although even there he is recognized. Producer Robert Greenhut was in Central Park one time and looked up to see him going to and fro with his head bowed. Worried that something was wrong, he called Woody on the phone to be sure he was okay.

The shower has turned out to be one of his most useful thinking spots; it is certainly a place one can expect not to be interrupted. It is particularly good in cold weather. "This sounds silly," he says, "but I'll be working and I'll want to get into the shower for a creative stint. So

I'll take off some of my clothes and toast myself an English muffin and give myself a little chill and then I can't wait to get in the shower. I'll stand there in the steaming water for thirty or forty minutes, just plotting a story and thinking out ideas. Then I dry myself and flop on the bed and think there."

Another help is for him to hear himself say the problem aloud. "It takes it out of the realm of fantasy, it becomes concrete. I'll call Mia and talk to her about the problems. Now, there's no way she can solve them because she doesn't have the faintest knowledge of what I've been thinking for the past several days. But hearing myself say it is a big help. I just have to be wary of the little Sartrean trap where I've already made up my mind and I'm presenting the problem in a way to get her to agree with me."

He credits Danny Simon with teaching him that "writing doesn't come easy. I learned to get at it early in the morning and work at it and rewrite and rethink and tear up my stuff and write it again. I was brought up in a hard-line approach—you never wait for inspiration, you have to do it and force it until you get it right. I think it's been proved a million times from amateur filmmakers to Buñuel that if you have a good script and you shoot it in a poor way, you can still have a movie that works. Whereas if you have bad material, you can shoot the eyes out of it and most of the time, no matter what style you bring to it, it doesn't work."

Of the early *New Yorker* casuals, each was different, of course, but all were somewhat the same in that they were short, funny, and to the point. His first collection, published in 1971 with the rather Perelmanesque title *Getting Even*, was a best-selling compilation of seventeen of them. *Without Feathers*, published in 1975, had a broader scope of writing and included two plays, *God* and *Death*. (An entry in "Selections from the Allen Notebooks": "How wrong Emily Dickinson was! Hope is not 'the thing with feathers.' The thing with feathers has turned out to be my nephew. I must take him to a specialist in Zurich.") *Side Effects*, published in 1980, gathers the last stories he has written. Of the sixteen in the book, a dozen fulfill his intent of writing just for laughs; the more laughs, the more successful the piece to him. But there are real short stories, too, the result of the same desire he has shown in his films to not do the same thing again and again.

"I would like to develop as a writer," he said just before *Side Effects* was published. "I'd like to do amusing short stories and, hopefully, an amusing novel. The thing I don't want to do is have years and years pass and just keep doing casuals; fifteen years after you've started, the subject matter changes but you're still writing the same thing. If you look at Benchley and Perelman—and they're the best, bar none, they're absolutely brilliant—they were writing the same thing after twenty-five years. If I was them, I would rather have experimented with short stories and novels; it would have interested me." Woody has stopped writing casuals, he says, "because I don't want to look up on the bookshelf one day and see ten collections of basically the same thing."

"The Kugelmass Episode," "The Shallowest Man," "The Condemned," and "Retribution"—all of which appeared in *Side Effects*—are notable exceptions to most of his other pieces, which are for the most part shorter and directed completely toward the laugh. These are stories with real, if exaggerated characters, and they are complex, with many characters and turns of plot. "Retribution," for example, is the story of a love triangle whose sides are a man, a mother, and her daughter. It begins:

> That Connie Chasen returned my fatal attraction toward her at first sight was a miracle unparalleled in the history of Central Park West. Tall, blond, high cheek-boned, an actress, a scholar, a charmer, irrevocably alienated, with a hostile and perceptive wit only challenged in its power to attract by the lewd, humid eroticism her every curve suggested, she was the unrivaled desideratum of each young man at the party. That she would settle on me, Harold Cohen, scrawny, long-nosed, twenty-four-year-old budding dramatist and whiner, was a *non sequitur* on a par with octuplets.

However notable such exceptions may be, they are still short, humorous pieces and similar enough to what Woody did in the ten years before them that rather than continue in the same vein, he will wait until he is less active as a filmmaker and therefore has more time to devote to more complicated works such as a novel. For now, he has stopped.

Woody finished writing *Don't Drink the Water* before leaving for London to do *Casino Royale* in the spring of 1966. He had worked on it over a couple of years for Max Gordon, who had retired years before but constantly threatened to abandon his leisure to produce one play or another, none of which he ever did. He and Woody corresponded regularly during the filming of *Pussycat* about the play, but in the end Gordon decided against taking it on because he felt there were too many problems with the structure and the characters. Whether this was truly the case or simply a way for him not to come out of retirement is debatable but unanswerable. "There are some people who feel there is no play in the world I could have given Max that he would have done," Woody says. "It also could have been just plain good judgment by him. He was a guy who had done many classy productions and he sensed that this one was not ready. I don't really know. David Merrick, on the other hand, did it immediately, and was happy to do it."

Don't Drink the Water chronicles the misadventures of a New Jersey caterer and his family on vacation in an unnamed Iron Curtain country who are mistaken for spies—the father has an unerring eye for military installations as the background for snapshots—and who take refuge in the U.S. Embassy. Also in sanctuary is the narrator, a priest who has been there so long he has mastered some magic tricks— mushrooming flowers and the like—but failed to perfect others, such as getting out of a straitjacket. When Woody started to write plays, he would ask himself what successful production his idea resembled. *Don't Drink the Water* is based on the premise of a family living together in close quarters and getting on one another's nerves, a source of comedy that worked wonderfully in *You Can't Take It with You*. Woody drew on that and on the structure of *Teahouse of the August Moon*, the John Patrick comedy about American army officers on Okinawa after World War II. While willing to draw on established plays for structure, Woody was unwilling to be influenced by plays on the boards while he was writing, so for about a year before *Don't Drink the Water* opened he went to none. Instead, he would walk around the theater district with Louise and say, "When my play is produced . . ." (His unwillingness to have his vision interfered with extends to not wearing sunglasses because of the alterations they make in color and light.)

"I used other plays as guidelines for structure in the beginning but now it's in me, it's second nature," Woody says. "I don't have to think about it, I feel it. I remember Noël Coward giving advice to a young playwright—in *Present Laughter*—about how to learn to write plays. He said you have to live and breathe the theater, get a job as a stage manager, anything, keep reading plays. And this is what I would tell someone, say, if they wanted to develop a feeling for jazz. You could hear some of the best clarinetists in the world and they wouldn't play New Orleans jazz as authentically as I play it, even though they tower over me. If you just adore something and immerse yourself in it for years, eventually it seeps in in a way that can't be codified. You just find it becomes your idiom of expression. And it's the same with writing. That's how it happened to me. Construction for me is innate now. But there was a time when I wasn't so confident. Now I've written so many things over the years—twenty movies and three plays and many other kinds of story. There have been a number of unproduced plays, and my other one-act plays like *Death* and *God*. So now I structure something by feel. I don't craft it as consciously."

From the start, the only person Woody envisioned as the father was Lou Jacobi, the mustachioed, sad-eyed personification of the self-made Jewish character at the heart of this cartoon. Gordon had agreed with Woody but Merrick at first did not; he wanted a more commercial, less pronouncedly ethnic actor. In the end Woody prevailed, but then while in London for *Casino Royale*, Merrick cabled him that he wanted Vivian Vance (of *I Love Lucy* fame) for the female lead, even though Woody had written the part "with a more Jewish character in mind." Merrick was adamant that she would both play the comedy perfectly and have great marquee value. Woody finally agreed although he later said it was a mistake, not because there was anything inherently wrong with Vivian Vance as an actress, "just that she was the wrong person for the character. It was a crass attempt at commercialism rather than correct casting. It would have been just as wrong to cast Kim Stanley. David was trying too hard to Anglicize it. He isn't anti-Semitic but he has an aversion to anything too Jewish." (The same problem carried over to the film version, which starred Jackie Gleason. "I adored him," Woody says. "He's a genius. But he's the wrong guy.")

One person left over from the Gordon days was the director, Bob Sinclair, who, although his credits included such Gordon-produced hits as *The Women*, *Pride and Prejudice*, and *Dodsworth*, had not directed a play in the approximately thirty intervening years. Still, as Woody had had several talks with him about the project, he felt obliged to keep him. Besides, Sinclair was alleged to be a protégé of George S. Kaufman, "but that," Woody said later, "was loose talk."

The first out-of-town performances were in Philadelphia, where the reviews were mixed. The laughs were big but they couldn't hide that the production was a shambles. "The direction was the worst in the world," Woody says. "Nobody knew what to do. People were standing around. It was a nondirected play." It became officially nondirected when Sinclair was fired, even though no other director could be persuaded to take over. Woody stepped in briefly to direct, working especially with Tony Roberts (who played the ambassador's aide) on a bit of business where he fell over a couch in the middle of an embrace with a woman. "It was very funny and he would do it over and over again and we'd laugh," Roberts remembers. "He would always look clumsy. He is as artful at that sort of physical comedy as Charlie Chaplin was. And of course I couldn't do it. I don't know, I was too big, or I didn't look right, and eventually we just dropped it."

Woody also rewrote whole sections of the play alone in his hotel room. The cast, playing half a new version that didn't quite match the remaining half of the old version, would get line changes at noon for a 1 p.m. performance. In the way good actors can, they learned them lightning fast but it almost didn't matter—hardly anyone came to see the play; one Saturday matinee not quite six rows were filled. Meanwhile, it was impossible to get a seat to see *Breakfast at Tiffany's*, a musical starring Mary Tyler Moore and also produced by Merrick. (That play was a hit in Boston, too, but closed during previews on Broadway.)

The show began its turnaround when Stanley Prager agreed to take over as director. His greatest contribution was to bring enthusiasm, confidence, and competence. "He was not a master director," Woody says, "but he was a breath of fresh air. His energy alone was a boost. He came in and said, 'Okay, let's get this going. We've got to give the material a fair shake.' And everybody did."

Prager reblocked and restaged the play and the troupe moved on to Boston, where Woody came down with a high fever and incipient pneumonia. He stayed in his suite at the Ritz, running up "an enormous bill for juices and poultices," but kept working on the play; it was there he got the idea to make the priest the narrator and then, he says, "the show started to coagulate. But the laughs were always in it, even though there were weak spots and it was soft as a blob."

Part of the softness came from the cast. It took three changes of actors to get an acceptable ingenue; the part of the ambassador took several changes to fill properly. In all, there were thirteen cast changes, the most major being the replacement of Vivian Vance with Kay Medford. "Suddenly, the mother became a hilarious character," Woody says. Still, problems seemed to continually befall actors secure in their roles: Richard Libertini, who played the priest/narrator, collapsed one night and couldn't go on; the night before opening in Boston the wife of one of the leading actors died and the stage manager had to play the part. And in the midst of this, Merrick considered closing the show and reopening it in a theater in Florida he had dealings with, where there would be less pressure in readying the play for Broadway.

Woody and Merrick, who has a reputation for imperiousness, got along well, at least for the most part; for despite his imperiousness, he is also a terrific producer who got Woody what he wanted when he wanted it. Yet he could be, Woody says, "like the angel of death. He'd come to the show and say, 'Oh, they're going to back the scenery truck up to the theater on Monday.'" He came to a performance in Boston and walked out. Woody called him in New York the next day. "How can you do that?" he asked. "These people have worked hard." Merrick listened and, Woody says, "was very docile, very nice. I liked him. The only problem was when he strongly disagreed with you. Then he would be an awful bastard. But he wasn't that way normally. I found him charming, funny, witty, and intelligent. He had this reputation of being a devil, though, and I guess he liked to act it out."

One such instance occurred two nights before the show opened in New York. Woody suggested having the dictator say to Lou Jacobi, "Are these people Jewish?" in a scene where the father became angry at him; it made the scene more provocative. Prager liked the idea but not Merrick.

"Well, look, I'm the writer of the show," Woody told him.

"Okay," he answered, "but if that line plays, I'm firing the director."

(Woody had some revenge in Washington, D.C., a couple of years later when *Play It Again, Sam* was in out-of-town tryouts. Merrick, resplendent in a well-tailored blue suit, suggested to Woody, who was unresplendent in his corduroys, that he change a line. "David," he said, rejecting the idea, "I've made over a million dollars in my life by not listening to men in blue suits.")

Such confrontations were the exception rather than the rule in Woody's dealings with Merrick, who for the most part he found "a very good producer to be in a stressful situation with. He was for the most part a regular and nice guy. One Sunday we were watching a football game on TV and he said to me, 'Do you know why I went into this business? To meet women. I was a lawyer. How many beautiful women do you think you meet when you're a lawyer? So I started producing shows.' "

On opening night on Broadway, November 17, 1966, Woody and Mickey Rose went to the Morosco Theater on West Forty-fifth Street and looked at the set, then they went to the Automat and had dinner. Afterward they wandered over to McGirr's Billiard Academy and shot some billiards. Jack and Jane Rollins had a party following the show and Woody went there to wait for the reviews, which were mixed but good enough to have people buying tickets for the next year and a half. (In contrast, the night *Play It Again, Sam* opened, he went to dinner after the show with some friends at the now defunct Broadway hangout Dinty Moore's, stayed with Louise Lasser—they were separated but still friendly—and had his first report of the good reviews from a stranger on the street who congratulated him as he walked home the next morning.)

The play's great appeal was that its audience identified with the characters, however burlesqued they were, just as Woody's cabaret audience identified with his exaggerated monologues. Had the show not been forced to move to another theater twice during its run, it would have played longer than the eighteen months it did.

Not that *Don't Drink the Water* is the apogee of playwriting. The story is thin and the structure flimsy. But it *is* funny. "I wrote it for laughs," Woody says. "I didn't know how to survive any other way, and Lou Jacobi and Kay Medford were hysterically funny. Lou got every laugh and twenty more from his body language. He's a funny human. It played like a house afire. It was so farcical and silly; it was reminiscent of the Kaufman things without his finesse."

Part of the criticism the play received was that the incessant humor prevented the show from being strengthened, a criticism that should not be confused with saying the play was too funny for its own good. "The legend that a show of this sort can have too many jokes for its own good is just that, a legend. Aristophanes would surely have clouted the man who suggested such a thing," Walter Kerr wrote in *The New York Times* shortly after the play opened. "What actually happens is that the theatrical current stops flowing, the stage doesn't fill to the water-mark. The one-liners are coming thick and fast, and the reservoir is emptying steadily. Comedy, like any other kind of theater, needs an interior impulse. The impulse comes from the story line and bubbles up into situations that would be funny even if the lines were as straight as can be. . . . It's the set-up that counts, not the spangles."

Kerr may have been right—his criticism is another lesson in the importance of a strong straight line—but the audience didn't care. "The laughs were *enormous*," Woody says. "Stagehands who had been at the Morosco Theater for thirty years said they had never heard so many laughs. Laughs are what the thing floated on. It had nothing else going for it but that. Yet I know it was full of weaknesses of the worst kind. I was just jumping into the water to get my feet wet. I haven't read the play in years. It's probably dreadful beyond words—but full of funny lines. I remember when Neil Simon came, he roared at a strictly ad-lib line I came up with at rehearsal. [The daughter falls in love with and becomes engaged to the ambassador's hapless aide, and as the mother and father are about to be whisked out of the country the mother tells them]: 'And while we're on the submarine, cable us your silverware pattern.' It was also a big laugh in the show. It was just a laugh machine and I never had any doubts about it even if we were playing to six rows of people."

Now that Woody had, as he said, gotten his feet wet in the theater, he was ready to immerse himself in a play that showcased his talents as a performer as well as a writer. Much of *Play It Again, Sam* was written in 1968 while he was staying at the Astor Towers in Chicago during a booking at Mister Kelly's. *Play It Again, Sam* is the story of Allan Felix, a critic for a highbrow film magazine, who fails with women when he tries to be something he isn't and who learns with the help of the ghost of Humphrey Bogart that success comes only when one is himself. A mark of the humor and gentility of the play is that although the woman he succeeds with is his best friend's wife, there is nothing smarmy about the fact. That the protagonist's name is Allan is not coincidental. Woody has always liked his name (whether fore- or sur-) and chose Felix because he feels he is lucky, like Felix the Cat. (Felix, of course, means lucky.)

As in many of his works, Woody used magical effects in *Play It Again, Sam*. Characters appear and disappear in flashback and real time, and Bogart reincarnate is a nifty illusion (and also Jerry Lacy, who played him, *looked* like Bogart reincarnate). Yet however central Bogart is to the piece, he was a late addition. Woody—who says he is a chronic daydreamer—began writing about a film critic who had fantasies. One day he wrote, "Humphrey Bogart comes," because the walls of Felix's apartment had many posters from Bogart films. A few pages later he thought to himself that it would be nice to bring Bogart back, and soon he was a major character, the man of the world who offers Allan advice on women. Woody's ability to make Bogart so believable a character comes from the important role films played in his youth, and still play in his life. Bogart and dozens of other stars were nearly everyday staples for him and a familiarity formed. Writing "Humphrey Bogart comes" was for him more a case of calling on a friendly icon than a stretch at theatricality. In a sense, Woody's affinity with the films and film stars of his childhood is not unlike a virtuoso musician's affinity with a composer whose music he loves to play. ("The first Humphrey Bogart movie I saw was *The Maltese Falcon*," Woody wrote in a *Life* magazine cover story in March 1969 entitled "My Secret Life with Bogart." "I was ten years old and I identified immediately with Peter Lorre.")

Throughout his adult life he regularly frequented the revival houses in Manhattan to watch favorite old films. Then in 1979, after *Manhattan* was released, he acquired the ultimate filmgoer's toy: his own screening room, which takes up half the space in his office/editing room complex, formerly a ladies' bridge club in a swank Park Avenue building. The comprehensive editing facilities allow him to cut his films, rerecord dialogue, and lay in a music track without in a sense leaving home. The screening room not only allows him to watch dailies and work-in-progress versions of his current film in a comfortable place available anytime he wants; it doubles as a private theater. The first summer he had it, he watched a favorite movie nearly every day. Jean Doumanian and her companion Jacqui Safra would come often—this was before Woody met Mia and (unrelatedly) before he had an ulcer problem—and the three of them passed those days sipping a bottle or two of, say, Romanée-Conti and watching films in a private version of the dark, air-conditioned theaters of his youth. Because there are so many old films he likes and so few new ones he cares about (although he can get a print of any current movie whenever he likes, and he watches many of them), it remains a great pleasure for him, one he shares with Mia's children. Often they will come on a weekend and view a film while Woody works in the next room, editing his own.

"Each of us in his life has certain inexplicable fond memories," he once said. "You don't know why you have them, it's just a warm meaningless moment or something. And I've noticed a large amount of mine are connected with movies. I remember going to the movies in Manhattan during the blizzard of '47 to see *Dick Tracy Versus Cueball*. I remember going to see *The Boys in the Band* with Diane Keaton and waiting on line at the Tower East theater [in Manhattan] on a snowy day. It is a very pleasant memory I have with her. I remember Mia and me when I first met her driving to a screening at the Paramount building at night and seeing a lot of cars and celebrities pull up and me having my phobic reaction of 'Let's not go in, let's pass this.' So we took a detour and went right over to the Regency, which was then a revival theater, where we saw the second half of a wonderful, by virtue of nostalgia, Esther Williams film. I remember one gray morning when I was a young kid knowing that at one o'clock when the movie opened I was going to see a Charlie Chaplin film. I remember the day before I was bar mitzvahed, a Friday, I went by myself after school to the movies and saw *Canon City*, a semi-documentary about a jailbreak.

"I can only think the reason movies play so strongly in my memory is the contrast between real life in general and my real life specifically. The intense experience that one gets, that I got, in a movie house was so enormous, so gigantic if you measure what real life is and what mine was. Even now, as recently as four or five years ago, I remember one blistering summer day that Mia was in town with the kids. We went to my screening room and made the whole day out of watching the first two *Godfather* films. It was a day well spent. No doubt, too, I have something of an inborn sense of drama."

Woody's ability to translate his intense feelings about the movies into a theatrical piece, combined with his creating a stage character that drew on the persona he had established as a stand-up, make *Play It Again, Sam* a dual treat. Bogart and the theme of *Casablanca* provide a nostalgic comfort and frame of reference for the audience, and Woody's take on the age-old dilemma of a guy who can't get a girl makes it current. When Linda (Diane Keaton) asks a despondent Allan Felix if all he does for dinner is heat TV dinners and he answers, "Who bothers to heat them? I just suck 'em frozen," he is able to transform his nightclub monologue into action of the most beguiling kind.

While the play (and the 1972 Herbert Ross–directed film that was made of it) is utterly contemporary, Woody's writing style was heavily influenced by plays presented by the Group Theatre in the 1930s and early 1940s, productions written by, among others, Eugene O'Neill, Clifford Odets, and Maxwell Anderson. Woody says that he is "a product intellectually, artistically, emotionally—and for better or worse—of that group of sort of New York playwrights. They were influenced in turn by Stanislavsky and Chekhov and that era of theater. It's that group of people that I'm always comfortable with, that I know about, and that my work is very influenced by if I don't force a change. Theirs was the era of the well-made play, three- or two-act plays with a certain old-fashioned construction. It permeates my work in one way or another. I say for better or worse because it leads you to a kind of dialogue-oriented piece which is natural to the theater but less natural to film, so for me to do a movie that's filmic requires my forcing myself into a slightly alien direction. I would have been, I think, very happy and functioning well in the 1920s and '30s along with all those people. I would have been one of them, I think. Either minor or slightly better than minor, I can't evaluate where, but it would have been in that theater group of Kaufman and Robert Sherwood and Odets." (Jo Mielziner, an icon of those decades, designed the sets for *Don't Drink the Water*.)

The craftsmanship of Odets and the others rubbed off on Woody because when he began to write, what he read all the time and what he saw as an audience member was the tail end of that group of plays. "The fact is," he says, "if left to my own devices, and if it wasn't that cinema has gone beyond that and the dictates of the art form has its own set of rules—it's become much more elastic—my tendency is always to write something with a very old-fashioned construction whether it's serious or comic. You really see it, no matter how I dress it up."

Woody is not alone in his predispositions. Ingmar Bergman was also very influenced by the theater, and he surmounted it with the development of his superb cinematic style. Many of Woody's films—*Hannah and Her Sisters, Crimes and Misdemeanors, Manhattan, Annie Hall,* and *The Purple Rose of Cairo*, for instance—have a well-made-play quality about them. And *Play It Again, Sam* is a much-better-made play than *Don't Drink the Water*.

Around the time that *Play It Again, Sam* opened, Woody was quoted as saying he wrote it to meet girls. There was a grain of truth in that; he never hesitated to throw in another part for a beautiful woman. And why not? After predictable and not unusual trouble as a teenager in meeting girls and having them like him, here was a chance to write whatever scenario he wanted for himself. That scenario, from the first draft of *What's New, Pussycat?* through *Play It Again, Sam* and many of his films, allowed him to win the girl even if he doesn't always keep her in the end: Allan gives up Linda as Bogart does Ingrid Bergman in *Casablanca*; Ike loses Tracy in *Manhattan* after he won't commit to her; Alvy keeps Annie only as a friend in *Annie Hall*. The one film in which he never wins the girl for even a while is *Crimes and Misdemeanors*, where he tries with all his heart but fails.

But of all the women in *Play It Again, Sam*, the one who matters most is, of course, Diane Keaton. The play marked the beginning of a love affair that continues today as a very close friendship. They had never met when she came for her first audition. She had been suggested for the part by Lucian Scott, her drama teacher at Orange Coast Junior College in California; Scott had also taught Joe Hardy, the director. Hardy remembered having seen and having liked her as Maria in a college production of *The Sound of Music* and more recently in *Hair* on Broadway. Another supporter was Sanford Meisner of the Neighborhood Playhouse, who also taught Diane and whom Woody remembers calling her "the most talented girl in New York." After three or four callbacks, she read a scene with Woody, whom she remembers being "as scared of me as I was of him." He also thought she might be a little too tall, because neither he nor Hardy wanted the joke to be that he was shorter than the girl. In the end, her talent overcame their fears.

At least insofar as her being the right person for the part. Their characters' affinity for one another is based in part on their manifest neuroses. Once Woody knew Diane was the best Linda possible, he had an attack of self-doubt, which made a nice match for her own sense that "I always feel insecure."

"She was so nice and so pretty, I thought to myself, 'Gee, I hope I'm not a disappointment to her. She's done Broadway and I've never done a show. I hope I'm going to be good enough for her,'" Woody remembers feeling. In an uncharacteristic lack of confidence about his work, he also had grave doubts about himself as the writer of the play. He never doubted that he could get laughs from the audience, but he wondered whether he had written three acts that worked as a whole.

Rehearsals began without any of these fears being spoken. For that matter, Woody and Diane barely said anything at all to each other apart from their lines. He was concerned with memorizing his, because he had never done this before; a play was a much different thing than a monologue. And Diane was terribly shy. She came to work, worked hard, and as soon as she was done, left without a word to anyone in the company of a young man who came for her every day.

The cast member who had the most fun was Tony Roberts, who played Linda's husband, Dick. There were a half dozen great-looking women in the show besides Keaton. Woody didn't like to mix business and pleasure, but Roberts, he says, "was like a kid in a candy store." Woody did mix enough pleasure with business to become close friends with him, something he had not done when Tony played in *Don't Drink the Water*; Woody was much more removed from the cast as solely the writer than he was as writer and fellow actor.

Woody did, however, begin to date a woman who had auditioned for the show and been offered a small part, which she turned down. (He and Louise had just separated.) The night before one date, Woody and Diane had to rehearse late and went out for a bite to eat at Jim Downey's, a now defunct restaurant on Eighth Avenue. As they sat and talked for the first time without benefit of lines, Woody found her "completely hilarious, I just couldn't stop laughing." Before long he was wondering why he was taking out the other woman the next night instead of her. One reason, he told himself, was the young man who met her every night and who he assumed was her boyfriend. Later he learned he was only her manager.

Then during tryouts in Washington, D.C., he invited her to dinner after a show. They saw more and more of each other, and a little while after they returned to New York, she moved into his apartment, where she lived for a year. By the time the film version of *Play It Again, Sam* was made in 1972, they were no longer lovers but still the best of friends, chatting happily between takes about favorite flavors of ice cream. As with Harlene, "we just grew apart," Woody says. "She had come to New York and was completely naïve, with no experience. She was in her early twenties and I was one of the first important relationships in her life. She was a maturing person developing very pronounced likes and dislikes of her own. She developed interests in areas that did not particularly interest me, nor did some of mine interest her. She was starting to get interested in painting and photography and graphic arts, and she began to spend time in places like California and the Grand Canyon and Santa Fe. She became a sophisticated woman and developed a million needs and plans, and I had my own plans—a number that coincided and a number that didn't. We parted amicably." The sum of their friendship is that they can and do talk about anything; Woody is particularly interested in her opinions. He talks with her at length about his projects, and she solicits his thoughts on hers.

"Keaton was a major contribution to my life in an artistic way," he said one day after speaking with her on the phone about possible actors for *Crimes and Misdemeanors*. "She helped my taste develop a lot, and there is a lot of her influence in my taste. She is someone who was completely her own person artistically right from the start. When I first met her, as young as she was she would never hesitate to express her likes and dislikes, no matter how against the grain they may have been. If she liked something unpopular, she liked it with no defensiveness; that was just it. And if she didn't, you could tell her all day long that, say, these plays of Shakespeare are masterpieces, and if she didn't like them, she just didn't care. She had utter, total conviction in her own taste—and her own taste was superb. She knows who the good actresses and actors are, and what the good plays are, and what the good paintings are, and who's funny and who's not. There's just some unclouded instinct in her that's never been messed up by peer pressure.

"She was a supporter of, I think, the best instincts of mine. When I first screened *Take the Money* for her before it came out and she told me that it was good, that it was funny, that was all I needed to hear. I knew it would have its place if it was liked or not liked. And I've felt this down through the years. When she's liked things of mine, they're worthwhile. She's always had absolutely great artistic instincts. Now she's not always available to see my films before they're finished. If I bring her in after it's completely finished, she'll want to be encouraging and supportive. But if she sees it before it's completely done, she has no compunction about saying, 'This is great and this actress is great and this little story is terrible and you've got to fix this up and I don't buy that for a second.' She's always a very important critic for me," a fact made evident by the look on his face when he turns to her for her reaction after seeing a rough cut of one of his films. His usual politely inquisitive demeanor when soliciting opinions from most other friends and acquaintances gives way with her to a look of anxious anticipation coupled with a hope to please.

Their new relationship had no deleterious effect on how they performed their roles in *Play It Again, Sam*, which opened February 13, 1969, at the Broadhurst Theater on West Forty-fourth Street. The difference, they both agree, came when one had to play with the other's understudy. "It was artificial," Woody says. "I was much more real than my understudy and she was much more real than hers. They were doing it from the outside, and that was a big difference."

The inside nature of Woody's and Diane's response to each other had certain pitfalls. One was that Diane could make Woody laugh as hard onstage as off. There were evenings during the run of the play when he would be so convulsed with laughter that he would have to sit still and wait to get control of himself. Then she would begin to laugh. Because of the lighthearted nature of the show, the audience was seldom aware of their problem; if they picked up on it at all, the laughter seemed a natural extension of the action. Which was a good thing, since there was a lot of extraneous laughter among Woody and Diane and Tony. (An example of this on film is the scene in *Annie Hall* where Alvie and Annie, both squeamish in the face of crawling crustaceans, attempt to prepare a lobster dinner at a beach house. It was the first scene shot for the movie and neither Woody nor Diane was acting. Their laughter was completely spontaneous, and it gives the scene a vitality that cannot be planned.)

"If Woody blew a line, he just went up," Keaton said several years after the run of the show. "He couldn't continue the scene. Tony and I could mess up a line and go on, but not Woody. And then you started laughing. The discipline some nights was really bad. Tony once had his pants off when Woody came offstage for a glass of water, and Woody was laughing so hard when he came back on that he couldn't talk. And then a couple of nights, Woody and Tony agreed beforehand that Woody would do Groucho and Tony would do Sydney Greenstreet." On other nights, circumstances acted independently to break them up. The wonderfully theatrical William Ritman–designed set allowed characters to appear like magic. Spotlights directly overhead had three lighting levels and walls had spaces that couldn't be seen from the audience. If Woody was talking, say, stage left, the woman he was talking about could appear stage right center. Or a character could turn and disappear into a wall. When Woody talked about rowboating in Central Park, a rosewood-and-leather chair suddenly became a dinghy. All this was perfect when properly used. But one night Diane was supposed to make an exit through a door and made it instead through a wall.

Although he tailored the character of Allan Felix to his own strengths and abilities ("I am that character. I wrote it for me as natural as could be," he once said), Woody had some initial difficulty making the transition from monologue performer to actor interplaying with other actors. "He thought he would be doing routines," Hardy says. "In a short period he learned you can't do routines in a stage play. What I really had to do was get him to be enlarged as an entity on the stage." Part of that entailed Woody's learning to respond to the audience not as a single performer but as part of a whole with an internal reality that is a step removed from the audience. For instance, one night while the play was in out-of-town tryouts, Tony Roberts was supposed to appear in a fantasy but he missed his cue and was still in his dressing room. Woody had no idea what was going on or what he should do, and he began to look around, helpless. In a few more seconds, "I would have lapsed into the instincts of a stand-up comedian who has direct contact with the audience and said, 'Look, folks. I'm sorry. I don't know what's happening here,' and made a joke. But the actress onstage, who was experienced, picked up and charged on with the next line and kept on going."

Roberts was "amazed that whenever anyone missed an entrance or blew a line, Woody was completely unable to improvise anything at the moment. He would have to leave the stage, or he would turn upstage and be at a loss for words, perhaps even broken up with laughter. Which was quite terrifying for a normal actor to confront. But his mechanism was to *be* Allan Felix, not pretend to be Allan Felix, which is what the rest of us were doing: We were pretending to be these people he's invented, and he *was* one of them. So when the story didn't continue for a moment, it was existentially dumbfounding to him. Whereas the rest of us were capable of thinking up an ad-lib."

For all that, Woody found performing on the stage much less nerve-wracking than performing as a stand-up. For him it was like the difference between playing solo and playing in a band: The group is playing and it just happens that people are watching. "You're doing what you're doing. It's not at all bothersome. I could drift into the theater with my corned beef sandwich and sit onstage and hear the audience out there and the stage manager saying, 'House to half,' " Woody once said, chewing on an imaginary sandwich. "And then him saying, 'House out,' " he added as he mimed putting the sandwich away. "Whereas I couldn't eat for three hours before I went on in a nightclub because of the direct contact I'd have with the audience. You come out and you're talking to *them*. But in *Sam*, it was me coming out and talking to Keaton and Tony Roberts and us just having a good time onstage.

"I can feel the anxiety I had before doing a monologue now as I talk about it," he continued, a little discomfited. "I remember sitting backstage so many times with Keaton in Vegas and as soon as we heard Edie Adams going into a certain song, it meant she had one more before I was introduced. I'd start to get tense. It's just Pavlovian. It's so silly, because I knew they loved me, my reviews were good, they'd booked me in places because they liked me, the people were there to see me, I killed them every night. It didn't matter how far into my engagement I was. It could be a Thursday night my third week there and I'd know I was going to do great because I did great the show before and the night before and the week before. But it still got to me. Once I hit the stage, though, I calmed down. There might have been some residual nervous energy but I was totally impervious to any tension whatsoever. Even at the beginning. It was all anticipatory anxiety."

This did not mean that Woody was impervious to nervousness before the show opened. His pre-opening-night jitters even led in part to his friendship with Roberts, who was, after all, initially *hired* to play his friend, and continues to play that part in Woody's movies. Their conversations onscreen and off are fast, they are full of insults, they are full of sport smarts—and in real life full of shortcuts in their discussion of people and events that neither one of them would want anybody else to hear. "They are the reflections of two street-smart guys, one from Brooklyn, one from Manhattan, jousting with each other," Roberts says. Yet all through the months of rehearsal and tryouts and the eighteen months *Don't Drink the Water* ran, there was virtually no personal relationship between them. Once the show was launched, in fact, Tony never saw Woody at a performance. The comfortable sense they have with each other onscreen jumped over into real life through Woody's discomfort before *Play It Again, Sam* opened on Broadway.

"The reason I got the persona I have as Woody's friend in his films is because it got a chance to develop during *Play It Again, Sam*. He would come into my dressing room and pace the floor and be scared, and I suddenly saw him emotionally naked," he adds. "I felt very secure in the play because I knew if I knew my lines and I knew my blocking and I had rehearsed a certain amount of time, that I would have appropriate opening-night jitters but that my energy would get focused the moment the curtain went up and I was onstage. I knew what to do. I had done it before. You thought about your next line and you focused on the other person and you heard your voice come out of your mouth and you would eventually relax and you'd love it. That's why I act. So I'd be nervous, but I'd also think, 'Ooooo, this is the good stuff.' Woody, on the other hand, was like somebody going to the guillotine. He *hated* doing it."

At least until he started doing it every night. Then nervousness was replaced by either the laughter with Diane and Tony or anger at the occasional unresponsive audience every show has. "You get angry," he says, "because you figure, 'Gee, I've played the show thirty-six times in a row and everybody laughs and now we're doing the same thing and they're just sitting out there dead.' You think, 'Get with it. You paid to see the show and we're doing it well and we've done it this way every night, what's the problem?' " As he soon learned, there often wasn't any problem. "You'd come out for your bow and the applause was thunderous and it turned out they were loving it throughout the whole show. I learned not to quit just because there weren't any laughs." He also learned how to zip through those performances with poor audience response, sometimes cutting off ten minutes from the usual playing time while still protecting the laughs. It was a variation on a lesson he had learned as a stand-up, when on slow nights he would wait for the laugh and find it not coming: He'd pick up the slack and go on to the next line, often to find that the response was barely improved. "You'd work for their energy," he said one day. "You couldn't do your usual pauses because you weren't getting the usual laughs and your hour act was over in thirty minutes." He paused. "I just want to add that when this happens, you're usually dying."

Just as performing onstage is different from doing a nightclub routine, so is acting in a film different from acting in a play. "Onstage, you get to know the place so well that you can think about anything when you perform," he continued. "I've been onstage in the midst of a scene getting big laughs and thinking as I spoke my lines, 'Hey, this is a pretty well-written scene. I think I constructed it well, but maybe I should have done . . .' " Actors commonly tell stories about how, say, Laurence Olivier would be moving an audience to tears while thinking about the laundry returning one fewer pair of underwear than he sent out that morning. "It's true," Woody says. "When you're doing a play you can easily keep most of your mind on the play while part of it wanders. But it's different in a film, where you do such short bursts of scenes. To me, it's a pain in the neck to have to act in a movie. I enjoy setting the thing up, but then I have to put on my costume and the collar itches, and then I have to get in front of the camera and dredge up the energy to act startled when she pulls out a knife. It's such an effort. But one reason I can switch on and off like that is that it's like playing poker for money or not for money. When I'm playing for money, or if I'm at a party and I want to impress someone, there's a switch that goes on. Another thing that helps me turn on immediately on the set is that I wrote the material and have more understanding of it than most actors. I'm writing to accommodate already existing feelings. I try not to write something I can't do."

In *Oedipus Wrecks* there is a scene at the end where Sheldon Mills (Woody) comes home to find a goodbye letter from Mia Farrow's character. Their relationship has been under stress ever since Sheldon's mother disappeared in a magician's Chinese box at a magic show, only to reappear in the sky above New York, the world's biggest busybody mother. ("This film is going to resonate in Israel," Woody said one day during its making. "It'll be the *Gone With the Wind* of Israel.") In desperation, Sheldon enlists the help of a seer played by Julie Kavner. It turns out she is a fake but a well-meaning and sweet one, who sends Sheldon home with the remains of a chicken dinner she makes for him. After Sheldon sadly reads the letter, "All the Things You Are" swells up behind the scene. He remembers the chicken, unwraps the aluminum foil, pulls out a leg dripping with pan jelly, and holds it under his nose with all the tenderness and emotion as if it were a single rose from Grace Kelly. The scene is poignant and funny, and was shot long before Woody knew what music would go with it, which would have made things easier for him.

"I made the shot knowing there's going to be a sweet piece of music there," he explained one day. "I'm just acting at the time, the way any actor would. I'm picking the leg up and I know I've got to smell it and make it romantic-looking. I'm"—he laughed—"pretending. I'm not thinking at the time that I'm the character and I'm not thinking, 'Oh God, I love her.' I'm thinking, 'Okay, I've waited enough time. I've dropped the letter and now I'm standing there and this is going to get boring if I don't move now; it seems enough time to notice the chicken. Keep it like this, don't be too feminine about it.' I'm not thinking motivation, I'm thinking mechanics.

"But that's easy if one can do minimal acting, which is what I do. I can't play Richard III or Chekhov. The acting I do is limited but it's very simple for me. When I was Danny Rose, I had to walk down a hallway and learn that my act is leaving me and respond to it. You see it on the screen and it's a nicely acted moment. I have this little tiny range, and those things that I do, I know I can do because I wrote the script. I don't give myself anything beyond my capacity as an actor, and that which I can do is a cinch. I can do it on call morning, late at night, over and over if I have to. It's like someone who can sit down and draw a rabbit. I'd spend all day and not be able to do it; or it's like writing a joke. People always ask, 'How do you write jokes?' If you can write them, there's nothing to it."

One of the reasons Woody likes to make films with actors he knows and trusts—like Louise Lasser and Diane Keaton and Tony Roberts and for the past eleven years Mia—is that he has so much confidence in them that he has only to worry about himself and the technicalities of filmmaking: Is the camera placed at the optimum angle? Are the actors moving too far? Does the set look right?

There are large differences between directing a play and directing a film: A play is on a much more human scale; there are no machines to interfere and no seventy-five crew members hauling set decorations and lighting equipment; the production hinges only on writing and actors; the action is enclosed in one place, a rehearsal hall, where the weather doesn't matter and there are no locations problems.

On the other hand, for good or ill a play is at the mercy of the actors. The director sees them do something wonderful in rehearsal and then prays they can repeat it time after time in front of an audience; good stage actors can balance control and spontaneity.

In film, it only has to happen once. And after it's captured on celluloid, the director and editor and special-effects technicians can enhance the whole in a dozen ways in the cutting room. "The director," says Ulu Grosbard, who directs both plays and films, "is a midwife in the theater. It's just the actors and the audience once the play is running."

There is a difference, too, in writing a play and writing a film, at least for Woody. Woody's film scripts are guides rather than molds. He rewrites and reshoots constantly during the course of filming and actors are encouraged to change their lines (but not their meaning) if they find it more comfortable to deliver them in some of their own words. He even does not hesitate to call a short halt in shooting a scene so he can rewrite dialogue. And so a screenplay is less a piece of writing for him than a stage play. Once he has worked out the idea of a screenplay, Woody has a draft written within a month or six weeks; the aim is for form more than it is for content at that point and so the exercise is more a necessary step than a creative pleasure.

In the past when Woody worked on a vehicle for himself he liked to write with a collaborator, as he did with Mickey Rose (*Take the Money and Run* and *Bananas*) and Marshall Brickman (*Sleeper*, *Annie Hall*, and *Manhattan*). In those instances, they talked out scenes together and worked out dialogue as they walked around New York. Two people talking have the structure of normal conversation, something that is hard for one person to create alone in a room. Brickman, who has written and directed several films of his own, says, "When you're alone, you're forced to be slightly rhetorical with yourself and reflexive. You have to ask yourself questions: What would I do? What would the character do? I sometimes find myself writing these questions out in order to create a feel of a collaborator in the room."

Woody did the actual writing of the first draft of the films he did with Rose and Brickman, although he says their contribution to plot and dialogue was equal to his. They also helped fit the action and the dialogue as snugly as possible to the Woody Allen persona. Final decisions were Woody's, as was the final draft. As Brickman points out, "The stuff was geared to the best use of Woody as a screen personality, and he was the best judge, obviously, as the writer and the director."

Brickman began his career playing banjo in a folk group called the Tarriers which was managed by Rollins and Joffe. During a Greenwich Village coffeehouse engagement in the mid-sixties, Woody was the opening act for them. Brickman was the one who talked while the others tuned up, because, he says, he could talk and tune up a little faster than the others. He was also the funniest. Charlie Joffe suggested that Woody and Marshall get together, and the two hit it off. Rollins and Joffe did not think that *The Filmmaker*, their first collaboration, was special enough to produce, but they liked *Sleeper*.

Over the several years of their collaboration, Woody and Marshall were often-seen fixtures of the Manhattan scene as they walked the streets working out their scripts. Part of Brickman's contribution was to try to impose a detailed structure. "I would try to go from A to B to C to D," he recalls. "I make physical analogies and analogies to science and architecture. That's how I remain on the face of the earth rather than flying off into space. For Woody, perhaps, structure is less dominant, less important. What were important for him were the individual moments and the leaps, which really are his special and unique talent. *Annie Hall* is the perfect example. I don't think anybody else could make a film like that. Maybe Jean-Luc Godard in some other universe, somebody who had a kind of audacity and creative ability to make those leaps where a word triggers a scene and goes somewhere else. That's representative of Woody's kind of mind. He's very intuitive. I was always trying to back in logically. In other words, to think of an idea for a scene or an idea for a line, I would always try to reason it out: Well, what would the character do? Maybe if that, then therefore. And Woody would sit and look at me and say, 'Yeah, but would it be funny if the guy had a rabbit suit on?' or whatever. It wouldn't be a rabbit suit, though, it would be something better. The point is, he would always have some sort of intuitive leap that would have within it the thing that was wanted. That's one of his real gifts. In order to exercise it, to use it, you have to have real courage.

"A joke is something that has an element of surprise to it and some kind of truth and an as yet unforeseen connection between two things. Woody has a way of finding it. Here's an example. One time we were walking down the street and we saw somebody. And I said, 'Isn't that Jack so-and-so?' And he said, 'Yeah. He got divorced.' And I said, 'Didn't he use to have a mustache?' And Woody said, 'Yeah, his wife sued for the whole face and settled for the mustache.' It's a big talent to apply that way of thinking to problems of structure or character, to surprise and remain within the framework and also be interesting."

Woody's single deficiency, according to Brickman, is not intellectual but rather gastronomic. "He has no idea how to order pizza. He has plain cheese pizza. In *Italy* they don't even have plain cheese pizza. It's like a canvas without the painting on it, with just the base, the primer. But it hasn't held him back. Einstein was also very simple. There is a famous story about his visiting a friend. He came down in the morning and said, 'Shaving soap *and* hand soap? Needlessly complicated.' So maybe the plain cheese pizza is an attempt toward a kind of simplicity in all things, starting with pizza."

For all the benefit Woody derived from his collaborations on screenplays, a stage play is strictly a solo venture. "The fun of a play is writing it," Woody says. "You've got to wallow in it. Writing a play with someone else would be like calling in another director on a film. I like the pure pleasure of waking up in my house, having my breakfast, going into a room by myself, and writing. For three months you get up and just write. I'm much looser in a room by myself because I'm not in contact with the real world. It's when you go into rehearsal that the real world hits you. You watch and listen to lines being done and you realize that they are sentimental and mawkish and not funny." Once the real world hits, though, Woody tears into the play and rewrites again and again.

A case in point is the work he did on *The Floating Light Bulb*, a play that to a certain extent, with its desperate home life and gentleman caller, is a tragicomic Brooklyn version of Tennessee Williams's *The Glass Menagerie*. Director Ulu Grosbard felt the father was not properly written and the two of them grappled with his relationship to the main story, integrating his life away from the scenes at home by going back and forth to them.

"What struck me as extraordinary in working with Woody was his willingness to tackle problems and his speed," Grosbard said after the play opened. "He made substantial changes—five drafts from our first meeting to opening. We'd meet on a Thursday and by Monday morning he had done a major rewrite. My experience often is that a playwright will change seven lines and consider it a rewrite. In rehearsal I found him more than ruthless with his own stuff, sometimes overly so because it was my fault or the actors' that was causing the trouble. He was always ready to accept blame on his end. He'd go to the dressing room and come back with four choices for a change."

Woody willingly accepts the blame for faults in his films, too, saying that with the freedom he has from Orion, in the end it is his shortcomings that prevent the movie from coming off as well as he had hoped. In placing himself in line for the blame—or credit where events work well—Woody totally absorbs himself in the production. In turn, he expects his collaborators to be as committed as he is. It is a high expectation, if only because no one can be as committed to a project as its creator. "We were rehearsing long hours," Grosbard says. "He couldn't grasp when we were close to previews that the cast was exhausted." Work on the text of the play continued until a few days before previews began and then the play was set. Woody, too, had done all he could do with it, despite some lingering sense that the play did not work as well as it could. "The problems we had were rooted in the premise somehow," Grosbard says. "I don't know that we ever solved it. We went as far as we could. Woody's strength in that play is a sense of theater, a sense of reality about the characters, letting the humor come out of a genuine situation and the structure of the play rather than from one-liners. It was truth that was funny and painful at times. It was also great theater with the magic." Grosbard adds that "Woody was very open in terms of the work, but he was not personally accessible." That included his not being around for the opening night, April 27, 1981. Woody and Jean Doumanian and Jacqui Safra flew to Paris that day. This was not a personal slight to the cast, however. Woody tries not to be around when anything of his opens, and so was out of town, for instance, when *Manhattan* premiered.

"It's the most pleasant thing to be nowhere in the vicinity of the earthquake," he says, "to not be exposed to any of the material. I don't have to hear how great I am, or how terrible I am." He always expects a disaster. "I'm always bursting with enthusiasm and security when I start off on a film. I never think it's going to be anything but wonderful—until I'm finished and I see what I have. And then I think, 'My God, what was I thinking? I must have been completely insane. How did I ever think I could fob this off on a rational public?' *Manhattan* is a perfect example. They put me on the cover of *Time* and of *The New York Times Magazine*, and they said it was the greatest. But two weeks before that happened, if United Artists had said, 'Well, tell you what we'll do. If you'll do two films for us for nothing, we'll burn the negative of this one,' I would have said, 'Okay, you have it.'" In fact, he seriously considered offering to do another film for nothing if they would not release *Manhattan*.

Take the Money and Run, like *Play It Again, Sam*, was written specifically for Woody to star in; so much so that "Woody" rather than "Virgil Starkwell" was typed above the lines in the early drafts of the script. "Woody," in fact, was used for all his characters through *Everything You Always Wanted to Know About Sex*.

During the period when Woody made his first several films, he was very much in the grip of wanting to be a screen comedian, and primarily being in films that presented him as a screen comedian. "Those early films do that and that's what they were for," he explained one day during the making of *Oedipus Wrecks*. "I always thought of myself as a comedian. Not to be pretentious about this, but the way you take the Chaplin character or the Keaton character or the Bob Hope character,

I thought of my character on the screen. And over the years I hope I've grown. Not everybody thinks I've grown, just as some people talk about Fellini, and say, 'Well, we loved *La Strada* and *Nights of Cabiria* and *I Vitelloni* and those films where you see a story and it is moving and interesting. But when you get on to this business of *Satyricon* and *Roma* and the opera picture, it's not for us.' I feel that I've grown with my films and I don't feel the same commitment to that comic character. When I wrote *Hannah and Her Sisters*, I could have played either role, mine or that of Hannah's husband, the Michael Caine role. The past few years of my life, I haven't cared about presenting myself as a comedian. When there's a role for me, I do it. But there was nothing for me in *Radio Days* [he was, however, the narrator, and the whole movie is really about him], there was nothing in *September*, there was nothing in *Another Woman*. There happens to be in this little picture. And I'm going to write something that I appear in for this fall because I feel that I don't want to take advantage of my relationship with Orion. [The film he wrote was *Crimes and Misdemeanors*.] So I don't think about that anymore. I don't think the films should be a vehicle for a comedian. Just the opposite."

Steven Spielberg has said that filmmakers make the pictures that they liked to see as youngsters, a notion, Woody says, "I agree with completely. When I started making pictures, I was interested in the kind of pictures I enjoyed when I was younger. Comedies, real funny comedies, and romantic comedies, sophisticated comedies. And as I got a little more savvy, that part of me which responded to foreign films started to take over."

At the time he wrote *Take the Money and Run*, though, he was thinking strictly in terms of a vehicle for himself and his comic persona. The question was, who would direct him? There had already been talk about him directing a film (the abandoned Robert Morse project that eventually became *Bananas*), but at first Woody did not think he was eligible to direct this one. Jack Rollins was a little wary of his doing it; he thought Woody might be perceived as being an egomaniacal boy genius who wanted to write, star in, and direct his films. While this is precisely what Rollins envisioned Woody eventually doing, it seemed to him a bit early. But no one could decide who should direct. There was some thought of Val Guest, one of the several directors of *Casino Royale*, who had directed Woody's segment. Then Jerry Lewis was sent the script, which he said he wanted to do. (Woody had long been a fan of his; when he and Diane Keaton were dating, he took her up to the Catskills to watch him perform.) So Woody went out to Los Angeles and met with Lewis at his home. Lewis thought the film should be in color whereas Woody favored black and white, more in keeping with its *March of Time* documentary style. Still, they had a cordial meeting filled with general agreement, and afterward Lewis drove Woody back to his hotel. But then United Artists, rather surprisingly, decided not to take Lewis on, and Charlie Joffe told all the studios interested in the project that Woody should direct it. When Woody was asked why he thought he could do it, he replied: "I think I can make it funny."

In the end, Palomar Pictures agreed to give Woody a budget of $1.7 million and the former nearly failed motion picture production student was on his way to becoming what no one else in his class was: a motion picture maker. He consulted a few film directors for advice, among them Arthur Penn, who had just directed *Bonnie and Clyde*, but he read very little about filmmaking: "I have no technical background; it's a mystique promulgated by the film industry that technical background is a big deal. It's common sense when you look through the camera. You can learn about cameras and lighting in two weeks. The question is, do you want to take the time to get people who are not only very talented, but whom you can work with well, too?" Which is what he has done from the start. "I'm surrounded by lots of expertise on my films. I can tell those guys what I want and then go back and shoot it again the next day if I have to." He does not mean, however, that a great editor and a great cameraman can give a poor director a great film.

What he also surrounds himself with is an excellent cast, one that *looks* authentic as well as acts well. For small parts, Woody has never hesitated to use amateurs. The result is that the characters look like real people and not like actors trying to play real people. In *Take the Money and Run*, for instance, the tellers in the bank were played by schoolteachers, the insurance salesman was an adman, and one of the men on the chain gang was a porn store owner.

As the beautiful heroine that every comedy needs, in this case a sweet and cheerful laundress named Louise, Woody found the epitome of the soulful type with long dark hair he was crazy for as a teenager in Janet Margolin, whom he interviewed over lunch at the Russian Tea Room, down the street from the Rollins and Joffe offices. "She was so beautiful," he remembered twenty years later, "I went back to Rollins and Joffe and just sat there for ten minutes staring into space and speaking Hindu, Swahili." (In the film Virgil is so taken by her that he says, "After fifteen minutes I wanted to marry her. After thirty minutes I'd completely given up the idea of snatching her purse.")

Take the Money and Run was shot in San Francisco, in the summer of 1968, with the prison sequences filmed at San Quentin. The prison authorities and even the inmates were cooperative but there was one caveat: "The guards told us, 'If you're held hostage we'll do everything we can to get you out short of opening the gates,'" Mickey Rose says. "We went nowhere without a guard. But one day we walked across the yard with a guard who turned out to be an actor in costume."

The film is a mosaic of visual, cinematic, and verbal gags and many were made up on the spot: Louise visits Virgil in prison in the standard scene where they sit on either side of a screen. She pushes a hard-boiled egg through the screen as he catches the pieces. Meanwhile in the background a prisoner and a visitor are each manipulating a ventriloquist's dummy. Working in the prison laundry, Virgil comes upon a brassiere among the dirty clothes. He looks at it, then with a shrug tosses it into the washer with the rest. Virgil volunteers to try an experimental vaccine in return for possible parole. "The experiment is a success," the narrator says, "except for one temporary side effect. For several hours he is turned into a rabbi." Virgil ineptly works a shirt-folding machine, a scene conceived when Woody saw the apparatus. One easy one (on paper, anyway), in which a chicken was supposed to walk across the prison yard during a breakout and a voice-over would say to Virgil, "I'm Ed," was scrapped when the chicken—the prop department had figured they would need only one—wouldn't budge. Interviews with Virgil's parents (disguised in glasses with false noses and mustaches attached) and associates are interspersed. A music teacher recalls how Virgil studied the cello but "he really had no conception of how to play. He blew into it." Scenes such as one of a chain gang parody *Cool Hand Luke* and *The Defiant Ones*, among other movies. And there are blackout sketches (which depend more on the writing than on the acting), the most famous being the scene where Virgil gives a bank teller a stickup note.

TELLER

What does this say?

VIRGIL

Uh . . . can't you read it?

TELLER

Uh . . . I can't read this. What's this . . . "act natural"?

VIRGIL

No, it says, "Please put fifty thousand dollars into this bag and act natural."

TELLER

It does say "act natural"!

VIRGIL

(Looking at note) Uh . . . "I am pointing a gun at you."

TELLER

That looks like "gub," that doesn't look like "gun."

VIRGIL

(Studying note with teller) No, that . . . that's "gun."

TELLER

Uh . . . no, that's "gub" . . . that's a "b."

VIRGIL

No . . . that's an "n" . . . that's . . . uh . . . "gun."

TELLER

(Signaling to another teller) Uh . . . George, would you step over here a moment, please? . . . What does this say?

GEORGE

"Please put fifty thousand dollars into this bag and abt natural." What's "abt"?

VIRGIL

"Act"!

TELLER

Does this . . . does this look like "gub" or "gun"?

GEORGE

"Gun," see? But what's "abt" mean?

VIRGIL

"Act." That's "act natural." It says, "Please put fifty thousand dollars into this bag and act natural."

TELLER

Oh, I see . . . this is a holdup.

VIRGIL

Yes.

TELLER

May I see your gun?

VIRGIL

Oh. *(Reaching under jacket and partially lifting out gun in his belt)*

TELLER

Well, you'll have to have this note initialed by one of our vice presidents before I can give you any money.

VIRGIL

Please. I'm in a rush.

TELLER

I'm sorry, but that's our policy . . . the gentleman in the gray suit.

Virgil goes to the vice president and the same argument ensues. Soon everyone in the bank is involved with trying to decipher the note. The sketch ends with Virgil calling Louise from the police station to say he can't make their date that day, and as he tells her, "Why don't I give you a call in, um . . ." the cop next to him says, "About ten years."

The film closes with Virgil back in a prison cell. He was locked up earlier for having tried to rob an armored car—with a stolen gun that turned out to be a cigarette lighter. Virgil had almost succeeded in an attempted escape with a gun carved out of a bar of soap and colored black with shoe polish, but unfortunately it was raining heavily and by the time he got across the prison yard to the gate with his guard hostages, all that was left of the gun was a handful of suds.

Now Virgil is in for attempted robbery, having been nabbed by his intended muggee, an out-of-uniform policeman who recognizes Virgil from their childhood marching band. Virgil has been sentenced to eight hundred years but, ever hopeful, he confidently says that with

good behavior he can cut the time in half. Asked by the narrator if he
has any regrets about choosing a life of crime, Virgil says,

> I think that crime definitely pays, and that . . . uh . . . you know
> . . . it's great . . . the hours are good, and you're your own boss,
> and you travel a lot and you . . . you get to meet interesting people
> and . . . uh . . . I just think it's a good job in general.

NARRATOR

What about your cohorts . . . what ever happened to them . . . all
the guys you've been associated with in various gangs?

VIRGIL

A great many of them have . . . uh . . . become . . . uh . . .
homosexuals, and some of them have entered politics and sports.

NARRATOR

Well, how do you manage to spend your time in prison . . . do
you have any hobbies or anything?

VIRGIL

I do. I . . . I . . . I've been working on . . . I . . . I've been doing
a lot of stuff in shop, actually, and . . . uh . . . I'm very skilled with
my hands. I . . . uh . . . Do you know if it's raining out?

Finding an appropriate ending has been a problem of Woody's
from his first film on. The planned ending for this one had Virgil
machine-gunned à la *Bonnie and Clyde*. After the funeral, Louise stays
behind. Suddenly she hears from the grave, "Psst. It's me. Get me out."
But even with the funniness of him really being alive, the bloodletting
was too harsh an ending for a comedy.

There were other problems, too. As Woody was learning how to
direct a film, he was also learning how to edit one. He tried to put *Take
the Money and Run* together himself with the assistance of editor James
Heckert, but Woody says, "Although it was reasonably well edited, it
was dying" until Ralph Rosenblum, who had edited *A Thousand Clowns*
and *The Producers* and *Long Day's Journey into Night*, came along. "It
was like a human being without the heart. I was making all kinds of
terrible mistakes. I didn't put music into many of the scenes, so they
just played coldly and dryly," he said while editing *Oedipus Wrecks*.

(That day he had the idea of putting Gene Krupa's "Sing Sing Sing" behind his character's watching in horror as his mother and aunt make an unannounced visit to his law office. The beating of the tom-tom signals trouble when his secretary interrupts a meeting with the head of the firm to tell him of the visit, and then Benny Goodman's clarinet swings up as the scene cuts to the long hallway where the two little old ladies wearing *Cats* buttons march inexorably toward him. "Ominous," Woody said, red-faced with laughter as he watched it with the music for the first time.)

In order to get an audience's reaction to *Take the Money and Run*, Woody screened the picture several times for soldiers gathered from the USO. As the film was still in a rough-cut version, there were no titles, no sound effects, no music—and there was no explanation of this to the audience. Perhaps a dozen young men watched each screening, invariably in stone-faced silence. Woody was crushed afterward each time. "I didn't know what I was doing," he now says. Then Rosenblum came in on the picture. "Look," he told Woody, "you've thrown out a ton of funny material, and you've got to put a piece of music behind that," or "You can't put a dreary, dirgelike piece behind this." In one such scene, Woody prepares himself for a date with Janet Margolin (his clothes hang in an old refrigerator, his shoes are in the freezer). He turns on the bathtub, gets into the shower, and does various pieces of business—puts on his pants, looks in the mirror, tries to be suave—yet playing behind that was a gloomy, sad piece of music. Rosenblum replaced it with a piece of Eubie Blake ragtime and said, "Look. Look what happens when you put a piece of lively music behind it." Woody saw. "The whole thing just came to life. I was suddenly just bouncing along. It made all the difference in the world. And there are a million little things I just didn't know. Probably seventy-five percent of the movie that was released is from my first edit, but what Ralph did was the difference between living and dying. My version was sure death. I edited it but I didn't make it alive. Ralph made it breathe. I feel he saved me on that picture."

Rosenblum suggested that Woody use pieces of a long interview with Virgil's parents (most of which had been cut out) as a funny bridge between segments that did not naturally flow into each other, and that he add more of narrator Jackson Beck's interviews with Virgil to link the mélange together. Narration is a favorite tool of Woody's. In *Zelig* and *Radio Days*, it is the cement that binds the story.

Woody's ability to go into a corner and quickly write whatever dialogue or narration was needed on scraps of paper was matched by composer Marvin Hamlisch's ability to come up with appropriate music in short order. (Hamlisch, who had been a rehearsal pianist until scoring *The Swimmer* and *Take the Money and Run*, later wrote the score of *A Chorus Line*.) But despite their similar ability to work fast with brilliance, the two were a personality mismatch, an example of the singularity of genius. Where Woody is invariably calm and patient, Hamlisch had endless questions to which he wanted immediate answers.

He "got in the habit of making frequent calls to the cutting room," Rosenblum wrote in his memoirs, *When the Shooting Stops*. "Incapable of withstanding a moment's wait, he would insist on playing new arrangements right over the telephone, as Woody and I, our minds elsewhere, struggled to be receptive. 'Marvin was wonderful,' says Woody, 'but he really used to drive us crazy. He'd call six, eight times a day, obsessed about everything and nervous about everything. Could I come over and hear a piece of music, could Ralph come over, what kind of cue for this section, would I buy this piece of music, does this sound good, should it just be piano, should it be piano and trombone, should it be funny, could we extend the scene a little bit 'cause it would help—a million questions about everything.'" Their worst moment, according to Rosenblum, was at the recording session for the ballad Hamlisch wrote for the main title sequence. "Woody's impassive reaction—'What was *that*?' he shrugged when the band finished playing—had so upset the young composer that when Allen left the room, Marvin lay down on the floor and wept."

None of this should undermine the importance of Hamlisch's contribution to the movie (and later to *Bananas*, which Rosenblum calls "one of the great unacknowledged film scores"). Comedy demands accompaniment and the music is a great, almost subconscious part of *Take the Money and Run*. (A bad score undermines comic effect, detracting from the jokes or overemphasizing them; it does everything but support them.) Woody places such high value on scoring that the vast majority of his films use music selected by him. He has had Dick Hyman arrange songs and write some original music for *Radio Days* and *Zelig*, for instance, but in the main Woody relies on standards from the first half of the century for accompaniment. He realized he could provide the music for his movies after Rosenblum introduced him to the concept of using a record to augment scenes in *Take the Money and Run*. Now, apart from the obvious strength of beginning with a solid story and script, Woody feels that "frame to frame, the score and the performances in my films are strong. I may write it wrong, but in those two areas I do very well."

Yet his talent as a scorer of movies is widely overlooked, or is so taken for granted that it passes unremarked. Music is such an integral part of Woody's presentation of a film, and his use of tunes from 1900 to 1950 so pronounced, that it is possible to recognize a Woody Allen film from the score alone. While he likes to cite Ingmar Bergman as a paragon of filmmaking, he differs from him in at least one major way: "Bergman says that he stopped using scoring because the combination of music and film was barbarous. 'Barbarous' was really the word he used. I'm the opposite."

After *Take the Money and Run* was reedited by Rosenblum and Woody (and after it was praised by Diane Keaton), it was shown to Palomar executives, who sat as stone-faced as the troops rounded up at the USO did at their screenings before the film was recut. After the first reel, one executive turned and asked Mickey Rose, "Are the rest of the reels like this?" There was talk of not releasing the film but Charlie Joffe persuaded them to give it a shot. Two prints of the movie were made and it opened on August 19, 1969, at the 68th Street Playhouse, a small theater on the East Side of Manhattan that often shows art and foreign films. But if the Palomar executives didn't get the movie, Vincent Canby and most of New York did. "The nicest surprise of *Take the Money and Run* is that it shows [Woody] has been able to complement visually the word-oriented humor of the writer-performer. . . . Allen has made a movie that is, in effect, a feature-length, two-reel comedy—something very special and eccentric and funny," Canby wrote in *The New York Times*. In another piece the following Sunday, in which he couldn't have known how correct he was, he added, "Like a nightclub monologue, the movie has a sort of loose-leaf form. You have a feeling that scenes and, perhaps, entire reels could be taken out and rearranged without making much difference in total impact, which is good because it all looks so effortless. Allen and Mickey Rose . . . have illustrated in fine, absurd detail the world that Allen has been talking about all these years." *Take the Money and Run* broke the record for ticket sales at the theater.

United Artists executives were so impressed by the movie that they wanted to sign Woody to do films for them, especially since they had blown the opportunity to do *Take the Money and Run* by offering only $750,000 as a budget. At a rally in 1969 for John Lindsay at Madison Square Garden, Charlie Joffe ran into David Picker, then UA's president. As they chatted under the grandstand, Picker asked what kind of deal Woody wanted to come to UA and Joffe said, "Two million budget, total control after you approve the story idea, and a three-film contract."

"Fine," Picker said. "Get your lawyers on it." And they shook hands in agreement. The only addition to the agreement was that if a film went over budget, Woody and Rollins and Joffe would cover the excess out of their fees: $350,000 for Woody as writer, director, and actor; $125,000 shared by Rollins and Joffe as producers. (UA would pay anything in excess of their fees and the fees would be recovered if the film turned a profit.) In addition there was $200,000 and $50,000, respectively, deferred until the film recovered its cost—at the time, generally 2.7 times the actual production cost (it is less than that in this age of fifty-million-dollar movies). Woody also was given 50 percent of the net profits, which he shared with Rollins and Joffe and others. Despite the rising cost of films and the higher salaries paid to other directors, Woody refused to renegotiate the contract for seven years, other than to let Rollins and Joffe wangle another $25,000 in production fees. And however attractive 50 percent of the net seems, Hollywood bookkeeping has myriad ways to stop films from ever showing a profit. It is unlikely, for instance, that *Take the Money and Run* will ever technically be in the black.

Happy with his deal at UA, Woody went in with his first script, a drama called *The Jazz Baby*. "The guys were white-faced," Woody recalls. Rollins and Joffe weren't excited about it either. They wanted Woody to establish himself better before branching out. (By the time he wanted to make *Interiors* in 1976, they were both supporters of his dramatic efforts.) Picker and his associates knew Woody could hold them to the contract and do the film, and told him so, but they also said that such a film just wasn't him. Woody didn't push them. "I'm not going to make a film by force," he said. "If you don't want to make this, forget it." He went home and two weeks later came back with *Bananas*.

The chairman of the board of UA was Arthur B. Krim. In 1951, he and Robert Benjamin came to the once-powerful company founded by Charlie Chaplin, Mary Pickford, Douglas Fairbanks, and D. W.

Griffith, which now was losing $100,000 a week and was effectively bankrupt. Chaplin and Pickford were in such disagreement over the running of the company that they no longer spoke to each other, but they didn't have to to know it needed new management. They found that in Krim and Benjamin, both lawyers with film business experience. With the company on the brink of receivership, however, the two needed some inducement to try to salvage it. They agreed to take over in return for a guarantee of 50 percent ownership if they turned a profit in any of the first three years of their stewardship. Due largely to their vision and their compelling personalities, they turned one the first year. (In 1956, with the help of some partners, they bought the other half of the company from Chaplin and Pickford.) They were helped by the 1948 United States Supreme Court ruling known as the Consent Decree that prohibited film studios from also owning movie theaters. The automatic markets that had allowed the studio system to thrive were over. By fortuitous timing, UA's ownership of neither a film production facility nor any theaters meant they did not have to suffer through the corporate overhaul that dismantled the studios, and they were not holding tracts of land and buildings that required vast sums for upkeep and taxes. Krim and Benjamin saw how to turn what for decades would have been a terrible disadvantage into their salvation.

Krim's and Benjamin's good names among bankers made loans available to keep the company going. Then they set themselves up as financiers and distributors of films. In return for money to make a movie and to compensate for the risk of their capital, UA would share in the profits from rentals of the film to theaters. This was revolutionary in that before the Consent Decree, studios pocketed production fees and studio overhead charges and had only small distribution expenses because they owned the theaters their films played in. As a result, the studios, not the individual producers, made most of the money. Now the producers, stars, and financiers stood to profit. The age of the independent producer, such as Charles Feldman, began.

In *Final Cut*, Steven Bach's account of UA's resurrection under Krim and Benjamin and its demise after the disaster of *Heaven's Gate* in 1980, he writes: "The most potent and enduring of lures and legacies Krim and Benjamin were to contribute to producers, United Artists, and, eventually, the industry [was] independent production in an atmosphere of autonomy and creative freedom. This laissez-faire approach to production—more than the careful distribution, more than the absence of overhead charges, more even than the promise of profits—was the distinctive difference that would make UA first unique, then the pacesetter for the industry."

It is not that Krim and Benjamin allowed producers to do whatever they pleased. Contracts were stringently written and UA retained vast rights of approval of the projects and those involved in them. But they were not the dictators who had run the studios, and thus whatever independence they offered looked even better by comparison. They also had a strong sense of what would make a good film and what wouldn't, and that sense extended to attracting people of high talent. The films that were made under UA's aegis ranged from *The African Queen* to *Around the World in 80 Days*; from *Some Like It Hot* to *West Side Story*; from *Witness for the Prosecution* to the James Bond and Pink Panther series.

The sense of autonomy and creative freedom that became the hallmark of UA is what made Krim so attractive to Woody, and is what has made Krim's support so valuable to him. Krim's respect for Woody's talent—and the unparalleled freedom Krim has granted him—has allowed Woody to grow as an artist without corporate interference from his backers.

Krim first met Woody in 1964, when he was chairman of a group of heavy-hitter Democratic contributors called the President's Club and Woody performed at a fund-raising event for Lyndon Johnson. They had more contact after Woody signed with UA, although initially Woody dealt mainly with David Picker. By the time Woody made *Love and Death* in 1974, however, he was dealing more and more with Krim, who recognized him as unique. Complications kept arising in Woody's deal with UA, such as his not wanting to have his movies shown on TV or airplanes, and they had to be adjudicated by the chairman. Krim conceded Woody the points and over the years has made allowances for him that he has made for no one else, because he believes "we can say with total credibility that we do it for Woody because he's special."

In 1978 Krim and four of his top executives left UA and formed Orion Pictures Corporation, with Krim as chairman of the board. UA had merged with Transamerica Corporation in 1967, but by 1974 the marriage was in trouble. In early 1978 Krim was quoted in *Fortune* as saying, "You will not find any top officer here who feels that Transamerica has contributed *anything*." John Beckett, Transamerica's chairman, responded: "If the people at United Artists don't like it, they can quit and go off on their own." They did. Woody would have preferred to follow Krim, but he still had two films left on his UA contract and felt he should honor it.

"I see you've formed this Orion company," Woody said to Krim one day when he met him on the street.

"We call it 'Waiting for Woody,' " Krim answered.

UA offered all sorts of blandishments to persuade Woody to stay, but when he has a choice, his allegiance has always been to people rather than companies, and in 1980 he moved to Orion. Orion had their own bank line to finance their films but they were also in an agreement with Warner Brothers, whose money they were in a sense using. Krim and Orion said to Woody, "Make whatever you want to make, within a certain budget." Warner Brothers, however, was not as keen on Woody as Orion was and the latitude Orion insisted on giving him contributed to the two companies' decision to dissolve their partnership.

Krim, a courtly man in his early eighties, likes to say that he came into the movie business with Charlie Chaplin and will go out of it with Woody Allen. Woody in turn feels Krim has had a large and positive effect on his career and is very comfortable with the personal and business relationship they have. Krim early on felt that Woody does "this very offbeat, talented work and we were able to establish it as such without causing concerns with our other producers." Now, he says, "I feel that because Woody has been with us so long, it is a motivation for other top creative people to come to us." He feels that Woody's special status is earned and accepted. "He just has a unique talent. Why was Rembrandt special?"

"Oh, sure," Woody said when told this. "Like Rembrandt, they're going to wait until I'm dead to make any profit off my pictures."

Woody's current and long-standing deal with Orion pays him 15 percent of the gross receipts, which he splits with Rollins and Joffe as well as Robert Greenhut, who has produced all his films since *Annie Hall*. Greenhut, a tall, lean man of about fifty who is known as Bobby and whose desk is a poker table, has the face of an acolyte and the mind of a winning horse player. In 1976 he was associate producer for Rollins and Joffe on *The Front*, the first non-Allen-written film Woody played in (Walter Bernstein wrote it, the late Martin Ritt directed). Besides producing fifteen of Woody's pictures, he has also produced, among other films, *Arthur, Big*, and *Working Girl*.

One of the lessons Woody learned from *Take the Money and Run* is that you can never have enough jokes for such a movie, and so for *Bananas* he and Mickey Rose loaded up even more. He also took others wherever he could find them. An elderly string quartet accompanying a palace dinner pantomimes playing their instruments because the fiddles rented for the scene had not yet arrived by the time everything was ready to shoot. Rather than being in documentary style, this film had a more conventional look. "Instead of using a hand-held camera, this time we used a fixed camera and hand-held actors," Rose says.

The film also had Woody's first cinematic dream sequence: Monks are carrying a man on a cross. As they stop on the street to back into a parking space, another group of monks carrying a man on a cross try to take the space and a fight ensues. Dreams proliferate in Woody's movies but he has surprisingly little use for real ones. The closest he comes to using them is to let his unconscious work on problems as he sleeps; when he gets into bed, he thinks of a problem in a script he's working on in the hope his mind will sort it out during the night.

"Nothing I've ever written has ever originated in a dream in any remote way," he said one day while talking about director Robert Altman, who had a dream and made the deal for *Three Women* based on it ("with an option on two other dreams, I guess"). "I like to use dreams occasionally in my work because you can be very graphic. I did remember my dreams when I was in psychoanalysis and I was making an effort to remember them. But when I saw how wasted that effort was, I stopped remembering them. The first time you're in psychoanalysis and dreams are interpreted for you, with you, there's a sort of exhilarating feeling that you're putting a puzzle together. But I found in years and years and years of treatment that apart from the puzzle pleasure, the play pleasure of doing that, it had absolutely no resonance in any way in my life. I never learned a scintilla about myself from a dream."

A scene in *Annie Hall* combined flashback action with daydreaming. Alvy and his second wife, Robin, are at a typical New York West Side party full of bookish types and urban intellectuals. Alvy has escaped to the bedroom, where he is watching the New York Knicks play a basketball game as Robin walks in.

ROBIN

Here you are. There're people out there.

ALVY

I can't believe this—the Knicks were fourteen points ahead—now they're two points ahead.

ROBIN

Alvy, what is so fascinating about a group of pituitary cases trying to stuff a ball in a hoop?

ALVY

It's physical . . . One thing about intellectuals—they prove that you can be brilliant and have no idea of what's going on. On the other hand . . . *(Clears his throat)* the body doesn't lie—as you know. *(Grabbing her, pulls her down on the bed)*

ROBIN

Alvy, stop acting out . . .

ALVY

Come on—it'll really be erotic—all those Ph.D.s in there discussing modes of alienation and we're quietly humping.

ROBIN

Don't—you're using sex to express hostility.

ALVY

Why do you always reduce my animal urges to psychoanalytic categories? *(Clears his throat)*, he said, as he removed her brassiere—

ROBIN

(Annoyed) Alvy, there are people here from the *New Yorker* magazine—my God, what would they think?

The scene in the movie ends here, but Woody shot more:

(Robin leaves. Alvy checks last look at game on TV. We see game and it is Knicks vs. a real team—)

ALVY

(Mutters as he watches) Intellectuals—where does it get you—

ANNOUNCER'S VOICE

Knicks' ball—out of bounds—Jackson to Bradley—shot! No good! Rebound—Kierkegaard—
CUT TO *set where this is happening.*

ANNOUNCER'S VOICE
(Cont.) Passes to Nietzsche—fast break to Kafka! Top of the key—
it's Kafka and Alvy—all alone—they're both gripped with anxiety—
and guilt, and neither can shoot! Now Earl Monroe steals it! And
the Knicks have a four-on-two—

The deleted part with Alvy playing was filmed in Madison Square
Garden, where Woody has season courtside seats. He is a lifelong basketball fan and his favorite player at the time of *Annie Hall* was Earl
Monroe, whose playing he found "poetic"; now the player he most
enjoys watching is Detroit's Isiah Thomas, whom he calls "a latter-day
Monroe." (Each, by the standards of the game, is small but both have
amazing grace.) For many of the crew, being on the floor of the Garden
with Knicks players was a dream come true, and they took every opportunity to shoot baskets. Woody, who is a good schoolyard player,
also had ample opportunity to turn daydream into reality but in a telling
choice preferred to keep the perfection of the fantasy, unless its real-
ization could also be perfect. "I resisted the temptation to shoot," he
recalled one day. "It was a pleasure I denied myself. My feeling was,
it had to be all or nothing—sign me to a contract or no shot at all."

Woody first presented himself to the public as an amusing fellow intent
on causing laughter, but little in life is what it seems. Just when people
thought they had him pegged, he transformed himself. For all of
Woody's low regard for *Everything You Always Wanted to Know About
Sex*, it proved his ability to make a film look any way he wanted it to,
and the fact was not lost on him. Where until then he had been happy
to concentrate on the jokes, now each component of a film was of equal
importance to him. In 1973 he burst from his chrysalis. During the
making of *Sleeper*, film editor Rosenblum telephoned producer Jack
Grossberg from New York to ask how Woody was coming with the
filming in Los Angeles. "Slowly," was the answer. Woody constantly
wanted sets rebuilt, props enhanced, scenes reshot. This movie would
look a lot different from any before it. "How so?" Rosenblum asked.

"The butterfly has come out," Grossberg told him, "and he has
red hair."

Part
Five

The Million-Dollar Finesses

Thank God the public only sees the finished product.
—Woody Allen, while editing CRIMES AND MISDEMEANORS

Among Woody Allen's many talents is his ability to incorporate mimicry with creativity. He learned the cadences of Bob Hope, the language of S. J. Perelman, the style of George Lewis, the outlook of Mort Sahl, the obsessions of Ingmar Bergman, the zaniness of the Marx Brothers, the soulfulness of Buster Keaton, the existential dilemma of Jean-Paul Sartre, the exaggerated exoticness of Federico Fellini, along with a score of additional influences, and (as they had built on others) he mixed their essences with his own to produce a unique sensibility.

When he talks about his work, it is full of references to these people who were once heroes to him but now for the most part are peers; he knew and was admired by Perelman and Groucho, he knows and is appreciated by Sahl and Bergman. When he invokes, say, Bergman, it should be heard as his aspiration to achieve a comparable body of work, not as the voice of a Brooklyn boy full of adulation for someone far superior to himself. For when historians write their books on films in the last third of the twentieth century, Woody's will surely be among the handful that stand out. *Alice, The Purple Rose of Cairo, Stardust Memories, Zelig, Radio Days, Manhattan*, and *Crimes and Misdemeanors*, among others, capture life in original and arresting ways.

It is not that every film of his is a masterpiece. Some, like *A Midsummer Night's Sex Comedy*, are trifles. In others, such as *September*, the dramaturgy does not deliver the intended impact in full. Yet whether an individual film works in all aspects, each of them succeeds on one level or another, and when they fail, they fail interestingly and with a certain flair. In no case has the viewer wasted an hour and a half. It is easy to be entertained by a Woody Allen movie and equally difficult to be bored, because an intelligence and a vision are always on display.

His achievements in mid-career are already impressive, and at the rate he works, he will easily turn out twenty or thirty more pictures. The twenty Woody Allen–written and –directed films to date are an eclectic mélange of subjects and styles. There have been outright comedies (*Bananas*), straight dramas (*Interiors, Another Woman*), pseudo-documentaries (*Take the Money and Run, Zelig*), surrealist fantasies (*Stardust Memories, The Purple Rose of Cairo*), social observation and romance (*Annie Hall, Manhattan*), a droll recollection of the joys of radio (*Radio Days*), shaggy-dog stories (*Broadway Danny Rose, Oedipus Wrecks*), an idyll (*A Midsummer Night's Sex Comedy*), a send-up of erotic mores in a parody of a variety of film genres and directorial styles (*Everything You Always Wanted to Know About Sex*), what he calls his "novels on film" (*Hannah and Her Sisters, Crimes and Misdemeanors*), a play on film (*September*), a futuristic fantasy (*Sleeper*), a comic-book *War and Peace* (*Love and Death*), and a meditation on whether one is a user of or a giver to the world (*Alice*).

He has grown from a comedian translating a monologue into film in *Take the Money and Run* to a character using a vast array of film techniques (split screen, cartoons, flashback, narration, stream of consciousness, fantasy) to tell his story in *Annie Hall* to an ironic commentator on values and artistic fulfillment in *Crimes and Misdemeanors*. The cinematography he has used to show his stories ranges from the crude, hand-held-camera style of *Take the Money* and *Bananas* to the deeply contrasted, Ansel Adams–like black and white in *Manhattan* to the cartoon brightness of *Radio Days* and *Alice* to the autumnal richness of *Hannah, Another Woman*, and *September*.

In his films he has joked, whined, probed, questioned, and laid bare human frailty and foolishness, meanness and hope. He has shown that fantasy is in the end defeated and ruled by reality in *The Purple Rose of Cairo*, paid homage to the virtue of loyalty in *Broadway Danny Rose*, dissected the insidiousness of self-absorption in *Manhattan*, described the redeeming nature of love in *Zelig*, held that hard as we may try, we cannot escape our emotions in *Another Woman*, and sought God thinking Him not there in *Crimes and Misdemeanors*. He has tried to capture the big game of family relations in *Interiors* and net the butterflies of an August day in *A Midsummer Night's Sex Comedy*.

He has dealt comically and dramatically with murder, morals, insanity, desire, hope, conscience, the unpredictability of love, and what makes life worthwhile in a hostile universe. Most of his films make people laugh not only at characters on the screen but, they soon realize, also at themselves. Others touch the nerve of self-realization in dramatic ways. Almost all of them share a single result: They make the viewer think. Sometimes one leaves the theater feeling he has nibbled a minnow, only to realize later that he has swallowed a barracuda, for the subjects of his films, no matter how they are presented, are thorny and basic and they play again and again in memory. His movies are so full of detail and observation that subsequent viewings reveal new insights.

The earliest films sought laughs, not thought. *Take the Money and Run* (1969) and *Bananas* (1971) are, he feels, funny in a sort of infantile or youthful way. "They trade," he says, "on what Noël Coward called the talent to amuse." *Everything You Always Wanted to Know About Sex* (1972) is technically well made, though Woody feels it was an unworthy undertaking. The film germinated from his seeing a Johnny Carson interview with the book's author, Dr. David Reuben, on *The Tonight Show*. When asked if sex is dirty, Reuben used a line of Woody's from *Take the Money*: "It is if you're doing it right." Where his first two movies were crudely shot, *Sex* is a compendium of cinematic techniques. One episode of the film parodies horror films; another imitates the style of director Michelangelo Antonioni. *Sleeper* (1973), which followed it, was much more a complete story than his others, and it was an effort on Woody's part to become a more proficient filmmaker, though he refers to this story of a contemporary man out of place in a futuristic society as "kinderspiel, silly child stuff."

Love and Death (1975) played with the issues of murder, war, social responsibility, God, and, of course, love and death. It is also a very funny movie, "my funniest picture to that time," according to Woody, "but its approach to the audience is on a kidding-around level."

Annie Hall (1977) vaulted him from a comedian admired by a respectable number of filmgoers to an Oscar-winning filmmaker embraced by a broad audience, though markedly so, in Woody's view, only after the Academy Awards. In technical terms he ranks the film among his half dozen best, but he holds the story at arm's length. "It massages the prejudice of the middle class," he has said. "It's nothing to be ashamed of but nothing special. It's still the area of romantic comedy and 'relationships,' which I mean pejoratively; not relationships like *Anna Karenina* or *The Red and the Black*."

He followed with *Interiors* (1978), the drama that mystified those in his audience who had pigeonholed him as a comedian. Some critics complained that he had made the film in bad faith, that he had broken some sort of moral contract with his audience, but to him it was nothing of the kind: He wanted to establish himself as a dramatist. He and his audience both had a good time with *Manhattan* (1979). Woody found it "indulgent, sensual fun to play with that view of Manhattan and that Gershwin music." The movie incidentally fulfilled his urge to show New York City in a pronounced, glamorous way. "Now whenever I do show it," he says, "I show it nicely, but that's strictly en route to the movie itself. I had a real urge to show New York as a wonderland and I completely exorcised that feeling in *Manhattan*." He has not, however, exorcised his desire to make his movies in New York, close to home. He attributes part of this to laziness but more of it to an indigenous homing instinct he notes in the work of directors such as François Truffaut, Jean Renoir, Fellini, and Bergman. "The directors I respond to so much are personal filmmakers, and they seem to have their work intimately connected with their lives." (He, however, is rooted in a city; they are more rooted in their countries.)

Other films have at least temporarily sated other urges. After *Stardust Memories* (1980) he didn't want to work in that baroque style for a while, though he does again now. He considers this his best film by far to that point, yet it was greeted with a collective gasp from many viewers and critics who thought Woody was mocking them in his Fellini-like use of actors with uncommon or even distorted faces who grasped and clawed at his character. To him, the film was about a comedian and filmmaker on the verge of a nervous breakdown who saw the world in a distorted way, and he succeeded in direction and style to step up to another level, however mixed the result for his audience. It is a film that has held up very well and that often pleasantly surprises viewers who see it today with a different perspective.

A Midsummer Night's Sex Comedy (1982) was a breather, a whimsical comic turn not very well received. To many people, it seemed like a step backward for him, yet it actually was a steppingstone to what he feels is a good period, and he has affection for it. If he has any reservations about *Zelig* (1983), his tale of someone who becomes like the person he is talking to, it is that the technical achievement—the inserting of Leonard Zelig into vintage newsreels or fabricated ones that look old, the sound, and making the film seem a decades-old documentary—was so flamboyant that it obscured the points he was trying to make about a man afraid to be himself.

He likens *Broadway Danny Rose* (1984) to *A Midsummer Night's Sex Comedy* in that it was "a little idea." He wanted to make the film

In Paris, ready to shoot his first scene with Peter Sellers
in *What's New, Pussycat?* "Think I'm scared?" It was also
his twenty-ninth birthday—December 1, 1964.

On the set of Annie Hall with Helen Ludlam,
Diane Keaton, and Colleen Dewhurst.

Bottom: Dylan Farrow (now renamed Eliza by Mia) visiting her father on the set of *Another Woman.* *Below:* Herbert Ross making a point while directing *Play It Again, Sam* in San Francisco.

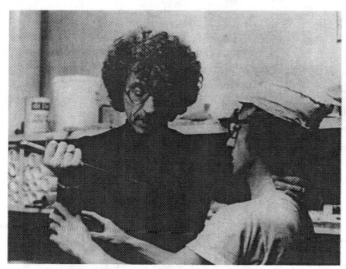

Directing a scene at the comics' table in *Broadway Danny Rose*. Woody's father is against the wall.

Tony Roberts: one of his leading men.

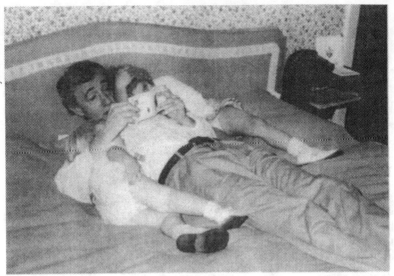

Top: With Satchel and Dylan, Salzburg, 1989. *Above:* In the rain in Leningrad, 1988; left to right, Lark Previn holding Satchel, Woody with Dylan, Fletcher Previn, Daisy Previn, Soon-Yi Previn, Moses Farrow, Mia. (Note: In 1993, Dylan's name was changed to Eliza, and Satchel became first Harmon, then Seamus.)

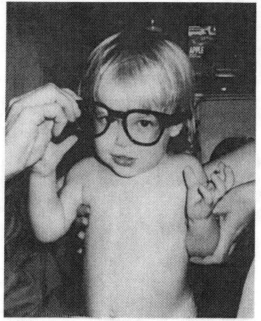

Above: Satchel Farrow, now Seamus, 1989.
Left: With Mia in Venice, 1988.

With Dylan, now Eliza, Venice, 1989.

so Mia Farrow could play a brassy character, and he had long had in his mind the story of a manager who nurtures his clients, only to be abandoned by them in the first flush of success. Woody feels it was nicely executed in general and is largely entertaining.

He was initially drawn to *The Purple Rose of Cairo* (1985) because he came up with an ending that was realistic, not escapist. The film grew from that. It was a technically complicated picture in that characters on the screen talk with people in the audience, and one character steps out of the black and white of celluloid fantasy into the real world of complex shades and colors. There, when he tries to pay for something, he literally and figuratively learns that the currency of the movies is worthless. It is one of Woody's favorite films.

In *Hannah and Her Sisters* (1986) he used a novelistic style to tell the story of a large group of intertwined characters. In one memorable shot, the camera circles the table where the three sisters talk over lunch, and as it goes around the table, each woman and her relation to the others is revealed. It was a very popular movie—for Woody, "always a dubious sign"—but he feels it is a somewhat middlebrow picture. What disappointed him was his inability to successfully write the ending he wanted. Ideally, Hannah's husband would still be infatuated with her sister, who is now in love with someone else, but he was unable to make it work on film. The result was a movie that ended like almost every movie, with happy endings all around: Hannah and her husband are secure, and the characters played by Woody and Dianne Wiest, supposedly unable to conceive a child, find that they have. It was too neat and tidy a finish for him. Life is more ambiguous, more unpleasant than that, and life is what he wants to accurately portray.

The lighthearted *Radio Days* (1987) is one of Woody's favorites. Its aim was modest, a picture done for fun, and successfully so; with sets and costumes and especially with music, he evoked an era.

From the broad and scattered canvas of *Radio Days*, filled with tenuously related stories, in *September* (1987) he went to a small summer house in which a half dozen characters play out their drama. Chekhov in the Colonies. It was a play he wanted to shoot as a movie, yet "I knew," he says, "very few people would like it because when you see something like this done on its most successful level, it's not widely seen because plays and movies are very different." Still, the idea made an interesting artistic challenge, and for Woody that made it a worthwhile effort.

Another Woman (1988) seemed in the shooting as if it would fulfill

Woody's goal of making a successful serious film, and one that did not have him in it. But after he was done he called it only "an improved picture. Like *September* and *Interiors*, its aims are high in terms of wanting to say something in a dramatic way." He believes, however, that "I wasn't good enough to have it rise to the level I wanted."

The forty-minute burlesque *Oedipus Wrecks* (1989) took a monumental number of reshoots and many, many attempts to get the effect of a mother who vanishes, then reappears as a gargantuan kibitzer in the sky. (John Mortimer wrote that the story could have been written by Nikolai Gogol.) "Do I see my fees flying out the window?" he asked one day as he set out to do still more work. The film was one-third of *New York Stories*; Martin Scorsese and Francis Ford Coppola directed the two other pieces. It is a fantasy on the ties that bind mothers and sons, a subject that few contemporary filmmakers could explore as amusingly and as seriously as he. He takes a son's worst fear and wrings laughter from it.

The success of *Crimes and Misdemeanors* (1989) made Woody reevaluate it: "When I put out a film that enjoys any acceptance that isn't the most mild or grudging, I immediately become suspicious of it. A certain amount of positive response makes me feel comfortable and proud. Then beyond that, I start to feel convinced that a work of any real finesse and subtlety and depth couldn't be as popular as it is."

Shortly after the movie opened—he was already filming *Alice* (1990) by then—Woody was glum. "People who have no concept of films or artistic maturation, or of my films, said to me, 'I like that film. It is your most mature film.' And they don't have the slightest idea. Last night someone was telling me they had seen it at a screening in Hollywood, on the Bel Air circuit at somebody's house. A number of celebrated names were there who all loved the film and they were happy to see it fourth on the charts businesswise in the United States. Ahead of it were three films of really moronic content. They were saying this, of course, all to make me feel good. And I was so depressed.

"Mia asked, 'What are you thinking of?' I was sitting in the corner. 'Why such a long face?'

"I said, 'I know I must be doing something wrong if my film is being viewed in some Hollywood character's screening room and a group of people there are saying, "It's his best film," when many of the things I attack are what they stand for.' If it really was a wonderful film, I feel it wouldn't get that interest."

Woody's harsh summary of his films and his distrust of anything more than faint praise of them might sound like the whining of an ingrate, as if he is saying to his large and loyal audience that they are fools for liking his work and in the process making him wealthy and revered. It is not what he intends. Self-deprecation has long been his style; what established him as a comedian was his stance as a guy who has a lot to complain about. It should be remembered, too, that he is someone who covered his ears when audiences applauded his stand-up act, a man who is embarrassed by a request for an autograph. As he has said, it may well be that as a child he wanted adulation so fiercely that getting it as an adult makes him recoil at what he perceives as the venality of his own desire. But whatever the root, to borrow one of his lines, Woody does not tan in the bright sun of approbation, he strokes. In *Annie Hall*, Alvy Singer says:

> There's an old joke. Two elderly women are at a Catskills mountain resort, and one of them says, "Boy, the food at this place is really terrible." The other one says, "Yeah, and such small portions." Well, that's essentially how I feel about life. Full of loneliness and misery and suffering and unhappiness, and it's all over much too quickly.

Then he adds what is the telling line:

> The other important joke for me is one that's usually attributed to Groucho Marx, but I think it appears originally in Freud's *Wit and Its Relation to the Unconscious*. And it goes like this—I'm paraphrasing: "I would never want to belong to any club that would have someone like me for a member."

Woody Allen is an artist whom many want to freeze in the familiarity of outlandish comedy. Yet being a comic was always to him only a step on the way to other achievements, and his films for the past fifteen years have been a wide mix of comic notions and dramatic themes. When his mother told him to aim high, she may have meant it only in the context of his becoming a successful joke writer while still a teenager, but the guiding principle of his career is that he aims high—always higher than where he is. For a public that likes to categorize and put people in niches, this is a mixed blessing. One knows what to expect from a Marx Brothers movie—or from a Bergman movie—but one doesn't know what to expect from a Woody Allen movie, because there is no such thing as a Woody Allen movie in terms of easy categorization. A Woody Allen film has nothing to do with persona and everything to do with creativity. A Woody Allen film is one which is imaginatively written, beautifully photographed, and well acted. It may be comic or dramatic or both. The Woody Allen character appears in many, but when he does, he is part of the whole, not the whole movie. Yet that character has so powerful a hold on many viewers' recognition and expectation that he obscures the artist behind him. If one were to see for the first time and without credits *Interiors*, *Manhattan*, *The Purple Rose of Cairo*, and *Crimes and Misdemeanors*, to pick four more or less at random, they would recognize the actor in two of them but likely never suspect they all were made by the same person.

Woody may carp about his perceived failures, but he also talks about people viewing his films a hundred years from now, and he cannot feel that badly about them if he has one eye on how they will play in five generations. His hope is that in retrospect the complaints about whether he made a comedy or a drama will be put aside and that his progress will be noted when all the films are seen as a whole that built on itself.

His malaise reflects his own sense of dissatisfaction with his work, for however high he aims, in his eyes he falls short. Beneath the carping, there is this request: "Look, that film may have been okay, but I've got an idea for a *really* good one." And though he says, "I'm not so far away in my own feelings from people who criticize me the harshest," he also says, "I'm appreciative of the praise I get. I would feel good if I'm half as wonderful as people sometimes think I am. I'd like to believe some of the nice things written about me. Part of my problem is my own subjectivity. I think of an idea for a film, I write it and rewrite it and work on it, nose to nose with every frame for a year. By the time I'm done, I have so many angry memories of things that went wrong, that didn't work, and that I had to compromise on. But it comes out and people go into a movie theater and pay their seven bucks and sit down with no idea of what I was trying to achieve. They say, 'Hey, this is entertaining; it's a fresh idea and it looks good.' I'm not saying my work is degenerate or insulting to the intelligence, it's just less than what I wanted it to be."

His reservations and criticisms aside, Woody and his films are very highly regarded within the motion picture community. There are two annual events one can count on in the film business: Woody Allen will make a movie and the Academy of Motion Picture Arts and Sciences will hand out Oscars, many times to him or to people in his films. Woody has been nominated for best director five times (*Annie Hall, Interiors, Broadway Danny Rose, Hannah and Her Sisters, Crimes and Misdemeanors*) and won once, for *Annie Hall*; has been nominated for writing the best original screenplay nine times (*Annie Hall, Interiors, Manhattan, Broadway Danny Rose, The Purple Rose of Cairo, Hannah and Her Sisters, Radio Days, Crimes and Misdemeanors, Alice*) and won twice, for *Annie Hall* and *Hannah* (only Billy Wilder with thirteen nominations and three awards has more); has had two films (*Annie Hall* and *Hannah*) nominated for best picture and won once, for *Annie Hall*; has been nominated for best actor once, for *Annie Hall*; in all, ten of his fifteen movies made between 1977 and 1990 were nominated for something.

As everyone knows, despite however many nominations he has, Woody will not campaign for them, nor will he attend the ceremony— or any awards ceremony. For that matter, he will not allow ads to herald the nominations or awards in or around New York City or Los Angeles; nor does he allow quotes from reviewers to appear in ads in those cities. Oscars (and quotes) mean so much added business for both the distributor and the theater owners, however, that he has had to allow them to be placed in other cities, where he won't see them. He has also won four Writers Guild of America awards (and been nominated ten other times) as well as its most prestigious Laurel Award for Screen, given for a body of work, virtually always at the end of a distinguished career, not in the middle of one. In addition, he has won many foreign Academy Awards. None of this array of hardware is in his apartment. Some are with Rollins and Joffe but the bulk he has had sent to his parents. For all the distinction and value the Oscars and other prizes may have, Woody does not like the idea of trying to win any of them.

"There are two things that bother me about [the Academy Awards]," he said in 1974 after Vincent Canby had written a piece wondering why *Sleeper* had received no nominations. "They're political and bought and negotiated for—although many worthy people have deservedly won—and the whole concept of awards is silly. I cannot abide by the judgment of other people, because if you accept it when they say you deserve an award, then you have to accept it when they say you don't. Also, it's hard not to get a slightly skewed feeling about the Academy Awards because apart from the ads and the campaigning and the studio loyalties, its a popularity contest really, because if the picture is not seen well or didn't do very well, its chances are hurt."

Yet one would have to be a Tibetan holy man not to derive *some* satisfaction from an Oscar, especially if one has spent a life as enmeshed in the movies as Woody's. And he admits that. "You take some pleasure but you have to be sure to keep it very much in perspective," he said after receiving the nominations for *Crimes and Misdemeanors*. "You think it's nice at the time because it *is* going to mean more money for your film, but as soon as you let yourself start thinking that way, something happens to the quality of the work."

One of his most pleasant fantasies when he was a boy in Brooklyn just starting out in show business was to follow in the footsteps of his idol Bob Hope, who hosted the Academy Awards telecast so wonderfully for so many years. "I'd watch them still if he did it," Woody has said. "Nobody could do those name jokes and MC like him." But when Woody was invited to host the show after he began to make films, he turned down the offer, to his great sorrow. "I know I could kill that audience," he said many years ago. "Sometimes I say to myself, 'Well, you don't even have to present one or accept one or get involved, but you can certainly perform on it, go out and do ten minutes and really break it up and you'll be seen by more people than will see your movies for the next twenty years.' But I can't bring myself to do it."

More recently he added, "What can you say about a system where an American cinematographer like Gordon Willis receives in his brilliant career in films, which is enviable the world over, one side-pocket nomination for *Zelig*, of all the ones. Of course, that was a technical achievement that had to do with him and the labs and the editing. It was a combination of everybody working together. But he's done superb photography on a large number of other pictures and he doesn't get a nomination for *The Godfather* or for *Manhattan*. How can you have any positive feelings, or how can the whole thing have any credibility? I find it hard to accept so much of what they extol and what they ignore."

When Woody returned home in 1975 from making *Love and Death* in France and Yugoslavia, he vowed he would never work outside of New York again. He had been away from home for a large part of two years, first filming *Sleeper* in Colorado and Northern and Southern California. His next film—as an actor only—was *The Front* (1976), the Walter Bernstein script about blacklisting directed by Martin Ritt, which was shot in New York. He settled into his Manhattan routine—dinner out seven nights a week with close friends such as Tony Roberts, Diane Keaton, Michael Murphy, Marshall Brickman, and Jean Doumanian. He dated regularly but no one often. For several years until he began to see Mia, there was a succession of women in and out of show business whom he saw a few times at the most.

He even stepped out one night with the President's wife. Woody was First Lady Betty Ford's escort to a 1975 benefit for the Martha Graham dance troupe. Mrs. Ford is a former Graham dancer and Woody is a big admirer of the choreographer. He wanted to get as much publicity mileage for the troupe as he could, and he came up with the idea of wearing black high-top sneakers with his tuxedo; he hadn't worked all those years for a press agent for nothing. The picture of the two of them was printed around the world, as was his straight-faced summary of his relationship with Mrs. Ford: "We're just good friends."

Not long after returning from Europe, Woody conceived *Annie Hall* with Brickman. Much of what Woody brought to the first draft was a murder mystery he had thought up sometime before. In one scenario a college philosophy professor named Dr. Levy would be found dead, an apparent suicide by leaping from his office window. Annie and Alvy were the characters in this version, too, and Alvy, aware of the professor's outlook on life, believed suicide was an untenable choice for him. They would prove it was murder. (Dr. Levy showed up a dozen years later in *Crimes and Misdemeanors*, this time an actual suicide. Lawyers for the publisher of Primo Levi, the Italian chemist who wrote eloquently about his survival in Auschwitz and who committed suicide in 1987, inquired if Woody was invoking him. Woody is an admirer of Levi's work, but he says that until their letter he made no connection between the two. Levy had been sitting around in his mind all those years and finally there was a chance to use him.)

The murder mystery began the same way as the finished film does, with Annie and Alvy meeting in front of a movie theater and arguing. Then it continued with their shenanigans as they tracked down the murderer. One alternative to using the Levy character was to have them return home after the film and become involved with their next-door neighbor, who is killing his wife. From there it metamorphosed into a period piece, a farce that took place in Victorian England. Woody went off to write it, but the day he began he said to Brickman, "Do we really want to write this? Do we want to go to Boston to shoot this and work in costumes and deal with all those problems? Let's do a contemporary story."

The story then evolved into a stream-of-consciousness illustration of what went on in the mind of Alvy Singer, a man incapable of experiencing pleasure; the love story was but one part of the whole. In the first draft, Alvy has just turned forty and is trying to sort out how he has become what he is. In quasi-Proustian flashbacks and flash forwards, associations are made that trigger other scenes and memories. It was a very novelistic, impressionist look at a character. For months the title was the name of his disease: *Anhedonia*. But the story had no dramatic drive; unlike a novel, a film exists in time and an audience needs a sense of forward movement. After Woody edited the film and screened it, audiences wanted to get past the other parts and back to the love story, which had a definite dramatic tension and drive to keep it afloat and the audience involved. Thus is art transformed.

Woody would still "love more than anything else in the world to do a murder mystery. That would be my gift to myself." He doesn't do it because he feels it's too trivial—he likens it to airport reading—and yet he has ideas for good ones. "I make a value judgment," he says. "I don't say what I do is so superior. I *try* to do superior work. I'm not saying that I don't strike out, but my attempt to begin with is higher than that. I'm going to insult all the mystery writers in the world, but to me a mystery story is still a second-class kind of thing no matter how you look at it. And I love them.

"People say to me, 'Oh, don't be silly. Look at Alfred Hitchcock.' I find that second-class stuff. It's great, but as he said, 'Some films are slices of life. Mine are slices of cake.' And that's what his films are: slices of cake. People will say *Macbeth* is a murder and *Crime and Punishment* is one, but I make a differentiation between those and what I'd like to do. In those, the murders are incidental to the drama; they're deep human and philosophical and spiritual dramas, and the murder becomes the vehicle from which these deep actions and ruminations spin off. That's not what films like *The Maltese Falcon* are, where the emphasis is on the who done it and why. Costa-Gavras did a wonderful one called *The Sleeping Car Murders* and it's superb. But it's a genre piece.

"I'm torn because I think I could be very funny in a comedy mystery and it would be enormously entertaining in a totally escapist way for an audience. But I can't bring myself to do that. This is part of my conflict. My conflict is between what I really am and what I really would like myself to be. I'm forever struggling to deepen myself and to take a more profound path, but what comes easiest to me is light entertainment. I'm more comfortable with shallower stuff," he said. Then, with a laugh, "I'm basically a shallow person."

Woody became a cartoon character while he was making *Annie Hall*, though not from the process itself. In 1976, *Inside Woody Allen*, drawn by Stuart Hample with jokes in part from Woody's collection that he jotted down on scraps of paper, premiered in 180 newspapers in sixty countries. It ran for eight years. Hample, a cartoonist who is now a playwright and screenwriter, became friendly with Woody in his earliest days as a performer. Woody says Hample, along with Diane Keaton and writer Pat McCormick, is one of the best laughers to have in the audience when performing in a nightclub ("they make up for a hundred people in terms of contribution"). Hample suggested the strip, and Woody, along with Rollins and Joffe, thought that it would be a good way to promote himself.

Every Saturday when they met to talk over the jokes and look at the sketches (Woody was as rigorous about every creative detail as he is with all his projects), Hample brought a sheaf of newspapers and stories related to the strip. Once he came with some Brazilian papers that gave it front-page coverage.

"Isn't that great?" Hample asked Woody.

"How do I know? I don't read Portuguese."

"You don't *have* to be able to read it to see they ran your picture and comic strip on the front page."

Woody looked silently at the paper for a minute. "I don't see the word *juif*," he said, then added, "Why am I always popular in countries where they torture people?"

The strip was widely read in the United States, too. Mary Beth Hurt used to call her mother in Iowa every Sunday. During one call while she was making *Interiors*, her mother asked what she was doing.

"I'm in a movie."

"Whose?"

Woody Allen

"It's written and directed by Woody Allen."
"Oh, I know him. He's the man in the funny papers."

Woody's return to New York in 1975 coincided with his attaining a new level of confidence in his work. Rollins and Joffe had provided him with great creative and psychological support all through his days (and nights) as a stand-up comedian and through the making of *Love and Death*. When he began to make films, he showed them his scripts as soon as they were completed, although in a somewhat unorthodox way: He would invite them up to his apartment, then have them read the script one at a time so that there would be no possibility of collusion in their reaction. Then all three would discuss it, often for hours. Apart from urging him to forget making *The Jazz Baby*, and the script he had written with Marshall Brickman called *The Filmmaker* that they had not been keen on, they were pleased with his growth. Rollins especially was supportive of Woody's risk-taking; although he is knowledgeable about and a great fan of comedy, he knew Woody was capable of more than sticking to just one kind of film. "He pushed me," Woody says, "to always be deeper, more complex, more human, more dramatic—and not to rest comfortably." Woody finds Jack a good theoretician, and the two of them, he says, "would speak endlessly about these matters. Then Charlie would go in and make a deal and get six times as much as we thought was possible."

Along with the support he still gets from Rollins, Woody feels he is also one of his harshest critics. "I've always said when the day comes that Jack and I agree that I've made a fabulous film—if that day should ever come, because neither of us has thought so yet—that we will know it as surely as those critics who have been rough on me over the years will know it, too."

But by the time he was ready to make *Annie Hall*, Woody's confidence in his writing had grown to the point that he did not feel the need to show anybody his scripts. Now he surprises Rollins and Joffe with the nearly finished film. Each brings to it a fresh eye that Woody trusts, and there is time to incorporate suggestions they may make, especially Rollins, who sees an earlier version than Joffe. Joffe moved to Los Angeles in the late 1970s to oversee the expansion of the office and to semi-retire. At one point Joffe felt that Woody had grown past whatever help he might offer and thought of withdrawing from any official connection with his movies. (All Woody Allen pictures are billed "A Jack Rollins–Charles H. Joffe Production" and Joffe was the on-set producer of four of the films through *Manhattan*.) "It may cost me millions of dollars," Joffe told him, "but the truth is, it's not a challenge for me to work on your films. What do I add to your filmmaking now?"

"Retire if you like from the other parts of the business," Woody told him, "but I want to know you're there."

In 1990 Rollins and Joffe sold the by-then-large agency to their associates and went back to their two-man partnership. Their only clients now are Woody, David Letterman, and comedian Rick Reynolds. Joffe has remained in Los Angeles, overseeing Reynolds's development. Rollins is still in New York. Woody calls on him when he has a problem that has no definite answer but rather requires the best use of judgment to act on. Joffe's greatest asset is that he is totally conversant with the intricacies of film deals, and Woody relies on his knowledge. Woody had almost hourly contact with the two during his first years as a performer, but his days of hanging around the Rollins and Joffe suite, looking down onto Fifty-seventh Street and assessing pretty women with Joffe, are long over. Woody talks by telephone several times a day with his secretary, Norma Lee Clark, to check on calls and mail, but months—years—can pass without his going into the office or their seeing each other. The same is true with Rollins. In a sense, Rollins and Joffe did a perfect job of parenting. They took a shy would-be performer who was so uncomfortable in crowds that he tucked himself into Joffe's back when they entered a restaurant, and they nurtured him until he grew into a giant—an industry. And then they let him go his own way, with the knowledge that they are always there for him.

The only time Woody ever really gave them concern was when he made *Stardust Memories*, which was released in the fall of 1980. Sandy Bates, a comedian and filmmaker played by Woody, is hounded by studio executives, his fans, his secretary, and his agent, all of whom have one compromise or another for him to make. Many viewers and critics were shocked by what seemed to be Woody's sourness toward them. They were wrong—Woody has always praised the support of his managers, his secretary, and his film studio and been grateful for his audience—but for a while Rollins and Joffe wondered, too. "When I walked out of the first screening," Joffe said in a *New York Times* interview after the movie came out, "I found myself questioning everything. I wondered if I had contributed over the past twenty years to this man's unhappiness. But I talked about it with my ex-wife, my kids, who grew up with Woody, and I talked with Woody himself for hours. He said to me, 'Does that really seem like the way I feel?' " Joffe then realized that people don't remain in bad business relationships for twenty years and that Woody was not hounded as Sandy Bates was. Woody knew that his playing Bates would cause people to draw some connection to him, but he was surprised by how completely they did. It was a case once again of Woody's persona overriding him in people's eyes.

It was also, however, an instance of what seems an unreflective side of his personality, because he arguably should have realized more clearly how the film would be viewed regardless of his intentions. Another version of this is how he deals with actors. For all his years of analysis, Woody has a certain blindness to the effects of his artistic vision, a vision that to one degree or another is indicative of his feelings and experiences. His increasing proficiency in all aspects of his filmmaking coupled with his own minimalist character has brought about a narrowed-down, streamlined process of working that year by year becomes even more internalized. This insulation and isolation—and self-sufficiency—may be what makes Woody Allen the artist different from other people. But it is what sets him apart from them, too.

Stardust Memories came right after *Manhattan*, in part the story of the relationship between a man in his forties and a teenager. Woody did casually date a younger woman at one point but he says that their activities were never like those in the film. If she looked anything like Mariel Hemingway, it would be easy to understand his interest. There have been a great number of beautiful actresses in Woody's movies but, he feels, Hemingway's beauty was not done justice in the way she was photographed in *Manhattan*. When he mentioned this to *New Yorker* film critic Pauline Kael, she dismissed his complaint; Hemingway certainly looked great in the film ("You're God's answer to Job," Woody tells her in one scene). Then some time later Kael saw what he meant. "You're right," she told him. "I saw her in a restaurant the other night. She's a goddess."

Woody and Mariel enjoyed doing *Manhattan* together and they became good friends. After the film was completed, she suggested that he come out to Idaho, where she is from, "and see how we live. Dad will be there and [Mariel's sister] Margaux and her boyfriend. Just come out and take a look at it." He accepted and admits that if it had been a man instead of a woman doing the inviting, he would never have gone. "The truth of the matter," he said some years later, "is I adored them all but I couldn't take that kind of environment."

It's too bad Woody had moved on from doing stand-up by the time he went to Idaho; his account of the trip would have made a nice routine for his act. It also is a good example of his normal conversation with people he knows well, in which he never tells jokes or stretches for a laugh but is funny because his perspective is different from anyone else's: "I went out there, my heart in my mouth. I had to fly someplace and then take a small plane to Ketchum, where she met me. So she drove me to her house in the middle of snow. And her family are all very athletic. Now I'm athletic, too, but it's a different kind of athletics. So I got there at three in the afternoon and we all sat around and chatted with Mom and Dad. And then we had dinner. Her father had shot dinner and you could hear the buckshot bouncing out of my mouth onto the plate. Bang, bang . . . you know.

"Then after dinner, as was the custom, she and her dad went for a long walk. I went with them. And we walked down the road, so cars with their bright headlights occasionally would come past, and that's always scary. This was in the middle of Idaho and it's freezing and the dog is running along with us. We took a long walk, like a mile and back. You know, they always have those kinds of names for things. Like 'We walked him to Grover's Creek and back,' or whatever. And I went to bed and the next day I got up and had breakfast with the family and we were sitting around and chatting. And we had lunch with Margaux and her boyfriend, whom she was to marry. And everything was fine.

"And then they took me for a hike in the snow, and that's when I started to get a little panicky. I was in good physical shape, that wasn't the problem. First of all, I was hiking, I hadn't brought any boots with me, so I was in these Stone Free shoes that are all style and made of cardboard. And they hiked me up over a mountain. At first you go and you go and you have to huff and puff because you're walking through high snow. And then after a while you turn around and there's nothing behind you as far as the eye can see but snow. You can't see the house and you're beyond a point of no return. It's a panicky feeling. And her dad is walking and peering through binoculars at the fauna. 'Oh, look,' he'd call out, 'there's a yellow-bellied sapsucker,' or whatever. They'd walked it a million times but it was a big deal for me. I mean it was up a mountain.

"That night during dinner she was telling Margaux, 'We walked him over Blind Man's Creek,' and everyone was laughing. I couldn't believe people did this sort of stuff. I went to bed that night and I thought to myself, 'This is not for me. I don't want to eat buckshot and walk over snow-laden mountains.'"

He survived the visit and has fond memories of the family. "I rarely see Mariel now," he says. "I wish I had a part for her. She's a wonderful actress. A natural."

Since around the beginning of 1980—about the time he began to see Mia Farrow—Woody has taken the fourteenth-century philosopher William of Ockham's doctrine that all unnecessary parts of a question are to be eliminated and applied it to himself. Ockham's Razor has become Allen's Law. The result is that Woody's life and work have microscoped. The acquisition of his editing room and screening room in 1979 allowed him to do all things connected with assembling his films in one place. Mia narrowed his attentions to one woman. No longer willing to travel to make his movies, he does all his shooting within driving distance of Manhattan. His daily life has evolved (or devolved) to the point that virtually every moment can be spent at work, with Mia and the children, or on such self-enrichment as practicing on his clarinet or reading. He takes no vacations apart from the occasional three-week trip to Europe with the family, during which he invariably does some writing and gives interviews in connection with a current film. This unglamorous and somewhat obsessed life is desirable because almost all extraneous distractions have been removed, therefore allowing him to concentrate on the making of his films while in the prime of his creative and physical ability to realize them.

This simplification of his life has not prevented complex personal changes, and it may well have enhanced them. His relationship with Mia Farrow is the longest and most involved of his life. His love for her brought him first into family life and then in 1985 to the most elemental change of all, his embracing in every way a child. The emotional depths that are opened by fatherhood cannot be plumbed without experiencing it. Yet these changes are more reflected in his outlook and his sentiments than they are in how he goes about his filmmaking, which is a steady evolution. Rather like a superb chef with a sauce, he has reduced his method to its essence. To see how he works, it is not necessary to trace his pictures chronologically. Rather, attitudes that shape one are abundantly clear in another.

Actors who have had no experience with Woody are almost always surprised by the absence of rehearsals before he shoots a scene. Even actors who have made films with him are sometimes surprised, too, but what he relishes is the spontaneity of their performance. "There is no theoretical point of view to my not rehearsing," he said during the filming of *Another Woman*, "but everything looks stale to me if I do it very much. So I don't look at the script after I write it. I mean, I write it and give it one look. Then I like to go and see what happens the first time actors do it." If he needs to, he can always rehearse it on the set with them. But he doesn't like to rehearse unless he has to. "Bergman likes to rehearse. But the reverse is better for me. It's part of our temperaments. He's a great artist and"—he gave a little laugh—"I'm not. Maybe it comes from his background in the theater and doing drama basically, while my roots are in comedy. In a comedy, you like that first time, before it gets stale. I'm probably wrong about that because Chaplin did scenes a hundred times. But I like to simplify things."

Woody clarifies the characters to himself as he goes along because, for him, writing the script is not the same as writing the movie. He writes a script so the film can be cast and costumed, so locations can be found or sets built. But really, he writes his movies as he makes them. Take, for instance, Frederick, the moody artist played by Max von Sydow in *Hannah and Her Sisters*. As he always does after he finishes the first draft of a script, Woody sat and talked with casting director Juliet Taylor about the characters and who might play them. After considerable conversation and tossing around some names she suggested von Sydow. He was someone Woody had not even remotely considered, but as soon as she mentioned him, he knew von Sydow was right. The part grew from there, beginning with his name, which Woody changed from Peter because Frederick was more in keeping with von Sydow's European looks and accent. He also became considerably older than Hannah's sister and his companion, Lee, played by Barbara Hershey, and very angry. Then the loft the location manager found for their apartment helped change a dramatic scene because Woody found it so visually strong when he went to shoot there.

Thus sometimes Woody is almost as uneducated as his actors when it comes to the fine points of their characters. "I know when there's a false step," he says. "I can see it in the dailies when something's wrong. But I don't always know exactly what I'm doing. I just know when it's not right. So I'll say to an actress with a question about her character, 'Just do what you're doing at the moment.' "

Hannah, for example, was a character Mia Farrow never understood, not at the start and not at the finish. Neither she nor Woody could ever figure her out. They could never decide whether Hannah was indeed a lovely, nice person who was the bulwark of the family and the spine who supported everyone else, or whether Hannah had a darker side. "At times, I didn't think she was nice, and at other times I did," Woody says. "Mia was always looking to me for guidance and I could never give it to her. I could just say to her, 'Well, play this scene and let me see as you play it instinctively and maybe I can change something.' But I'm in the dark a lot of times that way."

Elementary acting classes teach the importance of trust between players, but few ever have to so totally put their trust in a director as they must do in Woody. "I like it," he says, "when the actor comes in, if he has any questions, he can ask me, 'Am I a good friend of these people?' and I can tell him. And if he's doing something wrong, I can say so. It's really very simple if they'll just listen. But that simplicity is not always satisfying to the actor. The actor sometimes wants more. But telling them never helps."

Very simple for the director. Very nervous-making for the actor, even though there are no bad performances in Woody's movies; he protects his actors well, never leaving them looking or sounding awkward. Woody lays whatever shortcomings the film or the characters have at the feet of the writer and the director. He feels he has no excuses for why his films are not better except for his own inability "to be good enough, or not deep enough on subjects." He is solely responsible for the movie. An actor can rest assured that when he sees the picture, there will be nothing on the screen to embarrass him from a performing point of view; Woody has cut pieces out of pictures from quite important actors and actresses. If they have a lapse even for a moment, they won't find it in the finished film.

Sam Waterston has been in four of Woody's films and has learned that "the spontaneous, natural event seems what he wants to capture on the screen without anybody really knowing even that it happened. Woody is sometimes chatty with people before a take to make it impossible for you to plan what you're going to do." Waterston's first day of shooting on *Crimes and Misdemeanors* began after lunch. He arrived in time for the hour-long break, during which he chatted with Alan Alda, who had shot only a few of his scenes. A couple of other actors who also had limited experience with Woody soon joined in, tentatively at first and then more frankly, talking about the lack of rehearsal and the paucity of information from Woody about who their characters were. That afternoon, for instance, Waterston, Alda, and Joanna Gleason, none of whom had spent any time with the others before, were scheduled to play close siblings. The actors "were bemused and curious as they described these events," Waterston said, "and I just nodded my head and said, 'Yup, yup, yup.' Alan Alda said, 'So what you're saying is, you get used to it.' And I said"—he let out a huge laugh—" 'No! No, you don't!' And I explained that although you don't necessarily get used to it, to the degree that you do you're expanding your liberty as an actor, your freedom to just put it out there.

"I have a feeling it's representative of his personality and also of how he thinks about the process of moviemaking in which acting is a job among the jobs. We are accustomed as a class to living in a deluded world where the actor is the center of everything while he is being used. I find Woody's approach so refreshing even though it is so unsettling. I think it is terribly good for me as an actor to do this because in the end it seems what he is asking for is the simplest things you think you mastered in the beginning classes of acting, and what he's saying is that there are not then layers that you add to that. It's these fundamental things: Being present. Telling the truth. Responding spontaneously to whatever happens. Not giving up if odd things happen. Hoping for accidents. The willingness to improvise. The willingness to walk on a threadbare tightrope without a net. To put yourself at risk. All those things that you do the basic exercises for. Those are the things he wants and those are the things we all practiced in grade school. But partly defensively and partly because people tell you it's good, you begin to develop layers and layers of control and you get accustomed to being more in charge of your performance than that. Some other types of moviemaking and some other types of performance, it's very appropriate to be more in control. But one should at least be able to do this, and it's hellishly difficult to do."

Woody says his style is more to correct than to direct: "I try not to tell the actors anything at all and just have them do it, because they're all very good. If they do the part wonderfully from the start, the best thing a director can do is get out of their way and let the vitality come through. But in a sneaky way, I'm doing something, and if needed, I help guide them to the best reading I can."

His method, however, could better be described by a magician's term: misdirection. His talking to actors just before a scene, his giving only those lines necessary to play the part, even his perceived aloofness serve to draw the actors' minds to things peripheral to the part. A good magician creates a diversion away from the illusion, then pulls the illusion off. It is the same with Woody's directing. While distracting the actors from the precise point at hand, he puts them in a position to deliver their lines and act their parts more spontaneously and with less forethought. Any good movie is in a sense a feat of magic. The director shows only what he wants the audience to see, then springs his revelations and surprises at the appropriate moment.

There is also something of the musician in Woody's approach, because, having written the dialogue, he has a sense of exactly how it should sound. (The actor who perfectly got the sound Woody wanted was Martin Landau, who grew up in Woody's neighborhood. Landau did not imitate Woody's voice, but he captured the tone of his childhood. "He had every nuance," Woody says. "It was like falling off a log for him. He sounds exactly as I wanted it said.") If he doesn't hear what's in his mind in an actor's reading, he will ask for it to be done again— and again and again. At first, he is generally encouraging; he'll say something like "Gee, that was great. Let's do it one more time and then we'll get out of here." Of course, it almost never is one more take. But Woody will let the actor do it several more times without comment in the hope that the troublesome dialogue will get a good reading. If that fails, he will say something along the lines of "Do it more angry." If the words still do not make the sound in his ear that he expects, he will not tell the actor, "Listen, say it this way," and then recite the line; that, he believes, would lead to conscious mimicry. Instead he will sometimes say, "Let me see the scene for a second. What have I got here?" Then he will take the script and read both parts aloud, presumably for his own edification but actually so the actor can hear him, in the hope that what will happen is he'll realize, "Oh, *that's* what the guy is thinking. He hasn't been clear in telling me, but now I see." He may also tell the actor to drop or change a particularly vexing line, and will sometimes whittle away half or more of a character's dialogue to facilitate the reading he wants. Yet despite all this, sometimes nothing works. He'll give an actor many takes; he'll be tactful. Then after ten or twelve or fifteen takes, he'll adopt a more impatient approach in the hope that since nothing else worked, this might. "I don't believe a word of that," he'll say. "Human beings don't talk that way."

Sometimes it does work. While filming *Interiors*, Woody said on occasion to Geraldine Page, "That was pure soap opera. You could see that on afternoon television." But the result, he says, is that "I think Geraldine Page in *Interiors* was the best that I've ever seen her. I don't say that because it's my film. I think while she was one of our greatest actresses, she did have a tendency to be theatrical and overact. Certainly she was over the top when she started to do the scenes in *Interiors* and I had to say, 'Do less.' " (Page received an Academy Award nomination for her performance.)

While making *A Midsummer Night's Sex Comedy*, Woody asked José Ferrer perhaps thirty times to redo the line "These are not my teeth," a funny phrase very dependent upon nuance. After several failed attempts Ferrer became somewhat angry with Woody, to Woody's great surprise. "I had a wonderful time with him," Woody once recalled. "I thought he was a total delight in every way. Just that once I asked him to do a line over many times. Finally he said to me [in good Ferrer imitation], 'Now I can't, you've turned me into a mass of terrors.' And I thought to myself, 'My God, you're *José Ferrer*. How can I turn you into a mass of terrors? You're this wonderful actor and all I'm doing is saying no, that's not really the way I wanted it, do it again.' So I guess I'm insensitive, because I just take it for granted that they should take it for granted.

"It will astonish me sometimes that an actor or an actress will tend to do a scene a certain way," Woody went on. "I'm always operating from the perspective of 'I've hired you because I think you're great. You've got the job. You can tell me if these lines are moronic and stupid.' And I want to be able to go up and say, 'Don't do it *that* way. They'll laugh at us if you do it that way.' There are certain directors, such as Sidney Lumet, who have affectionate relationships with actors, but I've never been able to work that way. I give as much contact as is required professionally. Socially is a whole other world; I know there's not a buoyant atmosphere on my set. But I almost always make the wrong assumption that the actor's going to be secure, that we can be open and critical of one another."

Gene Wilder, who portrayed a doctor who falls in love with a sheep (and winds up in the gutter, drinking from a bottle of Woolite) in *Everything You Always Wanted to Know About Sex*, described his experience with Woody and contrasted him with Mel Brooks in a 1978 *New Yorker* article by Kenneth Tynan: "Working with Woody is what it must be like to work with Ingmar Bergman. It's all very hushed. You and I are talking quietly now, but if we were on Woody's set someone would already have told us to keep our voices down. He said three things to me while we were shooting—'You know where to get tea and coffee?' and 'You know where to get lunch?' and 'Shall I see you tomorrow?' Oh, and there was one other thing—'If you don't like any of these lines, change them.' Mel would never say that. The way Woody makes a movie, it's as if he were lighting ten thousand safety matches to illuminate a city. Each one of them is a little epiphany, topical, ethnic, or political. What Mel wants is to set off atom bombs of laughter. Woody will take a bow and arrow or a hunting rifle and aim it at small, precise targets. Mel grabs a shotgun, loads it with fifty pellets, and points it in the general direction of one enormous target. Out of fifty, he'll score at least six or seven huge bull's-eyes, and those are what people always remember about his films." ("I hear there's a sense of enjoyment on Mel's set," Woody once said. "I hear the people on his movies love the experience so much that they wish it would go on forever." He smiled. "On my movies, they're *thrilled* when it's over.")

In many instances, Woody will first shoot a scene without saying much at all, because he knows the actors have determined how they want to play the part before coming to the set. He feels that when actors come in wrong, they almost always come in with the scene too broad. It's very rare that they're not doing enough. The cause, he suspects, is that they rush because they're nervous and they want to get the scene over with, rather than luxuriate in it and have a good time. "I know that problem because I used to have it on a nightclub floor," he says. "I used to want to get out there, get my act over, and go. It's only when you're really looking forward to the time spent out there that the performance works."

Very occasionally, every attempt by Woody to get the performance he wants fails. When that happens, after the day's shooting and without anger or embarrassment to the actor on the set, Woody will replace him. The unpleasant task of breaking the news to the actor's agent falls to Juliet Taylor, who then mounts a search for the replacement. She more often provides actors with the pat on the back they might need. "He's not an actor's director," she says. "But it's his personality, not a personal offense. So I do it. It's an important but small aspect of my job."

However wonderful some actors may be, though, there is not a great likelihood of many "method" actors appearing in a Woody Allen movie. For example, Woody adores the work of Robert De Niro but is skeptical about their working together. "He's as great an actor as there is, but I'm told he needs a lot of time to get into his character. And I say, God bless him, because what you get is a brilliant and wonderful thing. I just can't work that way myself."

One notable exception to Woody's reluctance to use actors who steep themselves in their character is William Hurt, who appeared in *Alice*. He was aware of Woody's approach but wanted the part anyway, to Woody's pleasure. "I always heard that he required a good deal of time and conversation and went into his character with a lot of analysis, but he was surprisingly accommodating," Woody said after the film was finished.

The way Woody deals with actors is influenced by his directing himself so much—he is the star of fifteen of his twenty films. The script is so clearly in his mind that Woody Allen the actor and Woody Allen the director need no intermediary. Even a major rewrite of a scene is no problem for him. He just scribbles the new dialogue (and often some alternative lines) on a scrap of paper or the back of an envelope, then pulls it from his pocket for a quick perusal before the shot. Woody finds it so easy to direct himself because, as far as he is concerned, he has written dialogue that is within his range, and he can hear himself if he delivers it badly. He is also acutely attuned to his persona and what he believes the audience will accept. His character in *Oedipus Wrecks* is a lawyer, and costume designer Jeff Kurland outfitted him with an array of suits from Paul Stuart, the upscale men's store in New York. The film's original opening had Woody in his psychiatrist's office, with his coat on, his tie straight, talking directly to the audience (actually to the psychiatrist, whom the audience sees in the next cut), setting out the premise of the movie. ("I'm fifty years old, I'm a partner in a law firm, I'm very successful, and I still haven't resolved my problems with my mother.") When he saw the dailies of the scene, however, his instinct was that the audience would not accept him in "these million-dollar suits," but it seemed as much to be a sense of his own self-image, too;

he never dresses perfectly. The scene was reshot with his coat off and his tie loose, the *Gentleman's Quarterly* edge off him. He also changed the chair he sat in from an overstuffed leather one with a high back to a smaller Queen Anne. He put the psychiatrist in the larger one.

If Woody's scene requires comedy, he is as precise as a ballet master or a maestro in its movement. Again in *Oedipus Wrecks*, there is a scene with the magician who has made Woody's character's mother disappear. They are backstage; the stage manager has some lines and stagehands do their work as Woody walks from the stage manager to the magician. Before a take, Woody said to the cast, "Lots of energy."

The magician waited a split second to begin his dialogue in response to Woody's, and Woody stopped the take. "There should be no air space," he said. "When the stage manager says, 'The theater won't take any responsibility,' the second he speaks, you speak."

They did it again. As Woody crossed over from the stage manager to the magician, he was supposed to graze a stagehand who had a bundle of rope over one shoulder. To someone with a less finely tuned eye for comic business, it looked fine, as if the stagehand was just a minor impediment on Woody's hurried way, but after three takes he was still dissatisfied. "This cross is hurting me every time. I'm always waiting for him. In order to make contact with him, I've got to stall." They did it again. This time the stagehand moved a moment earlier, and so small a difference made a big difference.

In *A Midsummer Night's Sex Comedy* Woody shot over and over and over again a scene where eight people are having four conversations. "Even after the film had been wrapped and edited, we went back into the woods to do that damned scene," Tony Roberts says. "It was like going back to sleep to the same nightmare." Woody wanted the dialogue to overlap and to have a natural feel to it, but at the same time there couldn't be any air in it, nor could there be any sense of deliberateness. "He wanted everything to be heard, but in a way that made the listener in the audience feel that maybe he was the only one who heard it," Roberts says. "So the viewer discovers these things and thinks he's seen more than was really intended. But Woody's point is to make you feel that way, that you just got it. When you go back to see them two, three, four times, you begin to see the amazing amount of art in it, that nothing is accidental."

That extends beyond just what the characters say. Woody's films are full of subliminal commentary about those characters—about what they like and don't like, what they eat and read. They are brand-name specific in their product and cultural references, and there are other cues. After *Radio Days* was released in 1987, critic Janet Maslin wrote in *The New York Times*, "It happens in *Hannah and Her Sisters* that Mia Farrow is seen reading Richard Yates's *Easter Parade*, a novel about two sisters and their lifelong rivalry, but [he] does nothing to call attention to the detail; it is simply there. Nor is it necessary to know that the Gershwin songs in *Manhattan* comment so aptly on the action ('Someone to Watch Over Me' for the night when Isaac finds himself falling for the abrasive intellectual played by Diane Keaton, 'But Not for Me' in his final encounter with the schoolgirl Tracy) to sense their profound effect on the film's mood."

Mia has told Woody that she feels he is hard on actors, that he can be intimidating and that he doesn't help them get performances. She believes that actors always try and want to do their best, that they want to take risks, and that Woody sometimes comes down on them too hard.

Woody disagrees. "I have unorthodox contact with actors but I do have a method. I'm not just hiring good people and am unable to relate to them. My approach may be strange and appear haphazard, but the performance I get from actors is one of the strongest things I do. I know Mia feels I can be intimidating, but if you look at my films over the years, let's say starting with *Annie Hall*, you'll find an enormous amount of very good performances from people. No matter what people might say about *Interiors* or *Stardust Memories* or *Another Woman*, they always extol the cast, because I can recognize terribleness. So Gene Hackman—not that he would worry—can come on the picture for his one week's work in *Another Woman* and rest assured that he will be protected, that he will not look bad. And over the years, people have looked very good. I don't think that Marty Landau or Alan Alda has ever looked any better than they did in *Crimes and Misdemeanors* [Landau was nominated for an Academy Award; Alda won a New York Film Critics Circle award], or Elaine Stritch in *September*, or Mariel Hemingway in *Manhattan*."

This is not just true with the well-known actors with large parts. A characteristic of Woody's films is the naturalness of people in small parts. "Take Hy Ansel," Woody said one day while casting *Alice*. (Ansel played an alert patient being operated on by Fielding Melish's father in *Bananas* and had a small part in *Radio Days*.) "Everything he reads is natural. There are some people, the moment you read them you know you can use them. Ira Wheeler is like that. He came in to do one line as the doctor in *Hannah* and the minute he sat down and read the line, it was a real human talking. He sounds like a person. Marty Landau, too, or Julie Kavner. When they talk, it just sounds right." He paused. "What happened to just normal communication?" Normal communication, of course, is the single thing he demands of his actors. Woody's characters speak idiomatically; they are meant to sound like people at a dinner table. The effect that he prizes in a performance is the spontaneous, natural moment that comes in unselfconscious conversation.

"Actors often make the mistake of just saying words—the screen is empty," he continued. "With Brando, so much is happening that you don't need words. It's luck. Some actors and actresses are just interesting to watch. There are lots of significant stars who do a good job—solid professionals who earn a lot of money. But you put the camera on a De Niro or an Al Pacino or a Gene Hackman, on Jack Nicholson or Dustin Hoffman or George C. Scott, and something happens. Joe Mantegna [whom Woody was then directing in *Alice*] has something. An odd style that's just wonderful."

Despite whatever apparent difficulties working with Woody can create, they are insignificant enough so that virtually any actor is eager to appear in his films, and for less money than he or she normally makes. It is understood in the film industry that there are regular budgets and then there are Woody's budgets. Both pay well but the regular ones pay much better. Using Woody's method of listing actors, an alphabetical list of those who have appeared in his films includes: Danny Aiello, Alan Alda, Alec Baldwin, Bob Balaban, Marie-Christine Barrault, Claire Bloom, Philip Bosco, Betty Buckley, Michael Caine, Zoe Caldwell, John Carradine, Jeff Daniels, Blythe Danner, Judy Davis, Sandy Dennis, Colleen Dewhurst, Shelley Duvall, Denholm Elliott, Stephanie Farrow, José Ferrer, Carrie Fisher, Joanna Gleason, Jeff Goldblum, Gene Hackman, Daryl Hannah, Jessica Harper, Kitty Carlisle Hart, Mariel Hemingway, Edward Herrmann, Barbara Hershey, Ian Holm, John Houseman, Mary Beth Hurt, William Hurt, Anjelica Huston, Lou Jacobi, Van Johnson, Carol Kane, Julie Kavner, Diane Keaton, Martin Landau, Louise Lasser, Karen Ludwig, Keye Luke, Joe Mantegna, E. G. Marshall, Michael Murphy, Lloyd Nolan, Jerry Orbach, Milo O'Shea, Maureen O'Sullivan, Geraldine Page, Bernadette Peters, Anthony Quayle, Charlotte Rampling, Tony Randall, Lynn Redgrave, Burt Reynolds, Tony Roberts, Gena Rowlands, Wallace Shawn, Cybill Shepherd, Paul Simon, Sylvester Stallone, Maureen Stapleton, Mary Steenburgen, David Ogden Stiers, Meryl Streep, Elaine Stritch, Max von Sydow, Michael Tucker, Gwen Verdon, Christopher Walken, Jack Warden, Sam Waterston, Sigourney Weaver, Dianne Wiest, Gene Wilder, and John Wood. (There are, too, the cameo appearances by notables playing themselves: Sandy Baron, Saul Bellow, Milton Berle, Bruno Bettelheim, Bricktop, Dick Cavett, Howard Cosell, Don Dunphy, Jackie Gayle, Morty Gunty, Irving Howe, Will Jordan, Marshall McLuhan, Corbett Monica, Jack Rollins, Bobby Short, Susan Sontag, and Howard Storm. Also, most of the Previn/Farrow children have been in at least one movie.)

Casting for Woody's films is a slow process that begins with the first draft of the script. The actors for some parts are already known: Woody's and Mia's roles are tailor-made, as are parts for such regulars as Dianne Wiest and Diane Keaton. But sometimes events force a change even in those parts. Mia was supposed to play the philosophy professor in *Another Woman* but suddenly she was pregnant. Wiest was to have played the part of the woman whose voice the professor hears through the air vent in her office in the building shared with a psychiatrist, but personal matters prevented her from taking the part. Woody rewrote the script and made Mia the now pregnant woman, necessitating a somewhat older actress for the professor, which brought in Gena Rowlands. The change had the benefit of allowing him to explore the issue of having children. Such cases are exceptions, though. Usually once a draft is done, Woody can start the long series of talks he has with Juliet Taylor about whom to cast. The parts for women are invariably easier to fill than those for men.

"With so many gifted actresses around, it's never a problem, it's a pleasure," Woody says. "But it's hard to find *just men*, not a gunslinger. There are a few. Sam Waterston in *September*. Denholm Elliott. But American actors, who are as great as any in the world, are not average men. They're so charismatic. We breed heroes. They're John Waynes and Humphrey Bogarts and Jimmy Cagneys. Our film history is mythology, whereas in Europe a lot of it is adult confrontational, a realistic story where you need a man. Our actors are too beautiful and charismatic. I learned this the hard way, by casting. I need regular fifty- to fifty-five-year-olds—but I can't find them easily. George C. Scott is a great actor who can be believable just as a regular man; Dustin Hoffman is so gifted and he's a wonderful comic actor, too.

"Sam is someone I've relied on at times for a guy next door, a regular, recognizable human being who is not a cowboy. You don't get the feeling that he carries a gun or beats up people. We don't have many regular people like, say, Fredric March. Sam is one of the few people out there." Which is why Woody prizes him, and why he has played a son-in-law in *Interiors*, an architect in *Hannah and Her Sisters*, an aspiring novelist in *September*, and a blind rabbi in *Crimes and Misdemeanors*.

The paucity of just-men American actors has led Woody to cast English actors in parts that didn't call for a non-American, for example, Michael Caine as the gloriously foolish husband in *Hannah*. (He won an Academy Award for best supporting actor. Dianne Wiest won for best supporting actress.) Woody found no American actor who could be a regular man who is an accountant. "American men are dangerous and potent," he says. "Michael can play a CIA agent or a comic role and he gets a great kick out of playing either. England has a tradition of men of all ages because of its vital theater, and the films are not always about gangsters or gunfighters riding into town. They're normal human beings." Normal, it should be clear by now, is his favorite word when it comes to describing what he wants from actors and their speech.

Sometimes, however, no matter how much he wants an actor to play in one of his films, he just isn't right for the part. Woody had for years admired Denholm Elliott—he had seen him as Krogstad in Ibsen's *A Doll's House* and in several films—and wanted to cast him in something. A part of the right age came along in 1977 as the father in *Interiors*, but as it was an American family, the part required an American, or at least a nonevident British, accent. The question was, could Elliott do the right accent? Actually, the first question was, could he be located?

"You could never find him," Woody said after Elliott appeared in *September*. "He was living in Ibiza and he had no phone, he had to be called at a bar at a certain time of day. I finally tracked him down and I said, 'Can you do an American accent?' And he said, 'Absolutely. Would you like me to do it?' And then he recited 'Hickory, Dickory, Dock.' But it was totally British," Woody said, breaking into an English accent as he repeated " 'HICKory, DICKory, DOCK.' I'm on the phone to a bar in Ibiza and he's saying hickory, dickory, dock and it is totally

English. And I said, 'Well, thanks very much.' And he said, 'Well, are you going to hire me? I'd like to know.' I said, 'Let me think about this.' " The part went to E. G. Marshall, but ten years later, Woody had a role for him.

Woody finds that there is a difference between what satisfies him in actors in a drama and what is acceptable in a more lighthearted film. *September*, with only six parts, went through a mass of cast changes, whereas not one of the scores of actors in the cast of *Radio Days* didn't work out. Considering the number of films Woody has done, he has replaced very few actors, but the pattern is that the replacements come in the dramas, not the comedies. He places the onus more on himself than on the actors. In *The Purple Rose of Cairo*, the part of the actor who comes off the screen was originally played by Michael Keaton, whose work Woody admires. But the movie takes place in the 1930s and Keaton is a wholly contemporary actor. His performance was fine, but after ten days of shooting, it was clear that he came across as an eighties character, not a thirties character, so he was replaced without acrimony by Jeff Daniels.

"A comedy is looser, it's rougher, it's not as varnished and finished a product," Woody says. "You don't have to be as perfect in a certain way. In a serious piece you're requiring the audience to go along with you and become emotionally involved, and you can't suddenly have somebody break that reality by giving a bad or unreal performance. So the best thing to do is cast wonderful people. But even when once in a while you do cast wonderful people, either because of my inability to direct them well or their inability to grasp this particular role, for some reason it doesn't come together. And your choice is to leave in a less than perfect performance, or a second-rate performance, or to make a change. And I always feel obliged to the people who are putting up the money for the film and for my own artistic integrity and to everybody involved to make the change. In a movie like *Hannah* or *Annie Hall* or *Bananas*, somebody can come on and the level of depth and sensitivity in their performance needn't be that high. It's people talking fast and bright and quipping and falling and running around, and you don't notice the imperfection so much because it's razzle-dazzle and jokes and silliness. But when you're doing drama, the camera is close and it's quiet and people make longer speeches and are more emotional. You're trying to suck the audience into that, and everybody has to be good. That's not always easy to get, for many reasons. Sometimes the structure of the story is at fault, or the lines are written badly. Sometimes the lines are written well but the actor's not clicking on it. Sometimes I can't communicate for some reason that I'm not seeing."

Once the main roles are decided, there is the task of finding a supporting cast who will provide the natural readings Woody wants. When he began making movies, Woody went to the office of casting director Marion Dougherty, who, with Juliet Taylor, her assistant at the time, would bring in actors. For the first few films, Woody was not a direct participant. He sat in a rocking chair at the back of the room while assistant director Fred Gallo or producer Jack Grossberg talked with the prospective actors. He would have been happier sitting behind a screen. It was a mark of his shyness at the time but it served a purpose: He could hear and see the actor without distraction. Even now that he talks directly with the auditioners, he says, "One-way glass would still be ideal. You can look without interruption."

Woody's interviews have become known as the shortest in the business. Prospective actors and actresses are usually in and out within three minutes, something they have been forewarned about. (Those who are asked to read a scene are in for no more than ten.) Interviews are now held in Woody's editing room/screening room complex. Juliet Taylor came one day, as she always does, with that session's roster of possibilities and a list of their credits. She goes to every Broadway and Off-Broadway play to look for talent and has been known to stop interesting-looking people on the street and give them her card.

(For *Stardust Memories*, which is full of people with odd, wonderful, and sometimes Hogarthian faces, two or three days of casting auditions were held in a nightclub on Manhattan's Upper West Side. Ads were placed in the papers saying there were parts available in a Woody Allen film and a few thousand hopefuls showed up. Taylor and others involved with the casting sat at a big table with Woody behind them, watching and looking for specific kinds of faces for specific scenes as they walked by and dropped off their pictures and résumés. TV crews came and filmed lines going around the block. There were a couple of security guards, because anyone could come in off the street, and they did, among them two women in hospital gowns, handcuffed together. People also brought Woody presents, such as a gigantic zucchini.)

Woody and his assistant Jane Martin were waiting for Taylor in the twenty-by-forty-foot screening room. Four avocado-colored plush velvet chairs are along both side walls, which are covered in the same material. On a raised platform under the projection window are two more on either side of a tan plush love seat with large, soft pillows, where Woody sits while a film is being shown. A console to modulate the sound and communicate with the projectionist is at the right side.

"I had a dream about you," Juliet told Woody after saying hello. His eyes lit up. "Your name was Frankie. It was very funny."

"Why?" he asked.

"Frankie is the name of my goldfish."

("It's so funny," Woody said later. "A beautiful woman says you were in her dream and your hopes go up—and you turn out to be her goldfish.")

As everyone settled in their seats, Taylor mentioned an actress who had read for Woody. "She knows she's up for a large part, but if you want to use her in the smaller, that's life."

"You know how I feel about life," Woody told her. Anyone who has seen *Annie Hall* knows how Woody feels about life:

Annie and Alvy browsing in a crowded bookstore. Alvy, carrying two books, Death and Western Thought *and* The Denial of Death, *moves over to where Annie is looking.*

ALVY
I've a very pessimistic view of life. You should know that about me if we're gonna go out, you know. I feel that life is divided up into the horrible and the miserable.

ANNIE
M'hm.

ALVY
Those are the two categories. . . . The horrible would be like, I don't know, terminal cases . . .

ANNIE
M'hm.

ALVY
And blind people, crippled . . . I don't know how they get through life. It's amazing to me.

ANNIE
M'hm.

ALVY

You know, and the miserable is everyone else. That's all. So when you go through life you should be thankful that you're miserable, because that's—you're very lucky . . . to be . . . *(Overlapping Annie's laughter)* . . . to be miserable.

Interviews were scheduled for every five minutes, a dozen or so in all. Word came that the first person had arrived and Woody said, "Let's get started. I can't bear that that woman's waiting out there." The young actress, one of several for the part of the young Gena Rowlands in *Another Woman*, came in. Woody had a picture of Gena rolled up in his hand to consult as he looked at each. He took what is his regular place, in the middle of the room and out of sight as one enters from the anteroom. As soon as the person comes into view, he walks to greet them. He said to the young woman (and virtually all who followed), "Hi, this is for a film that starts shooting October 13 and goes through Christmas or New Year. Juliet thought you might be right for one of the parts and today I just want to see how you look. I can let you know very soon, within a couple of weeks." The young redhead, nervous as most hopefuls are, stood quietly and then with hesitation answered, "Okay." Woody looked at her closely for a couple of seconds and then said, "Okay, thank you." She shook his hand and waved to Juliet on her way out. To another young woman who came in he said, "I wanted to see you live," looking closely at her. "Great," she answered, as she did to everything that required an acknowledgment. Not all were so reticent. When Woody told one auditioner, "I just wanted to look at your face," she shrugged and said, "Well, here it is." Woody smiled. "Thanks for bringing it."

As he waited for the next prospect and as he often does, Woody stood in his spot, his right foot tapping out the beat as he whistled a tune, this time a lively rendition of "Spicy Advice." A man came in and read a scene with Juliet. Woody listened in a chair at the other end of the room, his right hand an awning over his eyes, the casting call sheet and pictures in his left covering the rest of his face to the base of his eyes. ("Hiding," he explained afterward. "Just hiding.")

"He doesn't talk like a real person," Woody said after the man left. "I don't normally read people. We generally know them from other work. It's awful having to read. I could never get a job as an actor if I had to do it. The problem with most actors is, when they come in and just stand around talking, they're fine. Then they start to read and they shift into third gear."

To another actor, Woody explained that the character was "just a regular guy." The man read the part and left. "He was pretty good," Woody said. "He didn't immediately lapse into two hundred years of lessons. The question is, could he do it when the lights are on and everyone is there? But I've always thought if you can do it at a reading, you can do it anywhere. There's nothing more unnatural than coming into this ghoulish room, people looking at you, and having to act natural."

There was a break scheduled after several interviews. Woody rubbed his hands. "A luncheon sandwich," he said. In what has become a ritual, Jane Martin, a smart, trim woman in her early thirties who was Woody's assistant and confidante for six years, asked his pleasure; there are several restaurants nearby that deliver. He was pensive. "Turkey, tuna, crab, pasta . . ." she intoned. Juliet laughed. "I hear this every day," she said. Jane threw up her hands. "I say the same thing every day."

"I smoked a pack a day into my twenties," Woody said. "For lunch I'd go with a friend and have fried eggs and a double order of bacon, two cups of coffee, and a couple of cigarettes—and thought it was a healthful lunch. Then at three o'clock, the malted break." Not anymore. He has adopted a diet that limits animal fats and almost everything that even begins with any of the letters in cholesterol—although a slice of pie or cake will often find its way into a meal. Given a choice, he would eat steak every night. But convinced of red meat's ill effects, he has it maybe once a year.

Over the turkey sandwich he settled on, Woody marveled about Mia's ability to do such tasks as running a tractor and painting houses, and his total inability to do such things: When he was writing for TV, he invited another writer to dinner every three or four months, not because they were such good friends but because Woody could not change a typewriter ribbon and the man could. "After the meal I'd say, 'Oh, by the way, can you change this?' I could never do any of that stuff." His incompetence in the even vaguely technical was matched by his horror over Juliet's plan to sail in the Mediterranean with her husband. The danger of American urban life was enough for him. The notion that in such troubled times for Americans abroad anyone would willingly cruise off the coast of Greece on a seventy-two-foot boat mystified him.

"Sure," he said, responding to her notion that adventure is a pleasure, "but you could be home reading a book instead of languishing in a Lebanese basement, bound hand and foot."

The most important name not on the list of those appearing in Woody's movies is, naturally, Mia Farrow, who has had parts great and small in his last eleven films and who deserves a separate list just for the characters she's played. His collaboration with her redefines the term. From Tina Vitale, the Mafia moll of *Broadway Danny Rose*, to Alice Tait, the perfect Catholic girl in *Alice*, she has portrayed a broad spectrum of women that is testament to the range of her acting ability. Every movie of Woody's with the exception of *Take the Money and Run* and *Stardust Memories* has had a part (almost invariably the lead) for one of the three actresses whom he's been either married to or seriously involved with. Woody says the reason is uncomplicated: "I like to work with the people I know." That goes for the crew, too.

This combining of personal and professional lives is not unique; Charlie Chaplin and Ingmar Bergman, to name two directors, cast women who were part of their personal lives. No director, however, has done it so consistently as Woody. Louise Lasser starred in two films (and had a cameo in *Stardust Memories*), Diane Keaton in six (counting *Play It Again, Sam*), plus a *Radio Days* cameo. Actually, Woody was no longer romantically involved with either Lasser or Keaton when they appeared in his movies, though they remained close friends. His devotion to his leading ladies even after the romance had ended led him to joke once that he could end up like Erich von Stroheim's character in *Sunset Boulevard*, the director-turned-factotum for a reclusive movie actress (to whom William Holden says, "Say, you're Norma Desmond. You used to be big." "I *am* big," Gloria Swanson replies. "It's the *pictures* that got small"). "I've been crazy about the women I've acted with and I would be happy to end up as their chauffeur and houseman," Woody said. "I don't mind that, with any of them. It would be fine with me. Answering her fan mail. *Writing* her fan mail."

These three highly individual actresses also mirror the evolution of Woody's movies. His descriptions of the strengths of each are similar to the strengths of the films they appear in.

"Louise is a totally urban comedian. She is New York, she is Fifth Avenue. And with Louise, an enormous amount of it is in the context. She exudes wit and says things that are witty.

"Diane is strictly behavioral. She can make anything funny. Diane can tell you about going to the corner to buy the papers and you'll laugh because there's something behaviorally funny about her.

"Mia is entirely different. Mia is not primarily a comedian, although she has an extremely good sense of humor." Her range has been both a surprise to audiences who were accustomed to her playing doelike roles and a joy to Woody. One time when they were eating in a favorite Italian restaurant, she saw a woman in dark glasses with blond hair piled on her head, then turned to him and said, "Gee, I would like to play a woman like that once." From that came her splendid role and performance in *Broadway Danny Rose*. (Mia once commented to Chicago *Tribune* critic Gene Siskel about her perceived fragility: "Maybe it's my physical look that confused people. I was very thin. I know people think of me that way. That's why I kept my sunglasses on in *Broadway Danny Rose*, because I know my eyes are a giveaway; they're not tough. But I'm sure *I* am underneath.")

"She's an extraordinary actress," Woody continued. "And she's solid like a rock. She shows up and can always do it. If you ask her to play that shrinking character in *The Purple Rose of Cairo*, or the silly cigarette girl in *Radio Days*, she does it. If you ask her to play nasty, she does it. If you ask her to play something sexy, she does it. And she's real sweet. She'll come to the set and quietly do her needlepoint, and then put on her wig and dark glasses, or whatever, and just scream out the lines, and stick a knife in your nose—and then go back to sewing with her little orphan children around her."

While Woody and his cousin Rita had a wall plastered with movie stars' pictures when they were growing up, Mia had no need for such a thing; her mother *was* a movie star and many others were her friends. But in April 1979, at the end of a winter spent on Martha's Vineyard, she noticed a picture of Woody wearing a sweater and holding an open umbrella over one shoulder on the cover of *The New York Times Magazine*. She had met him in passing at a party in California several years earlier and they once corresponded, she to tell him that she enjoyed *Manhattan* and he to politely thank her. She had never seen him as a stand-up comedian but knew him a bit as a director, having seen two of his movies, the other being *Annie Hall*. She found his photo in the *Times* so attractive that she read the story through, which made her find him "immensely appealing. I thought he was neat." She tore the cover off the magazine, but didn't plaster it on the wall, at least at first.

Instead, she stuck it in her large *Random House Dictionary*. About seven years later (by then she and Woody had been together for about six) she came upon the photo and had it framed. "I'm not in the habit of saving pictures like that," she explained one day, "but I was a little lonely at the time and he had such an interesting face. It was a long winter," she added, shrugging. "Carly Simon was there sometimes. [The Simon Sisters had occasionally performed on the same bill with Woody when he was a stand-up.] She confirmed that he was very interesting."

That fall Mia was on Broadway in *Romantic Comedy*. One evening Michael Caine and his wife came to the performance and afterward the three went to Elaine's for dinner. Woody was there at his usual table. Caine stopped to say hello. He reintroduced Mia and pleasantries were exchanged. Some weeks later, Woody sent her an invitation to his New Year's Eve party ("I think practically everybody in New York got one," Mia says), and she came with Tony Perkins, who was in the show with her, and his wife. Woody pays attention to the smallest details of planning the rare big parties he gives—he stewed over the paper stock of the Cartier invitations for this one. But he is an almost invisible host. He likes to fill a grand place like the Harkness House, a mansion turned into a ballet school, with hundreds of guests but does not like to work the room, chatting with people. His rare parties are social magnets, the most sought-after invitation not only in New York but in Los Angeles as well, from where people call to say they'll just happen to be in New York the night of the event and is it possible for them to attend? Yet while one of the most important missions for the guests is to be seen and thus have their status credentials validated, one of the greatest desires of the host is to be away from the center. He politely greets everyone as they arrive ("If it's me meeting people at the door I have no entry phobia. The burden is on them"). Then once the throng is assembled, he more or less blends into the walls.

Mia had a good time but only a few words with Woody. Afterward, she sent him a note of thanks and a copy of Lewis Thomas's *The Medusa and the Snail*. Woody, who also received dozens of bottles of champagne and a gardenful of flowers from guests, had Norma Lee Clark call Mia ("Gracious person that I am," he says) to thank her and suggest that they have lunch sometime. In April 1980, Woody and Jean Doumanian and Jacqui Safra flew to Paris for some fun—which for him is to do what he does in New York, "except the visuals and the food are different": go to restaurants and movies, visit museums, and take walks.

Woody remembers that they left for France two or three days after the death of Jean-Paul Sartre (which was April 15). But before going, he invited Mia via Norma Lee to lunch at Lutèce. She later made a needle-point sampler of the date and event—April 17, 1980—that hangs on the wall outside his bedroom. When he returned, she was still in the play and he began to film the reshoots of *Stardust Memories*. Norma Lee again phoned invitations to Mia for dinner on the night her play was dark. Woody always had an early call the next morning, so the evenings were never protracted. Over the first several months of this routine, Woody never phoned Mia. He prefers not to speak on the phone to anyone unless he has to, and being invited via an intermediary didn't bother Mia. "She never mentioned it," Woody says. It was a slow courtship that apparently both liked. "We'd have dinner," Mia says. "And we're still having dinner."

For the first few years after their friendly dates turned into serious ones, Woody would get up in the morning, give her a call, and then work while she did her business with the children. Around 7 p.m., he would pick her up for dinner or the opera or a show or a movie, then take her home. Very often on the weekend, she would bring a few kids and stay at Woody's. But they both very much led their own lives. Then in 1985 they adopted Dylan, and after that Satchel came along. They have shared the pleasure of raising children.

Their relationship, which has lasted eleven years with no end in sight, is the longest either has had. By conventional standards it is hardly a conventional union. Then again, neither are they conventional people. They are not married, nor do they live together—their apartments face each other across Central Park. (Her apartment, which in addition to nine children and a daytime nanny houses an array of animals, was used for her scenes in *Hannah and Her Sisters*.) "It's sort of like just enough," Woody said one day in his apartment. "Perhaps if we were to live together or if we met at a different time in our lives, it wouldn't work. But it seems to be just right. I have all the free time I want and it's quiet over here, and yet I get plenty of action over there. I think it's because we don't live together and that she has her own life completely and that I have mine, that we're able to maintain this relationship with a certain proper tension. If we got married years ago and lived together maybe now we'd be screaming, 'What have we gotten into?' These things are so exquisitely tuned. It's just luck."

Few married couples seem more married, however. They are in

almost constant communication and there is what can only be called a
sweetness about them; at the few parties they attend they usually shyly
stand off in a corner, holding hands. And not many fathers spend as
much time with their children as Woody does: He is there before they
wake up in the morning, he sees them during the day, and he puts
them to bed at night. As each has been married and divorced twice,
experience has taught them that legalizing a relationship doesn't necessarily make it last, and Mia is fond of quoting a line about the often-
wed Alan Jay Lerner: "Marriage is Alan's way of saying goodbye." Both
also seem to have what they want. Mia, who was encouraged not to
work during her marriages to Frank Sinatra and André Previn, has a
full career yet can also be a full-time mother. And Woody, who spent
much energy in his earlier marriages and relationships both educating
his partners and being needful of their attention, has found a balance
with a wholly contained woman.

"Mia's been a completely different kind of experience for me,
because the predominant thing has been family. Which is odd to say
because she lives there and I live here," Woody said. When they began
to date, they would wave towels out the window as they spoke on the
phone, delighting in saying they could see the other. "First of all, she's
very supportive workwise. But she's introduced me to a whole other
world. I've had a child with her and we've adopted one. She's brought
a completely different, meaningful dimension to my life. Yet the two
of us have so little in common that it always amazes us. We're always
marveling on why we threw in our lot together and stayed together as
long as we have.

"I could go on about our differences forever: She doesn't like the
city and I adore it. She loves the country and I don't like it. She doesn't
like sports at all and I love sports. She loves to eat in, early—five-thirty,
six—and I love to eat out, late. She likes simple, unpretentious restaurants, I like fancy places. She can't sleep with an air conditioner on, I
can only sleep with an air conditioner on. She loves pets and animals,
I hate pets and animals. She likes to spend tons of time with kids, I
like to spend my time with work and only a limited time with kids. She
would love to take a boat down the Amazon or go up Mount Kilimanjaro,
I never want to go near those places. She has an optimistic, yea-saying
feeling toward life itself, and I have a totally pessimistic, negative feeling.
She likes the West Side of New York, I like the East Side of New York.
She has raised nine children now with no trauma and has never owned

a thermometer. I take my temperature every two hours in the course of the day." ("Here's a story of hypochondria," Woody said one day in his editing room. "The other day I noticed a little bump on my nose that was new. I went to the doctor, who said not to worry, it was only a piece of cartilage, there was no tumor or anything. Later I wasn't so sure and I called him. He said, it really is okay. But a couple of days later I went back to him again. He said the same thing." A few days later, Woody went back yet again. "After all," he explained, "why should a little piece of cartilage show up for no reason at all?")

"I can only think that what made us throw in our lot together is that the two of us met slightly later in life and that we both have our own developed lives—her with a major family and me with a career—and we don't share the same house. I'm able to live with it when she goes to the country for the summer. She's able to live with it that I don't. We both have our own lives and just enough intersection so that it's fun but not smothering."

If this has the ring of rationalization, it really isn't. "Perhaps the balance he gets from Mia is exactly the amount of love and support he needs, because his work sustains him in such a strong way that the average man doesn't get," their friend Tony Roberts says. "The average guy finishes at five o'clock and comes home and wants somebody there. Woody's mind is so filled with ideas and such an imagination that most of his time is spent with his work, like any artist. And she is the perfect woman to nurture him, nourish him, be beautiful for him—since she is one of the most beautiful women in the world, and one of the sweetest and the most capable. It's wonderful that she finds what she needs by relating to those nine children and still has something left over for him. He once said to me, 'I spend as much time with her as is good.' It reminds me of what David Selznick said about a movie when someone told him, 'You can't have a movie two hours and twenty minutes long. No one's ever heard of that. It's too long.' And he said, 'As far as what length is concerned, how long is it good? is the only question that matters. Is it good for fifty minutes or for four and a half hours?' I think that's how Woody and Mia approach their relationship. They're both flexible enough and mature enough to keep it alive in all the good ways."

Mia's first movie for Woody was *A Midsummer Night's Sex Comedy*, which was filmed in the summer of 1981. While they were shooting, a newspaper columnist, to Woody's dismay, printed that the film was called *Summer Nights* and that it was his homage to Bergman's *Smiles of a Summer Night* (which was adapted for Broadway as *A Little Night Music*). That erroneous notion persists to this day; the film, Woody says, "is one of the very, very few of Bergman's that I wasn't crazy about." Besides, he adds, "it's the dumbest thing I've ever heard. There's no resemblance between the two." He had just finished the script of *Zelig* and was faced with two weeks of waiting while it was budgeted. Then he thought to himself, "While I'm waiting, why don't I write something?" What he refers to as "this little summer pastiche" occurred to him. "I thought it would be fun to get some people in a country house and just celebrate summer—make it very beautiful, with butterfly nets and badminton courts and picnicking." It was set up as a sort of subproject for Woody to shoot while also shooting *Zelig*, and because of weather requirements, it was finished first.

That little summer pastiche was a horror for Mia, who felt she had the part only because she was Woody's girlfriend and was "paralyzed with insecurity. I could barely get through the day and I got an ulcer in the process." She redeveloped her confidence in time for *Zelig*, but for the first film, it was like *Pat and Mike*, the Katharine Hepburn–Spencer Tracy movie where she is a champion athlete who falters whenever her beau is around. And that was on the good days. "In my worst moments, I felt he's so good and I couldn't do it at all. I thought that I was just bluffing the other times I had acted and managed to fool everybody." She was convinced that she would disappoint Woody, and was so unhappy that she wanted to abandon her role. If she was going to work with him at all, she'd do it behind the scenes.

Woody did not fully understand her predicament. "I tend to be maybe a little abrupt sometimes," he said after the film was finished. "So I calmed her but I was not completely sympathetic, because I didn't realize the dimensions, the gravity. I knew she'd be wonderful in it. It never occurred to *me* she'd disappoint me. So I didn't think to myself, 'Oh my God, darling, are you upset?' It just never occurred to me for a second."

Mia's ease on the set now, however, is evident in her easy joking with the crew, who themselves banter constantly, and with Woody. On the first day of shooting *Another Woman*, Mia was on her mark, ready to film her first scene. Woody was off to one side, sitting on a pile of equipment.

"Ready!" assistant director Tom Reilly called to the crew. (Reilly, a Harvard man in his mid-thirties with the mien of a cross between a fraternity president and a drill instructor, runs the set. He oversees its preparation for a shot and, on Woody's signal, calls out "Action!" and "Cut!") Woody looked up at Mia.

"It makes *me* feel ready," he said. "It's been so long since I've worked as an actor, I hope I don't lose it."

She smiled at him.

"You look like a mermaid sitting there." He laughed.

"Luring sailors to the rocks with my voice."

Then in the moment before the camera rolled, she looked over to property master Jimmy Mazzola and told him, "I need a chicken, a live chicken, in four seconds."

Later in the film, just two or three weeks before she gave birth to Satchel, a dramatic dream sequence with Mia, John Houseman, and Gena Rowlands was being filmed in a lower Manhattan apartment. For verisimilitude, Woody prefers real rooms as opposed to constructed sets, but the downside in this instance was that the noise from the street traffic kept interfering. Sound recorder James Sabat, whose first movie with Woody was *Bananas* and who has been with him on virtually every one since, was continually annoyed by the sounds of trucks and buses and car horns that seeped into the background of the dialogue.

"We should shoot this on the BQE [the Brooklyn–Queens Expressway]," he muttered, and asked for a short delay while he went outside to investigate whether there was a way to avoid the racket. Assistant director Reilly looked around. "Where's Jimmy?" he asked. "He's gone out to check," someone said. "On what," Reilly replied, "his oil?" Sabat's problem did not ameliorate. He silently registered dismay with every take; his face grew redder and redder, his eyes squinched shut in pain at every noise, his slow burn reminiscent of Edgar Kennedy, the lemonade vendor frustrated by the Marx Brothers in *Duck Soup*. Even cinematographer Sven Nykvist began to watch him instead of the action, amused but sympathetic.

"This is terrible," Sabat told Reilly.

Reilly shook his head. "There are eight million stories in the naked city."

"And I get the worst."

Mia, whose start point for the shot was nearby and who had been watching the goings-on, turned to Sabat in commiseration. "The noise really is awful here," she said, her look of apparent empathy doubled by her extreme pregnancy. Then in perfect timing she added, "And you're going to look so terrible." She grinned wickedly as everyone laughed.

However poor their communication at the beginning of their collaboration, Woody's feelings for Mia are encapsulated in the narrator's description of how Leonard Zelig evolved from the Chameleon Man into his own person: " 'Wanting only to be liked, he distorted himself beyond measure,' wrote Scott Fitzgerald. One wonders what would have happened if, right at the outset, he had had the courage to speak his mind and not pretend. In the end, it was, after all, not the approbation of many but the love of one woman who changed his life."

A brief sketch of the woman who changed Woody's life: Maria de Lourdes Villiers Farrow was born on February 9, 1945, the third of seven children. As she could not pronounce Maria as a toddler, she called herself Mia. She grew up in Beverly Hills (with some years in England and Spain interspersed). Among her neighbors were Hal Roach and Rosalind Russell. Her godfather was George Cukor. For all the glamorous trappings of the Hollywood life she grew up in, her childhood was constantly marked by tragedy. Her brother Michael, the first child, died when she was thirteen; her father died when she was seventeen. When she was nine, Mia developed polio. She faced it bravely, and before going to the hospital she carefully wrapped up all her toys in newspaper for each of her brothers and sisters to give away, not knowing that they would have to be burned as a precaution against infection. She was in a ward with three children. One died. Another was in an iron lung outside the door. She recovered.

Her family was devoutly Catholic and she attended convent school. She toyed with the idea of becoming a nun, an idea her mother, despite her devoutness, didn't like at all, and one even the nuns weren't taken with. "Mia asks disturbing questions about religion," one of her report cards read. She was in all the school plays. "Mia is not attentive except when she's performing," another report card noted. Every Christmas, Mia wrote and directed a play starring the neighborhood children, who had to pay for the privilege of performing. She gave the money to the March of Dimes. As she grew older, she was taken with the notion of becoming a doctor and treating patients in the tropics. In the end, she didn't go to college. She had immediate success as an actress; after seeing her Off-Broadway as Cecily in her first play, *The Importance of Being Earnest*, Vivien Leigh said, "This is a star." In 1964 she was cast as Allison MacKenzie on the television show *Peyton Place*. Allison was a poetic-minded dreamer, a small-town romantic of little experience who sought love and the meaning of life, and she established Mia as a vulnerable character. "I still have a fondness for Allison," she has said. "Maybe that's why Cecilia [the dreamer she played in *The Purple Rose of Cairo*] seemed so familiar."

In 1966, at the age of twenty-one, she married Frank Sinatra, a friend of her parents. She played perhaps her most famous role (before doing Woody's films) in *Rosemary's Baby* in 1967. The marriage to Sinatra lasted two years. She took no alimony. They remain friendly. She spent some time wandering through India in search of spiritual enlightenment. Later, she married the conductor and composer André Previn and they settled in London. In accordance with his wishes she did little film work. They had three children and adopted three more. They were divorced in January 1979. She took no alimony. She attended Woody's New Year's Eve party in 1979 and soon was in the most improbable relationship either could imagine, to the point that each even found the other's name difficult. "What should I call you?" she asked him. "Just call me Woody," he told her.

"It felt awkward at first," she has said, "It's such an extreme name, too. I know he thinks my name is awkward to say. He rarely calls me Mia. I hear him refer to me as Mia, and sometimes if he has to get my attention, he'll call it, but he doesn't often say it."

Despite the vast differences in background and upbringing, each likes the family of the other. Her mother and sisters appear in his films. "Everybody loves Woody's father," Mia says. "His father's all around town. He knows so many people. We saw Kitty Hart one night. *She* knew his father, from the jewelry business. Woody was amazed. His mother has a rich vocabulary and she's fun to listen to. She's really colorful. His whole family strikes me as exotic because their world is so alien to me." ("Exotic?" says the narrator in Woody's story "Retribution." "She should only know the Greenblatts. Or Mr. and Mrs. Milton Sharpstein, my father's friends. Or for that matter, my cousin Tovah. Exotic? I mean, they're nice but hardly exotic with their endless bickering over the best way to combat indigestion or how far back to sit from the television set.")

They have developed into a formidable acting team despite Mia's early insecurity, and she enjoys doing comedy with him because "he's not broad at all in real life and it's a treat to see him do it in a scene." Occasional difficulties arise. "I think it's harder acting with someone you have an intimate relationship with," she says. "It's harder to release yourself from the bonds of your mundane reality into the scene with a person you know intimately and see—frequently is not the right word— incessantly. It's inhibiting, and that's what you have to fight. If Woody and I were in rehearsal for a play, it would be different than filming spontaneously. Then we would build a reality apart from others that would always be there for us to go to; you create this sort of island. But as we don't do that in films, I have to be a little more resolved in pulling away from our personal relationship. There is one other thing, too. Woody is also the director and so I know he is evaluating my performance at the same time he's acting with me, something quite apart from our relationship. I also know he's this director with a laser view, not only of what I'm doing but of his own performance and everything else that's going on in the scene, and I have to relegate that to the background.

"Woody's instinct for what is correct is unerring," she says. "He sometimes doesn't even let you finish the sentence if it's incorrect. The truth can only fit through a very narrow pass for him. Sometimes a scene can go for forty takes. Another time you'll be astonished because he does only one take of a very long scene, and you think, 'Are you sure? Did I say all the words?' And if that's the only scene you're doing with Woody, you'd think it's slipshod or something. I've seen other actors go, 'Is that right?' But they don't realize, you have to trust him. He has a great feel for what is true."

Between the fall of 1986 and the spring of 1990, a period of about three and a half years, Woody Allen wrote and directed five films, two of which he appeared in: *September, Another Woman, Oedipus Wrecks, Crimes and Misdemeanors*, and *Alice*. They were made on top of and sometimes overlapping each other. The period and the films encapsulate the variety of his ideas and cinematic styles, and they point to what he will try to do in the future.

To watch anyone at work on so many and such diverse projects is an uncommon opportunity. It allows an extended look at his method and a sense of how personality and art come together. This period was an especially interesting one to follow Woody through because it co- incided with two major personal events: his becoming a father and his turning fifty. Dylan arrived a few months before the birthday, Satchel when he was fifty-two. Aspects of these two themes run through *Another Woman*, made in the fall of 1987 when Mia Farrow was pregnant with Satchel. His family life and his work have become the boundaries of his life, and the fabric of his days is woven from the events in both.

However different the movies—they range from the straightest drama of *September* to the broadest comedy in *Oedipus Wrecks*—Woody's method of bringing them to the screen was constant. Thus while each film was quite different from the others, they were interchangeable in their making. How he casts and directs his actors, how he edits and rewrites and reshoots, does not change with the type of film he makes, and to see him at work in that wide group of areas is to understand his artistic and creative process.

When *Crimes and Misdemeanors* had its first day of shooting in the fall of 1988, the script was actually entitled *Brothers*. Before long Woody would learn that the title was already the property of a television show, but for the moment, anyway, that was unimportant. As Woody does not let out the titles of his movies until just before they are released, while in production all his films are simply known by the acronym for the Woody Allen (Fall, Winter, Spring, Summer, depending on the season) Project and are followed by the year to keep each separate. Thus this was WAFP '88, a film being made, as all his films are now made, by Untitled Productions, Inc.

The cast and crew had gathered in Greenwich Village at 8 a.m. at the (now gone) Bleecker Street Cinema to shoot Woody's first scenes with Jenny Nichols, who played his niece. A tank truck with pipes attached to make rain was by the curb but it wouldn't be needed; the sky was pouring. Inside, the popcorn machine in the lobby was busily spitting out fresh kernels, trying to keep up with the demand even at such an early hour; eventually it would serve as set dressing, and Woody and Jenny would need popcorn for one of their shots. In the theater itself, the crew went about their preparations and greeted each other. Most have worked together on Woody's films for ten years or more. "It's like the first day of school, but we've all been held back by the same teacher," said makeup designer Fern Buchner, who has done sixteen of his movies.

Often a first day on Woody's films ends with no usable footage, and despite a promising start, this day was no exception. The camera was set up to look into the faces of Woody and Jenny as they watched a movie and munched popcorn. Smoke cookies, so called because they look like round oatmeal biscuits and produce a thick haze when lit, were ignited and waved around so they would diffuse the stream of light from the projection booth and add atmosphere. They billowed up ominously in the back of the theater and assistant director Reilly said to the extras standing there, waiting to be seated as background, "Anyone who hasn't made a will, leave now."

They began to shoot. "That should be a good one," Woody said after the second take. "That's getting closer," he said after another. "A couple more," he said after yet another. Finally: "One quick one and we're done." ("[The French director] René Clair was a perfectionist," Woody said one day while choosing which of a group of takes he wanted to use. "Garson Kanin told me that he would shoot a scene twenty-five times and then say, 'Fine, that's exactly the way I want it. Now let's do one more, this one faster.' And always it was the fast one he wanted to use.")

None of these shots was quick enough, it turned out, and Woody returned several times to get the one he wanted. By the last occasion, weeks into shooting, he despaired of ever getting what he wanted.

Woody usually has periods of gloom during the shooting of every film, but at the beginning of *Alice*, a film with special considerations, his gloom was pervasive. At the end of the first week of shooting in the fall of 1989, Woody entertained the fantasy of stopping the movie and checking himself into the hospital, which would have allowed his production company to claim expenses from the insurer because of illness. (It costs about $100,000 a day to make Woody's movies—very low by today's standards.) The chromatic progression of his career mirrors the step-by-step way he likes to make his movies (and do everything else), and to him, the only steps this movie had taken so far were backwards. After six days of filming he had virtually no usable footage.

Alice is the story of Alice Tait (Mia Farrow), a faithful Catholic as a girl, who has been married for many years to a wealthy New Yorker (William Hurt). Her life revolves around extravagant consumption and constant physical pampering for her constant physical worries and complaints. One day she finds herself attracted to Joe (Joe Mantegna), the divorced father of another pupil in her children's school. Around the same time, she is persuaded by friends to see a Dr. Yang (Keye Luke), an acupuncturist and, it turns out, a specialist in arcane practices.

He prescribes herbs with decidedly magical effects: They make her invisible, they conjure up an old love who has died (Alec Baldwin), and they make her behave in wholly un-Alice ways. She has an affair with the father. She encounters her long-dead mother (Gwen Verdon). Wanting to be a writer, she meets her muse, a spectacularly flaky woman in fairy-princess attire (Bernadette Peters). She also discovers that her husband has been unfaithful to her often and for years, and she comes to see the silliness and emptiness of her life. Just when she decides to leave her husband for Joe, Joe tells her he hopes to reconcile with his ex-wife. But even though the effect of another of Dr. Yang's herbs makes any man who sees her fall desperately in love with her, she realizes she wants neither the husband nor the lover. Instead, being reminded often of her faith as a child and of the desire she had then to serve others, she abandons the false life of comfort and goes to work with the homeless. (What Alice becomes is not unlike what Mia is.) Both the way the character of Alice is written and how Mia plays her evoke a sense of Woody's out-of-synch film persona. The movie, by turns amusing, touching, and satiric, is elegantly shot. It is also filled with images, such as a confessional on the lawn of Alice's childhood home, that are among Woody's best. Employing many of his favorite techniques—flashbacks, magic, dreams, and fantasies—*Alice* manages to be both realistic in its satire and magical in its effects.

At the head of the first draft of the script that he sent to key crew members (it was entitled *The Magical Herbs of Dr. Yang* at the time, but Woody came to think that gave away too much of the story), he wrote, "Note: everything in this film must be extremely stylish; the shots, the locations, costumes, casting. Perhaps we should consider using lots of color rather than the usual autumnal hues. The net result should have a nice, cartoon-like quality, to some degree like *Radio Days*. We should allow for the possibility of an original score. Mia will play Alice Tait. The film begins with the usual CREDITS and then the OPENING SHOT will be a fantasy, although we won't know it at first."

Stylishness is an elusive quarry, never more so than when a single vision has to be translated by several others into cast and costumes, street scenes and sets, lighting and photography. And now, six days into the shooting of *Alice*, Woody had no usable footage. "The problem with this movie is that it could be told naturalistically or stylishly, and I want every shot to have style and not be too realistic," he said. "It's hard to be stylish, even on Madison Avenue. It's not opulence I want, just style.

Leopard coats and someone holding a small dog—an almost musical quality. Yet everyone missed just a bit in this. I had the camera in the wrong place, someone acted unconvincingly. It's so hard to get what I want. Theoretically I want to shoot everything over, and if I had twenty million dollars I could do that. But the film doesn't deserve to be made for twenty million. It deserves to be done for the twelve it has."

Little things drove him crazy. Mia took a walk in the park and her coat came open, and instead of just seeing a deep red coat, some of the white dress underneath was visible. It ruined the aesthetics for him. "I know it's obsessional but they all add up," he said. He was depressed and exhausted from bearing down on details. "I don't have the personality for general overall management of a situation," he went on. "If I'm remodeling or decorating a house, I want it done in a strict logical and chronological order. It's hard to think, 'Well, a year from now all these bricks will be covered up and this is coming from Paris and that from the store around the corner.' " It's the same with his filmmaking. He doesn't like to go on to the next thing until what he's working on is perfect—a process that guarantees self-defeat. The scene with Mia, for example. He reshot it and reshot again, so when he put it in the can waiting for the edit, he knew he had what he wanted. Yet very often a shot he has labored so hard over won't make the picture. He knows that he would be better off doing a rough shoot and then going back for what he finds he needs. But if at the end of a day he feels a shot is less than what he was trying to do, he doesn't sleep well.

"All this obsession," he continued. "It isn't perfectionism, it's obsession, compulsion—and all of that is no guarantee that the film is going to be any better. In bed the other night, I flipped the TV dial for fifteen minutes. I was so tired I couldn't read. The public television station was having a weekly Bergman festival and suddenly there were the opening credits of *The Seventh Seal*. I immediately turned past it; it was so threatening to me. I felt it would just alienate me from working on my own film. As I flipped through the stations, I had to look away every time I passed by the channel it was on. Bergman has the same feelings. He doesn't like to watch a decent film while making a film of his." Woody sighed. "I spend the whole day trying to shoot a walk and a little bit on Madison Avenue, and I see it all day long with its warts and imperfections and I never feel I got it right. Then at night I turn on the TV and here's this finished work with the imprimatur of being a classic. It's finished, edited, scored, and in a way it's fresh to me, at least as opposed to my own material. . . . The week before, I had the same problem with *Wild Strawberries*."

Most movies are diffuse entities. Usually one person writes it, another directs, a third has the lead, and overseeing the whole is a producer and/or a studio who will invariably have a hand (or a foot) in the final cut. With Woody's films, he performs all those functions, beholden to no one but himself. The result is a film that takes a crew of seventy-five to make but has a single sensibility behind it. Even Orion leaves him alone and simply deducts from his fees if he goes over budget; and unlike the case with many pictures, no actor in Woody's movies has more power than he. As there are no real checks on Woody save his own sense of responsibility and a budget with some flexibility, the collaborative egos of director and producer, writer and star, that fuel the progress of other movies are replaced in his by, well, a butterfly with red hair.

Woody has surrounded himself with talent to bring his sensibility to life. "There's nothing to produce other than him. You get him to show up, you've produced a Woody Allen movie," producer Bobby Greenhut says. "He's the star, the writer, the director. Most producing, you have to put elements together. He's a one-man band." Greenhut, who worries more than Woody does, calls the money from Orion " 'the grant,' as in 'the grant can run out.' My job now is ninety percent preproduction [hiring the crew, negotiating with actors' agents, arranging the locations] and ten percent making sure the distributor has what he needs to get the picture into the theaters. It used to be that I was around for every shot, but if I never came now I don't think it would matter. He doesn't need anybody. After years of doing this there's such a shorthand involved. I would say I was more valuable to him in the early days than now because he knows so much better how to do something and where to do it and how to approach material. When I did *Annie Hall* I had probably already worked on forty movies, whereas Woody had only worked on five. So I brought all that experience he didn't have. Now he's light-years ahead of me." One of Greenhut's roles is to tell Woody which film ideas can be done within the budget. He also does not hesitate to tell Woody when he thinks portions of a movie need fixing ("Not your best work," he said after a rough-cut screening of one film). They have a smooth relationship, although at times Woody can drive him to distraction.

During the making of *Oedipus Wrecks* in the spring of 1988,

Greenhut visited the set as Woody reshot a scene he had filmed a few days earlier. During a break, the two chatted as they sat at a table. "You've already broken your word to me," Greenhut told him. "You promised no reshoots on this picture."

"No, no," Woody said, shaking his head. "Reshoots are what you do *after* the picture is over. These are *corrections*." Greenhut dropped his head to the table, burying it in his hands.

Greenhut has assembled a company of able technicians who make their plans around Woody's shooting schedule and who know his methods and style. And along with production manager Joe Hartwick, he is adept at saving a little money here, a little more money there, to accommodate the reshooting that is an integral part of Woody's filmmaking. Portions of films were routinely reshot under the old Hollywood studio system, using the standing sets on the soundstages and the gaggle of writers and actors under contract and therefore always available. But as actors became more independent, locations replaced soundstages, and costs rose, it fell into financial, and therefore artistic, disfavor. The esteem in which Woody is held in the film community has changed the concept of reshoots from a mark of failure to get it right the first time to an essential part of the creative process. They are again a common part of filmmaking, though not to the extent Woody relies on them. For him, they are the same as a novelist's rewrites.

His continuous reshoots require that Greenhut and Hartwick be able to change shooting schedules and assemble props and actors on quick notice and with no downtime, something they are able to do with remarkable proficiency. But not without personal cost. Hartwick is especially disheartened when he sees a film that looked to be on budget slip away into a great lake of red ink despite his best efforts. The phone call that invariably comes from Woody saying which scenes need to be reshot just when it looks as though he is done and on budget always makes him wilt. "Here's the list," Woody will say, and Hartwick, expecting only one or two scenes, will say, "The *list*?"

"Joe," Woody will say, feigning surprise, "is anything wrong?"

The shooting of *Another Woman* wound to an end in January 1988 (although Woody did a few reshoots as he worked on *Oedipus Wrecks* during the spring). It was a movie that had taken Greenhut's and Hartwick's best resources and all their ingenuity to keep in financial line. Then just as it looked as if he were done, Woody decided to rewrite a scene he had already filmed and shoot it at a new location, in this instance the Union Theological Seminary in Manhattan. Hartwick and Jonathan Filley, who finds the locations, were talking in an auditorium next to the classroom where Woody was filming the scene (it was ultimately cut) on what was supposed to have been the last day of shooting, a Tuesday. Hartwick had finagled the budget so there was enough money to go through Friday; there were a couple of other scenes to redo as well. About ten feet above where they stood talking were two platforms with railings. "I'm usually optimistic but I think we can do it," Hartwick said. Filley shrugged and answered, "If we don't finish by Friday, you and I can come here on the weekend and hang ourselves from these platforms."

Gallows humor, real and figurative, is not a bad release from the pressure of filmmaking, especially from the making of Woody's films, for everyone connected with the project feels it. Woody wants from his crew a version of the spontaneity he wants from actors. "I'm always driving the production people crazy because I don't want to plan anything before I go to the set," Woody said in the winter of 1989 while shooting *Alice*. He is the opposite of directors such as Alfred Hitchcock, who came to the set with every shot planned out on a storyboard. Woody knows the script better than anyone and certainly has a general shooting plan. But he barely knows what the particulars of a day's filming will be and he says, "Ninety-nine point nine percent of the time I haven't the faintest idea what I'm going to do with the camera when I come to the set."

The night before, there was a problem because of his inability to decide how to shoot until he sees the readied set. Woody and the production crew had scouted the location with cinematographer Carlo Di Palma and Woody had commented in an offhand way, "Oh, great, we make a shot here, we put the camera there and they come out, it will probably look very good." It was a night shot, and in an effort to save time, the technicians prerigged the lights so that they would fall auspiciously for the shot Woody had mentioned. When Woody got there, however, he had a completely different feeling. And Di Palma, who also doesn't like to plan on anything, did, too. Woody knows that sometimes this is annoying to the production people, "especially if we're doing special effects. There are certain things they've got to know. They just can't do it any other way. Yet it's very hard for me to work that way."

On many occasions, not only will the setup be wrong but Woody will decide the whole location is no good. While making *Another Woman*, the crew set up what was supposed to be the first shot of Marion (Gena Rowlands), in which she would come out of a neighborhood delicatessen with instant coffee and such supplies for her new office, and then walk along the street. It was to be accompanied by her voice-over, introducing herself and explaining her work. A dolly track had been laid out on the sidewalk so the camera could be moved to capture everything in one long master shot. It was a cold day and Woody and cinematographer Sven Nykvist stood in the store looking out at the street, the latter looking serious but the former looking sour. Neither spoke. After all was ready, Woody sat on the camera seat and was dollied through the shot. Then he said, simply, "No," and stepped aside with Nykvist and assistant director Tom Reilly. The area, he said, did not offer the right look and the shot would use up too much film time to explain so little. There had to be a better way to introduce her. (In the film, she is first seen in her apartment, getting ready to go out. The shot includes photos of her family, whom she talks about in her voice-over, thus introducing not only herself and her work but other central characters as well.)

"Nine of hearts on this," Reilly called out to the crew. Without surprise or saying a word, they started to dismantle the equipment that had taken two hours to set up.

A hallmark of a Woody Allen movie is his use of master shots. Most films, especially those made by American directors, are a mélange of long shots, close-ups, and over-the-shoulder shots that cut back and forth between the actors. It allows the director to choose between a variety of readings and camera angles in compiling a scene, but the result is choppy in comparison to a master. Woody's films are a succession of scenes in which the people and the camera move to capture all the angles he wants. It is a graceful and technically difficult way to shoot; it requires technicians and actors to get every move and word right over a period of as long as five minutes. Roman Polanski is another director who uses masters, as he did in *Rosemary's Baby*. In comparing the two men, however, Mia says that where Polanski "would rehearse the whole scene for camera many times, with many, many takes, Woody doesn't rehearse it, even for camera that much. There are a couple of perfunctory camera rehearsals where half the time he doesn't even seem to be tuning in. And then you're just shooting. His wonderful masters are one of the things I really respect about his directing. They look great, it's fun to do them, and you never have the tedium that you get in other filmmaking where you're doing the scene again and again and you have to match your gestures from every angle."

Woody also does not hesitate to have actors speak their lines off-camera, something almost unheard of in Hollywood. Producers and studios feel that people pay to see the stars in movies and that the films should be full of close-ups to give them their money's worth, yet Woody will shoot scenes where actors move in and out of the frame. In doing so, he ignores the traditional view that in comedy the jokes must be delivered in good lighting and full frame and that in any film the actors should always be visible. He credits cinematographer Gordon Willis with teaching him the effectiveness of offscreen actors during the filming of *Annie Hall*. In an early scene, Annie sits up reading in bed after she and Alvy have returned from watching *The Sorrow and the Pity*, Marcel Ophuls's chronicle of a French town during the German occupation of World War II.

ALVY

(*Offscreen*) Boy, those guys in the French Resistance were really brave, you know? Got to listen to Maurice Chevalier sing so much.

ANNIE

M'm, I don't know, sometimes I ask myself how I would stand up under torture.

ALVY

(*Offscreen*) You? You kiddin'? (*He moves into the frame, lying across the bed to touch Annie, who makes a face*) If the Gestapo would take away your Bloomingdale's charge card, you'd tell 'em everything.

"I usually know how I want to shoot comedies," Woody says. "I knew in *Annie Hall*, for example, that when I meet Keaton, I want to see us playing tennis and I want it to be wide. And most of the time it was completely logical. But on this occasion I said to Gordie, 'Hey, if we shoot Keaton this way, I'm going to be offstage when I do my joke.' And he said, 'That's okay, they can *hear* you.' " It was a revelation for Woody. (In *Stardust Memories*, there are several instances where characters walk out of the frame and continue talking while the screen is filled with a static shot of a white wall.)

Woody has made most of his films with one of three of the world's finest cinematographers—Willis (among whose other work are the *Godfather* movies), who shot *Interiors, Manhattan, Stardust Memories, Zelig, Broadway Danny Rose,* and *The Purple Rose of Cairo*; Sven Nykvist (the cinematographer for more than a score of Bergman's movies), who shot *Another Woman, Oedipus Wrecks,* and *Crimes and Misdemeanors*; and Carlo Di Palma (the cinematographer for many of Michelangelo Antonioni's films), who did *Hannah and Her Sisters, Radio Days, September,* and *Alice.* Each has a different style.

When Woody started with Willis, he had made only five films. He had been trying to learn as he went along and wanted to improve himself as well as the look of the whole movie. *Everything You Always Wanted to Know About Sex* was an improvement on the crude but energetic look of his first two movies. *Sleeper* was an even bigger improvement. (David M. Walsh was the cinematographer for both.) *Love and Death,* shot in France with the Belgian cameraman Ghislain Cloquet, was yet another step ahead.

"It was always an interest of mine to develop graphics and not just shoot functionally," Woody says. "Gordon and I would come to a set and I'd tell him how I wanted to shoot it and most of the time he would be in agreement with me. But sometimes he'd say, 'No, it's going to be very pretentious if we do that,' or 'It's going to look very tacky later,' and he'd explain to me why he felt that way. And he was usually right. Rarely, when I felt that he wasn't making sense, I would either shoot it both ways or shoot it again after seeing it in dailies. But his instinct is so good that in almost every case where he corrected me on something, it was a good correction. ("Woody and I hate the same things and like the same things," Willis says. "Our minds are cross-indexed very well.") I've been lucky because I learned a lot from him and I learned a lot from [film editor] Ralph Rosenblum, and they're two masters in their particular areas."

Willis and Nykvist are in many ways opposites whose strengths Woody has put to good use. Willis sees the whole frame and is not concerned specifically with the actors. Nykvist, through his long association with Bergman, is preoccupied with the actors, the prerequisite with Bergman. Every scene is framed and lit to illuminate their faces, a style of shooting Nykvist refers to as "two faces and a teacup." Willis has a different approach than Nykvist and Di Palma, in part because European filmmakers have less money and less time to make films, and thus less time to set up their shots.

"Gordon's is a very American style," Woody says. "It's wonderful. He would have been sensational working with John Ford or someone like that. His shots are superbly lit, I mean like Rembrandt. He just loves to paint with light. Carlo, on the other hand, likes the camera constantly in motion and is between the two of them. Sven likes to be in motion but he is not as committed to it as Carlo is. Carlo is a very beautiful mood lighter" and is great with color. His mother was a florist and he grew up surrounded by the bright hues of flowers, which he credits with influencing his work.

Woody is interested in the actor, of course, but he has a bigger interest in the total frame than Sven. The two, however, collaborate easily and with almost total understanding. (Each has difficulty hearing with his left ear, and when they walk and talk together, they loop around each other, trying to get to the good side.) The cinematographer, with his sense of lighting and camera work, must translate the director's vision into what the audience sees. But Woody has found he needs to spend very little time talking about it with men as capable as Willis, Di Palma, and Nykvist. Before shooting *Another Woman*, their first film together, Woody and Sven had a couple of formal discussions lasting a few hours as they went through the script page by page, but their understanding came largely by osmosis. They went location hunting together, had dinner, saw a few movies. Some were Woody's—*September* and *Radio Days*, which Nykvist had seen with Bergman, who admires Woody's work—others were either films Nykvist had shot or current movies of some visual interest, such as *The Sacrifice, Fatal Attraction, Someone to Watch Over Me*, and *Orphans*, and their viewing led to conversations about what worked.

There were two major questions they had to resolve. One was whether the dreams and flashbacks that account for perhaps a third of *Another Woman* should be shot any differently than the real-time story. The answer, they decided, was no. Keeping them the same allowed for a fluid transfer from one to the other, in the way daydreams and recollections slip in and out of daily life.

The other question was tougher: Should the film be in black and white or color? Black-and-white films are, if not box office poison, at least box office indigestion. In the age of color TV, many filmgoers are put off by black and white, even though some of the most impressive and classic films have been shot in it. Still, Woody has not hesitated to use it when he thinks it's called for—*Stardust Memories, Manhattan, Broadway Danny Rose*, and *Zelig* are all in black and white (and hard to imagine being as effective in color), even if this meant some people decided against seeing them solely because they lacked color, at least in the customary sense. The black and white and grays of *Manhattan* make the viewer aware of what the term "silver screen" means. Woody's reaction is philosophical. "That's not the audience I want anyway. I figure I'm better off without them. They're no good with subtlety if something as broad as that is a problem," he says. Knowing the commercial difficulty black and white poses, however, Woody is not suicidal in employing it; he uses it only where he thinks the story is better told.

Which is why he finally decided to use color for *Another Woman*. After a while, he realized that many of his conversations with Nykvist while scouting locations had to do with color. ("No dangerous colors," meaning sharp reds and bright blues, Sven said of one location.) Woody had considered making an arbitrary choice to do the movie in black and white because he loves it. He felt on the plus side, some of the dream scenes would have a better feel; they wouldn't seem quite so literal. On the other hand, black and white can give a sense of restraint, and these were characters he wanted the audience to become emotionally involved with. He struggled to make the right decision for the material; even one percentage point either way would make it worth doing that way. Finally he could envision the whole story more in color, but mainly because black and white is a rarity now. "Black and white has a weight on the material because it's different these days," he said. "I don't want people to come in and sit down and be distanced. I want them to sit down and watch, not sit down and say, 'Gee, I wonder why it's in black and white.'"

Once he decided on color, Woody wanted the film to have the autumnal tone of many of his pictures (eye-diverting colors appear in those films only for effect—the red dress Maureen Stapleton wears in her first appearance in *Interiors* is a visual whirlwind). For *Another Woman* he originally wanted the costumes to be in neutral shades, with the exception of those of the main character, Marion. Hers were to be black, but the costume tests showed the problem with that: Gena Rowlands looked smashing while everyone else faded into frumpiness. Additionally, the look was too fashionable for a professor, so her clothes took on more muted and neutral tones. "It's hard to do a picture entirely in mud," costume designer Jeff Kurland cracked during the tests. (He won a British Academy of Film and Television Arts Award for his work on *Radio Days*.) Most of the clothes were one degree of taupe or another. "Fifty characters with changes. You think that's easy? I spent the weekend in the dye pot."

The effect of costumes and props on the feel of a film is generally overlooked by audiences but they are an integral part of the planning and design. Woody shot almost two hours of costume tests for *Another Woman*—half an hour more than the length of the finished picture. A look as specific as Woody wanted is easy to create in a studio (*September*, for instance, had a stylistic motif that was easy to control), but as soon as shooting moves to the street or into a restaurant, it is easy to get into trouble because it's impossible to repaint a city.

"You can control the look of a period film more—candlelight, what we would call antiques," Woody said while still trying to decide whether to film in color. "A modern house has TV, telephones, candies out, that sort of thing. A period room is very different—Tiffany lamps or kerosene lamps. They have a poetry not found in contemporary rooms. But here I'm in a contemporary situation, so I'm not sure that working in color will make an effective contribution. Black and white could." He had planned that Rowlands's first scene would show her walking in black-and-white clothes, but then he realized if she wore black all the time, the effect would be "arresting but also distancing."

In preparing for the film, Woody and Sven talked back and forth about technical details, drawing on their sensibilities and their experience, thinking cinematically even when their minds weren't directly on the movie. One day as they were being driven home through Central Park after several hours of location hunting, their car pulled up behind a taxi at a stoplight. The colors in the park had the drenched intensity of a clear late afternoon. The sun was bright but diffused with orange; the leaves on the trees a glossy green; the road black as licorice; the cab in front a brilliant yellow. The angle of the sun was such that the windows of the cab were darkened; it was as if no one was inside. Suddenly, the right arm of the woman passenger in the rear came up and rested on her head as each caught the light. She had tanned skin and red nails, their rich tones framed in the otherwise vacant window. "Look at that arm!" Nykvist exclaimed. "The car was empty and suddenly it's not!" Woody smiled. "It's Buñuel's arm," he said.

For all their similarity in vision, the two have opposite sensibilities about nature. While scouting the rural location that was used as the family's home in *Another Woman*, Nykvist walked into some calf-length grass and vines growing around a tree in the yard. He has a sturdy Nordic quality about him—he is over six feet tall with blue eyes, silver-blond hair, and a gentle face framed by a white beard. "Is Sven looking for angles or going for a hike?" Woody asked as he watched him. "Sven is a woodsman, he likes this kind of stuff. He likes the smell of hay," Woody went on, his distaste for all of those things plain. A moment later, Nykvist motioned for Woody to join him. "Angles. Just my luck," he said, quickly stepping through the growth. They conferred for a moment about the look of the house from that perspective, then Woody dashed out, stomping his feet as if he had just stepped in some wild animal's leavings. One more difference between Nykvist and Di Palma was evident. "Carlo is more from the Via Veneto," Woody said, still brushing himself off. "He would have walked around."

As is almost inevitably the case in any collaboration, Woody and Sven have had their occasional artistic differences. In *Another Woman*, for instance, there is a scene with Gene Hackman and Gena Rowlands by a window at the end of a hallway. It was not until Woody looked at the dailies that he realized how much Nykvist had lit it. "It's so light, so bright," Woody said. "I thought it was going to be dark up in that hallway, just light coming in through that end window. That's why I picked that hall, for the look." But Nykvist said, "If that was the lighting, we never would have seen the faces of the actors. It would have been a very pretty picture but we wouldn't have seen the actors' faces."

"I'm somewhere in the middle of Gordie and Sven," Woody said later. "I want to see the actors' faces to a degree, but I'm much more willing not to see them than Sven would imagine or Bergman would be. I'd be perfectly willing to do that scene where you didn't see the actors' faces, you just saw light coming through the window and they were dark; then as the camera moved in, you saw their faces a little better." (In *Manhattan*, which is shot in black and white, there is a visually stunning scene with Woody and Diane Keaton in the Hayden Planetarium. The audience sees a walk-through exhibit of the surface of the moon, then hears their voices, then sees the silhouettes of their faces in front of a dramatically lit large photograph of Saturn. There is an echo in it of director Orson Welles's and cinematographer Charles Lawton's famous shot in the aquarium in *The Lady from Shanghai*.)

For all the differences between Willis, Nykvist, and Di Palma, someone watching *The Purple Rose of Cairo*, *Crimes and Misdemeanors*, and *Alice* would be hard pressed to tell who shot which. The lighting of a film is the signature of men as capable as these three, but Woody's style of shooting has evolved to such a degree that now all his movies use long master shots, have a great deal of camera movement, and tend to be similarly lit in rich and subtle ways. No matter the cinematographer, Woody is adamant about not shooting scenes in direct sun because it takes away from the depth of contrast, even at the expense of waiting hours for overcast to return. While making *Broadway Danny Rose*, he and Willis spent a morning working on a funny shot of Danny driving his car, fumbling and bumbling, trying to pass a truck full of chickens, as in the old comedies. Three-quarters of a mile of main road by a river in New Jersey was closed by the police so they could do the scene. Lunchtime came. Woody and Gordon went off to a restaurant and during the break the sun came out. As they wanted a flat sky, they decided to linger over a glass of wine without bothering to call in. They had also neglected to say where they were going. Bobby Greenhut came by the set when lunch was supposed to be over to find police and seventy-five people standing by, a piece of highway locked up, and no director or cameraman. He was not amused. Assistant director Reilly was assigned to accompany Woody to lunch from then on and to make sure he reported where they went, which he does still.

Woody's development is indicated in the changes he has made in how he edits a film, changes that in some way also reflect the evolution of that craft. Films for years were shot by the director and a rough cut was assembled by the editor, who then showed it to him. That often is still the case today.

"When I started with Woody, he didn't know what you do in a cutting room," says Ralph Rosenblum, who edited his first six films. "He paid a great deal of attention, though. He's very smart and he watched very carefully. But if he had to sit in the cutting room for *Bananas*, we'd still be there. He wasn't prepared to deal with all the film he photographed. He knows comedy, God knows. But he didn't know any of the nuances of cutting, what to leave out, what to shorten, what to transpose. Of all the films we did together, *Bananas* was the hardest technically to edit. He had less control over what he was doing as a moviemaker. He was shooting skits. And he was less sure of himself. It wasn't a case of following the story, which was nonsense. It was a case of trying to preserve all of the various elements of some very funny skits. I hated it when I couldn't make some of them work. But he learned. Now he doesn't need anybody like me."

During the editing of *Sleeper*, Woody and Rosenblum each sat at a Moviola in Rosenblum's office, looking at pieces of film over and over again, trying to find the ones that played in the best relation to the others. They cut, spliced, respliced, and hoped for luck. Woody worked on one sequence, Rosenblum on the following. As each finished, he showed the other what he had done and they collaborated on changes. "Woody is the opposite of most writer/directors, who have trouble throwing something out," Rosenblum says. "His sense of ownership as the writer is nonexistent. He was ruthless in what he would throw out. In *Bananas* I was fighting to keep material in. After a screening he'd say, 'What's the matter with you? The audience didn't laugh. It's not funny. Throw it out. What do you care?' I said, 'It *is* funny.' " (Woody's most extreme reaction to footage was during the making of *Annie Hall*. The first day of shooting in Los Angeles, he saw the dailies of the last day's work in New York, among them a shot of Alvy in Times Square, torn over what to do about Annie, who has gone to California. He looks up at the sign that flashes the news in lights around the top of the Allied Chemical Tower. Instead of news, there is a message: "What are you doing, Alvy? Go to California. It's okay. She loves you." He hated the scene so much, he drove up to a reservoir and threw the reels in.)

Whole sequences of the story line were discarded as *Sleeper* was shaped to keep the film moving quickly. "Digging a grave at a cemetery would be funnier to watch than two guys cutting a comedy," Rosenblum observed one day as they waded through the 200,000 feet of film on 240 reels (about 35 hours' worth) that had to be reduced to around 90 minutes, which Woody has said with some seriousness may be the perfect length for a comedy. Most films use perhaps 150,000 feet of film and run 110 minutes. Many of Woody's movies run within five minutes of 90 minutes. The shortest is *Zelig*, 79 minutes; the longest, *Hannah and Her Sisters*, 107 minutes.

As he is with anything that interests him, Woody was a good student of film editing. "I think beginning with *Take the Money* he learned a little bit more about every aspect of moviemaking and I can't say that about anyone else I've worked with," Rosenblum says. "He learned more about photography, he learned about acting for films, he certainly learned more about editing. The first time he came close to being a pro was on *Sleeper*. There was more money involved and he was more ambitious in subject matter and technique. *Bananas* and *Take the Money* can be compared to the early Brian De Palma films. They were low-budget, 'New York' pictures like *Greetings* and *Hi, Mom*. They got good reviews but nobody would confuse them with a film, I think. *Sleeper* was Woody's first real film."

And *Interiors* was his first real test. It came on the heels of *Annie Hall*, which had won Oscars for best picture and best screenplay, a romantic comedy that affected a generation. *Interiors* was a leap into the deep sea of tragedy, and it took hard work on Woody's part to stay afloat. He rewrote and reshot and bore down on a film that is not one of Rosenblum's favorites, but it was a type of film he knew Woody longed to make.

"Even before he made a movie, he had that Bergmanesque streak," Rosenblum says. "He was going to make funny movies and pull the rug at the very end. I wasn't shocked by the original end of *Take the Money and Run* [where Virgil is machine-gunned], but I thought it was stupid. But that's something he has carried through all his movies and he will finish his life making serious movies. He says that comedy writers sit at the children's table and he's absolutely right about that. He wants to be remembered as a serious writer, a serious filmmaker. He managed to rescue *Interiors*, much to his credit. He was against the wall. I think he was afraid. He was testy, he was slightly short-tempered. He was fearful. He thought he had a real bomb. But he managed to pull it out with his own work. The day the reviews came out, he said to me, 'Well, we pulled this one out by the short hairs, didn't we?' " (During the final stages of readying the film, Woody turned to an acquaintance after they had watched a particularly dramatic scene. "It's always been my fear," he said. "I think I'm writing *Long Day's Journey into Night*—and it turns into *Edge of Night*." Despite its mixed reviews, Woody received Academy Award nominations both for directing and for writing *Interiors*.)

The lighthearted banter that carried along the more serious points of *Annie Hall* was absent from *Interiors*; by design, there is not a joke or funny aside in the story of an obsessive, minimalist woman named Eve and her family. (Eve was modeled on Louise Lasser's late mother; her father was the model for the cosmopolitan aspect of Judah in *Crimes and Misdemeanors*—that worldly ability to know who to see and what to do in any city.)

Woody has been criticized by some for trying to be too solemn in his most serious pictures. He disagrees. When he's writing comedy, it's fast and flippant and idiomatic and casual. He wanted to write a specific kind of drama in *Interiors*, *September*, and *Another Woman*, different from what, say, *Crimes and Misdemeanors* is. "I deliberately wrote a high-blown kind of dialogue," he says, "but it's the direction that gives them that quality more than the writing. It may be the wrong choice but that is the style I want those films to be in. The writing is not pompous or solemn, it's the mood of those pictures, the way I stage it and have the actors talk. I could have directed the three like *Crimes and Misdemeanors* so they would have been very idiomatic. But I deliberately did them in a more stylized way, and I tried to supplement that in the writing."

While he intended to give those dramas a different sense and sound, he acknowledges that his source for them may have given him a false ring for the dialogue. He saw the Russian and Swedish films that are his models with English subtitles, and it is their translated dialogue he imitates. He thinks that they might be more idiomatic in their original language and that he has therefore heard them in the wrong voice. "Take the last speech in the Russian *Uncle Vanya*," he says. "It's extremely poetical, and nobody talks like that, really. Yet that's how I was trying to write in those dramas. After I saw it, with Diane Keaton, it became a very important film in my life. But even among all the people I know in the film business—the directors and actors and New Yorkers—nobody saw it. So when I do a film and I want it to be like that, I've got to know going in that even if I achieve its superbness, that style of drama and that feeling appeal to very few people."

By the time he was editing *Interiors*, Woody had advanced to a point where, as Rosenblum said, he didn't need him anymore. He was by then essentially the supervising editor, a completely different circumstance than Rosenblum was used to. Still, he did—and does—need editing help and he was—and is—open to ideas. It was Rosenblum, for example, who had suggested using the music of Sergei Prokofiev in *Love and Death* rather than Stravinsky's, as Woody wanted, which Rosenblum argued was too strong. It was just help of a different sort that he needed. Woody did then and does now obsess over a snippet of film, and he happily will work until all hours. "I knew that come the end of the day, five-thirty, six o'clock, he wouldn't want to leave,"

Rosenblum says. "He would have stayed there until midnight or two in the morning. He told me toward the end of one of those pictures, 'I love to work. I'd work seven days a week. I don't care about hours. When we solve this problem, whether it's five o'clock or ten at night, then we move on to something else. Hours or days mean nothing.'" This was not the best working arrangement for someone used to the autonomy Rosenblum has had for the length of his career.

The degree to which Woody is in control of his artistic affairs, and has been really from the outset, was shown one evening during the editing of *Interiors*. A thunderstorm was in progress as Woody and an acquaintance were leaving the editing room with Rosenblum and his assistant Susan Morse (who is known as Sandy. She took over as Woody's editor on his next film, *Manhattan*, and has been his editor since). Woody offered them all a lift home and everyone got into the ivory Rolls-Royce he then had. As the three sat in the back, Woody, in the front passenger seat, picked up the then uncommon car phone and called Arthur Krim, at the time the chairman of the board of United Artists. The seeming incongruity has stayed with Rosenblum ever since. "What a fantastic visual scene," he recalled years later. "Here's this guy in his Army fatigues, riding in his limo and calling the head of UA. The world thinks of him as kind of a schnook who has trouble with women and machines and anything else, and instead, there's a major business tycoon sitting up there."

The fact is, he *was* even then a major business tycoon, a critical and commercial success. His previous film, *Annie Hall*, had won him Oscar nominations for best director, best actor, and best original screenplay, a triple play managed only once before, by Orson Welles for *Citizen Kane*. (He won all but best actor, Diane Keaton won for best actress, and the film was named best picture.) It also made a tidy amount of money for United Artists, as had most of his others. Rollins and Joffe, and Sam Cohen, his agent, who is considered the most powerful in the business, had secured for him a deal that guaranteed his autonomy. Woody had proved himself a responsible director who did not abuse his prerogatives, and he was held in high personal and artistic esteem. All of which made him, even after only five pictures, a force to be reckoned with by corporate chairmen. Woody's call to Krim that day was to let him know he would soon be able to see *Interiors*, a film Krim felt Woody had earned the right to make, even if such a movie was not strictly included in their deal.

In the years since, he has grown only more powerful. He has had offers to back him in the independent production of his movies. Studios have tried with considerable energy to pry him away from Orion and guaranteed him the level of independence he demands and enjoys. ("I always feel I'm an enigma in that sense," he says. "Not all my films make money and I have any number of neurotic proscriptions: No one can see the script, I sometimes make movies in black and white. Yet people say, 'That's okay, just do what you're doing.' It's amazing to me.") But however great a tycoon he is, he has maintained the sensibilities almost of someone who works out of his garage: happy in his projects, streamlined in his operation, removed from the usual bustle of business. His success and his deals and alliances not only give him power, they afford him protection.

The glamour of the movie business is almost always absent in a film's shooting and never present in its editing, yet editing is one of the most vital parts of a film's making. Woody's editing room, about two-thirds the size of the screening room, is a self-contained movie production studio. There are two Steenbeck editing machines, which hold a reel of picture and two of soundtracks and are faster and can accommodate more film than the old Moviolas; a Magnatech recorder for transferring dialogue, music, and sound effects onto thirty-five-millimeter tape—there are hundreds of records and fifty-four reels of sounds at hand to choose from: interiors, car crashes, and so forth; and there is a mixing board for equalizing the sound when a line is lifted from one take and inserted into the middle of another. Woody doesn't like to waste a minute and so the second Steenbeck (they cost about $30,000 apiece when they were bought in 1981) is used, say, if a scene is being cut on the first machine and he wants to compare other takes head to head; this can be done without dismantling the reel in progress. It also allows one of Sandy Morse's assistants to synchronize the soundtrack with the pictures of dailies without interrupting her work.

Woody sits beside her as they edit. On the wall above their heads are dozens of one-and-one-half-by-ten-inch cards held in by rails and stacked in columns. Every scene has a color-coded card to follow threads of the story, and it is placed to show its spot in the movie as it is currently ordered; a scene written for one part can easily end up in another. Other columns contain the lifts, scenes that have been dropped. An "R" in front means the scene is a reshoot. "RR" means it has been reshot twice. On each are a few words to describe the scene, preceded by the scene number, such as these among the couple of dozen in the lifts column:

RR22A   Ken and Marion. NG sex. "Hardwood floor type."
R32   Car int. Marion and Laura discuss philosophy.
50   Marion and Peter in Library—gossip.

Because Woody barely finishes one film before starting the next—and sometimes works on two at once—cards for several films are sometimes there. One day Woody glanced up to check on the order of something and looked at the wrong film.

"Wait a minute," he said to Sandy. "Where's ours?"

"There are three there, and they're *all* ours," she reminded him.

Woody worked evenings and weekends to prepare a rough-cut edit of *Another Woman* as he shot it, and on a Sunday afternoon while some of Mia's older children and a couple of their friends watched *Roman Holiday* in the screening room, Woody and Sandy and her two assistants worked on a scene in which Marion (Gena Rowlands) follows Hope (Mia). Marion has overheard Hope's conversations with her psychiatrist, and Hope's anxieties compounded by her pregnancy have awakened long-suppressed feelings in Marion. The two women have never met but Marion once snatched a glimpse of Hope as she left the building. Then one night she sees Hope on the street and follows her. Woody had Sven Nykvist shoot several angles of each woman with different-sized lenses and now he was trying to piece the scene into a dramatic whole. Fourteen takes, hung by a paper clip bent into a hook that went through a sprocket hole, dangled from a pole over the trim bin, which looks like a large canvas laundry hamper. Eight other reels of shots were on a counter nearby; three others were on the Steenbeck. Despite the seeming tangle of footage, the pieces of the film are kept in re-markable order; any take desired can be produced in seconds. Woody sat next to Sandy as they watched the shots, then he doodled on a pad as she spliced together new combinations.

"My inclination is to drop the hundred-millimeter shot forever," he said. "It makes it look as though Gena is closer than she is."

"Let's just look at it," she suggested.

It was a shot of feet. Mia's go into a shadow, the frame turns all black, then they come out. "Let's try beginning with her coming out of

the black," he said. But it didn't look right. "There's no sense of movement. Leave her going into and coming out of shadow." As each passed
in front of a lighted window in the next cut he said, "We're not creating
sufficient distance between them. It looks like Mia should be in the
shot with Gena."

They fiddled some more. Woody at the editing machine is like a
man in an emotional elevator—he goes high, he goes low, and he seldom
stays long in one spot. His highs, however, are hardly effusive. "That's
not so terrible" is his almost constant euphemism for "good." "We're
going to be fine because all these work together to one degree or
another," he said. "The question is, is there one combination that's
more fun than another? The first two cuts, you can get away with. On
the third, we need to do something. You want to see the distance
between them. The only shot we haven't looked at is the wide shot
from last week. Shall we look at it and see if it's magical?" It worked,
if not magically, but the next cut did nothing: "It's not sweet. . . ." After
a couple of minutes of contemplation he said, "Let's wait and think
about this." Then, resignedly: "The combined wisdom of the script girl,
myself, and Sven and we still don't have a piece of cake on this thing."

"It's not as bad as you think," Morse told him.

Woody tried again. "Let's talk this down. We could use Mia's feet,
then the last half of Gena's shot."

"The choices are the fifty and the hundred. There's also the shadow
[of Mia along the wall]."

"The hundred, the boat's sailed on at this point, but I'll see it if
you like." They did. He had an idea. "We could try Mia to Mia [two
different shots of her]—the hundred to the corner." While Sandy set
it up he said, "If this works we could be in much better shape. We
could go to the fifty and move the shadow to where you wanted to try
it, or switch it with the feet because the feet are less of a risk. If we
can get the fluidity of that cut it will help us."

While Sandy made the changes he told her, his voice touched with
marvel, "Sven said that when he and Ingmar were shooting *Scenes from
a Marriage*, they were obliged to shoot twenty minutes of usable film
a day. They'd come in in the morning, rehearse, shoot ten minutes, go
to lunch, rehearse, shoot another ten minutes. They had no money and
every single day they had to get twenty usable minutes."

The notion of such constraints and pressure made him grimace,
as did the recut after Morse ran it.

"Philosophically speaking here, you're not bothered that she goes off in this direction and then fishhooks in the other?"

"I guess I'm not reading it the way you are."

"That's great. It means it's not illogical."

"It would be a problem for me if there were an acute angle there."

They tried a sequence with Mia crossing the street, a cut just before she reached the corner, then picking her up in the crosswalk.

"This is going to work. I can just feel it," Woody said as Sandy turned on the machine. "That's better. The eye fluidizes." He smiled. "I'll buy that." But then he watched it again. The smile vanished. "It doesn't work. I'm going to have to shoot it again. We've tried every conceivable way and it's graceless."

"What about the wide shot and then the hundred?"

"Uh-huh. Let's take a look at that. What might also work, although I don't like to cut that way, is double-cutting the wide shot [cutting in and out of it twice]."

"If the cutting works properly here, then the logic is okay and Gena doesn't look like a fool coming to the corner."

By now they had spent two hours and twenty minutes on these few seconds of film. They looked at another version. Woody shook his head. "It's just not a nicely cut shot. I don't think it works. But you could try the shadow here to see if it works and get a sense of it." His smile came back as they watched the newest attempt. "I think this is going to work. We got lucky with that wall—the texture and geometry." He rubbed his hands. "I'm starting to feel better now," he said, pushing away from the table. "So the much-fussed-over hundred-millimeter shot finds itself in the trim bin, relegated to the outtake reel forever." He later reshot one of the cuts in the walk.

Such meticulous editing might seem like drudgery for so successful a person to be engaged in, but Woody's attention to editing contributes greatly to his accomplishment. He long ago learned the importance of rewriting from Danny Simon and has applied that lesson not only to the crafting of the script but to the splicing together of the frames of film. Under any circumstances, in creative work, anyway, success does not excuse one from the need to rewrite, reedit, and continually polish a piece until it is as seamless as it can be.

It was time for a short break. "Do I see a sandwich coming over the hill? Or is it through the heather?" Woody asked as he ordered "the same tunafish sandwich I've been eating for forty-five years and a cocoa-bean steak [a chocolate bar]." He looked around for Jane Martin, who had stepped out to run a quick errand. "I have to return some phone calls," he said, a bit at a loss; here were a few moments when he was doing nothing. "But I need Jane, and she's busy talking to her bail bondsman or something."

Woody hoped that *Another Woman* would establish him with a broad audience as a successful writer and director of dramatic films. Throughout its making he cautiously felt that goal was within reach. "Everything seems to be right about it," he said a couple of weeks into filming. "It has all the elements I want to project: a serious film, not realistic, a cameraman I've liked so much over the years, a tremendous cast. The experience of *Hannah* and *September* helped this to jell. The omens are that everything seems to be falling into place, I'm happier with early dailies than I almost ever am—and it may be one of those things that turns out to be one of the worst films I've ever made.

"This is clearly a movie," he continued. "*September* [which was about to be released] is intentionally a play on film, one set in four acts that companies could do on the stage. I've come a long way from *Interiors* in knowing what entertains more when you're not using comedy. This is a mass-audience business and *Interiors* did as well as those little foreign films I loved, even though I admit there were plenty of things wrong with the dramaturgy—for instance, I brought in the Maureen Stapleton character [whom the father marries shortly after divorcing his first wife] too late. But this is a big country and to be considered successful you have to do big business."

The idea for *Another Woman* began as a comic notion many years ago when Woody was interested in making a Chaplinesque movie. A man lives in a tiny, thin-walled room and overhears a woman talking about her problems. He solves them and becomes her dream man who can make all her wishes come true. Then he questioned the taste of eavesdropping; even in the most benign Chaplinesque way it seemed wrong. So he put the script away. Then years later he thought of it dramatically—a woman hears something through a wall. He wondered what would be interesting, what could she hear that would make such a difference? His first thought was that the overheard woman's sister and husband are having an affair. Then the listener goes home thinking how terrible this is—only to find that her own sister and husband are having an affair. But that became too Hitchcockian, so he used the sister motif in *Hannah*.

This notion continued to haunt him and for years he bore down on it, trying to make it work. Eventually he conceived of someone with a closed life, someone who kept a wall around her but now in her fifties couldn't keep emotions out; feelings started to seep in and resonate in all the characters in her life.

"Maybe I'll regret that I didn't do it as a comedy," Woody said. "But people have difficulty dealing with their feelings and still are extremely proficient in their intellectual work. Yet when it comes to their own emotions, they're not good at it. I'm probably as guilty of that as anyone."

When Woody and Sandy Morse have cut and spliced and rearranged scenes and still are uncertain how best to order them, they will slip into the screening room away even from their assistants and talk over how best to proceed. Several weeks later as they worked on the rough cut of *Another Woman* so Woody could decide what to reshoot, they had continual trouble with the last fifteen minutes of the movie. One Friday in the late winter of 1988, as they neared completion of the cut, Morse sat with a sandwich and a glass of milk while Woody paced back and forth as they discussed the problem. Every move they attempted led to another dead end, or left them no better off.

She suggested flipping some scenes and Woody recited their order to see if that worked. "Marion fights with Ken, they have dinner with the Bankses, they fight again, which is the opposite of the Bankses, who are a happy couple. She gets up in the night, has the memory of her first husband—she buys the mask as a present for him, she puts it to her face, he kisses her. . . . I love this, it's writing itself. . . . She goes into this place and meets Mia Farrow, she talks about missed opportunities, then she sees hubby number two with her friend. . . . This is just the way it was supposed to be. . . . She walks hang-dog to her studio, Mia sums it up, she goes home to Ken. . . . This is the way it was meant to work."

Morse was not so sure and expressed her reservations. Woody stood by the wall, writing on it with his finger.

"I hope it does work," he went on. "It's close. I hate to have to throw in the towel and admit I couldn't pull it off." He paused. "It may liberate that part of the picture, make it airier and lighter. I don't know if I buy it really, but I think it's worth looking at just for us."

"Let's try it."

"Let's. It means more moving of stuff, but if it dies on the Steenbeck, there's no need to screen it. We can put it back together." The two were now six inches apart, deep in concentration.

"But I don't think the long dream sequence going down the hall works," she said. (Marion sees Hope in the hallway outside her and her husband's bedroom.)

"No?" He paused again. "It's my favorite. I sometimes wish there was some way to make it go at the end."

"I feel I've walked into another film. I think it shows Mia's character as she was originally drawn, not as she is. I also have trouble with the dream where Marion pushes open the door and John Houseman is there." (In the middle of a psychoanalytic session with his and Hope's doctor.)

"That's another one of those cuts that we can play with and look at. I don't feel a flaw there. She opens the door and sees Mia and it's nice. It's one line of an analytic session that you don't draw anything major about her character from. What she says is psychological palaver that you would hear at a billion psychiatric sessions."

They continued for some time, Woody becoming less and less optimistic. "My own feeling is that I'm never going to get it to play," he finally said. "The trick now is to make it as least embarrassing as possible. I'm trying to figure out how to put the abortion scene [Marion flashes back on telling her first husband she had an abortion] back where it was originally scheduled."

Morse made notes in a loose-leaf notebook of text and cuts. Then she suggested starting the scene on a different line. Woody liked the idea and she went off to make the changes.

"This will be an experiment for Monday," Woody said. "If it doesn't work, we'll lock it the other way. Monday or Tuesday we'll lock it no matter what. I'll do all this and have two weeks of waiting until we reshoot. I can start on the new script [which became *Crimes and Misdemeanors*]. That would be very valuable."

During all his editing and rewriting and reshooting, Woody maintained the hope he had felt early in the picture's making, that it could be the dramatic breakthrough he'd envisioned. When in the spring he saw a nearly complete version with the editing staff and an acquaintance, he liked it so much that he thought it could almost be released as is. Then he showed it to select friends, something he does several times with every film. He finds their reactions helpful, especially their negative ones. Sometimes they have only a few problems, other times, many. The worst screening ever for Woody was one for *Zelig*. He thought he was nearly finished but, he says, "people hated it. When I told [Mia's sister] Stephanie Farrow that I was going to reshoot the dance scene and one or two others, she said"—he waved a hand dismissively— " 'Those are the *least* of your problems.' "

After the first screening of *Another Woman* for friends, Jean Doumanian said she found the film a little cold. Woody doesn't take everything to heart that people tell him, but something about her lukewarm response made him distrust his feelings. Just before the next he said, "If I had done this right, I would have made two movies—this, and a comic one where I overhear Keaton or Mia and run out and do whatever they want. That would be the one that makes money and is successful and this is the one that is cut up for guitar picks."

Again at the second screening, another friend said the film was cold, and explained in greater detail why. Later that night during the break between sets with his band at Michael's Pub, Woody sat somberly at his table. "I liked this screening the best of all as I watched it, but I started to change as I listened to that objection," he said. "I think I've blown it. I think I haven't made it imaginative enough. I could have made it more exciting. The characters can all be cool and the movie still hot as a pistol. The fun of, say, Bergman's movies is that, yes, they're heavy, but something is always going on."

His feelings grew harsher and before long he had abandoned all hope for the film, if only because his disappointment in missing his personal bull's-eye was so great. "It's cold, boring, ball-less. A cure for insomnia," he said after he screened it a few weeks later. "I was falling asleep after the first fifteen minutes. I kept feeling, 'Get past this and there's a terrific scene.' But no. The movie is like the music over the titles: wispy, unfocused. There's good acting but I didn't pull it off. It's too cold. A better person could make it work. *Wild Strawberries* is about a cold man and it's hot." He paused. Near success provides him no solace. "Well, no need to sit and beat a dead horse. It's old celluloid."

Another Woman was released to mixed reviews in the fall of 1988. Richard Schickel of *Time*, who is a career-long appreciator of Woody's work and whom Woody likes, raved about it: "The subtlety of its structure and the tender irony with which it contemplates an emotionally guarded woman being drawn into confrontation with her past demonstrates lucidity and compassion of an order virtually unknown in American movies." Vincent Canby gave it the most completely bad review he's given Woody: ". . . his most personal, most self-searching film. . . . Yet something vital is missing, and without it, *Another Woman* takes the breath away, both for the intensity of its grand aspirations and for the thoroughness of its windy failure," he wrote.

"I just didn't believe he knew a thing about those people and their world," Canby said later of Woody's portrayal of a philosophy professor and her physician husband. "I don't think he has any real feeling for the lives those people are living or even knows really how they live: How they get up in the morning, what time they get up, if they brush their teeth first, or anything. I think he misses in the same way Hitchcock said he missed when he tried to do a period film, because he said he wanted to know where they went to the bathroom, if they have toilet paper. And I think this world is to Woody as strange as any period world was to Hitchcock. It's almost as if he were ashamed of being the very special person, the very special talent that he is, living a very particular life that is like very few men's lives. When he tries to cast his concerns in the shapes or persons of people who do live rather conventional lives, those lives are as foreign to him and in some ways as exotic as the lives of people living in the mountains of New Guinea."

Woody's relationship with critics is one of both approach and avoidance. He is friendly with some, corresponds with others, but almost never reads their reviews of his films. He is given general reports from Orion about how a film fared with national reviewers and in individual cities. He also learns how his films opened from waiters, who are fast to tell him, "Hey, nice reviews." (But "it's not reviews that you want the congratulations for," he says. "It should be, 'Congratulations on your achievement in the picture.' ") He is well aware of the power of critics, and while he respects those who are serious students of and lucid writers on film (he does read their reviews of other people's movies), they constitute a minority. "You do all this work for what? So some guy on TV can give you three pineapples, or whatever," Woody said one day as he struggled with editing a scene.

He recognizes the pleasures of approbation and knows even more the necessity to stand up to sharp criticism. "You have to have a lot of guts to weather major negative reactions," he said after *Another Woman* came out. "I knew *September*, for instance, could get major negative reactions. Still, when I worked on it I thought, 'Well, you know, who cares? This is what I want to work on.' Then it opened and phone calls came in every day saying, 'Gee, they hated it in Boston. Gee, it's not working here, it's dying in Philadelphia, it's dying in Washington.' And review after review said, 'What does he want to do this for?' "

He turned around and did the same thing again, however, with *Another Woman*, knowing that he had at least a 50 percent chance of having that film largely judged a failure, too. "You have to be able to not let that faze you at all," he went on. "Because the temptation is, it's always more pleasant in the perquisites of life when the reaction is like it was for *Hannah*. You open a movie and your phone never stops ringing and people are saying, 'It's wonderful,' and Orion calls and says, 'We opened in St. Louis and you never did great here but this picture just broke every record.' There's a tremendous rush of attention and success financially and critically and you have to be able to keep that in perspective and not put any value on it whatsoever." He laughed. "Because otherwise you start working for that. You have to be willing to give up success. I had to be willing on *Another Woman* to hear my producer, Bobby Greenhut, call me and say, 'They've seen the picture and they don't want to give you the Beekman Theater. They don't want to give you the Tower East.' I'm used to anything I want in New York. Then they see that kind of picture and they think, 'No, we're going to die with this. We don't want it.' You have to be prepared for that, you have to say, 'Okay, I'll take a lesser theater.' The next time out you can't let yourself say, 'Well, I don't want to go through that again. I want to get a good theater, I want the movie to be successful. I don't want to alienate critics, I don't want to alienate the public.' You just can't think about that. Otherwise you're succeeding on someone else's terms."

One way he keeps his terms his own is to almost never read things written about him, or to watch broadcasts of the very occasional TV interviews he does. He did, however, in a moment of curiosity, read Canby's critique of *Another Woman*, the first review he had read in a couple of years. It was a bad moment to be curious because the review was so unfavorable. Yet his response to it was only mild disappointment, and it gave him pause. "Where I really started feeling strange was in my lack of affect. Here was a mini-crisis and I thought to myself, 'God, I've picked up this review from a man whom I like and respect and who always gives me such wonderful notices, and he hated this picture.'

Yet it meant so little to me. I didn't disagree with him or agree with him. And I wondered, 'Am I being irresponsible to Orion, that I make a picture with their money and just don't care about criticism for a second, just let it roll off my back? Am I missing something in life when I have such a lack of affect that I don't get a thrill when a picture's a hit and I don't care when it's not a hit?' "

The answer, he decided, was that these events were only a small part of the larger sum that is his career. He has been successful for so much of his life that individual successes have taken on a different perspective for him than they might for someone who produces less work and has not been revered as he has. Recalling the huge successes of *Manhattan* and *Hannah and Her Sisters*, he said, "You get up that day and the papers say the picture's great and people are in lines in front of the theater, which you don't see unless you bother to go look at them. I've done that in my life, when I first started, but I haven't done it since *Sleeper*. The truth is, nothing happens. I'm here at Mia's and I'm playing with Dylan or doing whatever I'm doing, and the movie's playing different places and people are seeing it. But I still have to go home and practice the clarinet.

"It isn't like when you are a kid and you read about show-business life in *Act One* [Moss Hart's autobiography]. He thought to himself, 'If I ever get out of this environment in Brooklyn, I'll have an opening night on Broadway. It'll be a hit, and the next day I'll be invited to dinner, and there'll be cocktail parties.' And of course, that not only doesn't happen, but in the few cases where it does happen, it doesn't mean anything and you find that you wriggle out of going," he said, amused. "It's not that your life changes that way. Your life does change professionally with the first hit or two, but I know that if *Another Woman* was as big a hit as *Hannah* or as much a financial failure as *September*, I'm still going to make my next movie. I'm not in that position where the bottom's going to drop out."

One of the benefits of working at the pace Woody does is that there is little time to brood over old projects, because a new one is always waiting to take its place. In the case of *Another Woman*, it was the editing of his segment for *New York Stories*, which had been shot in and around the reshoots of *Another Woman*. One day he stood by the turntable in the editing room, trying to find a piece of piano music to replace Frankie Carle's "If You Were the Only Girl in the World," which he was unable to use because the rights to it were not available. Beside him was a stack of twenty or so records that he had pulled out from the shelves that store several hundred albums, mainly of music from the 1920s through the early 1950s. He repeatedly picked up and dropped the arm into the groove of a possible replacement from Erroll Garner, Earl "Fatha" Hines, and George Shearing, among others, but to no avail. He found one "too baroque," another "too sweet," a third "like a cocktail bar." He wanted "a piece of the right age, not too old, not Fats Waller. I want a straightforward melody," he said as he put on another record.

Just then Mia came in with Satchel and he went out to meet them in the small entrance foyer that doubles as the office. Dylan was already there and earlier had delighted in making Woody run back and forth in the screening room. ("I'm running up and down while the picture's going into the toilet," he said midway through his own delight in chasing her.) Sandy Morse's then newborn son, Dwight, was also there, until recently a most unlikely place for such a gathering of children. Earlier, Jane Martin had answered the phone with "Manhattan Day Care Center."

For several days, the words "Oedipus Wrecks" in Woody's handwriting had been on a yellow Post-it on the desk-light base. He held it up to Mia.

"What do you think of this for a title?"

She smiled. "It's funny."

"I don't want to know if it's funny, darling, I want to know if it's a good title."

"Yes, but it may be an esoteric reference for most of the audience, especially for a title."

"I don't mind being esoteric—not that this really is. Besides," he said, disappearing into the cutting room, "I never feel comfortable when too large an audience knows what I'm talking about."

Woody relies on Mia as a sounding board not only for titles but for the nuances of characters he writes for her. He talks about whomever he is creating while in the process and solicits her reactions. She often has a helpful response. It was her suggestion, for example, that Marion's actions be directly instigated by hearing Hope through the wall. Their professional relationship is so intertwined with their personal life that Mia has based her career on a quite different set of assumptions than she did before taking up with Woody. Her experience was as a mainstream actress, subject to the whims of Hollywood. Now she knows there will be an interesting part for her every year. Also, Woody's means of operation are different in that his films are self-contained, their budgets are smaller than most, and his approach to publicity is constrained. He is unwilling to tout his pictures on the morning television shows, a prize booking by most standards, and he does not expect Mia— or anyone else in his films unless they want to—to engage in their promotion. On film she is, Woody says, "so movie-starish. The camera just consumes her," yet she is quite un-movie-starish in her career. She regularly is offered parts in other films, and says she would accept a truly spectacular role, but she is happy just doing her film a year with Woody, in a part sometimes large, sometimes small. Other than a lucrative day's work in London in 1983 for *Supergirl*, she has not made a movie for anyone else since they linked up.

Shortly after Dylan was born, Mia and Woody met Vladimir Horowitz and his wife at a dinner party hosted by Kitty Carlisle Hart. Wanda Horowitz is a direct woman: "Mr. Woody Allen," she said when they were introduced, "you look the same as you do in the movies. No worse, no better." (She had a small speaking part in *Crimes and Misdemeanors*.) And the concert pianist, it soon became evident, shared many of Woody's odd sensibilities. "I like him because he's crazier than I am," Woody said not long after they met. Woody should know. While he ate the same dinner every night for the six months he was in Paris for *What's New, Pussycat?*, Horowitz ate the same dinner every night for years, one almost identical to Woody's standing order: sole, boiled potato, asparagus vinaigrette, crème caramel. Despite the singularity of the courses, the Horowitzes also shared Woody and Mia's passion for finding great restaurants. So on the occasions when it was Woody and Mia's treat, Jane Martin would call Le Bernardin or whichever fabled eatery they were going to and tell them Horowitz's meal had to be just such a way. Then over dinner, Woody would send his driver out to get the first edition of *The New York Times* because, Woody says, "he *had* to have it every evening. While at dinner he thought about it from the start of the meal."

Horowitz's death in 1989 at the age of eighty-six was a loss of a friend for them and an uncomfortable reminder for Woody. Because of Horowitz's age, when they heard the news on TV they were "not exactly stunned but Mia and I were saddened. Within a minute we agreed to call Wanda. Then one of the kids ran into the room. The cat had jumped up on the kitchen table. We hurried to get the cat off while the other kids came marching in demanding dinner. Suddenly the enormity of the passing of a human life was becoming history. The more pressing trivialities of life interfered. Mia was immediately the hard-pressed mother, grabbing the cat and ladling out the pasta. 'See how life goes on?' she said to me. It's a concept that causes me great trouble when I stop to think about it, which is often. That is, just how fragile and fleeting life is in the relentless flow of minor necessities that make up day-to-day existence."

The absurdity of existence yet the necessity of active choice is an underlying principle of existentialists such as Sartre, whose writing Woody has been particularly drawn to since an early age. All of which adds just the right touch of goofiness to the summer evening in 1983 when, as Woody and Mia were having dinner at Elaine's, Sartre's long-time companion, Simone de Beauvoir, came in and was seated with a friend at a nearby table. Woody and Mia noticed her (despite its reputation as a literary hangout, he was more than likely one of the few in the restaurant who had read any of her books) but, disliking interruptions by others and not inclined to introduce themselves under any circumstances, they went on with their meal. After a while, owner Elaine Kaufman came over to say that de Beauvoir wanted to meet Woody. Woody tried to demur but Kaufman asked if he please would do it. As Mia was not included in de Beauvoir's request, she stayed behind. Woody, who says, "I'm not a meeter. I hardly say a word to anybody," went to the table and, standing beside de Beauvoir, "napkin in hand, said hello, asked what she was doing in New York, and ended with the usual 'Nice to meet you.'" In a newspaper interview a few days later and in a recounting in Dierdre Bair's biography, de Beauvoir said of Woody and Mia, "They had nothing to say to me and I had nothing to say to them. I like what Woody Allen does a lot but he doesn't know me or anything about me or who I am."

Woody was finally able to cast Denholm Elliott in *September*, the least financially successful of his works, released in 1987. (From a technical point of view, however, he was very successful in making a play work on film, avoiding the usual problem of repeated close-ups and a static camera. "I don't think I've ever seen a one-set play done as beautifully as a film," says Vincent Canby, who is not as enthusiastic about the writing. "He always allows you to have a sense of where everybody is in the room at any one time.") The movie, however, is a good example of how Woody reworks his pictures, of how he will recast parts if necessary, and of how he is attracted by a new challenge. If a horse player were to describe *September*, he would say it is by *Hannah and Her Sisters* out of *Interiors*. It centers on the wishful or actual relationships of six people in a summer house: a mother (Elaine Stritch) and her daughter (Mia Farrow), with a traumatic past which has caused great bitterness; the daughter's best friend (Dianne Wiest), whose own life is in turmoil and who has come for a visit; an advertising copywriter with aspirations of writing a book who has rented the guesthouse on the property (Sam Waterston); an older neighbor who yearns for the daughter (Denholm Elliott); and the mother's present husband, an earthy physicist (Jack Warden). The film takes place entirely in the house.

Woody had long wanted to make a chamber piece with a small cast in one location, and one way to do that is to work in play form. Unlike dramas which are written for the stage and then adapted for film, often with less than satisfactory results, *September* is a screenplay in every sense. "It was conceived for film," he said before it came out. "It was shot as a film is shot and therefore, I hope, is not stagey. The perspective of the audience is forever changing, whereas in a play it can't, and the camera can come in very close and can change a number of times within the same shot. Also, this film never has to live up to any success it had on the stage or any of the practicalities of the stage."

The story is a drama with flashes of comedy that spring from the characters' personalities. If that and the action taking place in the country sound reminiscent of, say, Chekhov or Turgenev, it was not completely unintentional, even though, considering his view of nature, a summer house is an unlikely spot for Woody's attention. Actually, the film was shot indoors on a soundstage.

It wasn't meant to be that way, though. The original location was to be Mia's country home in Connecticut. She is forever trying to get him there, to enjoy the pleasures of the outdoors (an aptitude test once showed she was most suited to being a forest ranger), and he is forever having a hard time doing that (no aptitude test would ever result in that for him). One day as they strolled around her place she said, "This would make a great setting for a little Russian play. It's just so perfect.

It would be fun to shoot up here. The kids would love it and you would have something to do all the time." Woody snapped at the bait. "I thought, 'What a Chekhovian atmosphere this is,'" he recalled later. "It's a house on many acres, isolated, by a little lake. There are trees, and a field here, a swing there. It suggested to me right away the kind of locale in the stories of Turgenev and Chekhov, which have a certain amount of comedy in them. It's not real comedy but, I guess, comedy of desperation and anxiety."

While Mia's country home was the inspiration for the setting, the story was one Woody had kicked around for years: when a traumatic incident occurs in one's life, there are those who are wrecked by it and others who are virtually unaffected. The interesting thing to Woody was not the incident itself—years earlier the mother's lover was killed, apparently by the daughter as a young girl—which was why he never showed it in flashback. What interested him was the long-term responses.

Although Mia came close to luring Woody into an extended stay in the country, nature, of all things, intervened. The timing of the film meant the shooting would be done in winter, and the bare trees and the cold were not the feel Woody wanted. Instead Santo Loquasto, Woody's former costume designer and present production designer, conceived a set that brings the audience into the rooms of a summer place built on a soundstage. (He received a British Academy of Film and Television Arts Award for his *Radio Days* sets.) The outdoors is never seen. Rather, it is suggested by light or dark behind closed venetian blinds and by sound effects and references in the dialogue. In the original design they tried to simulate the outdoors through the windows, and they brought trees into the studio. But Woody found that they gave an artificial quality to the piece—not photographically but in mood. He wanted to focus the attention inward and not have the interaction between the characters distracted by a beautiful sunset or by the rustling of trees. The more internalized the setting became, the happier he was. It was finally decided not to make any shots out the window or simulate the outdoors but to just stay, as the athletes say, within themselves.

The set was not all that evolved. Originally, the actors were Mia as the daughter, Maureen O'Sullivan as the mother, Dianne Wiest as the friend, Denholm Elliott as the physicist husband ("I'd *live* to play that part," he told Woody), and Charles Durning as the neighbor. The writer was Christopher Walken, whom Woody calls "one of my favorite actors. I used him in *Annie Hall* and was dying to use him again. I think he's a great, inspired actor." But as sometimes happens between directors and actors, after a few weeks of shooting, Woody said, "we couldn't get copacetic on what to do and decided that instead of his making concessions and my making concessions, we'd work on something else down the line." So Sam Shepard was brought on and in ten weeks the film was done. Sort of.

Once he began to edit it, Woody found that a number of speeches were too stagey and too long; that there were many structural problems slowing the action; and that the tension he wanted developed too late. Overall, this is not uncommon; he often rewrites as much as half a movie, as he did on *The Purple Rose of Cairo*. One thing that necessitates such massive reworking is his use of long master shots. If a scene is five minutes long but a three-second line is wrong, no amount of fancy editing can save the entire shot. Also, everything in this film was circumscribed by the set and its playlike quality. Problems that he found, such as how the characters were blocked, were as much those of the stage as they were of film. When he saw the first version, he found he didn't need some speeches while other things needed to be said that weren't. This is no different than any playwright with a show out of town who reworks the scenes in his hotel room in Philadelphia, except it is more cumbersome, and more expensive. As the set was still in place in the Astoria Studios, Woody decided that rather than fiddle with the parts, he'd shoot the whole thing over again. He says now that he'd like to film it a third time "to make some experiments and just see if other relationships can develop. But of course, that's pure fantasy."

Even one reshoot played havoc with the cast. When he decided to begin anew, Maureen O'Sullivan was hospitalized with pneumonia and Charles Durning was involved with a long-standing commitment to another project. Woody and Shepard had not been able to get copacetic on his playing of the part either, and Woody replaced him, which led to the harshest public assessment of Woody's talents by an actor. "[Woody Allen and Robert Altman] have no understanding of actors whatsoever," Shepard said not long afterward in *Esquire*. "They're pisspoor as actors' directors. They may be great filmmakers, but they have no respect for actors. Individually, each understands zip about acting. Allen knows even less than Altman, which is nothing." (Shepard's professional feelings about Woody are unrelated to his personal ones.

His father had a marvelous collection of old jazz records, and after his death Shepard gave Woody some rare Sidney Bechet recordings.)

Sam Waterston replaced Sam Shepard and Elaine Stritch replaced Maureen O'Sullivan. (There was only a day's time to outfit Elaine Stritch in her costumes, and she was at first not pleased with all of them. Woody, anxious to start shooting and impatient over the delay her displeasure caused, came in to mediate. She burst into tears. He was unmoved. "Don't cry, you'll only make me madder," he quietly told her. She stopped and things improved considerably from there.) The two actresses come from different backgrounds—Stritch from the stage, O'Sullivan from films—and they gave different performances. "Maureen, because she's older, was more vulnerable where Elaine was more in charge," Woody said after filming. "But both were good and that's why this could be played onstage in different ways." While the mother's part required little rewriting, the advertising man/aspiring novelist required many changes in character because, Woody said, "Sam Shepard's quality is that of a kind of inarticulate, attractive loner from the plains, whereas Sam Waterston has a more Eastern, Boston quality."

While *September, Hannah and Her Sisters*, and *Interiors* may have a similar genealogy, it is one more of inference than of direct lineage. "All were meant to be serious pieces that examine family relationships," Woody says. "*September* is less cerebral and much, much warmer than *Interiors* but not as warm and familial as *Hannah*, which is a more amusing movie because I'm in it and I play a comic character in a comic predicament, and Michael Caine's predicament as a man infatuated with his wife's sister is in its way comic, too."

Eight of Woody's film scripts from *Annie Hall* through *The Purple Rose of Cairo* have been published in book form and are obvious choices for texts in film-writing courses. He receives a steady flow of compliments for how tightly written his scripts are, and he can only be amused by the praise because he knows that they were shaped more in the rewriting and reshooting than they were in the original crafting. Some films have been given memorable touches by serendipity. The nearly three dozen quintessential New York images that open *Manhattan*—quick shots of the skyline, the Brooklyn Bridge, Broadway, joggers in the park, crowded sidewalks, Park Avenue, the Fulton Fish Market, and so on— end with eye-filling fireworks over Central Park. All the previous images were carefully selected and specifically shot. Then when the movie was nearly done, Woody learned of the impending pyrotechnics and he and Willis and a crew went to the Central Park West apartment of the parents of one of the production staff, where the cameraman hung out a bathroom window to record the display. Usually the refashionings and additions are more intentional, but however they come about, all of his films change considerably from writing to release. Some, such as *Annie Hall*, scarcely resemble what they began as.

Manhattan had a serious third-act problem, because many relationships were coming to a head but there was no confrontation between the two best friends who found themselves in love with the same woman. Marshall Brickman, who collaborated on this script with Woody, pushed him to write a scene where the two friends have it out face to face. Originally, they glanced off one another in a phone call, but on film the encounter did not have the desired effect. It's hard in the writing of a script to always find the balance between being just enough ahead of the audience so that they're interested, not being so far ahead that they are lost, and not, of course, being behind them so they already know or feel what they see. After seeing the film for the first time Woody and Brickman knew that something new had to be done, but one problem with the scene Marshall wanted was that Woody would be required to do on the screen what he never does in life: Yell and scream and get upset with a friend.

Brickman prevailed. Although a synopsis reads like a summary of a bodice ripper, the scene Woody wrote follows one in which Mary (Diane Keaton) tells Ike (Woody) that she is still in love with Yale (Michael Murphy). Ike has meanwhile ended his relationship with Tracy (Mariel Hemingway) on account of his newfound feelings for Mary, whom he started to see after Yale told him he had broken things off with her. In the awkward and miserable way of such events, Mary tries to apologize but Ike wants nothing of it. "I gotta get some air," he says, walking out into the street.

The camera stays on Mary for a moment; she still sits on the coffee table, one hand on her knee, the other holding her glass of wine.
    Marching music is heard as the scene shifts to Ike, walking quickly on the New York sidewalks, muttering to himself, gesturing, oblivious to the passersby. He enters a university, walking past two girls looking at a bulletin board. Still muttering to himself, he

marches to a classroom door. He knocks on its small window. Yale, teaching a class, turns and sees his friend. Ike motions to Yale to come over to him; he knocks again. Yale excuses himself to his students and walks out the door. The music stops.

IKE

(Whispering) Psst. I wanna talk to you.

YALE

(Standing by the door, still holding the knob) What're you doing here?

IKE

What do you mean what am I doing here? I spoke to Mary. Weren't you going to say anything?

YALE

(Softly) Oh, damn. I was gonna say something to you, but not—sssh, there's a class in there.

IKE

Yeah, so where can we go and talk?

YALE

(Motioning) Come here. Come here. Come here. Come here. *(Yale pulls Ike across the corridor to another classroom door; they continue to speak in low voices.)*

IKE

Where can we—where can we go speak?

YALE

How'd you get past the security?

IKE

What do you mean? I walked right past. *(Ike and Yale walk through the door to an empty classroom. It looks like an ordinary schoolroom, with its wooden desks and blackboard, except for the two skeletons hanging near the door; they seem to be observing the two friends as they talk.)* What are you telling me, that you're gonna leave Emily—is this true?—and run away with the winner of the . . . Zelda Fitzgerald Emotional Maturity Award?

YALE

Look, I love her. I've always loved her.

IKE

(Sighing) Oh, what kind of crazy friend are you?

YALE

I'm a good friend! I introduced the two of you, remember?

IKE

Why? What was the point? *(Chuckling)* I don't understand that.

YALE

Well, I thought you liked her.

IKE

Yeah, I do like her! Now we both like her!

YALE

(Looking away) Yeah, well, I liked her first.

IKE

(Reacting, incredulous) "I liked her first." What're you—what're you, six years old? Jesus.

YALE

Look . . . I thought it was over. You know, I mean, would I have encouraged you to take her out if—if I still liked her? *(Ike walks closer to Yale; he now stands next to one of the skeletons. As he talks, he shares the screen with the skeleton's skull, which looks as if it has a perpetual grin. Ike, deep in conversation with Yale, ignores his long-dead scene stealer)*

IKE

So what, you liked her. Now you don't like her. Then you did like her. You know, it's still early. You can change your mind one more time before dinner!

YALE

Don't get sarcastic about this. You think I like this?

IKE

How long were you gonna see her without saying anything to me?

YALE

Don't turn this into one of your big moral issues.

IKE

(Reacting, still standing next to the skeleton) You could've said
. . . all you had to do was, you know, call me and talk to me. You
know, I'm very understanding. I'd'a said, "No," but you'd've felt
honest.

YALE

I wanted to tell you about it. I knew it was gonna upset you. I—
uh . . . we had a few innocent meetings.

IKE

A few? She said one! You guys, you should get your story straight,
you know. Don't you rehearse?

YALE

We met twice for coffee.

IKE

Hey, come off it. She doesn't drink coffee. What'd you do, meet
for Sanka? That's not too romantic. You know, that's a little on
the geriatric side.

YALE

Well, I'm not a saint, okay?

IKE

(Gesturing to the skeleton) But you—but you're too easy on yourself, don't you see that? You know . . . that's your problem, that's
your whole problem. You rationalize everything. You're not honest
with yourself. You talk about . . . you wanna write a book, but, in
the end, you'd rather buy the Porsche, you know, or you cheat a
little bit on Emily, and you play around with the truth a little with
me, and—and the next thing you know, you're in front of a Senate
committee and you're naming names! You're informing on your
friends!

YALE

(Reacting) You are so self-righteous, you know. I mean, we're just
people, we're just human beings, you know. You think you're God!

IKE

I—I gotta model myself after *someone*!

YALE

Well, you just can't live the way you do, you know. It's all so perfect.

IKE

Jesus—well, what are future generations gonna say about us? My God! (*He points to the skeleton, acknowledging it at last*) You know, someday we're gonna—we're gonna be like him! I mean, you know—well, he was probably one of the beautiful people. He was probably dancing and playing tennis and everything. And—and—(*Pointing to the skeleton again*) and now—well, this is what happens to us! You know, it's very important to have—to have some kind of personal integrity. You know, I'll—I'll be hanging in a classroom one day. And—and I wanna make sure when I . . . thin out that I'm well thought of!

(*The camera stays focused on the skeleton, its full form shown now, as Ike leaves, then Yale*)

Woody has come to feel that he "muffed the scene. I needed something and I overcompensated. I made it too preachy." Even if that is so, what stands out most in it is the writing. It is evocative and funny and it tells a world about the two characters. But precisely because of that, it could appear in a novel as easily as it could in a film; its literary, not its cinematic, strength is what carries the viewer, which was Woody's intent. He became a director primarily to protect his writing. He has obviously been able to do that and he has managed it, he says, by "directing minimally to get the writing across. I've never wanted to put obstacles or flamboyant style between the digesting of the material and the audience." He cites how up to the present, anyway, he would never have made *Citizen Kane* in the baroque style Orson Welles used. Now, however, he would like to use more of the weapons of a filmmaker and employ emotional effects created by the camera to tell a story only in a way that can be done on film.

"There's no way that the experience you have in *Persona* or *Amarcord* can really be given to you in a novel," he has said. "You get it from a combination of music and casting and camera angles and makeup.

This sounds pretentious, but you're made to feel cinema acting on you; it's the experience of what's being done through film itself that gives you the emotional feeling you get while watching."

The closest he has come to doing that throughout a movie is in *Radio Days*, which has many moments that can only be told through a camera. The film is not so much plot and story and character as it is a series of incidents woven together. They each have a beginning, middle, and end, yet the viewer never feels he is starting over as they come along. *Stardust Memories* uses extreme casting and starkness to make visible the heightened, subjective view of a character's own distorted sense. And *Alice*, too, has dreams and images that are spectacularly cinematic. But *The Purple Rose of Cairo* and *Hannah and Her Sisters* and certainly *Crimes and Misdemeanors* could all have been written as novels, as could *Annie Hall*. One doesn't get that feeling from an Akira Kurosawa film such as *The Seven Samurai* or *Ran*, or from Bergman's *Cries and Whispers*, which is a drama almost without words. Though Woody has made twenty films, he hasn't yet used all the tools of a director. First he relied on comedy, which was his strength. Then he relied on writing, which was another strength. He has so far been unwilling to cut loose from scripts that are self-contained and rely more on directing to make movies that are effective because of the use of film and camera only. "I think that's important for me to do," he says. "It's hard for an American filmmaker, especially one with a reputation like mine, because people would come and they'd most likely be bored— unless I pull it off brilliantly, which most likely I won't."

Woody has changed no film more than he did *Crimes and Misdemeanors*. After he saw the rough cut, he threw out fully a third of the story and virtually rewrote it from scratch. In the original version, Halley (Mia) worked as a geriatric social worker instead of the television producer she was in the film; she was married to a magazine editor whom the audience meets, and was also having an affair with a man the audience sees briefly as Cliff (Woody) and his niece Jenny (Jenny Nichols) secretly tail her through Central Park; the documentary film Cliff makes so he can spend more time with Halley, with whom he has fallen in love, was of ex-vaudevillian patients in the nursing home where she works, not the funny and damning film-within-the-film he makes of his brother-in-law Lester (Alan Alda); and the ending had Cliff passing himself off as a TV producer at the climactic wedding in order to foster a liaison with an aspiring actress played by Sean Young, with whom he is caught in an indelicate position when a curtain in the ballroom is accidentally opened. The last shot was of him with Jenny, his only real friend, telling her that little girls are the hope of the world. In addition, the story line with Cliff and Jenny was much stronger, as was that of his romance-seeking sister, Babs. And the story of Judah (Martin Landau), who foresees his life being shattered if his former mistress, Del (Anjelica Huston), reveals their relationship and his slippery financial dealings with a charitable trust, had more impetus to it than the others. His was the center of the film—Judah and his actions bring to light deep questions of faith and morality.

"Well," Woody said after seeing the first rough cut of the movie at the end of March 1989, "the good news is, it's better than I thought, apart from some obvious cuts and trims. The bad news is, Mia's and my story doesn't work." Yet Woody was not distressed. "This may be the best I've ever felt at this stage. At least I don't want to blow the place up."

In what has become standard practice, Woody and Sandy Morse met in the screening room, where for the next several hours they discussed how to reshape the movie. Woody began with the ending. "We could cut from my despondency to Esther Williams on the movie screen, then cut to an exchange between me and Jenny—clumsily said, 'I'm getting on with my life,' and some notion of a happy ending. Then 'The End' from the movie on the screen. Not a Pollyanna ending but not one where we keep going down. We could also use *Yankee Doodle Dandy* or *It's a Wonderful Life*, although I'm sensitive to use that as the end to our movie. It's such calendar art and it may anger a lot of people because it's such a revered movie."

He moved on to Judah's story.

"Did we go too fast?" he asked her.

"You don't want lots of expositional material to slow things down."

"Right. There's a question of whether we're strong enough with the religious aspect at the beginning. Put another way, a clearer statement of the argument of the movie: No higher power is going to punish us for our misdeeds if we get away with them. Knowing that, you have to choose a just life or there will be chaos, and so many people don't do that that there *is* chaos—then go on to prove or disprove that."

He went on, thinking aloud, unhappy that in the first two scenes between Judah and Del, she's hysterical in each. He decided to write the two scenes as one. Then he considered a scene between Judah and his brother Jack (Jerry Orbach, who arranges for Del to be murdered). He was displeased with a guilt-stricken Judah saying, "How did we become what we are?" and wanted to redo it.

"Judah is secular but there is a spark of religion from when they drive it into you as a kid," he said. "I feel we're getting two blocks of information at the beginning: Judah and his secret [the affair with Del] and also the religious stuff. I want to make it all one at the start. Do I have her flash through his mind while he's making his speech?" (The film opens with Judah being honored for his charitable work.)

After about an hour and a half of this, they ordered out for lunch and then moved on to Mia. Woody paced the floor as he talked.

"What you want with Mia is the essential line: We meet, I fall in love. Finding out she is married is a stall but viable." He stopped to think, then said, "It's an artificially introduced obstacle—her husband that I don't know about. I meet a girl, someone you'd think too mature and sober for Lester and she winds up with him. Then I conveniently don't notice her wedding ring for at least a week. There's no other meat in the story with Mia. It's all the slow playing out of arbitrary information."

"All that it needs to me is some sense that she could come to you," Morse told him. "I wish you had more reason to hope than there is. I wish for more intimacy in the champagne scene [after Halley tells Cliff in his editing room that Public Television is interested in the film on Professor Levy that he has been shooting for years] and at the jazz club [where Cliff and his wife and Halley and her husband go one evening. In the final version of the film, the scene is with Cliff, his wife, Halley, and Lester]."

Woody shook his head. "There's no special plot with Mia here. It's all dredging up and trying to find stuff." He tried, unsuccessfully, several paths to find a way around. "The original notion was that she's married and having an affair. Why? And what does it give us? Is that more intriguing than what I have now? I open champagne, we drink, she says, 'Congratulations, I was talking to my husband about your film [on the professor].' I say, 'What does he do?' and you see my disappointment at discovering she's married. Or do I do another scene with Jenny where I say, 'She's the first woman who's interested me in years and she's married.' But if you go back to her having an affair, it leaves the problem of her character not being so nice. So if I rewrite in a radical way—which I'm willing to do—say she and her husband have a fight at the table at the jazz club . . ." He stopped in mid-sentence and shook his head. "I've elongated a scene when I only needed a cut and now I have no value in that scene."

He thought a moment. "She could go to the phone and I could feel sick and go to the bathroom, then something could happen between me and Mia at the phone booth, but what? Originally there was the information about her affair and this was a breakup cut." He took a drink from a paper cup of chicken noodle soup and thought some more. "Why doesn't she just say to me, 'I'm married but I'm not happily married'? Something's got to be clear for that segment. It breaks my heart that I can't follow her." The scene where Cliff and Jenny follow Halley through Central Park and discover her meeting the man she's having an affair with was both amusing and beautifully photographed. Woody picked up an overstuffed turkey sandwich and took out some of the meat. Then he began to redo scenes aloud.

"Judah finds Del's body, that dark segment. Then I'm filming Lester and he hits on Halley in a playful way." Woody played Lester's and Halley's parts.

" 'I'm going to Barbados again.'

"She says, 'I not only freckle, I hive.'

"I say to Lester, 'She's a married woman. She's not one of those bimbos you're always after. She's intelligent and not your type.'

"He says, 'She's not happy. I was passing the office and I heard her on the phone and they were yelling and later she was crying—I know all the signs.' "

He resumed his own voice. "Then you cut to the jazz club because something more revealing has given it resonance. I happen to know her husband is having an affair and I know about the argument. My looks at her are more 'What's the story?'

"Or maybe Lester wasn't so pointed." He again played his role and Lester's.

" 'She's not a doxy,' I say.

"[Pointing to his chest] 'I have a little ticker here. I know this woman's not happy. She's looking for something.'

" 'That's wishful thinking, Lester.' " He resumed his own voice once more. "It gives more resonance for Lester when she goes off with him."

Sandy shook her head. "I don't know why I'm ill at ease. It's too protracted maybe."

Woody nodded. "Yeah. It's more extra material. The surprise has got to be that she picks him. In comparison to Judah's story, I'm not getting big enough things happening." He sat down. There was a long silence. He tried out a couple of possible scenes with Lester and the professor but came up empty, then moved on to the scenes with Cliff's sister.

"I don't care at that point in the picture to go off on that subject," Sandy told him. "You and Mia are poised on the end of a diving board to take the plunge or not take the plunge."

"We need to touch base with Babs," Woody said. "I need her somewhere. I might need her as a confidante to me, not for her problems. What we need is a segment that includes Halley coming over to the cutting room to cheer me up; I get news of the professor's death; and some up thing to begin it, and try to get my sister and niece in there.

"Then there's the walk in the park with Mia [where she says she is going away for a few months to sort out her life and turns down his offer of marriage]. The truth is, it may not have enough feeling to it, where she says she's going away. I may have been better off drawing it out. I may have dumped it too quickly."

He took a bite of his sandwich, then reworked some scenes at the wedding before moving back to Cliff and Halley.

"Is there anything to this?" he asked, trying a new tack. "I'm married and I fall in love with Halley because my marriage is not a very happy one. And she's single and I'm falling for her and Lester is pitching her in a superficial way and finally she says to me, 'You're married,' and I think that's the thing standing in her way when she's really being polite. Then she goes to London to do a show on foreign people. . . ." He threw up his hands. "It's no good. It's too masochistic, like a German movie of the twenties."

After a long while of jumping from scene to scene, they moved back to the ending. Sandy suggested, "What about Jenny coming in and saying, 'Let's blow this joint. There's a great midnight movie.' " Woody brightened.

"That's better already. It's wrong for me to say, 'The future of the world is in little girls.' I have just been betrayed by Mia and embarrassed by Sean Young. I like the idea of an Esther Williams Technicolor extravaganza. People singing and dancing, then you cut back to the audience and I'm there. I do a couple of sentences, a positive statement. You want an *Annie Get Your Gun* ending, 'There's No Business Like Show Business,' Indians and cowboys. There's *Yankee Doodle Dandy*, but it's black and white."

"We can always get the colorized version," Sandy said slyly. Woody faked a smile.

By mid-afternoon, he had a pretty clear idea of what he needed to do. "This may be neurotic speculation," he said, "but I like to squeeze and squeeze until I've gone as far as I can. It would be self-destructive not to try." He shrugged. "The worst that will happen is that people will get upset with me and it will cost me money."

There were ten scenes to rewrite and reshoot, the availability of actors and locations to check on and arrange. "We just need a few little finesses," Woody said. A little grin appeared. "A million dollars' worth of finesses."

Besides his trouble in finding an appropriate ending for his films, Woody has almost as hard a time finding the right title. Some, like *Hannah and Her Sisters* and *Broadway Danny Rose*, came easily. *Annie Hall* arose only at the last moment, however, and *Zelig* was a great problem; *The Chameleon Man* and *Cat's Pajamas* are only two of the dozens of contenders that came out of the title derby Woody carried on with his friends. But none of those films were as hard to title as *Crimes and Misdemeanors*. Woody's original choice of *Brothers* neatly summed up the varied relationships of the characters, and when he learned he could not use it, he was at a loss.

After months of trying to find another title he liked, he sat one day at the desk in his cutting room. Time was running out and a choice had to be made soon. Sandy Morse sat in a chair a few feet away and they threw out whatever came to mind. *A Matter of Conscience* was suggested. Woody shook his head. "I don't like *A Matter of* . . ." He stared at the desk a moment, then looked up. "There's no one word that means the human condition, like 'fandango,' is there?"

He continued free-associating. *"Dr. Shenanigans."* He laughed. *"Decisions. Decisive Moments. Make a Killing. Two Lives. Anything Else.* [Each of the last two was briefly the title.] *Crimes and Vanity."* *Crimes and Misdemeanors* and its variant, *High Crimes and Misdemeanors*, had been early suggestions, but the first didn't really hit the points Woody wanted and the second smacked of Gilbert and Sullivan. The phone rang. It was Bobby Greenhut. They talked a minute, then Woody asked him, "I guess you don't like *The Lord's Prayer* as a title. Do you think it puts too much of a burden on the film?"

After Woody hung up, he took a legal pad and divided the page into sections. He wanted to make some connection between eyes and God and success, and the day before an acquaintance had told him of a quote from Aeschylus that had the hat trick: "Success in men's eyes is God." He had liked the idea but now laughed as he said, "I can hear it now." His voice became pompous. " 'The title is taken from Aeschylus.' " He wrote down prospective titles under the proper headings.

GOOD AND EVIL
Acts of Good and Evil
Moments of Good and Evil
Scenes of Good and Evil

EYESIGHT GROUP
The Eyes of God
Windows of the Soul
Visions of the Soul
Dark Vision
The Sight of God

HOPE
Glimmer of Hope
Hope and Darkness
Faint Hope

CHOICE
A Matter of Choice
Choices in the Dark
Decisive Points

He filled the bottom of the page with doodles as they talked.

"*Empty Choices*," someone said. Woody was unimpressed.

"That'll send them away with a big sneer on their face. It's like *Split Decisions*. Titles like that always sound like those other pictures—too commercial. But then [chairman of Walt Disney Studios] Jeff Katzenberg said over lunch the other day that you couldn't have three worse words than *Dead Poets Society*." He looked at his list. "*The Eyes of God. The Sight of God.*" He shook his head. "It's a little much to ask for the shopping-mall people to come and see."

There was yet another problem to solve quickly. At the end of the film, Ben, the blind rabbi played by Sam Waterston, dances with his daughter at her wedding as the music continues into the beginning of the credits. Woody had planned to use "Always," but when he heard Steven Spielberg was making a film with that title he checked with him to see if he intended to use the song. He did (although it turned out that Irving Berlin would not give permission to use it) and Woody said he'd find something else, a gracious act he now regretted because he couldn't find anything appropriate. An added problem was that with Ben's blindness, a title with "eyes" in it, such as "I Only Have Eyes for You" or "Jeepers Creepers," made an unintentional and inappropriate joke. (He ended up, however, using "I'll Be Seeing You" because he could find nothing better.) He and Sandy suggested songs to each other, occasionally getting up to check the backs of albums on the shelves in a large case against the wall or to look through the ASCAP title book. He knows virtually every decent song written between 1900 and 1950 and has used hundreds of them in his movies. He has also seen and reseen thousands of films and has retained their specifics with almost the same clarity as a chess grandmaster remembers thousands of moves.

"We've used 'Make Believe' before, in *September*," Woody said. " 'We'll Meet Again,' but Kubrick used it in *Dr. Strangelove*. It has the right sort of schmaltzy sound. 'Speak to Me of Love.' 'If I Loved You.' 'I Only Have Eyes for You.' " He laughed. "I keep doing that by accident. It's too bad. It's such a pretty, schmaltzy song. 'As Time Goes By' can't be used. 'I Dream Too Much,' we've used. I wouldn't want to use Gershwin because of *Manhattan*. Cole Porter is the wrong person for this end music. 'Falling In Love Is Wonderful,' but an Irving Berlin song can't go beyond the picture [and into the credits]. How about 'I'm Confessin'?' "

"That's in *September* also," Sandy told him.

"Okay." He paused. "I want something with the feel of 'Lara's Theme,' that's a waltz." He paused again. " 'I'll Be Seeing You' is in *Oedipus Wrecks*. 'You Are Too Beautiful,' we've used. 'Bewitched,' we used. 'Isn't It Romantic?' . . ."

"You don't think *that* would have gotten away." (It's in *Hannah and Her Sisters*.)

"Nothing by Vernon Duke? Certainly nothing by Duke Ellington. Too jazzy. Porter's too sexy, more of a Latin beat. That's not right. Anything of Leonard Bernstein's? 'On the Town.' 'My Sister Eileen.' There are so many to choose from."

So many everythings to choose from: songs, titles, feet of film. By the time Woody had a version of the movie he liked, there were fifteen large cardboard boxes filled with reels of discarded film along one wall of the screening room: the first story between Woody and Mia, his film of the people in the geriatric home where she worked in that incarnation, characters and scenes that had to be cut because of the relentless pace that film requires to keep the story moving ahead.

One bit of good fortune for Woody in the ending of this film is that, almost for the fun of it, he had shot a close-up of Judah as he sits talking with Cliff on a piano bench. The intention was to have a several-minute-long master of Judah wrestling with his guilt (and winning), but Woody decided the scene played too long after he first edited the movie. Having the extra shot allowed him to cut away to the ballroom and then back to the close-up of Judah as the two men discuss moral responsibility even if there is no God. It was good luck because without the close-up to come back to, the effect was to see two people, go away to other action, then come back to the two still in the same spot, as if the listener is held there by invisible hands on his lapels. "The Ancient Mariner problem," Woody calls it.

A friend of Woody's who had seen several versions of the film looked at the stuffed boxes after the last screening. "I got to know those people so well as they were," she said. "It's like their lives are erased."

"I'm sorry to lose them, too," Woody told her, "especially the second digression with my sister that we shot [in which she had a date with a seemingly eligible but, it is shown, loony man], but the demands of cinema took over. I can't go for another digression there as you could in a novel. It's too bad. I wanted to have more strands. And I tried not to make the ending too happy. That's what I didn't like about *Hannah*. I backed off from my original ending because *nobody* liked it."

Then he added, "I feel if I could have one more day of shooting with just the people I want . . ." His reverie was broken by knowing laughter from everyone in the room. Woody looked at them with wide eyes. "But I'm serious," he said. He always is. As every film is readied for release he asks the same rhetorical question: "Are we out of time yet?"

Just after Woody's fifty-fourth birthday he said to an acquaintance, "It's hard to conceive of myself as this age. I was always the sixteen-year-old prodigy." In the nearly forty years since his first joke was published, his output has been prodigious and varied but his outlook has remained unchanged in one basic way: His ambition has always exceeded his current success. One of his great contentments as an artist is his discontent; he draws his satisfaction from doing the most original work he can while aiming to do more than he has. His comic films have won him predictable acclaim. His dramas have been praised, too, but they have also brought the predictable criticism that a son of Brooklyn is trying to put on airs by steeping himself in European cinema. He finds such thought without merit.

"I do not feel that I am betraying my muse or that I am putting on the clothes of a foreign filmmaker," he says, adding that it is no more foreign for him to go in the direction of European filmmakers than it is to go in the direction of Americans. He is convinced that for any creative person to settle for what he can do most simply is to make too easy a choice; that leads to finding a safe niche and staying in it, for him an artistically unhealthy option. Most of the writers and directors he admires are foreign and to draw on work he loves is to him a healthy influence.

Among Woody's colleagues is a director who considers himself a commercial filmmaker, a manufacturer of entertaining movies. He enjoys success; if a picture of his opens and it is not successful, he is uneasy and depressed. The director wants the public and critics to like his films, and so because he has found a way to please them, he is unwilling to risk doing anything different for fear of alienating his audience. As much as anyone can be, he is assured of a hit year after year, and he seems content.

"Now, if that were me," Woody says, "I would kill myself."

From the earliest days in his career when he argued with Gene Shefrin over what kind of jokes to write, Woody Allen has not let his audience lead him. He says, "The vision of the audience is never as deep as the vision of the artist involved. They are always willing to settle for less than you want for yourself." He learned this at the start of his career as a moviemaker. When he shifted from movies like *Take the Money and Run* and *Bananas* to *Annie Hall*, he was immediately criticized. People asked him, "What do you want to do that kind of movie for?" And they told him, "My friends liked it but they liked the other kind better." Woody's response was and is to ignore such talk, and he knows that by doing so he has distanced himself in two ways. The first is to not be swayed by current style or the ideas of others. The second is to draw farther and farther away from the teenage and young adult market most movies aim for. One of the few expectations a viewer can bring to a Woody Allen movie is that it will reflect the dilemmas of its maker's age group, and so his films now are about people in their late forties and early fifties.

"Personally, creatively, I've isolated myself," he says. "I really don't read what's written about me. The less I hear about myself, the better. I work quietly in New York with my people and I'm isolated in terms of my films not being trendy or fashionable. I want to make my movies and that's it. Yet whenever you go in for any kind of change, it's a big problem. I think you have to do it, though. I also think that somewhere subliminally, even with people, for instance, *Another Woman* fails with, they know that there's something decent in the attempt. I think there's a sense that I'm working in a different area and what I think is a better area, and I hope eventually that it will pay off for a large number of people. I know I already have a certain respect because of the positive responses I've gotten on much of my work and the quarters they've come from. Also, I'm inundated by actors and actresses who want to work with me. Juliet Taylor constantly fends off people who want to be in my films and are willing, or say they're willing, to lower their prices. I think they do that because there's an appreciation of what my films try to be."

Woody is not without his great successes, of course. *Annie Hall, Manhattan, Hannah and Her Sisters,* and *Crimes and Misdemeanors* were big critical and commercial hits. But they did not, so far as he is concerned, delve into human nature as deeply as he would like. Along with more comedies and a musical he's been thinking of for some years, what he wants to make are films that "go for the highest sensibility. I tried that with *Interiors* and I missed. I wasn't equal to it. But maybe next time I will be, or maybe it will take me five more tries. But it's the goal that's important. With these kinds of films you're talking about the highest kind of achievement—like that of O'Neill, Chekhov, Bergman." There is a slight smile on his face when he says this. "I realize that is aiming high, but I think it's not a very satisfying accomplishment for me to aim at a more modest goal and achieve it."

The fact that he has never been completely satisfied with a piece of work does not mean he could never be, however harsh he is in assessing himself. His "biggest thrill would be to make a film that when I finish it I can say, 'This picture ranks with Buñuel's best and Bergman's and Kurosawa's.' That would give me a nice inner feeling of warmth. So far, I haven't even come close. I think I've made some decent movies and a larger number of okay movies, but I've never made a great movie. A great movie to me is [Jean Renoir's] *Grand Illusion,* or *Citizen Kane,* or [Vittorio De Sica's] *The Bicycle Thief,* or *Persona.*" He feels that *The Purple Rose of Cairo* is the best film he's made, and that *Zelig* ranks as one of his better efforts. He has always had great confidence in *Stardust Memories*, a very unpopular film. He also thinks somewhat well of *Annie Hall, Manhattan*, and *Hannah and Her Sisters*, his New York trilogy of romantic comedies. Those six, he says, and *Radio Days* are his best, and his achievement gives him some hope for even better work in the future. He concedes they are decent. They are just not good enough to rest his ambition on.

"They're not A films," he says of them, "they're B films, though not in the way one usually talks about B films as second features; they're all solid pictures, they work in terms of what they set out to do, and there's inspiration in some of them. But I don't have a *Wild Strawberries* or a *Grand Illusion*. I'm going to try before my life is over to rise to the occasion and make one or two that would be considered great by any standards: Where you see pretentious bores on cable television talking and they think it's great, and even the most irate critics think it's great, and the man in the street thinks it's great. It would lift up this body of work I have. Any artist—Fellini, Bergman—is in the same situation. They've made a large number of films. They don't always make *Amarcord* or *Cries and Whispers*. Some are truly great ones, like *The Seventh Seal*, some are quite above average, like *Winter Light*, and the rest are decent, but the whole body of work is lifted by these little shining stars. What I'm lacking in my group of films are those little pinpoints of light. Maybe now that I've moved into my fifties and I am more confident, I can come up with a couple that are true literature."

In the end, Woody did not have to check himself into the hospital during the filming of *Alice*. In the end, he got, as he usually does, the look he wanted and the performances he wanted. He reshot perhaps half the movie while making it, as he often does, and after he saw the first rough cut he rewrote the beginning and he rewrote the ending. The start of the movie did not establish quickly enough Alice's solipsistic, unrestrained consumer lifestyle, nor did it show the undercurrent of Catholicism that impels her to throw that extravagant but empty way of life aside. The finish had her in Calcutta, working in a shelter similar to Mother Teresa's; first in a ward so stylized it looked, as someone said, "like the Donald Trump Pavilion," then in a realistic one that still did not deliver the effect Woody wanted. He added a voice-over of Alice reading a letter to her sister saying she and the children would soon return to New York, but it could not bridge so wide a gap as she had leaped. In the end, he left her working with the homeless in New York, still within the city where her children attend school but far away from the world in which she had lived.

Around noon one day in May 1990, Woody finished the last of the edits that required him to be in the cutting room full-time for *Alice*. He went over to Mia's to see her and the children and have lunch, then walked back across Central Park to his apartment. In a month he would begin work in a rare acting-only appearance, starring with Bette Midler in Paul Mazursky's *Scenes from a Mall* (written by Roger Simon and Mazursky), and the first draft of the Woody Allen Fall Project '90 needed to be finished before then. As his films flow into each other, blurring the end of one and the beginning of the next, this bonus free afternoon was as good a time as any to start; under any circumstances, the notion of pausing to savor completion of a year's work is alien to him.

He went into the corner room where his typewriter sits on a table by a window overlooking the park and picked up a pen and a pad of paper. Then he walked on, past the bookshelves lined with novels, philosophy, magic, and poetry. He continued through a small room with bunk beds and a treadmill in it, and into the guest room, where the big brass bed he has composed on for years now has a single bed next to it, and where the closet is full of baby paraphernalia. For the next several hours he lay on the double bed, his face pressed close to the page, writing a film script in longhand.

Part
Six

Pride and Prejudice

Do you love the artist or the man?
— BULLETS OVER BROADWAY

Ten years in ten sentences: Woody began and ended the 90s with lead roles in pictures directed by Paul Mazursky (*Scenes From a Mall*) and Alfonso Arau (*Picking Up the Pieces*). *Central Park West* was produced off Broadway as part of *Death Defying Acts*, a trilogy of one-act plays also written by David Mamet and Elaine May; a New York opening of his two new one-act plays is planned for 2001. He rewrote *Don't Drink the Water* as a television movie, taking on the part of the father that Lou Jacobi performed so brilliantly on Broadway in 1966 and Jackie Gleason interpreted so awfully in the 1969 film, and starred with Peter Falk in a made-for-television version of Neil Simon's *The Sunshine Boys*. He provided the voice for Z4195, the worker in existential crisis in the DreamWorks animated film *Antz*. He acted in Bobby Farrelly and Peter Farrelly's *Stuck On You* (to be released in 2001). He had uncredited parts in Stanley Tucci's *The Imposter*, James Ivory's *A Soldier's Daughter Never Cries*, and Douglas McGrath and Peter Askin's *Company Man*. He appeared in *Light Keeps Me Company*, Carl-Gustav Nykvist's documentary about his father Sven Nykvist. He and his jazz band were the subject of the Barbara Kopple documentary *Wild Man Blues*. And he wrote and directed ten films, acting in eight of them. An entirely predictable level of work for a man who likens his work habits to those of a digger ant.

All of which has been largely obscured by two entirely unpredictable events: his relationship with Soon-Yi Previn and Mia Farrow's sudden accusation in the midst of a bitter child custody fight that he molested their adopted daughter Dylan. These interrelated stories supported an international and multimillion-dollar media frenzy for years as charge met countercharge and sensationalism overtook reason and fact. In their entirety, the events could easily fill a not-particularly-informative book. Here, a brief summary will have to suffice.

To help understand why the media frenzy occurred, it is important to remember how jarring the news of his private upheavals was to his public's perception of him. As mentioned earlier, because Woody is the writer and the director of his films and because he dresses in the same clothes and speaks in the same way as most of the people he plays, it is easy to see author and actor as the same person.

Woody recognizes the irresistible attraction to link the film actor with the movie character because film is a powerful associative medium: "The actor is playing out a myth for you. Not that this was true, but a fan of John Wayne's wouldn't want to know that in real life he was a sniveling coward. The reality is so intense in a movie that you can't abide it. So you don't want to know that I'm not the character that you see on the screen."

This is particularly true in his case. People knew that John Wayne, for all his iconic status, was not a cowboy or a marine in real life. Perhaps Cary Grant was thought to be as suave and urbane offscreen as he was in his movies, but no character and actor are more universally thought to be the same as Woody Allen and Woody Allen. He was seen as a funny, quirky observer of society. Woody/Woody was a questioner and a complainer and, beneath it all, a decent guy who articulated an attitude toward life that millions identified with. So when the real Woody Allen took up with his paramour's adopted daughter, then a twenty-one-year-old residential student at Drew University in New Jersey, some people were horrified and disappointed, both by the deed itself and by the fact that it was performed by someone for whom they had so much affection—and with whom they so closely identified. There was, as the psychoanalysts say, a loss of idealization. The Woody Allen character was viewed by many in a new and less adoring way, as was the man. Things the character did that were once considered affecting were now often seen as sinister, and the man's personal character was mangled in the headlines by his graphically public personal life. For some of Woody's fans, his relationship with Soon-Yi created such a discrepancy between what they perceived or imagined him to be that it has altered how they look at his films. For others, time has brought a large measure of understanding and acceptance at the end of a decade that has been a tumultuous saga, as well as a period of uninterrupted creativity.

Biographers of the dead are at the mercy of their own archival talents; biographers of the living are at the mercy of their subject's future as well as his present. The past allows perspective. The future is unknowable. And the present, however carefully observed, is sometimes misinterpreted because a beguiling appearance hides a more mundane actuality; when the reality emerges it can lead to a suspicion in the reader's mind that the biographer knew more than he chose to tell. When Woody and Soon-Yi's relationship became public knowledge more than two years after this book was sent to the printer, I was often asked if I had any inkling that it would happen, as if I could foretell events thirty months in the future. As Woody says, "There was no way even *I* could tell, let alone anyone else."

So the romance between Woody and Mia Farrow turns out to have been rather different than it appeared in 1990. On the last day I spent with them as the first edition was being readied for publication, Woody taught Moses basketball moves in his dressing room on the set of *Shadows and Fog* at the Astoria Studios in Queens. Driving back across the East River to Manhattan, he and Mia chatted amiably while Satchel rode on his lap. Dylan delighted in her father's presence. All seemed calm, all seemed bright. But clichés are overrated: What you see is not always what you get. Unbeknownst to anyone besides Woody and Mia and a very few close friends, their unconventional relationship had become stale. They had not married and, Woody said not long after *Sweet and Lowdown* was released, "What it boiled down to was that Mia and I had a very civil but burned-out relationship that wasn't going anywhere."

After Mia adopted Dylan in 1985 and Satchel was born in 1987, "the only thing that was holding us together was the children. There was really nothing else. Mia and I were friendly, but if there were no children involved, I wouldn't have gone over there and she wouldn't have much cared—without wanting to sound nasty about it. I would have seen her occasionally, and we would have had an amicable drift apart. There was a burned-out undercurrent, but there was no rage or hostility and there was great mutual professional respect. It was that way for a long time, at least five years and maybe more." Even so, Woody's love for Dylan led to his legally co-adopting her with Mia in December 1991, after Mia filed an affidavit with the court stating that he was an excellent father. At the request of Moses and Mia, he also became Moses's adoptive father. It was the first time in New York that an unmarried couple was permitted to jointly adopt children.

At the time it was easy to consider their uncommon relationship a fairy tale of film-world bohemia. They did nothing to advertise the distance between them, though in retrospect there were signals that their romance had become a civil practicality. While filming *Shadows and Fog* in the winter and spring of 1991, they posed on the set for a cover for *The New York Times Magazine* but were explicit in their request not to be photographed holding hands or otherwise touching. *Shadows and Fog*—with a cast that in addition to Woody and Mia includes Kathy Bates, John Cusack, Jodie Foster, Julie Kavner, Kate Nelligan, Madonna, John Malkovich, Donald Pleasence, Lily Tomlin, and Wallace Shawn—opened in France to considerable attention, but in the United States the film was a commercial flop that received respectful reviews. Woody was not surprised; he knew going into it that a black-and-white German Expressionist comedy/drama shot in artificial fog was not a likely crowd-pleaser. (It is based on his one-act play, *Death*, published in 1975.)

"I'm not so out of touch that I didn't realize I was making a film that wouldn't be user-friendly," he said after it opened. "I didn't expect there to be lines around the block. I knew it was not going to do very well—and it didn't. But I did make the film I wanted to make, limited only by my shortcomings as a filmmaker, and as a thinker, and as a writer. I had the fun for six months of doing an expressionistic film all on a set. I enjoyed showing mysterious streets with dramatic lighting and having dark shadows peek around corners and people getting strangled and Kurt Weill music in the background."

Some common themes of Woody's pictures over the years are marital stress, infidelity, whether to have a child, sexual yearning, and the unpredictability of love, as well as its reparability. That these may to some degree be themes of his personal life should not obscure the fact that they are also common themes in many people's lives, as well as in good drama. Their presence in a film does not mean that they should be used as a Rosetta Stone to Woody's psyche at the time of its making. With apologies to Leo Tolstoy, all happy marriages resemble one another, each unhappy marriage is unhappy in its own way, and it would be fortunate for a movie about an unadulterated happy marriage to sell eight tickets.

Husbands and Wives, released in the fall of 1992, is all about adulterous and stressed marriages. It is one of Woody's favorite films. Shot in a semi-documentary style with a hand-held camera and all the jerky motion that goes with it, the opening sequence is dizzying: It has a rough-cut look to it that gives the viewer a sense of walking in on the action. An interviewer (Woody's long-time costume designer and friend Jeffrey Kurland) asks questions offscreen. In the manner of Jean-Luc Godard's *Breathless*, scenes are cut in unlikely places, dialogue ends in the middle of a word, and the camera stays on the same person, omitting action while cutting from one piece of dialogue to another.

Which was Woody's plan. "I wanted to make a film that obeyed none of the niceties of filmmaking. I wanted to tell it as roughly as I felt like, and I did. It was one of those pictures like *The Purple Rose of Cairo* that from my point of view very successfully did what I set out to do."

Husbands and Wives was written in the summer of 1991 and shot that fall. In the opening sequence, Jack and Sally (Sydney Pollack and Judy Davis) tell their good friends Gabe and Judy (Woody and Mia) that they have agreed to divorce. The apparently happily married Gabe and Judy, horrified by the news, are at a loss to comprehend it. In the end, however, the passion that has driven Jack and Sally apart brings them back together, while Gabe and Judy's marriage cannot survive its lack of passion.

Beneath the surface of their placidity, Gabe and Judy are both restless. Judy has a covert longing for Michael (Liam Neeson), her coworker at a magazine. Gabe, a college professor of writing, is intrigued by Rain (Juliette Lewis), a talented and precocious student who tells him she has had several affairs with older men, including her psychiatrist and one of her father's friends. Later, he witnesses a humiliating confrontation between Rain and an older ex-lover who has not yet gotten over her.

As Gabe finds himself increasingly drawn to Rain, he tells the offscreen interviewer, "Everything about it was wrong, I know, but that did not deter me. If anything, maybe, as usual, there was something interesting."

"So what is it? You were on some self-destructive streak?"

"You know, I don't know. My heart does not know from logic."

After Rain kisses Gabe amidst thunder and lightning at her twenty-first birthday party, he says to her, "That was a great moment there, but I don't really think that we should follow up on it. . . . If things were different, if I was younger or you were older—if anything was different. Somehow I feel I know how this is going to come out."

The song that plays over the end titles is "What Is This Thing Called Love?" Some viewers might, naturally, make comparisons between aspects of the plot of the film and themes in Woody's personal life at the time. He denies there is any correlation at all: "The film was conceived and written before I began with Soon-Yi."

Husbands and Wives is notable for the amount of coarse and graphic language and for its physical combativeness; a screaming argument between Jack and his girlfriend Sam (Lysette Anthony) ends with him wrestling her into his car. These were all jarring departures from Woody's usual style, but they were departures with a purpose for a filmmaker who says, "I was experimenting. I felt that with the documentary style it should be open, sexually and linguistically. That interested me a bit for a few pictures"—*Mighty Aphrodite* (1995), *Deconstructing Harry* (1997), and *Celebrity* (1998) have similar language—"but now it's faded."

In January 1992, while in the middle of filming *Husbands and Wives*, Mia discovered sexually explicit Polaroid pictures of Soon-Yi on the mantle in the room Woody used for writing, mementos of an affair that he says had begun the month before. What remained of the relationship with Mia exploded, followed by a cavalcade of ugliness and judicial oddities.

Mia, shocked, devastated, and feeling betrayed, lashed out at Woody and Soon-Yi. She called Woody many times during many nights to scream at him and to threaten, among other things, "You took my daughter, and I'm going to take your daughter," meaning Dylan.

Woody clearly understood his situation and Mia's anger and says simply, "I didn't have a leg to stand on." But he hoped that the children would not be brought into what promised to be a terrible battle. They were. He clearly sowed the wind, but it was they who reaped the whirlwind. Mia told the children almost daily that Woody was "evil" and "the devil." One nanny reported that, within a month, five-year-old Satchel was saying, "My father is fucking my sister."

Attempts were made at a compromise that would allow Woody to see the children and for Mia to act in his next film, *Manhattan Murder Mystery*, and by the beginning of August, there was a tentative agreement between their lawyers. On August 4, 1992, Woody was at Mia's home in Connecticut for a regular visit with Dylan and

Satchel. After he left, a babysitter whom Mia had instructed to keep an eye on Woody claimed that the two of them were missing for at least ten minutes and that he seemed to have molested Dylan. Over two or three days, Mia made a videotape of Dylan saying what purportedly had been done to her, but it was filled with contradictions and appeared to have been heavily edited. Mia also had a physician examine Dylan for any signs of abuse. None were found. But by law the incident would now have to be investigated.

Woody's "last memory of Dylan is that my visitation with the kids was just fine. They both gave me a toy catalog, which I still have. I said, 'Check off what you want me to bring back.' And they first checked three things, then six, and soon everything in the catalog was checked. I said, 'I'm coming back on Saturday, I'll bring the toys. You want this doll's house, you want this train.' I kissed her goodbye—and I never saw her again in my life."

When Mia made her charges, Woody was more offended than outraged. His initial reaction was, "Nobody is going to take this seriously, it is too manifestly stupid," and that the issue would pass within a day or two. At first he saw no need even to hire a lawyer to defend him against the allegations. But eventually he had five, led by Elkan Abramowitz. At one point, his legal team arranged for him to take a lie detector test administered by the former FBI agent in charge of the Bureau's Polygraph Quality Control Program, which he passed.

Abramowitz also gathered testimony from expert witnesses. Kathryn Prescott, Woody's psychiatrist for twenty years, filed a two-page affidavit in which she stated that "There has never been any suggestion that Mr. Allen was suffering from a sexual perversion/deviant behavior." A week later, a similar affidavit was filed by Fred Brown, Professor Emeritus of Psychiatry at the Mount Sinai School of Medicine in New York City and a specialist in pedophilia. Dr. Brown, who had never seen Woody as a patient, wrote that his tests showed Woody is "child-like in his makeup" and that he has a personality marked by "obsessiveness, vulnerability to anxiety, discomfort with adults, and feelings of safety and security in the presence of children and young women. . . . Sexual abuse of a child and especially his daughter would be both alien and repulsive to Mr. Allen. [I] conclude . . . that the allegation made against him is false."

In September 1992, the Connecticut State Police opened an investigation into the charges and commissioned the Child Sexual

Abuse Clinic of Yale–New Haven Hospital to conduct interviews, perform tests, and make a judgment as to whether the allegations had any merit. That December, another expert witness weighed in on Woody's behalf. Richard Marcus was Commanding Officer of the New York City Police Department Manhattan Sex Crimes Squad, now known as the Special Victims Unit. After viewing the videotape Mia made of Dylan, he concluded that it "violates every rule" of reasonably objective questioning of a child in this circumstance. "Many of the questions are suggestive, and there are numerous gaps in the continuity of the videotape which give me cause for concern. . . . I find [Dylan's] specific references to 'daddys [sic] don't do this' and 'daddys don't act like boyfriends' very suspect." The tape, he concluded, "has not convinced me of the child's credibility."

Despite these statements, Acting Justice Elliott Wilk of the New York Supreme Court, who was presiding over the child custody case, ruled that Woody should not be allowed to see Dylan until the Yale–New Haven report was in. In March 1993, the doctors who conducted the study released their findings. It was their "expert opinion that Dylan was not abused by Mr. Allen . . . [and] that Dylan's statements on videotape . . . do not refer to actual events." They also concluded that Woody's "visitations with Dylan should be restored"; that "it is important for Dylan to have ongoing contact with" Soon-Yi; and that both parents and all three children (Satchel, Dylan, and Moses) receive psychotherapy.

Still, the damage to Woody had been done, and facts were by now immaterial to much of the public. As Woody's friend and collaborator Marshall Brickman says of Woody and Mia, "So here were these two stereotypes: the neurotic Jew—self-obsessed, intellectual, weird—and suddenly he's hooked up with this saintly, sort of virginal yet highly fecund mother. Who's going to lose in that kind of a contest? Talk about Greek irony, the whole thing is wildly ironic if you know even a little bit of it. It was a coming home to roost of the public images, and they really clashed."

In a scene in *Bananas*, Fielding Mellish is hauled into court. As played by Woody, he jumps in and out of the witness box, alternately the defendant and the cross-examining attorney. This becomes not only a travesty of justice, one of him declares, but "a travesty of a mockery of a sham of a mockery of a travesty of two mockeries of a sham."

Which is an apt characterization of Connecticut State's Attorney Frank Maco's announcement in September 1993 that, although he was dropping sexual molestation charges against Woody and closing his fourteen-month investigation, he nevertheless had "probable cause" to prosecute Woody, but would not do so in order to spare Dylan the trauma of testifying. (Woody's response: If Maco had any hope of making his case, he "would . . . proceed nonstop, even if it meant putting my little girl through a meat grinder.") Maco had already kept the case open for six months after the Yale–New Haven report had concluded that Woody was innocent. Now, if Woody wanted to defend himself in court, it would have to be in the court of public opinion.

Yet if Maco had evidence that Woody was guilty of molestation, not to prosecute so terrible an offense was misconduct on his part and a disservice to everyone including Woody, who would be in dire need of help. As it was, Maco claimed a victory without a trial or disclosure of any incriminating evidence.

Despite the recommendations of the Yale–New Haven report and testimony by two psychiatrists who had treated Dylan and Satchel and who felt that Woody should be allowed to see them, Judge Wilk still would not permit Woody to see Dylan. His decisions denying Woody custody or visitation seem based on the notion that Woody's taking up with Soon-Yi was so heinous that responsibility for whatever resulting misery the children experienced was his alone. Moses, caught in the middle, declared that he didn't want to see Woody. Wilk allowed Woody to see Satchel, but only with a court-approved supervisor present.

Those visits felt unnatural to Woody and must have felt the same to Satchel. At first, Woody had to travel to Mia's house in Connecticut to see the boy, where there was no comfortable place for them to be together. They would go to a local shopping mall for a while, then stop in a restaurant to get a slice of pizza. On the frequently hot and muggy days, they would just stay for a time in the air-conditioned car.

It was hardly better when Woody finally was able to have Satchel spend his two-hour visits with him in New York. The tension in the Farrow household and Mia's repeated condemnations of Woody to all the children left Satchel confused and agitated. Mia said that Satchel often became carsick during the two-and-a-half-hour drive each way.

Once he was at Woody's apartment, Mia would often call several times to speak to him. Weekend visits, which would have allowed two or three days to settle into a normal routine, were denied. Wherever they went for their hours together in New York—to the circus, for ice cream, to a restaurant, even to the bathroom—a supervisor accompanied them or took Satchel. When Satchel and his father moved from room to room, the supervisor moved from room to room with them.

At the end of 1995, the visits were suspended. Satchel, as with many children at the center of custody battles who constantly hear one side of the argument, adopted the view of the parent he lived with. When Satchel was said to complain that he didn't want to see his father, the judge refused to enforce the visitation rules, and so his alienation from Woody grew, to the point that he stopped seeing him altogether. Yet custody fights often include charges of abuse that are proved unfounded, and they are often based on behavior by one or both parents that is not the norm of society. A wise judge can find a way to leaven the unhappiness so that the children involved can recover a relationship with both parents.

In 1993 custody was awarded to Mia. The cost of all this to Woody has been about $7 million in legal fees. He still pays child support and has cared for his children in his will. The cost to the children has been immeasurable. They have been dragged through a vicious process that stripped them of their privacy, their father, and even a modicum of childhood innocence. (They have also been renamed, though for consistency I have used their original names. Dylan is now Eliza; Satchel was first Harmon, then later became Seamus.)

Woody hopes that when his children are grown, they will better understand what occurred and want to reestablish a relationship with him. Meanwhile, he says, "I want all of the children, and particularly Dylan because I had no contact with her, to know that she was not abandoned. That Soon-Yi and I did everything we possibly could to get her, to see her, to get presents to her, to have contact with her, to speak to her on the phone, to get tapes of my voice to her—which was denied—to do anything I could possibly do. I fought for years. I spent millions and millions of dollars. The only reason that we stopped is that we exhausted all avenues. There was nothing else we could do.

"I've been able to say this to some degree to Satchel and Moses. I was sending Moses some money in the mail on the QT for a while, but somehow Mia got wind of it, and I got a curt letter from Moses saying he doesn't want my money. But Dylan has to think, 'This guy went away on a Wednesday and I never saw him again.' Yet I did nothing for years but try and try."

The question, of course, is why would either Soon-Yi or Woody want to start an affair? Their relationship may seem an odd one, but to a man whose movies are all about the unpredictability of love, it is not. Nor is he "the slightest bit" concerned that many people are appalled by what they consider an inappropriate union.

"People have thought that I've been arrogant or have a blind spot. They write, 'He just doesn't get it.' And I want to say to them, 'I get it, I get it, I just don't agree with you. Is it possible that I could get it and not agree with you?' I chose this course of action and I feel it was a perfectly fine course of action for me to choose. You may not like it. My choice may be questionable to you. Fine. I don't want to debate it. I chose it. It was a woman over the age of consent who was no relationship to me. It was not my daughter, it was not my adopted daughter, and she is not a natural sister of Dylan, who was adopted from somewhere else.

"People can argue, 'Well, symbolically you're her father,' and that usually would be a very good point, but in this situation it doesn't happen to be true. Soon-Yi will tell you that she and Lark and Daisy and Fletcher and all those people never for a second thought of me in any paternal way. They thought I was a joke, they thought I was a silly person. Their father was André Previn. They knew it. They had no interest in me."

As for the argument that he has broken taboos, "Comedians are by nature enemies of boundaries," John Lahr wrote in a *New Yorker* article on Woody. "They live easier by the laws of joy which they create than by the laws of good behavior which society sets down. Their job description is to take liberties—something that the public applauds in art but abhors in life."

Woody acknowledges this. "I'm a dramatist and an actor, and it had a certain drama to it. In my life I've had affairs with people; I've been in situations that were tricky. I see these things happen other places, I write about them, I make them up. My whole life in different ways has been unusual." (For that matter, so has Mia Farrow's. When she married Frank Sinatra, she was nineteen, two years younger than Soon-Yi was when the affair began with Woody. And she very famously became involved with André Previn, who at the time was married to one of her best friends. A difference is the perceived level of taboo.)

It is ironic that at first neither Woody nor Soon-Yi thought their involvement had a future. The relationship deepened after the legal battle grew intense, and the pressure of notoriety bound them closer.

"It was truly two of us against the world," he says. "We couldn't go for a walk without television trucks and fifteen cameramen and reporters running along with us. But actually that was a time we really grew together. I got to know her very well, she got to know me; it was a forging experience, a cementing experience. It was sort of great in a way."

In the eight years Woody and Soon-Yi have been together, Soon-Yi earned a master's degree in special education from Columbia University and has become well-regarded for her teaching of learning-disabled children. She and Woody were married in Venice on December 22, 1997, and in 1999 they became parents of a baby girl they named Bechet, after Sidney Bechet. In the spring of 2000, they adopted a new-born girl, Manzie Tio, named for Manzie Johnson, Sidney Bechet's drummer, and Lorenzo Tio, who taught Bechet how to play. Most striking is that Woody seems more content than he has ever been, and he credits Soon-Yi with "opening me up more." In fact, he said, shortly before adopting Manzie, "I've finally found myself in the kind of relationship that I wanted to have, that I fantasized having when I was younger, but that always eluded me. In all my past relationships, there's been an element of planning. This one just evolved in the unlike-liest way imaginable with two of the unlikeliest participants. If some had said to me when I was in my twenties, thirties, or forties, 'You're going to have a serious, marital relationship and have a child with an Asian woman far younger than you who doesn't have the vaguest interest in show business and your professional interests,' I'd have thought, 'That's crazy. We wouldn't last fifteen minutes together.' But it didn't turn out that way. Soon-Yi has never seen three-quarters of my movies; she's never seen *Annie Hall*. She has no compunction about seeing a film that I've just finished and not liking it openly and just saying she was bored. There's no work connection in that sense at all."

Woody has a remarkable ability to compartmentalize his life. He says that in all the years of legal and public turmoil, "there wasn't a moment I was distracted from work. When I tell people, they think there's something wrong with me, that I'm cold and aloof and have a surprising lack of feeling, but it isn't so. I had the appropriate feeling at the time, but my work is a separate thing."

My work is a separate thing. The phrase perfectly sums up his artistic life. He has structured his life to use work as a death defier. If one is constantly busy, there is no time to consider the practical mortality of the present. So he sleeps seven hours a night, practices his clarinet an hour a day, makes a movie a year, begins work on the next one the moment he finishes the last, and fills in any gaps with other projects. The thirty theatrical and two TV films he has written and directed (he has also acted in twenty-eight of them and appeared in eighteen films and documentaries by other directors) make him the most prolific working American filmmaker. Which does not impress him.

"Productivity is an accomplishment of sorts," he says, "but it's the depth of the individual work that counts: James Joyce had a tiny output, but look at the depth. Writing is just something that I can do. I only wish I could write better."

This accomplishment did not happen by accident. Since he was a teenager, he has maintained a creative focus that has not been blurred by distraction, success, money, or time. For someone who is chronically concerned with health and mortality, writing creates an alternate life and an alternate time in which he, not nature or human events, is master. It is the perfect anodyne for his anomie. Work, he says, "is the thing that keeps me from becoming depressed and anxious."

Manhattan Murder Mystery (1993) was filmed during the time that the media heat surrounding Woody's personal life was at its whitest. It was based on an idea he developed many years ago that he thought Marshall Brickman should write and direct and he would act in. But after years passed without result, Woody suggested that Brickman give him the script back, and he would see what he could write for himself.

"I have to write a script for me," he says. "I really know what I want to do. But we collaborated on it in the planning, which for me—and for him and for any writer—is the tough part. The actual writing of the thing I like to do for myself because I like to write the dialogue I can say; I don't like to say somebody else's dialogue." Because Woody feels he has "a limited range as an actor," a lot of the parts that he plays are comics or writers or people that are professionally similar to him.

He says he could play "a teacher or a bookworm or a lowlife petty thief. I'm believable as those. But something like a soldier or an air traffic controller, I could never get the reality."

Woody particularly enjoys collaborating with Brickman because "he's so smart, so funny. Some of the best memories I have are times I worked with him, pounding the pavement or going to dinner and the two of us sweating out problems. Usually I do the typewriter work myself. I don't take notes; I'll usually hold onto the story. Marshall says, first you write your story [in your mind], and then you write it down, and I agree completely. I can write down a script in two or three weeks because all the hard work has been done."

Years earlier, Woody had denigrated the idea of a movie like *Manhattan Murder Mystery* as being too light a piece to do. But he indulged himself, and the result was what he envisioned. It is "the kind of picture I loved to get lost in as a kid. For me it was pure pleasure. That's probably where my intellectual and emotional level is really most at home. I had a wonderful time doing it."

The film is filled with Allen hallmarks. It was shot in his favorite weather—overcast or rain; there's barely a sunbeam to be seen. (He says he would like to make a picture called *A Rainy Day in New York*. Wherever the characters are—going in and out of offices and apartments and restaurants—it's always raining hard outside. "Of course," he adds, "the production people will say, 'You've got to be kidding.'") And a favorite cinematic effect of his in which characters talk to each other offscreen is carried farther here when Woody and Diane Keaton talk in bed for what seem to be fifteen seconds of totally dark screen.

Larry Lipton (Woody) is a book editor. His wife Carol (Diane Keaton) is an imaginative snoop. When their neighbor's wife suddenly dies but her husband Paul House (Jerry Adler) seems unaffected by her death, Carol becomes suspicious. She enlists the help of Larry's and her friend Ted (Alan Alda), a recent divorcee with an apparent crush on her. Larry, meanwhile, has potential trouble on his hands from temptress Marcia Fox (Angelica Huston), who is one of his authors and whom he wants to fix up with Ted. The four double-date and become caught up in Carol's suspicions. Eventually they find that House has indeed killed his wife, and he is about to kill them.

The climactic scene behind the screen of a movie theater mirrors the climactic Fun House/Hall of Mirrors scene in Orson Welles's *The Lady from Shanghai*—while *The Lady from Shanghai* plays on the screen. Sometimes instead of describing the details of a scene in his script, Woody will simply write, "We'll find some tour de force scene" and then say to his designer Santo Loquasto, "I've got to get some tour de force location." After *Manhattan Murder Mystery* was well under way, Loquasto found an old movie theater filled with mirrors, which gave Woody the idea for playing off the Welles film. This meant rewriting and reshooting earlier scenes so that House was a cinema owner rather than a stamp dealer, as originally written.

The film ends with a joke that started life in the middle of the movie, was later cut, then was resuscitated when Woody realized that it might provide a good exit line; it is an example of how well Woody and Diane Keaton banter. Larry and Carol are walking back to their apartment after escaping the theater unharmed and are talking about how serious Ted's crush on Carol might have been. Larry is dismissive of their handsome friend.

"Take away his elevator shoes and his fake suntan and his capped teeth, and what do you have?" he asks her.

Without skipping a beat she answers, "You."

Woody thinks that "there was real chemistry between Keaton and me. I feel that in that kind of relationship, in that kind of equation, we will always be great together." His original script called for him to play the snoopy and suspicious character and for Mia to play the more sober mate. But after everything between them fell apart and Keaton stepped in to replace her, he switched the character traits. "She is such a strong comedienne, such a vibrant comedienne, that the whole emphasis shifted, and she became the funny one," he explained after the film was completed. "If Mia had been in it, I would have been the funny one because I'm a more naturally comic person. But that equation is always great where Keaton has the mad lust to follow the guy and do all the things and I'm the one saying, 'Take it easy.' She's such a great maniac."

In *Deconstructing Harry* and *Sweet and Lowdown*, the artist who is the central character destroys his personal life for his work. In *Bullets Over Broadway* (1995), he gives up his work so that he can have a personal life. Woody collaborated on the script with Douglas McGrath (who in 1996 wrote and directed *Emma*). They knew each other socially through his former assistant Jane Read Martin; she and McGrath later married.

"I don't usually like to collaborate, but Doug is witty and a friend, and every five or six years or so you get lonely in the room and you want to have another human being for the fun of it," Woody said after the film was released. He showed McGrath several ideas he had and asked, "'Which one of these strikes you as most fun to work on?' And he said, 'The one where the gangster turns out to be the playwright.' And I said, 'Really? Because that's like third on my list.' I had a political idea that I thought he would warm to, and one of those personal ideas where he said, 'Ah, it's another of those films where you talk to the audience.'"

They worked together much the same way Woody does with Marshall Brickman. "Doug came over to my house. We chatted, chatted, chatted. Then he went off, and I wrote down the script and made the movie. It worked out very well."

Before Woody was willing to proceed with writing a script, every scene had to be worked out. McGrath describes how one idea was dropped: "We acted out each scene—acted in the loosest sense. Woody stood and gave a very animated performance of one story while I listened. After he finished I said, 'I think there's just something familiar about it.' He immediately slumped and said, 'I know, I know.' The great thing about it is that he wanted to fix it. He didn't want me to puff him up and say it was a great idea. He wanted the most blunt criticism I could give. The beauty of the way he works is all about getting the material right. It's not about cutting corners or fobbing something off."

Woody was in the midst of his custody battle with Mia, which produced daily headlines and sordid stories. "Needless to say," McGrath wrote of their collaboration in *New York* magazine, "it was an interesting time to write a comedy."

One day we were in the living room in our familiar positions: he pacing back and forth and coming up with good ideas, me slouched on the couch, hoping he'd keep it up. He was telling us a movie. This was the standard way he began: We would describe the movie to each other as far as we had it and then would try to see what the next scene should be. He began by raising his arms in a sort of Zorba the Greek-like attitude and snapping his fingers as if to signal the start of a show. Then he began: "It's the Roaring Twenties, and there's this playwright who thinks of himself as a great artist—"

The phone rang. He lifted his finger, indicating that he would be just a second, and took the call. He spoke in low tones, saying things like "a long history of mental problems . . . tried every drug known to man . . . private detectives. . . ." Then he hung up and turned back to me. He caught his breath, smiled, lifted his arms, and snapped his fingers. "Okay, Roaring Twenties, playwright, great artist, and he goes to a producer seeking a production of his play, but he wants to direct it himself to protect his artistic integ—"

The phone rang, and before I could blink, he was back on the line saying, "intensely claustrophobic . . . two red eyes at the window . . . sent her child to the *Post* . . . hairs in a glassine envelope." When he hung up the third time he didn't snap his fingers. He just smiled sheepishly and said, "Okay, let's get back to our little comic bauble."

The film is a comic meditation on art and artists. John Cusack plays the self-regarded great artist David Shayne, who writes in the style but not with the skill of Eugene O'Neill. He asks his girlfriend Ellen (Mary-Louise Parker) the question that becomes a theme of the film: "Do you love the artist or the man?" Jack Warden is his supportive producer Julian Marx, who puts up with Shayne's insistence on his artistic integrity in the face of chronic failure. The backer Marx finds for his play, *God of Our Fathers*, is a godfather named Nick Valenti (Joe Viterelli), who sees a chance to give his girlfriend Olive Neal (Jennifer Tilly) a starring role on Broadway, no matter that her stage experience to date has been as a stripper. Shayne is unsettled when he discovers who his angel is, but is comforted that he will be able to mount the show according to his vision. He is ecstatic when Marx lands Helen Sinclair (Dianne Wiest), a theatrical grande dame of the Gloria Swanson in *Sunset Boulevard* school who interrupts emotional moments with Shayne by placing her hand on his mouth and saying in sweepingly dramatic tones, "Don't speak!" He even accepts having Valenti's gunman Cheech (Chazz Palminteri) at rehearsals to keep an eye on Olive. (When he was casting the film, Woody had never heard of Palminteri, who had just written and acted in *A Bronx Tale*, but he recalls that "the moment he walked in the door I thought, 'This is the character I wrote. Just get a contract out quickly and sign him.'")

Olive, predictably, is a disaster. Cheech, unpredictably, is a natural playwright. Woody feels that he masked that unpredictability by using the technique of misdirection that he learned as an amateur magician, and Cheech is a sterling example of misdirection. He looks and talks like one imagines a hoodlum would, and for the first half of the film he behaves the same way. Then, after days of sitting quietly but menacingly in the theater as Olive's bodyguard, he calls out, "That line, it's gone to my head. It's stupid writing." Even then, no one watching thinks he's a writer. Only when his sensible little suggestion is followed by bigger and better ones made privately to Shayne does the audience realize that the real artist is the gangster and the self-proclaimed artist is just an ordinary soul. By the time the play is ready to open, it has been transformed by Cheech into his own creation, but it is being ruined by the hapless Olive. Cheech does the only thing he can: He shoots her and blames the killing on rival bootleggers. ("When I thought of bumping off Olive, that's when I knew I was going to go ahead with the story," Woody says.) Valenti discovers the truth and has Cheech gunned down backstage on opening night as the play ends in great triumph. Shayne is hailed as a new dramatic genius but knows the truth. "I'm not an artist," he tells Ellen, and asks her to marry him and move back to Pittsburgh.

The "don't speak" line delivered with such comic effect by Dianne Wiest (who won an Oscar for her performance) is a variation of Anna Magnani's reaction to learning her husband has been killed in *The Rose Tattoo*. "Magnani played that so dramatically," Woody says. "I thought it would be funny if Dianne did it. The more she did it in the movie, the funnier it was."

Woody helped her with the role as much or more as he has any actor. Normally he gives very little direction. He simply will ask for take after take until he sees what he wants. In this case, however, "I had to play a lot of that to show her. She kept saying, 'I can't do this. You've got to get another actress, I can't do this.' And I kept saying, 'Are you kidding? You're the greatest actress in the world. Where am I going to get another actress like you?' I wanted her to camp it up more than she was camping it up. I would come flouncing in and go, 'Oh, God!' And I would do the scene. And she said, 'Really, you want it that broad?' And I said, 'Yes.' But in her hands it doesn't look anything like I did it."

In 1994, Jean Doumanian asked Woody if he would like to contribute to an evening of one-act plays about death written by him, David Mamet, and Elaine May. In March 1995, the farcical *Central Park West*, his part of *Death Defying Acts*, opened off Broadway.

Michael Blakemore directed the three plays. Rehearsals were tense because neither Woody nor Elaine May was happy with his approach and had constant suggestions and rewrites. (Mamet, whose wife had just given birth, stayed at home.) *The New Yorker* published Blakemore's diary of the production, in which he offered unflattering anecdotes of the two playwrights on the scene. Woody took the criticism philosophically.

"Some of it was exaggerated in a comic way, but I don't think any of it was intended meanly. I can't even say that it was necessarily untrue. That's the way I work. I was constantly coming in with ideas and changes and gags. I'm always trying to improve what I've written." One thing in the story, however, embarrassed Woody "because he had it wrong. He wrote that I said to him to think of my play as *Who's Afraid of Virginia Woolf?* I'm smart enough and tasteful enough to know my play is not in the same universe as *Who's Afraid of Virginia Woolf?* He told me he was going to direct it like a drawing-room comedy. And I said, 'Don't. Direct it like it's *Who's Afraid of Virginia Woolf?* and then the laughs will come out.' When something is funny, you can direct it seriously and it will be funny or twice as funny. You don't try and make it funny."

Mighty Aphrodite (1995) is an example of how Woody's films sometimes coalesce from a variety of ideas he has played with for years; in this case, they deal with adoption, fate, and the use in a central role of the chorus normally seen in classic Greek drama. The film opens with and often returns to a Chorus in robes and masks declaiming, "Woe unto man!" Their leader is played by F. Murray Abraham.

The tale is thus: Lenny Weinrib (Woody), a Manhattan sportswriter, and his wife Amanda (Helena Bonham Carter), an art dealer with schemes for her own gallery, are in conflict over whether to have a child. Although at first Lenny is against adoption for "the same reason we don't lease a car—pride of ownership," they finally adopt a boy they name Max, who grows into an entirely attractive and intelligent seven year old.

By then, Amanda has less interest in Max and more interest in a wealthy potential backer with an eye for her. Lenny, with more time on his hands than is good for him, becomes obsessed with wondering who Max's undoubtedly cultured and smart biological parents are. After some comic sleuthing, he discovers that the mother (Mira Sorvino) is a hooker and porn actress who does some hairstyling on the side.

The Chorus envisions only trouble ahead for Lenny. Cassandra appears from time to time, warning "I see danger."

"You're such a Cassandra," she's told.

"I'm not 'such a Cassandra,'" she shoots back. "I *am* Cassandra. That's who I am."

Lenny arranges to meet the mother, Linda Ash, professionally known as Judy Cum. Without telling her that she is Max's mother, he tries to improve her life and get her out of prostitution. He eventually buys off her pimp with courtside tickets for New York Knicks games and fixes Linda up with Kevin (Michael Rapaport), a young boxer with good looks and no brains who says, "I've had sixteen fights, and I've won them all but twelve." But Max's plans go awry. Kevin is ready to marry Linda until he sees one of her films at a party thrown by his friends. Furious with disillusionment, he slugs her and goes back to the family farm. Lenny's marriage to Amanda is in little better shape as she seems destined to leave him for her wealthy backer. Linda and Lenny, talking about their woes, fall into mutual consolation and then into bed.

Despite Cassandra's predictions and the Chorus's worries, a *deus ex machina* ending brings happy resolutions. Linda meets a helicopter pilot who descends from the sky to make an emergency landing in a field at the moment she drives by. He doesn't care about her past and helps her start a hairdressing business. Amanda decides it is Lenny she loves. Everyone lives happy ever after.

But there is a surprise. Linda has a baby girl from her night with Lenny and doesn't tell him; now both don't know they are a parent of the other's child. A year or so later Lenny and Max are in F.A.O. Schwarz looking for toys, and there is Linda with her baby. Linda looks at Max and says, "He's so handsome. Amanda must be very beautiful." Lenny, looking at her baby, says, "And your husband must be so handsome."

Woody had written the Chorus to be part of *Retribution*, a short story about a man who falls in love with the mother of his girlfriend, that appeared in the *Kenyon Review* in the 1980. He thought that the story "had Greek contours. The Chorus would appear in restaurants and places in New York. I thought it was a good motif for comedy." But in the end it didn't work as he had hoped.

The adoption story, too, had its own separate life. "It may have been reinforced when Dylan came along," he says, but "I always thought it was an interesting thought to track down the parents." It was only when he came up with the business of Linda and Lenny being a parent of the other's child that the idea was viable. "Having her a whore did not occur to me until I was off and writing. I was going to make her an eye, ear, nose, and throat specialist on Park Avenue, but I couldn't get it to work unless I worked in extremes. It was too tough a piece of writing for me."

It was also a tough piece of casting. The part of Amanda was unfilled until casting director Juliet Taylor suggested Helena Bonham Carter, who made her reputation in such genteel films as *A Room With a View* and *Howard's End*. When Woody met her "she was someone I had just seen in those bonnet pictures." She read for him in a very good American accent, and he immediately thought she was "just right. She was beautiful and she was classy."

Woody had such difficulty finding all the right actors that he went to England to look for, among others, the Chorus Leader. Among those he interviewed were Sir Ian McKellen and Sir John Neville. "Juliet and I had a meeting up in the hotel with all the peerage of the Crown," he said one day, laughing. "I'm reading these Lords and Sirs one after the other. Of course they were all great, but none of them had that delivery I wanted. Finally I went to an American, and the person that seemed best to me was F. Murray Abraham. He had enough Shakespearean authority, but he also spoke like a Brooklyn guy."

Perhaps the toughest role to fill was Linda. He tried a number of American and English actresses; Mira Sorvino was among those who had auditioned in New York. She happened to be in London at the same time Woody and Juliet Taylor were there and called to ask if she could audition again. They invited her to come by the hotel. When she removed her coat, she was in perfect costume for the role.

"It shows you how little foresight people—in this case, I— have," Woody continued. "It's the same thing as Sylvester Stallone. I was making *Bananas* and asked the casting people to send me a couple of gangsters, and they sent Sylvester Stallone and another kid. I said, 'This is not what I meant. This is nothing.' And they said, 'Please, Mr. Allen, give us a chance, let us make up.' They came back in sixty seconds, and I realized what a schmuck I was. I realized then that I had no foresight or vision whatsoever. So the minute Mira walked in, I thought, 'She looks like a little hooker. It's perfect.' She looked appropriate for the part without being too vulgar. Then she read, though not in the voice she used in the film; but her acting was so good and convincing even without the voice." She won an Oscar for her performance.

Much of the credit for taking the edge off the profanity in *Mighty Aphrodite* goes to her because, Woody says, "She brought a lightness to it, she played it like such a cartoon." A key element of her hilarious and touching performance is her high, thin voice that sounds as if she breathes helium. "That voice was all her, she had it from the first day. I had some uneasy moments about it during shooting, though I didn't tell her. I thought, 'My God, if they don't buy into the voice, I'm really out of it.' But I went by my old instincts. I thought, 'I'm a regular audience member and I buy it.' And I was right, the audience did buy it. But it did cross my mind that we're really out on a limb with this."

When *Mighty Aphrodite* came out, many people jumped to the conclusion that this was Woody's way of trying, as he puts it, "to set the record straight about my time with Mia, but it had zero to do with my life in any way. People like to draw the connections. They did it with John Cusack in *Bullets*, with Sean Penn in *Sweet and Lowdown*— Pauline Kael even did it with Mary Beth Hurt in *Interiors*. One of the pieces of evidence she adduced for her case that Mary Beth was me was that she wore my colors and tweed jackets, but she was the one in the plot with no talent whatsoever and couldn't express herself. I don't have that problem. I was much closer to Geraldine Page [who played the obsessive-compulsive mother]—and Keaton [who played a poet], maybe, but Geraldine Page more.

"You can make all those connections, but to me they're meaningless. People always ask if I choose a certain story to create a particular point for the audience. And I'm thinking, 'You're giving me too much credit.' I finish a movie, and I go into a room and I think, 'What movie do I want to do next? Do I have an idea in my notes that works, or do I have to sit and sweat out a new idea?' There's no ulterior motive other than great thankfulness that any idea comes at all. What works best for the story is what I care about. I'm happy to play a mealy-mouthed louse if it works in a good film."

That notion of what works best for the story is what impressed Douglas McGrath when he collaborated with Woody. "He is very considerate of the audience in the best way. Whatever is written cannot be a repeat of something before, and it has to advance the story. He is ruthless about his material." When Woody screened the final version of *Bullets Over Broadway* for him, a favorite scene had disappeared.

"What happened to it?" McGrath asked.

"We didn't need it."

"But it was funny."

"It was funny, but it was not necessary," Woody explained. "Each movie has a certain amount of time the audience can give it. A scene may be funny where it is, but if the movie is too long overall, you lose the audience at the conclusion."

For many years, Woody has talked about his desire to write an original musical. The problem is, the kind of music he likes went out of fashion forty or fifty years ago, and he has no desire to make a picture with a contemporary score. In *Manhattan* he was able to use many songs by George and Ira Gershwin to enhance the story, but that only whet his appetite for a more ambitious work.

"I got lost in the shuffle of contemporary music," he says. "I'm sure it's me, but I like to think it's not. I love to see someone like Billie Holiday or Frank Sinatra singing a Cole Porter tune or a Jerome Kern tune or Gershwin, quietly, and you can hear the lyric and hear the melody. Today you see four guys with guitars and 10,000 people lifting their friends up over their shoulders, and the music is amplified beyond belief, and they dress silly and smash the guitars. It just doesn't mean anything to me. It's clear that I've been left behind."

In 1996, however, Woody was able to realize at least part of his ambition with *Everyone Says I Love You*. (The title is from the Burt Kalmar and Harry Ruby song in the 1932 Marx Brothers film *Horse Feathers*.) Whereas he has no use for contemporary music, contemporary society is his bread and butter. An admirer of "old musicals about family life," he thought that a film about wealthy residents of the Upper East Side of Manhattan in the 1990s would be very different. Instead of a nuclear family of long standing, this one would be a combination family from divorces, with prior husbands and prior wives. What he ended up with was a modern equivalent of the sophisticated and luxurious Manhattan life he dreamed of as a result of all the movies he saw as a child.

Woody plays Joe, a writer who lives in Paris—this is a romantic comedy—and who is the prior husband of Steffi (Goldie Hawn), a do-good liberal now married to Bob (Alan Alda), a lawyer who is happy to turn their home into a plush salon. Joe and Steffi have a daughter, DJ (Natasha Lyonne), who overhears the psychoanalytic confessions of Von, played by Julia Roberts. (Overhearing a psychiatrist was a serious device Woody had used a few years earlier, but he felt that it had comedic possibilities he could use "in a minor way so people wouldn't think this was the comic version of *Another Woman*.") Joe contrives to meet Von in Venice (a city that Woody loves as much as it loves him. At the 1995 Venice Film Festival, he was given an honorary Leone d'Oro for his body of work). Joe wins Von by seemingly miraculously knowing her every desire, then loses her when she finds it is better not to have your deepest dreams realized. The film ends with Joe and Steffi and Bob and all the extended family at a costume ball at the Ritz Hotel in Paris, with everyone wearing Groucho Marx glasses—and with Woody doing a perfect imitation of him.

Julia Roberts was an ideal object of affection; Woody found her "a wonderful actress and terrific to work with. I did have to lean up to kiss her, of course, which is one of the, you know, annoying things in life." (Of Angelica Huston in *Husbands and Wives* he once said, laughing, "There was a scene that was cut out of the picture where I kissed her. She had to sit on the sofa so I could walk by and do it"— here he laughed louder—"because if you think Julia Roberts was tall, it was like trying to kiss, I don't know, Kareem Abdul-Jabbar.")

Casting Drew Barrymore as the debutante Skylar, however, was going against type; a more obvious choice might have been Gwyneth Paltrow. Woody worried at first that her having played tougher women and her penchant for body art might work against her being accepted in the role by the audience. But, he says, "I heard from everyone that had worked with her that she was so talented and so dedicated that she would make the part work. She came in and I liked her very much, and she read wonderfully and I figured, we could cover her tattoos."

Edward Norton, who gained an Academy Award nomination in 1999 for his portrayal of a neo-Nazi in *American History X*, was one of "a million guys that I didn't know" when he came in to audition for the part of Holden, Skylar's preppy suitor. But "he was so talented, the second he read the part, as far as I was concerned, he had it. No one had read it before with any reality or conviction. He read it and he was like a real person doing it."

Woody cast the film with no regard as to whether the actors could sing; when he auditioned people, he never mentioned the film was a musical. "It never occurred to me to tell anyone that it was," he said after its release, somehow without seeming disingenuous. He was the only one connected with the movie who took so relaxed a view, and he seems to have relished the fits he gave various production people.

"The people in the music department were saying, 'They can't sing!' and the distributors were saying 'They can't sing!'" he recalled with what can only be called glee. "And I kept saying, 'Yes, I know, that's the point. If they sing as well as they could in the shower, as well as you and I could sing, that's the idea. I don't want Edward Norton to start singing and sound like Pavarotti.'"

He was casting for believable actors, not singers, though some, among them Alan Alda and Goldie Hawn, can sing quite well. Even English actor Tim Roth, who played the tough ex-convict Charles Ferry, managed a perfectly fine American warble, although Woody says that music director Dick Hyman kept saying, "'He can't sing! He can't sing!' and I kept saying, 'It's okay.'" Unless, he quickly added, "it really put a spear through your heart. I mean, if someone's voice had been like caterwauling so it's punishment, we wouldn't have used it." The only member of the cast who wasn't up to it was Drew Barrymore, who told him, "I'm tone deaf, I can't do it." She requested that her song be dubbed.

Everyone Says I Love You is shot in deep and luscious colors. "It's one of those movies you can make look very rich," he says. Whereas a realistic movie that takes place on the streets of New York needs a plainer look to keep a sense of reality, those same streets in a musical or a period piece are a different matter "because everything's so romanticized." A scene in which Joe and Steffi, two Americans in Paris, walk on the quay by Notre Dame and then break into a dance in which (aided by an unseen crane and harness) they leap higher than even Gene Kelly could have dreamed, is drenched in what would seem the reflected light of a billion-carat canary diamond.

"I lucked out that Goldie was available," he says. "She is one of those people that can do it all."

Followers of Woody's work who were prone to look for autobiography in *Husbands and Wives* had a referential field day with *Deconstructing Harry* (1997), originally called *The Worst Man in the World*. Harry Block, whom Woody has called "a nasty, shallow, superficial, sexually obsessed" writer, barely fictionalizes his life in his work and richly earns the enmity of those who once loved him.

In Harry Block, Woody had an idea he "thought was funny. You'd see a guy who I could play—a New York Jewish writer—and you would watch the guy and learn about him, but learn about him through what he wrote. You'd see his short stories and excerpts from his novels, and that would tell you about him. I thought that had a certain cleverness to it, and it would give me a chance to do a number of little comic pieces that wouldn't sustain for a whole movie but can be funny in short stories." One is a scene in which a man borrows a friend's apartment for a rendezvous with a prostitute; unfortunately, it is the very afternoon that Death has on his calendar to take the friend, and how does one explain to Death that he's come for the wrong person? Another is about an actor, played by Robin Williams, who suddenly finds that he is out of focus. Not in the camera lens, but in real life. He is a walking blur.

Woody says that "I could be walking around on the set and someone would say, 'I can't get focus on that.' And the cameraman would say, 'He's a little soft. Let's call the lens company.' Then you don't even think of it, but it becomes part of the experience and makes a funny sketch."

As for Harry, "I tried to get somebody else to play it—I tried to get everybody else to play it. I knew if somebody else played it, they'd say it was me anyway, but I thought it could be played better than I could play it. I first went to Robert De Niro. I went to Dustin Hoffman. I went to Elliott Gould. I went to Albert Brooks. I spoke to Dennis Hopper. And many others. I couldn't get anyone to do it for one reason or another. One person wasn't available, one person wanted too much money, somebody else didn't want to play it because he thought he was too young for the part. Finally, maybe less than two weeks before shooting, I said I'd play it. The content of the film expresses something people feel is my philosophy of life because I'm the writer, but if it was more amusing for the lead character to express the opposite point of view, people would think that's what I think."

One critic wrote of a scene in which Harry has a prostitute over to his house and tells her he doesn't want to talk about Proust with her, "the last thing in the world I'd want to do is talk Proust with Woody Allen." But that misses the point entirely. Harry is fictional and is an authority on Proust; Woody, who merely plays him, has never professed himself an authority. "But they don't see the difference," he says.

One of Woody's greatest pleasures continues to be playing New Orleans jazz. His regular Monday night performances have shifted from Michael's Pub to the Carlyle Hotel, and the few score people who can be crammed in are able to observe him playing with his eyes downcast but his heart in flight.

In his daily practices at home or at his editing offices, he regularly tries different pieces of equipment. "I need a good mouthpiece and reed to bail me out when I play," he explained one day after doing his scales. "Really talented horn players are not so dependent on reeds. Sidney Bechet could scrape a mouthpiece on the pavement to widen it and get a better sound than I can get if I have it doctored in a laboratory. I'm always searching for the perfect horn and reed. Buffet made me a clarinet that I play most of the time these days. It's good, in tune, and pretty. I've played cheaper ones that are more alive but not in tune, and I'm not good enough to play them when they're out of tune. Once when I went in to pick up my horn after I had had it cleaned and repaired, I asked, 'Will I sound better?' And the repairman said, 'Yes, but not as much as you'd like.'"

For some time, he and his banjo player Eddy Davis had talked of doing a jazz tour, and in 1997 Jean Doumanian contracted with Academy Award-winning documentary film maker Barbara Kopple to make a film of the band's sold-out tour through Europe.

For all its sprightly performance pieces, the film is less about music than it is about Woody and Soon-Yi; after seeing it he said, "To Soon-Yi and me, it's like a home movie about the trip." In fact, it does show them to be comfortable and having fun together. He is heard to introduce her to someone in a large crowd as "Soon-Yi Previn—the notorious Soon-Yi Previn." She is shown telling him to at least say hello to the other band members and not talk just with Davis.

Woody wore a microphone sixteen hours a day, and Kopple turned on her camera whenever she felt like it. "I think we came off the way we were," he says. "I came off for what I am: a low-energy, slightly depressed person who can be amusing although eccentric. For instance, I was nervous about going on stage, and I must have my own hotel living space and a private bathroom. A Spanish director said to me that most people try to come off well in a documentary, but he said, 'You tried to do the opposite.'"

Celebrity (1998) is about just that. "Everybody was suddenly a celebrity, every plastic surgeon and model and athlete," Woody said after it was made. "I thought it would be a fun subject to fool around with." It stars Leonardo DiCaprio, Kenneth Branagh, Charlize Theron,

Judy Davis, Melanie Griffith, and Bebe Neuwirth, along with a number of celebrities along the line of Donald Trump playing themselves. Woody was fairly happy with the film, which, though it received mixed notices, was not a financial success, something he finds ruefully amusing: "I make the first DiCaprio film after *Titanic*, and it didn't make a dime."

Many people criticized what they thought to be Branagh's doing an imitation of the Woody Allen character—which he arguably was—and of the man, which he definitely wasn't. The midlife crisis the Branagh character goes through was appropriately comically played by a forty-year-old. If Woody, then sixty-two, had played the role, the story would have been much darker and without humor.

Celebrity is in black-and-white, even though making such a film is, Woody says, "a pain in the neck. The labs are so unsuited to black-and-white, and there are so many technical problems: static on the film; edits come out; and you have to have the whole film coated because the temperature of the lamp melts the black-and-white stock going through the projector." But he says he chose it because he thought it would give it "a nice, glossy, journalistic feel. It wasn't a warming film that would be helped by color." Plus, he has always loved New York in black-and-white; much of the story takes place late at night; and he was working with the talent of Sven Nykvist, one of the great black-and-white cinematographers.

Woody found two actors new to his films particularly good. "Charlize Theron has screen humidity, as I like to call it. It comes from within. She's great looking and has a lot of justified confidence. She knows how to present herself. Add up her looks and confidence and talent, and you have a winning package. And Leonardo DiCaprio is not a flavor of the month; he's up there with the best of them—De Niro, Pacino—a great natural. Apart from being good looking, he's a tremendous actor. He's real and full of intensity and is a great improviser. His instincts are beautiful."

Sweet and Lowdown (1999) is a lighter and much reworked version of *The Jazz Baby*, a script Woody wrote more than thirty years ago. His first version of the story of a self-destructive jazz guitar genius named Emmet Ray is so unrelievedly bleak that he realized he would have to inject some spirit if the film had any chance of working. As it formerly existed, all the audience would have been left with was "a big ladle of masochism, of Germanic Emil Jannings masochism."

As played by Sean Penn, Ray is still self-destructive, egocentric, and a part-time pimp. But he has a quixotic and amusing quality that makes him raffish and sad rather than pathetic. Penn learned the fingering for the songs Ray is seen playing, and he would play, say, *Limehouse Blues* while waiting to rehearse a scene. Woody found him to be "amazing. He's devoted. His ability as an actor carried him through to what a musician should be." He balanced those conflicting characteristics so well that he received a Best Actor Oscar nomination for his work.

Penn had often said that he wanted to be in one of Woody's films, and Woody was eager to have him play Ray. But because in at least two prior instances when he wanted to use Penn he was unavailable, Woody considered Johnny Depp and Nicolas Cage as possibilities, and would have done it himself if no one else had been available. When Penn turned out to be free, Woody looked no further. He has great admiration for Penn's abilities and feels that "most of the time he brought his genius—and it is genius—to the acting. Ninety-five percent of the time he made everything sing great."

There were, however, a couple of scenes Penn didn't get to Woody's liking, and he shot them over many times. The most noteworthy takes place in a poolroom with two prostitutes Emmet runs. At first, following Woody's original script, it had taken place in a hotel room, where Emmet has to intervene in a fight between one of the women and a client.

"He just wasn't getting the comic nuances the way I heard them in my mind," Woody said later. "I've always felt that if you scratch the surface of a scene that's not working, ninety-nine percent of the time it's the writing. Once in a while it's the acting, once in a while it's the directing, but almost always it's the writing. So my feeling is, I was saddling him with material that if he wasn't getting, nobody would have gotten. I rewrote it each time and finally changed it to the poolroom. But Sean was always ready and never said, 'Hey, I've done this scene three times.' He always gave me more than I dreamt of. Get an actor to do those lines the way he does them, it's a treat, like having an atomic weapon."

Another formidable weapon was Samantha Morton, the young English actress who plays Hattie, the mute girl Emmet wins, then foolishly discards to his eternal regret. When Woody saw her in *Under the Skin* (1997), he knew that she was right for the part. Morton, who comes from a small town in rural England, was twenty years old when Woody asked her to come in for an interview, and she is an example of how fame can be silted over by generations. She had never seen any of his films and told *Variety* that her first reaction was, "So who's Woody Allen?" Once that question was answered, she came to meet him in New York where, Woody recalled, "I told her, 'I would like you to play this like Harpo Marx.'

"And she said, 'Who's Harpo Marx?'

"And I said, 'Harpo Marx, the Marx Brother that doesn't speak.'

"And she said, 'Who are the Marx Brothers?'

"I realized how old I was. I told her she should see the Marx Brothers because she would like them, and I hired her. She went back to England and she did see the Marx Brothers. The next time I saw her was on the set. She did a perfect impression of Harpo Marx. I had to explain to her, 'I don't want you to really act like Harpo Marx, but that's the general idea I'm going for, that mute character.'" He paused. "As opposed to Johnny Belinda."

While Morton never spoke a word with her voice, she said tomes with her eyes and body language. In one scene where Emmet tells her his band is going to Hollywood to play a small part in a movie and says knowingly that there are ways to steal a scene, Morton does exactly that; Hattie's reaction is what the audience watches.

Hattie's "not a quiet person," Morton told *Variety* after she was nominated for an Academy Award for her work in the film. "She just doesn't have the ability to speak." As for working with Penn, she added that she appreciated his virtues only after "I came back to England and started working with really crap actors. It was like having a boyfriend and taking him for granted until you break up."

In May 2000, *Small Time Crooks* opened. Financially, it was by far the most successful Allen film in years, with approximately $15 million in U.S. box office receipts alone in its first two months. It is an out-and-out comedy in the family of *Take the Money and Run* and *Bananas*, with the added value of Woody's thirty years' maturity as a writer and director. Over the years, Woody has worked with many of the best cinematographers, and for *Small Time Crooks* he used Fei Zhao, who established his reputation in China. (The first English-language film he made was *Sweet and Lowdown*.)

Ray Winkler (Woody) is a dishwasher and ex-con with what he

thinks is a sure-fire scheme that will enable him and his manicurist wife Frenchy (Tracey Ullman) to move to an easy life in Florida. With his dimwit cronies Denny (Michael Rapaport), Tommy (Tony Darrow), and Benny (Jon Lovitz), he plans to rent a store, then tunnel into the bank two doors away—not unlike Edward G. Robinson and his cohorts in the 1942 film *Larceny, Inc.*, written by S. J. Perelman. As the sun sets behind Ray and Frenchy while they talk on the roof of their apartment building, he persuades her to bake and sell cookies as a front. Business immediately takes off, and soon Ray hires Frenchy's even dimmer-witted cousin May (Elaine May) to keep up with demand. Of course, nothing goes as planned: The shop's success leads to lines down the block; a policeman likes the cookies so much he drops by all the time; and when the gang who couldn't dig straight comes up through the floor of a neighboring shop instead of the bank, the cop is right behind them with a gun.

Ray convinces the officer (Brian Markinson) that while robbery was clearly their intent, they actually stole nothing. The cop thinks for a moment, then says he'll let them off for a piece of the action, which he can sum up in one word: "Franchising."

A year later, Sunset Farms is so big and successful that Steve Kroft is doing a *60 Minutes*-type piece on it. Frenchy, a former stripper, wants to buy respectability by becoming a patron of the arts and throws elaborate dinner parties cooked by their chef (Isaac Mizrahi) in their hideously over-decorated Park Avenue apartment. Ray wants only a cheeseburger.

David (Hugh Grant) is an art dealer with an eye on a big score who becomes Professor Higgins to Frenchy's Eliza Doolittle. She rewards him with lavish presents, including the Duke of Windsor's fabulously expensive Cartier cigarette case. When it is clear that she has fallen for David, Ray says that they don't need a lawyer, she can have everything. While in Venice on a European trip with David (they stay in separate rooms), Frenchy receives a call to immediately come home, where she is told that the company's accountants have stolen everything. On learning this, David's gentlemanly façade evaporates, showing him for the cad he is. When Frenchy asks for the cigarette case back, he sneers, "I think not, my love."

Ray, meanwhile, has had another brainstorm, which is to steal the gigantically jeweled necklace of a socialite whom he and Frenchy have come to know. He has a duplicate made up in Chinatown that he plans to switch at a party, but he becomes confused between the real and the fake. After Ray hears that Frenchy has lost everything, he goes to console her. Then he pulls out the necklace, which she immediately spots as glass. But Frenchy saves their figurative cookies when she produces the Duke's cigarette case, which she was able to lift from David's safe because Ray had taught her how to crack one. Florida will be theirs after all.

"Richard Schickel wrote a very nice essay about me, saying that my audience left me at a certain point," Woody said while talking about once again playing the kind of character his audience first fell in love with. "And I thought that was the one thing he had wrong. It was that I left them, they didn't leave me. They were very nice, and if I had continued to live up to my end of the contract, they showed no signs of wanting to leave me and be anything other than a nice, affectionate audience. I was the one that moved in a different direction, and a good sized portion of them felt annoyed and betrayed. They didn't like it when I did *Interiors* and *Stardust Memories*. One critic said that *Interiors* was an act of bad faith. I tried to make a serious film, and if it didn't work, it didn't work. I completely respect those people for whom it didn't. But it wasn't in bad faith. Then *Stardust Memories* put people off, and over the years the audience got more and more picky with me, more and more annoyed when I didn't keep repeating earlier successes.

"*Small Time Crooks* was fun for me to do. It was an old idea of mine that was lying around for years that I also felt was funny, or charming at least, but trivial. It's one of those films that has a good premise to it and if I can work it out, fine, but in the end it's never going to be *Rashomon*. I thought it was amusing that these people buy a store to rob a bank, and the store turns out to be a success, and they don't realize what they have. I named the character May when I wrote it, and Elaine May was the first choice, as was Tracey. Elaine's a real pro. She shows up on time, she knows her lines, she can ad lib creatively, but if you don't want her to, she won't. She's a dream. She puts herself in your hands. She's a genius. It's in her voice. Tracey's also a genius. They are two hilarious women." As for Grant, Woody would like to write a film centered on a character played by him.

Jean Doumanian and Woody have been the closest of friends for nearly forty years. In the early 1990s, she formed her own film production company, Sweetland Films, and in 1993, Sweetland became the production company for Woody's films. When the two friends joined forces, they did so knowing that someday they might have a substantial business disagreement. When Woody's desire to be paid more than the low seven figures guaranteed him became a problem, they chose friendship over business.

"It's difficult when you're dealing with friends," he said shortly after their parting in March 2000. "They want to give more, I want to make more, but I don't want to take it from them. Before it got to be unpleasant, we both felt we're good friends and love each other, and we wanted it to stay that way." She will continue to do theater projects with him.

For the forty-eight hours between the time Woody and Sweetland decided to end their seven-year partnership and his William Morris agent John Burnham arranged a new deal with DreamWorks, "I kept thinking I was like the character in Saul Bellow's novella, *The Dangling Man*," he said with amusement a week later. "I felt I had to write something." What he wrote was the second of the two one-act plays he expects to have produced in New York in early 2001.

Over the past several years Woody has built a relationship with Jeffrey Katzenberg of DreamWorks. Besides Woody's vocal work for the studio in the animated film *Antz* (1998), DreamWorks made a distribution deal for *Small Time Crooks* through Sweetland. The DreamWorks agreement is a three-picture distribution deal, with the fees for U.S. rights for all three films paid in advance by DreamWorks. German distributor VCL Film + Media AG has announced that it will pay close to an estimated additional $50 million in advances in return for foreign distribution rights. Woody has all the freedoms that he has had for decades, which is to say total control of the film from writing to casting to editing. Because his own company, Gravier Productions (named after a New Orleans street), will make the movies, he will earn a considerably higher fee and also will own his films, as he did at Orion. He also feels that he has found a comfortable artistic home.

Despite his freedom to make whatever movies he wants, Woody says that Katzenberg and his partners "take it on faith that I'm not going to walk in there and lay on his desk, you know, *From the Life of the Marionettes*. They know I'm not going to go crazy. I'm going to do the films I've been doing for years. Some are more commercial, some are less commercial. And I'm mindful of their needs. They want me to be in at least half the films. To me it never makes a difference if I'm in them or not. I couldn't care less if I was never in another film as an actor in my life; the only reason I do them is if I can't get anyone better. I know that they prefer funny films to a deadly serious film, and for me to act in many of them. I don't mind that at all. I have a slew of comedies I've wanted to do." His first film will be *The Curse of the Jade Scorpion*, with a cast that includes himself, Helen Hunt, Charlize Theron, Dan Aykroyd, Wallace Shawn, Elizabeth Berkley, and David Ogden Stiers.

One winter's day not long after Woody had finished mixing the sound on *Small Time Crooks*, he returned to the sublet apartment he and Soon-Yi and Bechet were living in while their new Georgian town house a mile up Fifth Avenue was renovated. The buyers of the duplex penthouse Woody had lived in for nearly thirty years had taken it over and were enjoying its sweeping view of Manhattan. "Believe me, for me to give up my apartment and move takes a very influential spouse," he said with a laugh. "I really thought I was in that place for life. It was a unique apartment. But now we have a child and a nanny and need more room," and soon they would have another child.

That evening, he was scheduled to speak at a Carnegie Hill Community Association meeting, the residents' group in his new neighborhood. Many home owners, Woody among them, were trying to persuade the City to prevent construction of a seventeen-story apartment building at the corner of 91st Street and Madison Avenue. He later shot and narrated a two-minute video of the neighborhood to show to the Commission. The tape garnered a great deal of attention, including stories in *The New Yorker* and the *New York Times*.

"More people want to see this than they do my movies," he said after yet another request came in from Europe. His involvement brought to mind a line from Liam Neeson's character in *Husbands and Wives*: "I don't believe in capital punishment except for some New York builders."

Talking about his involvement (the project was eventually rejected) got him to thinking about how he has created a small personal universe. "I wish I had a personality that could have participated more gracefully in life," he said. "When I look around and see colleagues of mine, they have more rounded existences. They have many friends in show business, they have people over to the house, they go over to people's houses, they dine out with people all the time, they go away on vacations with people, they become politically active or active in these social functions that could be anything from the Academy Awards to the AIDS Foundation. They're more rounded, deeper citizens of the world than I am. I'm sort of removed from that, living my own existence. I managed somehow to strategize my life so that I could live it within the confines almost exclusively of Manhattan's Upper East Side. There are enough restaurants, my screening room is here, I play jazz at the Carlyle, I practice at home, I make all my pictures in New York. I venture out, but I come back. I've moved after thirty years now, but virtually in the neighborhood. People I know have a much bigger agenda.

"So I've been blessed in being able to lead a certain kind of limited life—which may be why I have a limited audience. The earthly things don't pleasure me enough. I enjoy playing music, and I enjoy writing stories and putting them on—or even just writing them. And I enjoy watching sports and spending time with a few friends, Soon-Yi being one of them, and my daughter. But it's a funny existence. I've been immune to criticism, and"—he laughed—"I've been immune to pleasure."

He is hardly a typical, well-rounded adult. When asked what he thought of Dr. Brown's description of him being childlike in nature, he said it's "not that far off. I've always gotten along with kids and always played with kids and always liked them. I do have anxiety in the presence of adults. I have my entering phobia and general anxiety about not just crowds, but going to a dinner party or other such things. I've always struggled with that.

"Comics are like that a lot of times. What happens to a comic is when you start out you are childlike. And many remain childlike their whole life, and actually remain physically youthful into old age. Comics are childlike in that they are suing for the approval of the adults. They are supplicants. And then what happens is, they make it and they become a thousand times more wealthy than their audience, more world traveled, more educated, more experienced, more sophisticated, and they're no longer the supplicant. They've dined at Buckingham Palace and the White House, they have chauffeured cars and they're rich—and suddenly it becomes difficult to play that character, because you don't feel it; it's artificial. Then different things can happen. You can become less amusing, or you can become pontifical.

For those that do retain their childlike qualities, other problems arise because it becomes unbecoming to see guys sixty, seventy years old walking on the sides of their feet.

"I think its affected me to a certain degree. When I was twenty years old, I used to sit with my girlfriend in the Thalia or the New Yorker theater on a Friday night watching foreign films, and I used to think when the lights were on between features, 'My God, I could get up on stage here and just fracture these people. They would think I'm so funny.' I would have been the darling, the court jester.

"Then over the years I gained a certain amount of success—financial success and critical success and personal success—and I've tried for better or worse to elevate my work. And while sometimes I make it, that's also where I'll strike out in my most embarrassing ways. It's very hard to keep it all in balance and not become a pontificating ass. That's why so many actors and actresses make fools of themselves on talk shows, using their celebrity to wax profound on issues that are beyond them."

Soon-Yi and Bechet arrived home, and Woody took the year-old baby in his arms. The two of them are pleasures he is not immune to. With evident affection he spoke to Bechet in a mixture of American sing-song and French endearments. After Soon-Yi took her to the playroom, he reflected on his career. Perhaps it was the effect of the transitional surroundings, but whatever the cause, he found himself difficult to categorize.

"I fall between two stools," he said. "I'm not an artist really. I don't have the sufficient genius or the sufficient intellect. And I'm not commercial either. People who came up with me—Barbra Streisand, Bill Cosby, Robin Williams a tiny bit after me—own their own airplanes, have hundreds of millions of dollars, and are beloved. I'm not remotely in that category, not remotely [although his new film financing deals should move him to a less remote category]. And then there are the kind that are genuine artists whose level of work I can aspire toward but not really achieve, like Bergman or Fellini. I feel I've made no real contribution to cinema. Martin Scorsese or Francis Ford Coppola, just to name two gifted contemporaries, have. Not only are they fine directors, but they've made significant stylistic contributions that have influenced people. Stanley Kubrick has influenced people. I haven't been any kind of an influence, and maybe it's just as well.

"That's why it always struck me as strange that so much attention was paid during my crisis with Mia. And even when someone will write about my films positively or negatively and make a big fuss, I think, 'What are we talking about here?' I'm not someone who has a big audience. My films have not been the talk of the country where they're a social phenomenon. They're modest pictures done for modest budgets making extremely modest returns and making no real ripple in the business. You can see every third director is imitating Martin Scorsese, and he deserves to be emulated. But young directors are not running out imitating me and shooting films the way I shoot them.

"I believe that," he continued. "When I watch *Magnolia* or *Boogie Nights*, I see Scorsese's influence all over them; I see Scorsese's influence everywhere. I see it in Spike Lee. I see Oliver Stone's influence and Francis Coppola's influence. And it's deserved influence. I think that I'm sort of—without the special genius that he had—like Thelonious Monk in jazz, who was just a separate thing apart; nobody really plays like Thelonious Monk or wants to, although I think he was great. [Woody's artistic philosophy is also like Monk's, who said, "Don't play what the public wants. Play what you want and let the public catch up."] Whereas Bud Powell or Carl Silver or Oscar Peterson, they were tremendous influences. I'm not saying this out of any false modesty, I assure you. When I see other films, and I see a lot of other films, I just don't see anything that looks like I've influenced it."

He is not completely wrong. While other directors do emulate Woody—Nora Ephron and Albert Brooks come quickly to mind, as do Whit Stillman (*Metropolitan*) and Hal Hartley (*Henry Fool*)—he's right in saying that he is not widely imitated. There is no clear, direct line of influence from Woody to another director, as there is, say, from Ernst Lubitsch to Billy Wilder. Even when Woody shows the influence of directors he admires, such as Bergman and Fellini, his films are still personal and reflect his own sensibility so strongly that directors who try to imitate him run the risk of looking like Kenneth Branagh in *Celebrity*: someone doing an excellent job, but who is also a constant reminder of someone else.

Whatever his influence, there are many notable and revered directors others don't imitate. Few casual moviegoers know the films of Kenji Mizoguchi, whose work is at least the equal of Akira Kurosawa's. Yes, while Kurosawa has had great influence, Mizoguchi, who died in 1956, had little. As for American directors, apart from a few famous shots, no one much copies Orson Welles, whose morally complex movies are too ambiguous for mainstream Hollywood. Woody's sensibility, too, does not fit the Hollywood commercial template all that well. Yet his work is so distinctive that his signatures can be found in most American movies made in the last twenty years; perhaps that is why he has found studio support for his thirty-one feature films and counting.

He has clearly increased the vocabulary of romantic comedy. He has made the nerdy, offbeat anti-hero into a leading man. He has perfected the use of long master shots in which a whole scene is filmed without cutting from one take to another. He has turned narration and voice-over into character, and speaking to the audience natural. And he has had a tremendous influence on

Woody has become more than influential: He has become referential. "Zelig-like" is a common phrase; lines from his films and stories are regularly quoted; when bran was declared not to have proven anti-cancer value, the *New York Times* accompanied the story with a still from *Sleeper*, in which science in the future has proved that steak and chocolate are good for us.

In discussing himself, he was serious and sincere in an offhand, matter-of-fact way, but he quickly added that "I don't want to seem like I'm complaining, because I've had this blessing. When I was a kid, I used to run into the cinema to escape—twelve or fourteen pictures in a week sometimes. As an adult, I've escaped into making the films I want to make. For a year I get to live in that world of gangsters and showgirls, or neurotics, or heroes, or murderers, or suave wits, or whatever I want. I get to pick the costumes and the locations and the musical backgrounds. I've escaped into a life in the cinema, on the other side of the camera from the audience."

Filmography

1965   *What's New Pussycat?*
   Director: Clive Donner
   Screenplay: Woody Allen
   Producer: Charles K. Feldman
   Cinematographer: Jean Badal
   Principal actors: Peter Sellers; Peter O'Toole; Romy Schneider;
        Paula Prentiss; Capucine; Woody Allen; Ursula Andress;
        Louise Lasser
   Color, 108 minutes. Distributed by United Artists

1966   *What's Up, Tiger Lily?*
   (An imaginative dubbing of the 1964 Japanese film *Kiniko Kizi*,
        by Senkichi Taniguchi)
   Additional sequences written by: Woody Allen
   Screenplay and voice-overs: Woody Allen; Len Maxwell; Frank
        Buxton; Mickey Rose; Louise Lasser; Julie Bennett; Bryna Wilson
   Producer: Reuben Bercovitch for Benedict Productions
   Principal actors: Woody Allen; Tatsuya Mihashi; Mie Hama;
        Aiko Wakabayashi; Tadeo Nakamaru; Susumu Kurobo
   Color, 79 minutes. Distributed by American International Pictures

1967   *Casino Royale*
   Directors: John Huston; Ken Hughes; Val Guest (for Woody
        Allen's sequences); Robert Parish; Joe McGrath

Screenplay: Wolf Mankowitz; John Law; Michael Sayers; Billy
   Wilder; Ben Hecht; Val Guest; Terry Southern; Joseph
   Heller; inspired by the book *Casino Royale* by Ian Fleming
Producers: Charles K. Feldman and Jerry Bressler
Principal actors: David Niven; Peter Sellers; Ursula Andress;
   Orson Welles; Woody Allen
Color, 130 minutes. Distributed by Columbia

1969   *Don't Drink the Water*
   Director: Howard Morris
   Screenplay: R.S. Allen; Harvey Bullock; after the play by Woody
      Allen
   Producer: Charles H. Joffe
   Principal actors: Jackie Gleason; Estelle Parsons; Ted Bessell;
      Joan Delaney; Michael Constantine
   Color, 100 minutes. Distributed by Avco Embassy Pictures

1969   *Take the Money and Run*
   Director: Woody Allen
   Screenplay: Woody Allen and Mickey Rose
   Producer: Charles H. Joffe for Palomar Pictures
   Cinematographer: Lester Schorr
   Production designer: Marvin March
   Costume designer: Erik M. Hjemvik
   Editors: James T. Heckert and Ralph Rosenblum
   Music: Marvin Hamlisch
   Principal actors: Woody Allen; Janet Margolin; Marcelle Hillaire;
      Jacquelyn Hyde; Louise Lasser; narrated by Jackson Beck
   Color, 85 minutes. Distributed by 20th Century–Fox

1971   *Bananas*
   Director: Woody Allen
   Screenplay: Woody Allen and Mickey Rose
   Producer: Jack Grossberg for Jack Rollins and Charles H. Joffe
      Productions
   Cinematographer: Andrew M. Costikyan
   Production designer: Ed Wittstein
   Editors: Ron Kalish; Ralph Rosenblum (associate producer)
   Music: Marvin Hamlisch

Principal actors: Woody Allen; Louise Lasser; Carlos Montalban;
    Natividad Abscal; Howard Cosell; Sylvester Stallone
Color, 81 minutes. Distributed by United Artists

1972 *Play It Again, Sam*
    Director: Herbert Ross
    Screenplay: Woody Allen, after his play
    Producer: Arthur B. Jacobs for Apjac Productions; Charles H.
      Joffe, executive producer
    Cinematographer: Owen Roizman
    Editor: Marion Rothman
    Music: Billie Goldenberg; additional music by Oscar Peterson
    Principal actors: Woody Allen; Diane Keaton; Tony Roberts;
      Jerry Lacy; Susan Anspach
    Color, 86 minutes. Distributed by Paramount

1972 *Everything You Always Wanted to Know About Sex But Were
Afraid to Ask*
    Director: Woody Allen
    Screenplay: Woody Allen, loosely inspired by the book by Dr.
      David Reuben
    Producer: Charles H. Joffe for Rollins & Joffe and Brodsky-
      Gould Productions
    Cinematographer: David M. Walsh
    Production designer: Dale Hennessy
    Costume Supervisors: Arnold M. Lipin; G. Fern Weber
    Editor: James T. Heckert
    Music: Mundell Lowe
    Principal actors: Woody Allen; Louise Lasser; Gene Wilder;
      John Carradine; Lou Jacobi; Anthony Quayle; Lynn
      Redgrave; Tony Randall; Burt Reynolds; Jack Barry; Erin
      Fleming; Robert Q. Lewis; Heather McRae
    De Luxe Color, 87 minutes. Distributed by United Artists

1973 *Sleeper*
    Director: Woody Allen
    Screenplay: Woody Allen and Marshall Brickman
    Producer: Jack Grossberg for Jack Rollins and Charles H. Joffe

Productions; Marshall Brickman and Ralph Rosenblum, associate producers
Cinematographer: David M. Walsh
Production designer: Dale Hennessy
Costume designer: Joel Schumacher
Editors: Ralph Rosenblum; O. Nichola Brown; Trudy Shipp
Music: Woody Allen, playing with the Preservation Hall Jazz Band and the New Orleans Funeral and Ragtime Orchestra
Principal actors: Woody Allen; Diane Keaton; John Beck; Mary Gregory; Don Keefer; Eric Lax (voice of the police)
De Luxe Color, 88 minutes. Distributed by United Artists

1975 *Love and Death*
Writer and director: Woody Allen
Producer: Charles H. Joffe for Jack Rollins and Charles H. Joffe Productions
Cinematographer: Ghislain Cloquet
Production designer: Willy Holt
Costume designer: Gladys de Seconzac
Editor: Ralph Rosenblum
Music: Serge Prokofiev
Principal actors: Woody Allen; Diane Keaton; Georges Adel; Harold Gould; Jessica Harper; Alfred Lutter III
Color, 85 minutes. Distributed by United Artists

1976 *The Front*
Director: Martin Ritt
Screenplay: Walter Bernstein
Producer: Martin Ritt for Jack Rollins and Charles H. Joffe Productions; Charles H. Joffe, executive producer; Robert Greenhut, associate producer
Cinematographer: Michael Chapman
Editor: Sidney Levin
Music: Dave Grusin
Principal actors: Woody Allen; Zero Mostel; Herschel Bernardi; Michael Murphy; Andrea Marcovicci; Remak Ramsay
Color, 95 minutes. Distributed by Warner-Columbia

1977   *Annie Hall*

   Director: Woody Allen
   Screenplay: Woody Allen and Marshall Brickman
   Producer: Charles H. Joffe for Jack Rollins and Charles H. Joffe
       Productions; Robert Greenhut, executive producer
   Cinematographer: Gordon Willis
   Production designer: Mel Bourne
   Costume designer: Ruth Morley
   Editor: Ralph Rosenblum
   Music: Selected by Woody Allen
   Principal actors: Woody Allen; Diane Keaton; Tony Roberts; Carol
       Kane; Paul Simon; Colleen Dewhurst; Janet Margolin; Shelley
       Duvall; Christopher Walken; Marshall McLuhan; Sigourney
       Weaver; Walter Bernstein; John Doumanian
   Color, 93 minutes. Distributed by United Artists

1978   *Interiors*

   Writer and director: Woody Allen
   Producer: Charles H. Joffe for Jack Rollins and Charles H. Joffe
       Productions; Robert Greenhut, executive producer
   Cinematographer: Gordon Willis
   Production designer: Mel Bourne
   Costume designer: Joel Schumacher
   Editor: Ralph Rosenblum
   Music: Selected by Woody Allen
   Principal actors (in alphabetical order): Kristin Griffith; Marybeth
       Hurt; Richard Jordan; Diane Keaton; E.G. Marshall;
       Geraldine Page; Maureen Stapleton; Sam Waterston
   Color, 83 minutes. Distributed by United Artists

1979   *Manhattan*

   Director: Woody Allen
   Screenplay: Woody Allen and Marshall Brickman
   Producer: Charles H. Joffe for Jack Rollins and Charles H. Joffe
       Productions; Robert Greenhut, executive producer
   Cinematographer: Gordon Willis
   Production designer: Mel Bourne
   Costume designers: Albert Wolsky and Ralph Lauren
   Editor: Susan E. Morse

Music: George Gershwin
Principal actors: Woody Allen; Diane Keaton; Michael Murphy;
Mariel Hemingway; Meryl Streep; Anne Byrne
Black and white, 96 minutes. Distributed by United Artists

1980 *Stardust Memories*
Writer and director: Woody Allen
Producer: Robert Greenhut for Jack Rollins and Charles H.
Joffe Productions; Jack Rollins and Charles H. Joffe,
executive producers
Cinematographer: Gordon Willis
Production designer: Mel Bourne
Costume designers: Santo Loquasto and Ralph Lauren
Editor: Susan E. Morse
Music: Selected by Woody Allen
Principal actors: Woody Allen; Charlotte Rampling; Jessica
Harper; Marie-Christine Barrault; Tony Roberts
Black and white, 89 minutes. Distributed by United Artists

1982 *A Midsummer Night's Sex Comedy*
Writer and director: Woody Allen
Producer: Robert Greenhut for Jack Rollins and Charles H.
Joffe Productions; Charles H. Joffe, executive producer
Cinematographer: Gordon Willis
Production designer: Mel Bourne
Costume designer: Santo Loquasto
Editor: Susan E. Morse
Music: Jakob Mendelsshon
Principal actors (in alphabetical order): Woody Allen; Mia Farrow;
Jose Ferrer; Julie Haggerty; Tony Roberts; Mary Steenburgen
Color, 87 minutes. Distributed by Orion Pictures and Warner
Brothers

1983 *Zelig*
Writer and director: Woody Allen
Producer; Robert Greenhut for Jack Rollins and Charles H.
Joffe Productions
Cinematographer: Gordon Willis
Production designer: Mel Bourne
Costume designer: Santo Loquasto

Editor: Susan E. Morse

Music: Original compositions by Dick Hyman; others selected
by Woody Allen

Principal actors: Woody Allen; Mia Farrow; contemporary interviews with Susan Sontag, Irving Howe, Saul Bellow, Bricktop,
Dr. Bruno Bettelheim, Professor John Morton Blum

Black and white, 80 minutes. Distributed by Orion Pictures and
Warner Brothers

1984 *Broadway Danny Rose*

Writer and director: Woody Allen

Producer: Robert Greenhut for Jack Rollins and Charles H.
Joffe Productions; Charles H. Joffe, executive producer

Cinematographer: Gordon Willis

Production designer: Mel Bourne

Costume designer: Jeffrey Kurland

Editor: Susan E. Morse

Music: Selected by Woody Allen

Principal actors: Woody Allen; Mia Farrow; Nick Apollo Forte;
Sandy Baron; Corbett Monica; Jackie Gayle; Morty Gunty;
Will Jordan; Howard Storm; Jack Rollins; Milton Berle

Black and white, 85 minutes. Distributed by Orion Pictures

1985 *The Purple Rose of Cairo*

Writer and Director: Woody Allen

Producer: Robert Greenhut for Jack Rollins and Charles H.
Joffe Productions; Charles H. Joffe, executive producer

Cinematographer: Gordon Willis

Production designer: Mel Bourne

Costume designer: Jeffrey Kurland

Editor: Susan E. Morse

Original music: Dick Hyman

Principal actors: Mia Farrow; Jeff Daniels; Danny Aiello; Dianne
Wiest; Van Johnson; Zoe Caldwell; John Wood; Stephanie
Farrow; Alexander H. Cohen; Camille Saviola; Karen
Akers; Milo O'Shea; Deborah Rush; Irving Metzman; John
Rothman; Michael Tucker; Annie Joe Edwards; Peter
McRobbie; Julia Donald; Edward Herrmann

Color, 81 minutes. Distributed by Orion Pictures and Warner
Brothers

Filmography

1986 *Hannah and Her Sisters*

Writer and director: Woody Allen

Producer: Robert Greenhut for Jack Rollins and Charles H. Joffe Productions; Jack Rollins and Charles H. Joffe, executive producers

Cinematographer: Carlo Di Palma

Production designer: Stuart Wurtzel

Costume designer: Jeffrey Kurland

Editor: Susan E. Morse

Music: Selected by Woody Allen

Principal actors (in alphabetical order): Woody Allen; Michael Caine; Mia Farrow; Carrie Fisher; Barbara Hershey; Lloyd Nolan; Maureen O'Sullivan; Daniel Stern; Max Von Sydow; Dianne Wiest

Color, 107 minutes. Distributed by Orion Pictures

1987 *Radio Days*

Writer and Director: Woody Allen

Producer: Robert Greenhut for Jack Rollins and Charles H. Joffe Productions; Jack Rollins and Charles H. Joffe, executive producers

Cinematographer: Carlo DiPalma

Production designer: Santo Loquasto

Editor: Susan E. Morse

Music: Selected by Woody Allen

Principal actors (in alphabetical order): Mia Farrow; Seth Green; Julie Kavner; Josh Mostel; Michael Tucker; Dianne Wiest

Color, 89 minutes. Distributed by Orion Pictures

1987 *September*

Writer and director: Woody Allen

Producer: Robert Greenhut for Jack Rollins and Charles H. Joffe Productions

Cinematographer: Carlo Di Palma

Production designer: Santo Loquasto

Editor: Susan E. Morse

Music: Selected by Woody Allen

Principal actors: Mia Farrow; Denholm Elliott; Dianne Wiest; Sam Waterston; Elaine Stritch; Jack Warden

Color, 82 minutes. Distributed by Orion Pictures

1988   *Another Woman*
　　Writer and director: Woody Allen
　　Producer: Robert Greenhut for Jack Rollins and Charles H.
　　　　Joffe Productions; Jack Rollins and Charles H. Joffe,
　　　　executive producers
　　Cinematographer: Sven Nykvist
　　Production designer: Santo Loquasto
　　Editor: Susan E. Morse
　　Music: Selected by Woody Allen
　　Principal actors: Gena Rowlands; Mia Farrow; Ian Holm; Blythe
　　　　Danner; Gene Hackman
　　Color, 84 minutes. Distributed by Orion Pictures

1989   *Oedipus Wrecks* (in *New York Stories*)
　　Writer and Director: Woody Allen
　　Producer: Robert Greenhut for Jack Rollins and Charles H.
　　　　Joffe Productions; Jack Rollins and Charles H. Joffe,
　　　　executive producers
　　Cinematographer: Sven Nykvist
　　Production designer: Santo Loquasto
　　Editor: Susan E. Morse
　　Music: Selected by Woody Allen
　　Principal actors: Woody Allen; Mia Farrow; Mae Questel; Julie
　　　　Kavner
　　Color, 39 minutes. Distributed by Touchstone Pictures

1989   *Crimes and Misdemeanors*
　　Writer and director: Woody Allen
　　Producer: Robert Greenhut for Jack Rollins and Charles H.
　　　　Joffe Productions
　　Cinematographer: Sven Nykvist
　　Production designer: Santo Loquasto
　　Editor: Susan E. Morse
　　Music: Selected by Woody Allen
　　Principal actors: Woody Allen; Mia Farrow; Martin Landau;
　　　　Angelica Huston; Alan Alda; Claire Bloom; Jerry
　　　　Orbach
　　Color, 104 minutes. Distributed by Orion Pictures

Filmography

1990 *Alice*
Written and Directed by Woody Allen
Producer: Robert Greenhut for Jack Rollins and Charles H.
  Joffe Productions; Jack Rollins and Charles H. Joffe,
  executive producers
Cinematographer: Carlo Di Palma
Production designer: Santo Loquasto
Costume designer: Jeffrey Kurland
Editor: Susan E. Morse
Music: Selected by Woody Allen
Principal actors: Mia Farrow; Joe Mantegna; Keye Luke;
  William Hurt
DuArt color, 106 minutes. Distributed by Orion Pictures

1990 *Scenes From a Mall*
Director: Paul Mazursky
Screenplay: Roger Simon and Paul Mazursky
Principal actors: Woody Allen; Bette Midler; Bill Irwin
Color, 87 minutes. Distributed by Touchstone Pictures

1992 *Shadows and Fog*
Writer and director: Woody Allen
Producer: Robert Greenhut for Jack Rollins and Charles H. Joffe
  Productions; Jack Rollins and Charles H. Joffe, executive pro-
  ducers
Cinematographer: Carlo Di Palma
Production designer: Santo Loquasto
Costume designer: Jeffrey Kurland
Editor: Susan E. Morse
Music: Selected by Woody Allen
Principal actors: Woody Allen, Mia Farrow, David Ogden Stiers,
  John Malkovich, Madonna, Donald Pleasence, Lily Tomlin,
  Jodie Foster, Kathy Bates, John Cusack, Philip Bosco, Kate
  Nelligan, Fred Gwynne, William H. Macy, Julie Kavner,
  Wallace Shawn, Kenneth Mars
Black and white, 86 minutes. Distributed by Orion Pictures

1992 *Husbands and Wives*
Writer and director: Woody Allen

Producer: Robert Greenhut for Jack Rollins and Charles H. Joffe
Productions; Joseph Hartwick and Helen Robin, co-producers;
Thomas Reilly, associate producer; Jack Rollins and Charles H.
Joffe, executive producers
Cinematographer: Carlo Di Palma
Production designer: Santo Loquasto
Costume designer: Jeffrey Kurland
Editor: Susan E. Morse
Music: Selected by Woody Allen
Principal actors: Woody Allen, Mia Farrow, Sydney Pollack, Judy
Davis, Juliette Lewis, Lysette Anthony, Liam Neeson, Blythe
Danner
Color, 107 minutes. Distributed by TriStar Pictures

1993 *Manhattan Murder Mystery*
Director: Woody Allen
Screenplay: Woody Allen and Marshall Brickman
Producer: Robert Greenhut for Jack Rollins and Charles H. Joffe
Productions; Helen Robin and Joseph Hartwick, co-producers;
Thomas Reilly, associate producer; Jack Rollins and Charles H.
Joffe, executive producers
Cinematographer: Carlo Di Palma
Editor: Susan E. Morse
Costume designer: Jeffrey Kurland
Production designer: Santo Loquasto
Music: Selected by Woody Allen
Principal actors: Woody Allen, Diane Keaton, Alan Alda, Anjelica
Huston, Jerry Adler, Ron Rifkin, John Doumanian
Color, 104 minutes. Distributed by TriStar Pictures

1994 *Bullets Over Broadway*
Director: Woody Allen
Screenplay: Woody Allen and Douglas McGrath
Producer: Robert Greenhut for Sweetland Films; Jean Doumanian,
J. E. Beaucaire, executive producers; Helen Robin, co-producer;
Thomas Reilly, associate producer; Letty Aronson, Jack Rollins
and Charles H. Joffe, co-executive producers
Cinematographer: Carlo Di Palma
Production designer: Santo Loquasto
Costume designer: Jeffrey Kurland
Editor: Susan E. Morse

Music: Selected by Woody Allen
Principal actors: John Cusack, Jack Warden, Dianne Wiest, Chazz
        Palminteri, Joe Viterelli, Jennifer Tilly, Rob Reiner, Mary-
        Louise Parker, Stacy Nelkin, Annie Jo Edwards, Harvey
        Fierstein
Color, 98 minutes. Distributed by Miramax Films

1995   *Mighty Aphrodite*
        Writer and director: Woody Allen
        Producer: Robert Greenhut for Sweetland Films; Jean Doumanian,
                J. E. Beaucaire, executive producers; Helen Robin, co-
                producer; Thomas Reilly, associate producer; Letty Aronson,
                Jack Rollins and Charles H. Joffe, co-executive producers
        Cinematographer: Carlo Di Palma
        Production designer: Santo Loquasto
        Costume designer: Jeffrey Kurland
        Editor: Susan E. Morse
        Original music: Dick Hyman
        Choreography: Graciela Daniele
        Principal actors: Woody Allen, Mira Sorvino, Helena Bonham
                Carter, F. Murray Abraham, David Ogden Stiers, Olympia
                Dukakis, Danielle Ferland, Claire Bloom, Jack Warden,
                Michael Rapaport
        Color, 95 minutes. Distributed by Miramax Films

1996   *Everyone Says I Love You*
        Writer and director: Woody Allen
        Producer: Robert Greenhut for Sweetland Films; Jean Doumanian,
                J. E. Beaucaire, executive producers; Helen Robin, co-
                producer; Letty Aronson, Jack Rollins and Charles H. Joffe,
                co-executive producers
        Cinematographer: Carlo Di Palma
        Production designer: Santo Loquasto
        Costume designer: Jeffrey Kurland
        Editor: Susan E. Morse
        Original music: Dick Hyman
        Choreography: Graciela Daniele
        Principal actors: Woody Allen, Natalie Portman, Goldie Hawn,
                Alan Alda, Julia Roberts, Edward Norton, Drew Barrymore
        Color, 101 minutes. Distributed by Miramax Films

1997   *Deconstructing Harry*
 Writer and director: Woody Allen
 Producer: Jean Doumanian for Sweetland Films; Richard Brick,
  co-producer; J.E. Beaucaire, executive producer; Letty
  Aronson, Jack Rollins and Charles H. Joffe, co-executive pro-
  ducers
 Cinematographer: Carlo Di Palma
 Production designer: Santo Loquasto
 Costume designer: Suzy Benzinger
 Editor: Susan E. Morse
 Music: Selected by Woody Allen
 Principal actors: Woody Allen, Caroline Aaron, Kirstie Alley, Bob
  Balaban, Richard Benjamin, Eric Bogosian, Billy Crystal, Judy
  Davis, Hazelle Goodman, Mariel Hemingway, Amy Irving,
  Julie Kavner, Eric Lloyd, Julia Louis-Dreyfus, Tobey Maguire,
  Demi Moore, Elisabeth Shue, Stanley Tucci, Sunny Chae,
  Robin Williams, Hy Anzell, Scotty Bloch, Philip Bosco,
  Robert Harper, Shifra Lerer, Gene Saks, Howard Spiegel
 Color, 95 minutes. Distributed by Fine Line Features

1998   *Antz*
 Directors: Eric Darnell, Lawrence Guterman, Tim Johnson
 Screenplay: Todd Alcott & Chris Weitz & Paul Weitz
 Producers: Brad Lewis, Aron Warner, Patty Wooten for
  DreamWorks SKG and Pacific Data Images; Penny
  Finkelman Cox, Sandra Rabins, Carl Rosendahl, executive
  producers
 Production Designer: John Bell
 Art Director: Kendal Cronkhite
 Editor: Stan Webb
 Original Music: Harry Gregson-Williams, John Powell; additional
  music, Gavin Greenway, Steve Jablonsky, Geoff Zanelli
 Voices (in alphabetical order): Woody Allen, Anne Bancroft, Danny
  Glover, Gene Hackman, Jennifer Lopez, Grant Shaud,
  Sylvester Stallone, Sharon Stone, Christopher Walken
 Color, 87 minutes. Distributed by DreamWorks Distribution L.L.C.

1998   *Celebrity*
 Writer and director: Woody Allen
 Producer: Jean Doumanian for Sweetland Films; Richard Brick,

co-producer; J. E. Beaucaire, executive producer; Letty Aronson, Jack Rollins and Charles H. Joffe, co-executive producers

Cinematographer: Sven Nykvist

Production designer: Santo Loquasto

Costume designer: Suzy Benzinger

Editor: Susan E. Morse

Music: Selected by Woody Allen

Principal actors: Kenneth Branagh, Judy Davis, Leonadro DiCaprio, Melanie Griffith, Joe Mantegna, Bebe Neuwirth, Winona Ryder, Charlize Theron, Isaac Mizrahi, Gretchen Mol. As themselves: Donald Trump, Mary Jo Buttafuocco, Joey Buttafuoco, Anthony Mason

Black and white, 113 minutes. Distributed by Miramax Films

1999 *Sweet and Lowdown*

Writer and director: Woody Allen

Producer: Jean Doumanian for Sweetland Films; J. E. Beaucaire, executive producer; Letty Aronson, Richard Brick, Jack Rollins and Charles H. Joffe, co-producers

Cinematographer: Fei Zhao

Production designer: Santo Loquasto

Costume designer: Laura Cunningham Bauer

Editor: Alisa Lepselter

Original music: Dick Hyman

Principal actors: Woody Allen, Sean Penn, Samantha Morton, Uma Thurman, Gretchen Mol, Tony Darrow, Nat Hentoff, Douglas McGrath, Mr. Spoons

Color, 95 minutes. Distributed by Sony Pictures Classics

2000 *Small Time Crooks*

Writer and director: Woody Allen

Producer: Jean Doumanian for Sweetland Films; J. E. Beaucaire, executive producer; Letty Aronson, Richard Brick, Jack Rollins and Charles H. Joffe, co-executive producers

Cinematographer: Fei Zhao

Editor: Alisa Lepselter

Music: Selected by Woody Allen

Principal actors: Woody Allen, Tracey Ullman, Elaine May, Hugh Grant, Michael Rapaport, Jon Lovitz, Tony Darrow, Elaine Stritch

Color, 94 minutes. Distributed by DreamWorks Distribution L.L.C.

Acknowledgments

It took Woody Allen no time at all to agree to this book and its scope, but nearly four years to answer the last of my constant questions. I am grateful to him for many reasons, among them his forbearance, in that initially we thought it would take only a year. He entertained me the whole time with constant cooperation and without complaint as we dug into his past more deeply and surveyed his work more broadly than either of us had anticipated. All books should be as interesting and enjoyable to research.

Mia Farrow graciously put aside her innate sense of privacy and thereby opened many windows onto Woody. This book would be as diminished without her insight as it is enhanced by the photograph she took for its jacket.

Reconstructing a person's life and giving it a proper dimension requires information from many points of view, and more than a hundred people gave me theirs. Among others, I am thankfully indebted to Letty Aronson, Irene Weinstein Aronson, Judi Swiller Davidson, Marion Drayson Holmes, Elliott Mills, Mickey Rose, and Jack Victor for reliving their and Woody's childhood; to Tad Danielewski, Coleman Jacoby, Mike Merrick, Gene Shefrin, and Danny Simon for recounting 1950s gag and television writing; to Mitchel Levitas and Len Maxwell for re-creating Tamiment; to Norma Lee Clark, Charles Joffe, and Jack Rollins for showing me Woody's emergence as a performer, and for years of many kindnesses; to Art D'Lugoff, Jan Wallman, and Fred

Acknowledgments

Weintraub for a sense of the cabaret scene in the 1960s; to Dick Cavett, Jean Doumanian, and Tony Roberts for describing a friend; to Walter Bernstein and Marshall Brickman for giving a sense of collaboration; to Susan Morse and Ralph Rosenblum for access to their editing rooms; to Stuart Hample for remembering everything and telling it all; to Richard O'Brien for clipping everything and sharing it all; to Alan Alda, Karen Ludwig, Elaine Stritch, and Sam Waterston for the actors' view, and to Ulu Grosbard for a director's; to Sven Nykvist for two faces and a teacup; and to Robert Greenhut, not least for a nice poker game.

Besides allowing me to use many of her candid snapshots, Jane Read Martin answered more phone calls in three years than a directory assistance operator. She did so with such efficiency and good humor that my work was made much easier. Also, Amy Johnson stood in for several months of relief. Thank you. Brian Hamill and Kerry Hayes kindly let me use some of their photographs, and I am grateful to them. Thanks, too, to Fern Buchner, Michael Caracciolo, Kay Chapin, Carlo Di Palma, Jonathan Filley, Michael Green, Romaine Greene, Joseph Hartwick, Linda Kirland, Bill Kruzykowski, Jeffrey Kurland, Mark Livolsi, Santo Loquasto, James Mazzola, Dick Mingalone, Ray Quinlan, Thomas Reilly, Helen Robin, James Sabat, Julie Sriro, Juliet Taylor, Carl Turnquest, Jr., and all the others in Woody's crew who let me roam among them and who treated me so well.

If a fact or even a person needs finding, no one can do it faster or better than Linda Amster. My thanks are numbered by my nearly countless calls to her. One fact I did not need to look up is that it helps to have good friends who are also good writers. Jamie and David Wolf and David Freeman read my manuscript and made many helpful suggestions, as did Joseph G. Perpich. They have my most affectionate thanks, as do Jane Clapperton Cushman, my agent and friend, who always gives the right advice, and Judy and Donald Simon, who always give a great send-off. As ever, I am grateful to Dorothy Lax for her constant motherly support.

Jonathan Segal of Alfred A. Knopf is a master at turning a chapter into a piece of origami if necessary to get it to work better, and he demonstrated once again that real editing did not end with the passing of Maxwell Perkins. His rigorous criticism and amiable encouragement improved both my thinking and my writing. Among others at Knopf, my gratitude to Ida Giragossian, Karen Mugler, and Iris Weinstein, as well as to Carol Devine Carson and Chip Kidd.

It is not hyperbole to say that Arthur Gelb is responsible for my doing this book. For years he pressed me to undertake it and for years I argued that for better or worse, I had already written about Woody and had no desire to make a career of him. "Woody's changed and you've changed," he said over and over. "It's an opportunity that seldom comes along." He has more good ideas in an hour than many people have in a month. I hope he still feels this was a good one. I am very grateful for his perseverance.

Carol and Arthur Sulzberger gave me a key to their apartment for what originally were to be a few research trips to New York but turned into fifty over a period of almost four years. They treated each visit as if it were the first, welcoming me with open arms and wonderful dinners. They made me feel as if I had never left home.

My wife, Karen Sulzberger, gladly helped pack up baby and belongings so we could spend several months in New York at the start of this project, then after we returned home she held all together (including, at the end, a second child) while I made those fifty trips. Her always helpful comments on drafts made me clarify what I knew but the reader didn't. These are but three of the scores of reasons this book is dedicated to her.

Acknowledgments for the Second Edition

My boundless thanks to Andrea Schulz, editor of Da Capo Press, for her enthusiasm for this book and for her patience and talented editing, and to Jane Snyder, fixer extraordinaire.

Index

Index

Index

Index

Index

CPSIA information can be obtained at www.ICGtesting.com
Printed in the USA
LVOW101957071011

249617LV00001B/1/A